THE ULTIMATE PLANT-BASED DIET COOKBOOK FOR BEGINNERS

800 Delicious and Healthy Recipes for Plant-based homemade Meals |
With 28-day Meal Plan to kickstart your plant-based lifestyle

D1567142

Beth B. Orlowski

Disclaimer Notice:

Please note the information contained within this document is for educational and entertainment purposes only. All effort has been executed to present accurate, up to date, reliable, complete information. No warranties of any kind are declared or implied. Readers acknowledge that the author is not engaged in the rendering of legal, financial, medical or professional advice. The content within this book has been derived from various sources. Please consult a licensed professional before attempting any techniques outlined in this book.

By reading this document, the reader agrees that under no circumstances is the author responsible for any losses, direct or indirect, that are incurred as a result of the use of the information contained within this document, including, but not limited to, errors, omissions, or inaccuracies.

Table of Content

Chapter 4 Lunch Recipes 35

Chapter 5 Vegetarian Mains....... 63

Chapter 6 Dinner Recipes.......... 87

Chapter 7 Sauces, Broths, Dip and Dressings 115

Chapter 8 Smoothies, Beverages and Desserts 126

Chapter 9 Snacks and Sides ...145

Introduction

   A plant-based diet or a plant-rich diet is a diet consisting mostly or entirely of plant-based foods. These are foods derived from plants with no animal-source foods or artificial ingredients. While a plant-based diet avoids or has limited animal products, it is not necessarily vegan. It's a diet derived mostly from plants, including fruits, vegetables, nuts, seeds, legumes, and grains, with few or no animal products. It also means choosing whole, unprocessed foods as much as possible and avoiding highly processed foods. This way of eating comes with a lot of benefits for your body, your wallet, and the environment. The idea of giving up meat, dairy, and eggs may feel overwhelming. But you can still enjoy many of your favorite foods—all it takes is some creativity, which is where this book comes in. There are tons of substitutions you can make so you don't feel like you are missing out. And, in most cases, the plant-based substitute is far healthier than the original.

   There are lots of Health benefits in eating a plant-based diet. Studies have found that a plant-based diet can reduce the risk of Type 2 diabetes, heart disease, certain cancers, and other illnesses. It can also control or reverse chronic illnesses and inflammation. Many people report having more energy and an easier time managing their weight after switching to a plant-based diet. For more information on plant-based health benefit of the more expensive items you can put in your cart, so you'll happily notice your grocery bill decreasing after switching to a plant-based diet. Eating plant-based is far less expensive than a meat-based diets .There are many environmental benefits to following a plant-based diet. Raising livestock is one of biggest contributors to greenhouse gas emissions. In fact, one serving of beef creates more greenhouse gas emissions than 20 servings of vegetables. For this reason, avoiding animal products is a great way to reduce your carbon footprint Also, no animals will be harmed in the making of your meal Even if animal welfare is not your main motivation, and we think everyone can get behind the idea of coexisting on a more peaceful planet and not causing suffering.

Chapter 1 The Whole Food-Plant Based Diet

When we hear the word "diet," we immediately think about meal plans, sad-looking dinner plates, and giving up foods we enjoy. The whole-food, plant-based diet is not a weight loss program intended to take away the enjoyment we get from food. Instead, it's a way of eating that focuses on natural, plant-based foods that are not heavily processed to give your body plenty of vitamins and minerals. It's a way to bring life to your meals through colors, flavors, and variety. This way of eating is centered on understanding and harnessing the nutritional benefits from plants, including vegetables, tubers, fruits, seeds and nuts, whole grains, and legumes such as chickpeas and lentils

100% Plants

The foundation of this diet is using plants and plant-based ingredients as the primary or sole source of nutrition. Plants provide the vitamins, minerals; phytonutrients, protein, and fiber you need to maintain health and fight off illness. These natural ingredients give you everything your body needs while being both visually pleasing and delicious.

Whole Foods

Whole foods are foods eaten in their natural state, or as close to it as possible and that haven't been treated with chemicals, refined, or enhanced through industrial means. These foods are easier for your body to digest and benefit from, while being lower in calories, higher in fiber, and more conducive to maintaining a healthy body weight. Some examples of whole foods are fruits, vegetables, nuts, seeds, legumes (beans, peas, lentils), and whole grains (brown rice, quinoa, oats). Eating whole foods has been shown to lower the risk of heart disease and diabetes, and, in some cases, reverse these complications

SOS (Salt, Oil, Sugar)

Salt, oil, and sugar are all linked to health complications and are the three main additives common in processed foods. The sections here break down the risks. Salt, also referred to as sodium, is added to processed foods to lengthen shelf stability and add flavor. Consuming excess sodium increases blood pressure, which increases your risk for heart failure, stroke, stomach cancer, and kidney disease. Around 30 percent of Americans will develop high blood pressure in their lifetime, and minimizing sodium is a way to decrease your risk for health complications. The consumption of oil has increased dramatically in the last 50 years as more food products have been created. Even though less-refined oils like olive oil contain heart-healthy omega-6 and omega-3 fatty acids, the overconsumption of oils promotes heart disease. Additionally, most oils, like corn, canola, and soy, are created using a high-heat process, which oxidizes the oils and creates free radicals that can lead to cancer. Most food products today have highly processed oils added to them, or these oils are used for cooking. Sugar shows up in the most unexpected packaged food products, like peanut butter, soup, marinara, and even bread. In the United States, added sugars account for nearly 20 percent of daily calories for adults, putting people at risk for type 2 diabetes, heart disease, acne, and certain cancers. Making your own food from natural ingredients is a simple way of eliminating the dangers accompanied with consuming added sugar.

PLANT-BASED DIET VS. VEGAN DIET

You may be wondering how "plant-based" differs from "vegan." These two terms have a lot of overlap, but they aren't exactly the same. Veganism is deeply tied to animal rights and excludes all forms of exploitation and cruelty to animals—for food or any other purpose. This means avoiding animal food products as well as animal-derived consumer goods, like leather and products tested on animals. Those who eat a plant-based diet are primarily concerned with nutrition and health. A plant-based diet includes little to no animal food products, but people following a plant-based diet may not necessarily avoid animal-derived consumer goods from a food standpoint, "plant-based" implies a diet that embraces whole foods and avoids highly processed foods. Some products that technically qualify as "vegan" would not be embraced by plant-based eaters because they're highly processed. For example, Oreos do not contain animal products, which mean they are vegan. However, someone who identifies as plant-based wouldn't eat Oreos. A plant-based diet focuses on whole foods, like fruits and vegetables, and less-processed food and vegan replacement foods like meat substitutes

Plant-Based Diet	Vegan Diet
Eats little or no meat, dairy, eggs, fish, and seafood	Avoids meat, dairy, eggs, fish, seafood, and bee products
May use animal-derived consumer goods or products tested on animals	Avoids all animal-derived consumer goods and products tested on animals
Avoids highly processed foods	May include highly processed foods
Diet choice motivated by health and wellness	Lifestyle choice strongly linked to animal welfare

Scientifically Proven Benefits of a Plant-Based Diet

Study shows that Diet is the biggest predictor of early death. A classic American diet that's high in saturated and Trans-fats, sodium, and processed meat puts you at a disadvantage when it comes to health and longevity, while a diet that promotes whole foods and plant-based ingredients appears to have the opposite effect. As the following studies show, adopting a plant-based diet may help reduce the likelihood that you'll need medication, lower your risk of obesity and high blood pressure, and maybe even help prevent or manage type 2 diabetes and heart disease. In a review published in July 2019 in JAMA Internal Medicine, researchers found that following a plant-based diet (one that included foods like fruits, veggies, legumes, nuts, and whole grains) was associated with a lower risk of type 2 diabetes. The nine studies involved about 307,100 participants, and were adjusted for factors such as smoking status and exercise frequency that otherwise could have affected the results. Researchers therefore deduced that the lower risk was due to participants' diet choices.

The reason for this lower risk of type 2 diabetes may be improved function of beta cells, which help produce insulin (the hormone that keeps blood sugar levels stable). Past research has noted that as type 2 diabetes progresses, beta cell function declines — and this can cause dangerous fluctuations in blood sugar levels. But a randomized trial published in February 2018 in Nutrients found that after just 16 weeks following a plant-based diet, participants had better beta cell function and insulin sensitivity compared with the control group — not to mention improved body mass indexes (BMIs) and less belly fat. A plant-based diet can help you manage your weight, and may even lead to weight loss if you follow it in a healthy way. "Most people [who transition from a typical American diet] also start to feel like they have more energy," she adds.

A plant-based diet could be helpful for both your body and your mind. One study published in September 2019 in Translational Psychology set out to answer that question, and the results turned out mixed. While researchers concluded that this diet is beneficial for boosting metabolism, managing weight, and reducing inflammation (especially among people with obesity and those with type 1 and type 2 diabetes), they didn't confirm whether this diet can positively affect mental function. Don't rule it out yet, though — the researchers noted that there's plenty of potential for future studies to explore the subject further. And if you're not ready to give up on animal proteins just yet, don't worry. Another study, published in August 2019 in JAMA Internal Medicine, found that, while adding plant-based proteins to your diet can help lower your risk of cancer and cardiovascular disease, there was no increased risk associated with animal proteins. So while it's not necessary to completely eliminate meats and dairy from your diet, you can still lower your risk of certain diseases by making an effort to include more plant proteins. To set yourself up for success, make a shopping list heavy on produce, beans, and plant-based proteins to make sure you have plenty of options to reach for when you get hungry.

Keys to Meal Prep Success

Meal prep can take many forms. It doesn't have to be a three-hour cooking marathon on Sunday—although if that's what works for you, great! It's really just taking time to plan and make at least one recipe in advance.

Start Small

First of all, breathe! Meal prepping can be simple and fun! If you're a beginner, start by making one recipe at a time and saving the leftovers. For example, if you're cooking for one and you make a recipe that has four portions, you can eat one meal hot on Monday night when you make it and then have your Tuesday, Wednesday, and Thursday lunches ready to go. This way, you can quickly build up a supply, and then you'll be able to mix and match recipes so you don't get bored. If you cook another recipe on Tuesday night, you can mix and match the two recipes during the week.

Plan Ahead

Planning ahead is the biggest part of meal prep. You'll need to select your recipes in advance and allow time for grocery shopping and cooking. Choose recipes that are compatible in terms of ingredients and equipment needs. Your prep day will go more quickly if you can chop ingredients for multiple recipes at the same time— like dicing all your onions at once—and if you can use both your oven and stovetop simultaneously. Once you get in the kitchen, cook whatever takes the longest first. For example, if you want to prepare baked potatoes and broccoli, you would get the potatoes in the oven before making the broccoli.

Embrace Leftovers

Some people are hesitant to practice meal prep because the idea of eating the same food several days in a row or eating food a few days after it was prepared is unappealing. However, meal prep does not have to mean scooping a tired casserole out of the same pan night after night. Packaging your meals immediately in individual meal prep containers not only makes them easier to grab-and-go, it also helps to maintain freshness. You can also vary what you eat by making a variety of interchangeable items that can be repurposed.

Need-to-Know Nutrition!

Learning about all the vitamins, minerals, phytonutrients, and antioxidants from a diverse source of plants is one of the most exciting parts of transitioning to the whole-food, plant-based diet. We all know the adage: An apple a day keeps the doctor away. But we typically don't look beyond the singsong sentence. A fresh apple includes fiber for gut health and digestion; the phytonutrient quercetin, which has been linked to reducing the effects of asthma, certain cancers, and coronary heart disease; and polyphenol antioxidants, which can lower the risk of type 2 diabetes. Understanding the nutrition and positive effects of the whole-food, plant-based diet is powerful, and that knowledge will help you plan your meals to get the most from your food.

Protein, Carbs, and Fats

As you transition to the whole-food, plant-based diet, you might have questions concerning the macronutrients needed for a healthy body. Having even a general understanding of the three macronutrients is important for everyone.

Protein

Protein is essential for cell production and aids in feeling full longer. The recommended minimum protein intake is a modest 0.36 grams per pound of body weight, or, on average, 15 to 25 percent of daily calories from a protein source. This number fluctuates based on activity level, age, and sex.

Carbs

Carbs are the macronutrient most diets eliminate because they are commonly associated with weight gain. However, the recommended amount of carbohydrates for an adult is between 45 to 65 percent of daily calories (the amount in grams depends on individual caloric intake and will vary widely based on age, activity level, weight, and sex). The problem with carbs isn't in their nature; it's in their production. Refined grains, like those in white breads, have fiber and protein stripped, which causes them to be digested too quickly and leads to a rapid rise and fall of blood sugar. Whole food is unrefined and, therefore, contains the fiber necessary to promote even blood sugar levels and less frequent cravings for snacks.

Fat

Fat is misunderstood—good fats are a necessary macronutrient for brain health, nutrient absorption, and positive hormone production. Between 20 and 35 percent of your daily calories should be from fat for brain health and proper vitamin and mineral absorption (the amount in grams depends on individual caloric intake and will vary widely based on age, activity level, weight, and sex). However, it is easy to overdo the fat if you are cooking and baking with a lot of oil.

Vitamins and Supplements

The recipes throughout this book are stand-alone and are not a meal plan. As you plan your meals, consider diverse sources of macronutrients and micronutrients. By eating whole-food, plant-based meals, you will get a range of vitamins and minerals from a variety of vegetables and fruits. Yes, you can even get iron from dark leafy greens and vitamin B12 from plant-based sources like nutritional yeast and tempeh. However, it is beneficial to consider taking supplements or using fortified ingredients that contain B12 iron, and vitamins D and K2 as well as omega-3 fatty acids. Although it is possible to get all the recommended vitamins and minerals from foods, these just mentioned are often lacking for everyone, regardless of diet, according to medical research.

Food to Eat, Limit, and Avoid in Plant Based Diet

What to Eat and Drink	What to Limit/Avoid
Vegetables (including kale, spinach, Swiss chard, collard greens, sweet potatoes, asparagus, bell peppers, and broccoli)	Dairy (including milk and cheese)
Fruits (such as avocado, strawberries, blueberries, watermelon, apples, grapes, bananas, grapefruit, and oranges)	Meat and poultry (like chicken, beef, and pork)
Whole grains (such as quinoa, farro, brown rice, whole-wheat bread, and whole-wheat pasta)	Processed animal meats, such as sausages and hot dogs
Nuts (walnuts, almonds, macadamia nuts, and cashews all count)	All animal products (including eggs, dairy, and meat if you're following a vegan diet)
Seeds (such as flaxseed, chia seeds, and hemp seeds)	Refined grains (such as "white" foods, like white pasta, rice, and bread)
Beans	Sweets (like cookies, brownies, and cake)
Lentils	Sweetened beverages, such as soda, and fruit juice
Coffee	Potatoes and French fries (3)
Tea (including green, lavender, chamomile, or ginger)	Honey (if not vegan)

A Final Word on Plant based Diet: The plant-based diet is a category of diets that has this in common: All plant-based diets limit animal-derived foods in favour of plants. Instead of a diet centred on meat and dairy, the starring roles are played by vegetables, fruit, and whole grains. It's a fresh, flavourful approach to eating and has been shown to have significant health benefits, including weight loss and disease prevention.

Chapter 2 The Plant based Diet Action Plan

Stocking Your Plants Pantry

When it comes to plant-based eating, being organized and prepared is essential. These are our must-have ingredients that we always have on hand. You will add fresh fruits and veggies to your shopping lists when you go, but these are items that can stay in your pantry.

Oils and Vinegars	Nuts and Seeds
Apple cider vinegar	Raw almonds
Coconut amino	Raw cashews
Coconut oil	Nut butters
Olive oil	Pumpkin seeds
Red wine vinegar	or any seed you like
Condiments	**Gluten-Free Baking**
Ketchup	Blanched almond flour
Marinara sauce	Arrowroot powder
Mustard	Cacao powder
Soy-free vegan mayonnaise	Dairy-free chocolate chips
Sriracha sauce	Ground flaxseed
Grains and Legumes	All-purpose gluten-free flour
Canned beans (black, kidney, chickpea)	**Seasonings**
Oats	Cinnamon
Pasta (we like brown rice pasta best)	Ground cumin
Quinoa	Dried Italian herbs (rosemary, thyme, oregano, parsley, basil)
Rice(Use both white and brown rice, usually use long-grains such as jasmine or basmati)	Nutritional yeast
Sweeteners	Paprika
Coconut sugar	Black pepper
Maple syrup	Salt
Medjool dates	Ground turmeric

28-Day Meal Plan

Day	Breakfast	Lunch	Dinner	Snack/ Dessert	Motivational Quotes
1	Easy Granola Clusters	Grains and Spinach Salad	Veggie Barley Bowl	Hot Tropical Smoothie	Life changes very quickly, in a very positive way, if you let it.
2	Apple Muesli	Barley and Strawberry Salad	Indian Lentil Dahl	Pumpkin Smoothie	Food can be both enjoyable and nourishing.
3	Blueberry Oatmeal	Bulgur Salad with Cucumber and Tomato	Kale and Sweet Potato Quinoa	Kiwi and Strawberry Smoothie	I am a better person when I have less on my plate
4	Vanilla Steel-Cut Oatmeal	Roasted Root Vegetables	Brown Rice with Mushrooms	Easy and Fresh Mango Madness	If I don't eat junk, I don't gain weight.
5	Easy and Healthy Oatmeal	Cannellini Bean Gazpacho	Veggie Paella	Simple Date Shake	Keep an open mind and a closed refrigerator.
6	Breakfast Quinoa with Cherries	Kidney bean and Tomato Chili	Vegetable and Wild Rice Pilaf	Beet and Clementine Protein Smoothie	Start where you are. Use what you have. Do what you can.
7	Spelt Berry Porridge with Dates	Lentils and Mushroom Soup	Brown Rice with Spiced Vegetables	Pineapple Smoothie	The hard days are what make you stronger.
8	Vanilla Buckwheat Breakfast Bowl	Bean and Mushroom Chili	Spiced Tomato Brown Rice	Chia Fresca	My body is less judgmental of my diet than my mind is.
9	Potato Medley	Three Bean Chili	Noodle and Rice Pilaf	Veggie Hummus Pinwheels	Let food be thy medicine, and medicine be thy food.
10	Breakfast Quinoa with Peanut Butter	Thai Water Chestnut Stew	Easy Millet Loaf	Veggie Hummus Pinwheels	New meal; fresh start.

11	Maple-Cinnamon Granola with Dates	Vegetable Soup	Walnut-Oat Burgers	Easy Kale Chips	You didn't gain all your weight in one day; you won't lose it in one day. Be patient with yourself.
12	Flaxseed Pancakes	Vegetable Gnocchi Soup	Spicy Beans and Rice	Strawberry and Mashed Avocado Toast	Ability is what you're capable of doing. Motivation determines what you do. Attitude determines how well you do it.
13	Banana Blueberry Pancakes	Sumptuous Pea, Yam, and Potato Soup	Simple Baked Navy Beans	Cashew Queso	I always believed if you take care of your body it will take care of you.
14	Pumpkin Spice Muffins	Sumptuous Minestrone Soup	Vinegary Black Beans	Matcha Pistachio Balls	Looking after my health today gives me a better hope for tomorrow.
15	Blueberry Muffins	Summer Soup	Spiced Lentil Burgers	Oil-Free Green Beans with Almonds	You may be disappointed if you fail, but you are doomed if you don't try.
16	Spelt Berry Porridge with Dates	Simple Potato and Leek Soup	Pecan-Maple Granola	Garlicky Broccoli	Fitness is like marriage, you can't cheat on it and expect it to work.
17	Vegetable Hash Breakfast	Super Easy and Ritzy Borscht	Bean and Summer Squash Sauté	Roasted Root Veggies with Maple Syrup	Exercise should be regarded as a tribute to the heart.
18	Cinnamon Congee with Apricots and Dates	Pinto Bean and Avocado Salad	Peppery Black Beans	Baked Pears and Yams	If it doesn't challenge you, it doesn't change you.
19	Potato Medley	Endive and Green Lentil Salad	Walnut, Coconut, and Oat Granola	Crisp Onion Rings	It's going to be a journey. It's not a sprint to get in shape.

20	Tofu Breakfast Burritos	Lemony Millet and Fruit Salad	Peppers and Black Beans with Brown Rice	Easy Baked Sweet Potato Fries	Just believe in yourself. Even if you don't, pretend that you do and, at some point, you will.
21	Morning Carrot Oatmeal with Pecans	Asparagus Soup	Bibimbap	Apple Nachos	Nobody is perfect, so get over the fear of being or doing everything perfectly. Besides, perfect is boring.
22	Creamy Pumpkin Pie Oatmeal	Cannellini Bean and Carrot Soup	Lentil Burgers	Homemade Soft Pretzels	The secret of change is to focus all of your energy not on fighting the old, but on building the new.
23	Peach Strawberry Smoothie	Ritzy Summer Salad	Lentil Burgers	Chocolate and Almond Balls	You get what you focus on, so focus on what you want.
24	Tropical Spinach Smoothie	Bulgur Tabbouleh	Easy Chickpea Salad Sandwiches	5-Minute Almond Butter Bites	Yes, I can.
25	Spinach and Peach Smoothie Bowl	Brussels Sprout and Sweet Potato Salad	Smoky Tofu and Bean Bowls	Simple Showtime Popcorn	Don't stop until you're proud.
26	Spinach and Peach Smoothie Bowl	Spinach and Eggplant Salad	Mashed White Beans, Potatoes, and Kale	Tomato Garlic Swiss Chard	A little progress each day adds up to big results.
27	Cinnamon Applesauce Pancakes	Rice and Bean Salad	Smoky Tofu and Bean Bowls	Rhubarb and Strawberry Pie	It has to be hard so you'll never ever forget
28	Veggie and Tofu Scramble	Farro Salad with White Beans	Super Three-Bean and Grains Bowl	Crispy Almond Biscotti	The groundwork of all happiness is health

Chapter 3 Breakfasts

Easy Granola Clusters

Prep time: 5 minutes | Cook time: 1 minute | Makes 2 cups

1½ cups peanut butter
¼ cup maple syrup (optional)
1½ cups old-fashioned rolled oats
½ cup raisins
¾ cup flaxseed meal
¾ cup raw sunflower seeds (no shells)

1. Place the peanut butter and maple syrup (if desired) in a medium microwave-safe bowl. Microwave them on high for 30-second intervals, stirring between intervals, or until the mixture is well incorporated and smooth. Allow to cool for a few minutes.
2. Fold in the oats, raisins, flaxseed meal, and sunflower seeds and stir the ingredients until they are completely combined.
3. Spread the mixture evenly on a baking sheet and freeze for at least 25 minutes until firm.
4. Break it into clusters before serving.

Per Serving
Calories: 493 | fat: 31.0g | carbs: 49.8g | protein: 16.0g | fiber: 12.2g

Overnight Muesli

Prep time: 10 minutes | Cook time: 0 minutes | Serves 4 to 6

2 cups gluten-free rolled oats
¼ cup no-added-sugar apple juice
1¾ cups unsweetened coconut milk
1 tablespoon apple cider vinegar (optional)
1 apple, cored and chopped
Dash ground cinnamon

1. Mix together the oats, apple juice, coconut milk, and vinegar (if desired) in a large bowl and stir to combine.
2. Cover and refrigerate for at least 3 hours, preferably overnight.
3. When ready, stir in the chopped apple and serve sprinkled with the cinnamon.

Per Serving
Calories: 214 | fat: 4.2g | carbs: 28.9g | protein: 6.1g | fiber: 6.0g

Banana Muesli with Dates

Prep time: 5 minutes | Cook time: 0 minutes | Serves 2

1 banana, peeled and sliced
1 cup rolled oats
½ cup pitted and chopped dates
¾ cup unsweetened almond milk
¼ cup unsweetened coconut, toasted

1. Mix together all the ingredients in a large bowl until well combined and let soak 15 minutes, or until all the milk is absorbed.
2. Give it a good stir and serve immediately.

Per Serving
Calories: 391 | fat: 8.1g | carbs: 82.1g | protein: 10.5g | fiber: 13.0g

Stovetop Granola

Prep time: 5 minutes | Cook time: 10 minutes | Makes about 6 cups

5 cups rolled oats
¾ cup date molasses or brown rice syrup (optional)
1 tablespoon ground cinnamon
½ teaspoon salt (optional)
1 cup chopped dried fruit

1. Place the oats in a saucepan over medium-low heat and toast for 4 to 5 minutes, stirring constantly to prevent burning, or until the oats are lightly toasted. Transfer the toasted oats to a medium bowl.
2. Add the date molasses (if desired) to the saucepan and cook over medium-low heat for 1 minute. Stir in the toasted oats, cinnamon, and salt (if desired). Transfer the mixture to a nonstick baking sheet and allow cooling to room temperature.
3. When cooled, transfer the mixture to a large bowl and add the dried fruit and mix well. Serve immediately.

Per Serving
Calories: 327 | fat: 5.7g | carbs: 69.2g | protein: 14.5g | fiber: 14.9g

No Bake Peanut Butter Granola Bar

Prep time: 10 minutes | Cook time: 0 minutes | Makes 12 bars

1 cup packed pitted dates
¼ cup creamy natural peanut butter or almond butter
¼ cup pure maple syrup (optional)
1½ cups old-fashioned oats
1 cup coarsely chopped roasted unsalted almonds

1. Pulse the dates, peanut butter, and maple syrup (if desired) in a food processor until the mixture starts to come together and feels slightly sticky. Stop right before or as it starts to turn into a ball of loose dough.
2. Add the oats and almonds and pulse for 1 minute. Transfer the dough to a baking dish and cover with plastic wrap. Place in the refrigerator for 20 minutes until chilled.
3. Cut into 12 bars and serve immediately.

Per Serving
Calories: 182 | fat: 8.8g | carbs: 24.3g | protein: 5.1g | fiber: 4.2g

Vanilla Steel-Cut Oatmeal

Prep time: 5 minutes | Cook time: 40 minutes | Serves 4

4 cups water
Pinch sea salt (optional)
1 cup steel-cut oats
¾ cup unsweetened almond milk
2 teaspoons pure vanilla extract

1. Place the water and salt (if desired) into a large pot over high heat and bring to a boil.
2. Reduce the heat to low and stir in the oats. Cook for about 30 minutes until the oats are soften, stirring occasionally.
3. Add the milk and vanilla and stir well. Cook for about 10 minutes more until your desired consistency is reached.
4. Remove the cereal from the heat and serve warm.

Per Serving
Calories: 187 | fat: 0g | carbs: 28.8g | protein: 9.2g | fiber: 5.0g

Apple Muesli

Prep time: 5 minutes | Cook time: 0 minutes | Serves 2

1 cup rolled oats
½ cup raisins
¾ cup unsweetened almond milk
2 tablespoons date molasses or brown
rice syrup (optional)
¼ teaspoon ground cinnamon
1 Granny Smith apple, cored and chopped

1. Stir together the oats, raisins, almond milk, date molasses (if desired), and cinnamon In a large bowl and let soak 15 minutes.
2. When ready, add the chopped apple and stir to combine. Serve immediately.

Per Serving
Calories: 356 | fat: 4.7g | carbs: 79.9g | protein: 10.1g | fiber: 11.5g

Blueberry Oatmeal

Prep time: 5 minutes | Cook time: 5 minutes | Serves 1 to 2

1½ cups unsweetened coconut milk
1 cup old-fashioned rolled oats
½ cup fresh or frozen blueberries, thawed if frozen
Optional Toppings:
2 tablespoons chopped nuts
2 to 3 tablespoons granola
1 tablespoon maple syrup (optional)
2 tablespoons raw sunflower seeds (no shells)
1 tablespoon coconut shreds
1 teaspoon spices of your choosing (like cinnamon or pumpkin pie spice)

1. Heat the milk in a medium saucepan over medium-high heat until boiling.
2. Fold in the oats and blueberries and stir well.
3. Reduce the heat to low and let simmer uncovered for 5 minutes, or until the water is absorbed, stirring occasionally.
4. Remove from the heat and top with toppings of choice.

Per Serving
Calories: 273 | fat: 7.5g | carbs: 45.4g | protein: 14.4g | fiber: 8.5g

Easy and Healthy Oatmeal

Prep time: 5 minutes | Cook time: 5 minutes | Serves 2

1 cup rolled oats
Sea salt, to taste (optional)
2 cups unsweetened coconut milk or water

1. Cook the oats, salt (if desired), and milk in a small saucepan over medium-high heat. Bring to a boil.
2. Reduce the heat to medium and continue to cook for about 5 minutes, or until the oats have soaked up most of the liquid and are creamy, stirring occasionally.
3. Ladle into bowls and serve hot.

Per Serving
Calories: 300 | fat: 11.2g | carbs: 42.7g | protein: 15.8g | fiber: 7.2g

Slow Cooker Butternut Squash Oatmeal

Prep time: 15 minutes | Cook time: 6 to 8 hours | Serves 4

1 cup steel-cut oats
3 cups water
2 cups cubed (½-inch pieces) peeled butternut squash
¼ cup unsweetened coconut milk
1 tablespoon chia seeds
1½ Teaspoons ground ginger
2 teaspoons yellow (mellow) miso paste
1 tablespoon sesame seeds, toasted
1 tablespoon chopped scallion, green parts only

1. Mix together the oats, water, and butternut squash in a slow cooker.
2. Cover and cook on Low for 6 to 8 hours, or until the squash is tender when tested with a fork. Mash the cooked butternut squash with a potato masher or heavy spoon. Stir together the butternut squash and oats until well mixed.
3. Mix together the milk, chia seeds, ginger, and miso paste in a small bowl and stir to combine. Add this mixture to the squash mixture and stir well.
4. Ladle the oatmeal into bowls and serve hot topped with sesame seeds and scallion.

Per Serving
Calories: 229 | fat: 4.9g | carbs: 39.7g | protein: 7.1g | fiber: 9.0g

Multigrain Hot Cereal with Apricots

Prep time: 30 minutes | Cook time: 30 minutes | Serves 2

¼ cup long-grain brown rice
2 tablespoons rye
2 tablespoons millet
2 tablespoons wheat
berries
2 tablespoons barley
6 dried apricots, chopped
2 cups water

1. Rinse the grains and soak them in water for 30 minutes until softened and drain.
2. In a saucepan, add the soaked grains, apricots, and 2 cups of water and stir to combine.
3. Cook for about 17 minutes over low heat, or until the liquid is absorbed, stirring periodically.
4. Allow to cool for 15 minutes before serving.

Per Serving
Calories: 242 | fat: 1.6g | carbs: 50.5g | protein: 6.5g | fiber: 6.1g

Hot Breakfast Couscous Cereal

Prep time: 10 minutes | Cook time: 5 to 6 minutes | Serves 4

¾ cup water
½ cup couscous
¼ cup fresh-squeezed orange juice
2 tablespoons finely chopped blanched almonds (optional)
1 tablespoon maple
syrup (optional)
1 tablespoon frozen apple juice concentrate
1 teaspoon finely grated orange zest
Dash ground cinnamon

1. In a large casserole dish, add all the ingredients and stir well. Cover in aluminum foil.
2. Transfer the dish to a microwave oven and cook for 5 to 6 minutes on high heat, or until the water is absorbed, and the couscous is softened, stirring occasionally to prevent sticking.
3. Let sit for another 1 minute, covered.
4. Divide the cereal among bowls and serve hot.

Per Serving
Calories: 47 | fat: 0.3g | carbs: 10.3g | protein: 0.9g | fiber: 0.5g

Breakfast Quinoa with Cherries

Prep time: 2 minutes | Cook time: 20 minutes | Serves 2

1 cup water
½ cup quinoa
½ cup unsweetened fresh cherries
½ teaspoon vanilla extract
¼ teaspoon ground nutmeg

1. Combine all the ingredients in a large saucepan and cook over medium-high heat until boiling.
2. Reduce the heat, cover, and simmer for 15 minutes or until the quinoa is soft and the liquid has been absorbed.
3. Divide the quinoa between two bowls and serve warm.

Per Serving
Calories: 182 | fat: 2.7g | carbs: 33.0g | protein: 6.4g | fiber: 3.7g

Breakfast Quinoa with Peanut Butter

Prep time: 5 minutes | Cook time: 10 minutes | Serves 2

²/₃ cup quinoa flakes
1 cup water
1 cup unsweetened nondairy milk, plus more for serving
¼ cup raw cacao powder
2 tablespoons natural
creamy peanut butter
¼ teaspoon ground cinnamon
2 bananas, mashed
Fresh berries of choice, for serving
Chopped nuts of choice, for serving

1. Stir together the quinoa flakes, water, milk, cacao powder, peanut butter, and cinnamon in a pot over medium-high heat. Cook until the mixture starts to simmer, stirring often.
2. Reduce the heat to medium-low and cook for an additional 3 to 5 minutes, stirring frequently.
3. Add the mashed bananas, stir, and cook until hot.
4. Serve with the fresh berries, chopped nuts, and milk sprinkled on top.

Per Serving
Calories: 478 | fat: 16.5g | carbs: 69.6g | protein: 19.2g | fiber: 16.1g

Spelt Berry Porridge with Dates

Prep time: 5 minutes | Cook time: 55 to 62 minutes | Serves 4

2½ cups water
1 cup spelt berries
¼ teaspoon sea salt (optional)
⅛ Teaspoon ground cloves
⅛ Teaspoon ground
cinnamon
¾ cup dates, pitted and chopped
¼ teaspoon orange zest
2 cups unsweetened almond milk

1. Heat the water in a medium saucepan over medium heat and bring to a boil.
2. Stir in the spelt berries, salt (if desired), cloves, and cinnamon. Reduce the heat to medium-low, cover, and simmer for 45 to 50 minutes, or until the spelt berries are softened, stirring periodically. Drain as much liquid as possible.
3. Add the dates, orange zest, and almond milk into the pan and stir well. Continue to simmer for 10 to 12 minutes until thickened, stirring often.
4. Serve warm.

Per Serving
Calories: 303 | fat: 3.5g | carbs: 57.1g | protein: 11.0g | fiber: 6.9g

Date and Oat Flour Waffles

Prep time: 10 minutes | Cook time: 8 to 10 minutes | Serves 12

4 cups rolled oats
¼ cup chopped dates or raisins
¹/₃ cup whole-wheat
flour
½ teaspoon salt (optional)
5 cups water

1. In a large bowl, thoroughly combine the oats, dates, flour, and salt (if desired).
2. Add the water and stir until well incorporated. Pour the batter into a food processor and pulse until a smooth consistency is achieved.
3. Cook on High for 8 to 10 minutes in a waffle iron until done. Serve hot.

Per Serving
Calories: 169 | fat: 2.4g | carbs: 30.6g | protein: 6.8g | fiber: 6.1g

Quinoa Chocolate Porridge

Prep time: 5 minutes | Cook time: 30 minutes | Serves 2

1 cup quinoa
1 cup water
1 cup unsweetened coconut milk
1 teaspoon ground cinnamon
¼ cup raspberries
2 tablespoons walnuts
Pudding:
1 large banana

1 to 2 tablespoons almond butter, or other nut or seed butter
1 tablespoon ground flaxseed, or chia or hemp seeds
2 to 3 tablespoons unsweetened cocoa powder, or carob

1. Cook the quinoa, water, milk, and cinnamon in a medium pot over high heat and bring to a boil. Reduce the heat to low, cover, and simmer for 25 to 30 minutes, or until the liquid is absorbed and the quinoa is tender.
2. Meanwhile, make the pudding: Mash the banana in a medium bowl. Add the almond butter, flaxseed, and cocoa powder and stir to combine.
3. Spoon 1 cup of cooked quinoa into a bowl and place half the pudding and half the raspberries and walnuts on top.
4. Serve immediately.

Per Serving (1 bowl)
Calories: 391 | fat: 18.9g | carbs: 8.8g | protein: 12.1g | fiber:9.7 g

Peach Strawberry Smoothie

Prep time: 5 minutes | Cook time: 0 minutes | Serves 1

1½ cups unsweetened plant-based milk, plus more as needed
½ cup frozen peach slices

½ cup chopped frozen strawberries
½ cup pitted and chopped Medjool dates

1. Process all the ingredients in a blender until smooth and creamy. Add more milk if you like a creamier texture.
2. Serve immediately.

Per Serving
Calories: 455 | fat: 4.9g | carbs: 98.3g | protein: 4.9g | fiber: 11.4g

Cinnamon Congee with Apricots and Dates

Prep time: 8 minutes | Cook time: 20 minutes | Serves 4

2 cups water
4 cups cooked brown rice
½ cup chopped unsulfured apricots
½ cup dates, pitted and chopped

¼ teaspoon ground cloves
1 large cinnamon stick
Salt, to taste (optional)

1. Bring the water to a boil in a large saucepan over medium heat.
2. Once it starts to boil, add the remaining ingredients, except the salt, to the saucepan and stir well. Reduce the heat to medium-low and cook for 15 minutes, or until the mixture is thickened.
3. Season to taste with salt, if desired. Remove the cinnamon stick before serving.

Per Serving
Calories: 313 | fat: 1.9g | carbs: 68.8g | protein: 6.0g | fiber: 6.2g

Potato Medley

Prep time: 15 minutes | Cook time: 20 minutes | Serves 4 to 6

4 potatoes, peeled or unpeeled, cut into ¾-inch cubes
1 onion, cut into cubes (separate the pieces)
1 green bell pepper,

chopped into large pieces
4 cloves garlic, sliced
1 cup water, divided
2 cups thawed frozen or fresh corn
1 large tomato, diced

1. Combine the potatoes, onion, bell pepper, and garlic in a nonstick frying pan with ½ cup of the water. Cook, stirring, over medium heat for 5 minutes.
2. Add the remaining ½ cup of water to the pan. Cover and cook for an additional 10 minutes, stirring occasionally.
3. Add the corn and tomato, stir, and cook for another 5 minutes.
4. Serve warm.

Per Serving
Calories: 275 | fat: 0.7g | carbs: 60.1g | protein: 7.5g | fiber: 7.8g

Simple Tofu Scramble

Prep time: 5 minutes | Cook time: 15 minutes | Serves 2

½ red bell pepper, diced
½ yellow onion, diced
1 block firm tofu
½ cup unsweetened

plant-based milk
¼ teaspoon freshly ground black pepper
¼ teaspoon turmeric

1. In a nonstick skillet over medium heat, sauté the bell pepper and onion in a little of water for 3 to 5 minutes, or until the onion is translucent.
2. Break the tofu into small pieces and add to the skillet, along with the milk, black pepper, and turmeric. Stir to combine and continue to cook for an additional 8 to 10 minutes.
3. Serve warm.

Per Serving
Calories: 215 | fat: 10.0g | carbs: 11.8g | protein: 21.9g | fiber: 4.0g

Tofu Breakfast Burritos

Prep time: 10 minutes | Cook time: 10 minutes | Serves 6 to 8

¼ cup chopped green bell pepper
¼ cup chopped scallion
¼ cup water
1 tablespoon diced canned green chilies
1 tablespoon diced pimiento
1 pound (454 g) firm

tofu, crumbled
¼ to ½ teaspoon ground turmeric
1 tablespoon soy sauce
Freshly ground pepper, to taste
6 to 8 whole-wheat tortillas

1. In a nonstick skillet, sauté the green pepper and scallion in the water for 5 minutes.
2. Add the green chilies and pimiento and stir.
3. Add the crumbled tofu, turmeric, soy sauce, and ground pepper to the skillet, stirring well. Cook over medium heat for about 5 minutes until cooked through.
4. To serve, divide the cooked mixture evenly among the tortillas and roll.

Per Serving
Calories: 188 | fat: 8.3g | carbs: 17.5g | protein: 12.1g | fiber: 4.5g

Spinach and Peach Smoothie Bowl

Prep time: 10 minutes | Cook time: 0 minutes | Serves 2

2 cups fresh spinach
1 orange, peeled and segmented
½ cup water
2 cups sliced peaches, preferably frozen
1 ripe banana, frozen

½ cup sliced strawberries
¼ cup raw cashews
1 kiwifruit, diced
4 fresh mint leaves, chopped

1. Purée the spinach, orange, and water in a food processor until completely mixed and smooth.
2. Add the banana and peaches to the food processor, and pulse for a few times. The mixture should be thick and creamy. Stop to scrape down the sides as needed.
3. Divide the mixture between two bowls. Top each bowl evenly with the strawberries, cashews, kiwifruit, and mint leaves.
4. Serve immediately, or refrigerate to chill.

Per Serving
Calories: 377 | fat: 10.5g | carbs: 58.9g | protein: 11.9g | fiber: 9.8g

Spinach and Peach Smoothie Bowl

Prep time: 2 minutes | Cook time: 25 minutes | Serves 4

2½ cups vegetable broth
2½ cups unsweetened almond milk
½ cup steel-cut oats
½ cup slivered almonds

1 tablespoon farro
¼ cup nutritional yeast
2 cups old-fashioned rolled oats
½ teaspoon salt (optional)

1. Pour the almond milk and vegetable broth into a large saucepan and bring to a boil.
2. Add the steel-cut oats, almonds, farro, and nutritional yeast to the saucepan, and cook over medium-heat for about 20 minutes, stirring frequently.
3. Fold in the rolled oats and stir well. Cook for an additional 5 minutes until the oats are thick and creamy.
4. Sprinkle with the salt, if desired. Let the porridge cool for 8 minutes before serving.

Per Serving
Calories: 209 | fat: 8.2g | carbs: 22.1g | protein: 14.2g | fiber: 7.1g

Blueberry and Banana Quinoa

Prep time: 20 minutes | Cook time: 20 minutes | Serves: 2 to 4

2 cups unsweetened coconut milk
1 cup quinoa
½ cup frozen blueberries
1½ Teaspoons cinnamon
1 banana, sliced
Chopped almonds, for topping (optional)

1. Pour the coconut milk into a medium saucepan over medium-high heat and bring to a boil.
2. Gradually whisk the quinoa into the milk just as it begins to boil.
3. Reduce the heat to low, cover, and allow to simmer for 15 minutes until the quinoa can be fluffed with a fork.
4. Stir in the blueberries and cinnamon, and simmer for an additional 5 minutes.
5. Divide the quinoa between two bowls. Serve the quinoa with the banana slices and chopped almonds, if desired.

Per Serving
Calories: 273 | fat: 6.8g | carbs: 42.9g | protein: 10.2g | fiber: 4.8g

Citrus-Berry Breakfast Bowl

Prep time: 10 minutes | Cook time: 0 minutes | Serves 2

½ cup sliced strawberries
½ cup raspberries
½ cup blackberries
½ cup blueberries
1 grapefruit, peeled and segmented
1 tablespoon maple
syrup
3 tablespoons freshly squeezed orange juice (from 1 orange)
¼ cup sliced almonds
¼ cup chopped fresh mint

1. Combine the berries and grapefruit in a large bowl.
2. In a separate bowl, whisk together the maple syrup and orange juice until completely mixed.
3. Pour the mixture over the fruit and gently toss until evenly coated.
4. Scatter with the almonds and mint, then serve.

Per Serving
Calories: 157 | fat: 0.8g | carbs: 35.5g | protein: 2.5g | fiber: 7.3g

Creamy Pumpkin Pie Oatmeal

Prep time: 5 minutes | Cook time: 35 minutes | Serves 4

3 cups plant-based milk
1 cup unsweetened pumpkin purée
1 cup steel-cut oats
2 tablespoons maple syrup (optional)
1 teaspoon ground cinnamon
⅛ Teaspoon ground nutmeg
⅛ Teaspoon ground cloves

1. Bring the milk to a boil in a medium saucepan over medium-high heat.
2. Once it starts to boil, reduce the heat to low, and stir in the remaining ingredients.
3. Cover and cook for 30 minutes, stirring frequently, and serve.

Per Serving
Calories: 219 | fat: 4.9g | carbs: 38.0g | protein: 7.2g | fiber: 6.0g

Creamy Brown Rice Cereal with Raisins

Prep time: 5 minutes | Cook time: 10 minutes |Makes about 2 cups

2 cups water
½ cup uncooked brown rice
¼ cup raisins
1½ cups unsweet-
ened almond milk (optional)
½ teaspoon cinnamon (optional)

1. Add the water to a medium saucepan over medium-high heat and bring to a boil.
2. Meanwhile, pulverize the brown rice by using a high-speed blender or food processor. Grind until the rice resembles sand.
3. Once it starts to boil, gradually stir in the ground brown rice.
4. Add the raisins and reduce the heat to low. Cover and simmer for 5 to 8 minutes, stirring once or twice during cooking, or until the rice is tender.
5. Fluff with a fork and serve sprinkled with the almond milk and cinnamon, if desired.

Per Serving
Calories: 131 | fat: 1.8g | carbs: 26.5g | protein: 2.4g | fiber: 1.3g

Sweet Potato Oatmeal

Prep time: 10 minutes | Cook time: 20 to 22 minutes | Serves 2 to 3

1 large sweet potato, peeled and diced
1 cup unsweetened almond milk
1 cup rolled oats
½ cup date molasses
½ teaspoon ground ginger
½ teaspoon ground cinnamon
¼ teaspoon ground allspice
¼ teaspoon orange zest
Pinch salt (optional)

1. Put the diced sweet potatoes in a large pot of water and bring to a boil over high heat for about 10 minutes until softened.
2. Drain the sweet potato well and mash it with a potato masher or the back of a fork.
3. Transfer the mashed sweet potato to a small saucepan. Add the almond milk, oats, molasses, ginger, cinnamon, allspice, orange zest, and salt (if desired), and whisk well. Cook the mixture over medium heat for 10 to 12 minutes, stirring frequently, or until the oats are cooked through.
4. Divide the oats between two serving bowls and serve.

Per Serving
Calories: 400 | fat: 5.0g | carbs: 79.7g | protein: 9.2g | fiber: 7.1g

Cranberry and Protein Shake

Prep time: 5 minutes | Cook time: 0 minutes | Serves 3

¼ cup cranberries
¼ cup chia seeds, soaked in water for 20 minutes
¼ cup hemp seeds
2 cups unsweetened
coconut milk
1 fresh banana
2 tablespoons vegan protein powder (chocolate or vanilla flavor)
4 ice cubes

1. Put all the ingredients into a blender, and blend for 2 minutes until smooth and creamy.
2. Pour into three glasses and enjoy.

Per Serving
Calories: 326 | fat: 16.7g | carbs: 19.8g | protein: 23.5g | fiber: 6.7g

Pineapple and Mango Oatmeal

Prep time: 5 minutes | Cook time: 0 minutes | Serves 2

2 cups unsweetened almond milk
2 cups rolled oats
½ cup pineapple chunks, thawed if frozen
½ cup diced mango,
thawed if frozen
1 banana, sliced
1 tablespoon chia seeds
1 tablespoon maple syrup

1. Stir together the almond milk, oats, pineapple, mango, banana, chia seeds, and maple syrup in a large bowl until you see no clumps.
2. Cover and refrigerate to chill for at least 4 hours, preferably overnight.
3. Serve chilled with your favorite toppings.

Per Serving
Calories: 512 | fat: 22.1g | carbs: 13.1g | protein: 14.1g | fiber: 15.2g

Strawberry Chia Jam

Prep time: 10 minutes | Cook time: 20 minutes | Makes 2 cups

1 pound (454 g) fresh strawberries, hulled and halved
¼ cup maple syrup
¼ cup water
3 tablespoons freshly
squeezed lemon juice (from 1 lemon)
3 tablespoons chia seeds
1 teaspoon vanilla extract

1. Add the strawberries, maple syrup, water, and lemon juice to a medium saucepan over medium heat. Allow to simmer for about 15 minutes, stirring occasionally, or until the strawberries begin to soften and bubble. Use a spoon or potato masher to mash the strawberries to your desired consistency.
2. Add the chia seeds and continue stirring over low heat for 5 minutes. The chia seeds will help the jam achieve a gelatinous texture.
3. Add the vanilla and stir until combined. Remove from the heat and let the jam cool to room temperature. Stir again.
4. Serve immediately, or transfer to a mason jar and store in the fridge for up to 1 week.

Per Serving
Calories: 132 | fat: 2.5g | carbs: 25.7g | protein: 1.9g | fiber: 2.5g

Sticky Rice Congee with Dates

Prep time: 10 minutes | Cook time: 15 minutes | Serves 4

2 cups water
4 cups cooked brown rice
½ cup chopped apricots
½ cup dates, pitted and chopped
¼ teaspoon ground cloves
1 large cinnamon stick
Salt, to taste (optional)

1. Add 2 cups water to a large saucepan over medium heat and bring to a boil.
2. Add the brown rice, apricots, dates, cloves, and cinnamon stick, and stir well.
3. Reduce the heat to medium-low and simmer for 15 minutes, stirring occasionally, or until the mixture is thickened. Sprinkle the salt to season, if desired.
4. Let the congee cool for 5 minutes and remove the cinnamon stick, then serve.

Per Serving
Calories: 313 | fat: 1.9g | carbs: 68.8g | protein: 6.0g | fiber: 6.2g

Maple-Cinnamon Granola with Dates

Prep time: 10 minutes | Cook time: 10 minutes | Makes 6 cups

3 cups old-fashioned rolled oats
1 cup raw almonds, roughly chopped
1 tablespoon ground cinnamon
2 tablespoons maple syrup (optional)
6 dates, chopped
½ cup pumpkin seeds
½ cup raisins

1. Preheat the oven to 400ºF (205ºC). Line 2 baking sheets with parchment paper.
2. Stir together the oats, almonds, cinnamon, and maple syrup (If desired) in a large bowl. Evenly spread the oat mixture onto the 2 prepared baking sheets.
3. Bake in the preheated oven for 7 to 10 minutes until lightly browned.
4. Remove from the oven and allow to cool for 10 minutes. Once cooled, transfer to the large bowl, along with the dates, pumpkin seeds, and raisins, stirring until well incorporated.
5. Serve immediately or store in an airtight container.

Per Serving
Calories: 211 | fat: 9.1g | carbs: 25.8g | protein: 6.2g | fiber: 4.1g

Breakfast Quinoa

Prep time: 5 minutes | Cook time: 10 minutes | Serves 2

1 cup unsweetened almond milk
2 cups cooked quinoa
1 tablespoon defatted peanut powder
1 tablespoon cocoa powder
1 tablespoon maple syrup

1. Add the almond milk to a saucepan over medium-high heat and bring to a boil.
2. Reduce the heat to low, and add the quinoa, peanut powder, coco powder, and maple syrup while whisking.
3. Allow to simmer for 6 minutes, stirring frequently, or until some liquid has evaporated.
4. Remove from the heat and serve warm.

Per Serving
Calories: 340 | fat: 18.2g | carbs: 3.1g | protein: 14.2g | fiber: 7.1g

Brown Rice Breakfast Pudding

Prep time: 10 minutes | Cook time: 12 minutes | Serves 4

3 cups cooked brown rice
2 cups unsweetened almond milk
1 cup dates, pitted and chopped
⅛ to ¼ teaspoon ground cloves, to taste
1 cinnamon stick
¼ cup raisins
1 Granny Smith apple, cored and chopped
Salt, to taste (optional)
¼ cup slivered almonds, toasted

1. Place the brown rice, almond milk, dates, cloves, and cinnamon stick into a medium saucepan over medium-low heat. Cook for 10 minutes, stirring occasionally, or until the mixture is just beginning to bubble and thicken.
2. Remove the cinnamon stick and add the raisins, apple, and salt (if desired), and continue stirring for 2 minutes until the apple is tender.
3. Transfer to a bowl and sprinkle the toasted almonds on top for garnish before serving.

Per Serving
Calories: 375 | fat: 5.5g | carbs: 72.7g | protein: 8.7g | fiber: 6.8g

Easy Apple and Cinnamon Muesli

Prep time: 10 minutes | Cook time: 0 minutes | Serves 2

1 cup rolled oats
½ cup raisins
¾ cup unsweetened almond milk
2 tablespoons date

molasses (optional)
¼ teaspoon ground cinnamon
1 Granny Smith apple, grated

1. In a large bowl, combine the oats, raisins, almond milk, date molasses (if desired), and cinnamon. Stir until well combined and transfer the bowl to the fridge. Let the oats soak for at least 30 minutes.
2. Remove from the fridge and add the grated apple. Give it a good stir and serve immediately.

Per Serving
Calories: 325 | fat: 4.2g | carbs: 63.7g | protein: 8.8g | fiber: 10.1g

Blueberry Muffins

Prep time: 5 minutes | Cook time: 25 minutes | Makes 8 muffins

½ cup unsweetened plant-based milk
½ cup maple syrup (optional)
½ cup unsweetened applesauce
1 teaspoon vanilla ex-

tract
2 cups whole-wheat flour
½ teaspoon baking soda
1 cup blueberries

1. Preheat the oven to 375ºF (190ºC).
2. Whisk together the milk, maple syrup (if desired), applesauce, and vanilla in a large bowl until combined.
3. Stir in the flour and baking soda until no dry flour is left and the batter is smooth.
4. Fold in the blueberries and stir to combine.
5. Fill 8 muffin cups three-quarters full of batter in a muffin tin.
6. Bake in the preheated oven for 25 minutes, or until a toothpick inserted into the center of a muffin comes out clean.
7. Transfer to a wire rack and let the muffins cool completely. Serve immediately.

Per Serving (1 muffin)
Calories: 201 | fat: 1.0g | carbs: 44.9g | protein: 4.1g | fiber: 2.0g

Salted Caramel Oatmeal

Prep time: 5 minutes | Cook time: 15 minutes | Serves 4

4 cups water
16 Medjool dates, pitted and chopped
Pinch salt (optional)
2 cups steel-cut oats

Fresh berries, for topping (optional)
Sliced almonds, for topping (optional)

1. Put the water, dates, and salt (if desired) in a small saucepan over high heat and bring to a rapid boil.
2. Once it starts to boil, reduce the heat to low. Add the oats and allow to simmer for 10 minutes, stirring frequently, or until the oats are cooked through.
3. Divide the oatmeal among four serving bowls. Serve topped with fresh berries and sliced almonds, if desired.

Per Serving
Calories: 376 | fat: 2.1g | carbs: 84.9g | protein: 5.2g | fiber: 9.1g

Chocolaty Banana Breakfast Bowl

Prep time: 5 minutes | Cook time: 25 minutes | Serves 2

1 cup quinoa
1 teaspoon ground cinnamon
1 cup non-dairy milk
1 cup water
1 large banana
2 to 3 tablespoons unsweetened cocoa powder, or carob

1 to 2 tablespoons almond butter, or other nut or seed butter
1 tablespoon ground flaxseed, or chia or hemp seeds
2 tablespoons walnuts
¼ cup raspberries

1. Put the quinoa, cinnamon, milk, and water in a medium pot. Bring to a boil over high heat, then turn down low and simmer, covered, for 25 to 30 minutes.
2. While the quinoa is simmering, purée or mash the banana in a medium bowl and stir in the cocoa powder, almond butter, and flaxseed.
3. To serve, spoon 1 cup cooked quinoa into a bowl, top with half the pudding and half the walnuts and raspberries.

Per Serving (1 bowl)
Calories: 392| Total fat: 19g| Carbs: 9g| Fiber: 10g| Protein: 12g

Maple Sunflower Seed Granola

Prep time: 20 minutes | Cook time: 0 minutes | Makes 2 cups

1½ cups peanut but-
ter
¼ cup maple syrup
1½ cups old-fash-

ioned rolled oats
¾ cup raw sunflower
seeds
¾ cup flaxseed meal

1. Place the peanut butter and maple syrup in a microwave-safe bowl, and microwave on high in 30-second intervals, stirring well between each interval, until the mixture is completely mixed. Let it rest for a few minutes until slightly cooled.
2. Add the rolled oats, sunflower seeds, and flaxseed meal to the bowl, and whisk until well incorporated.
3. Transfer the mixture to a baking sheet lined with parchment paper and spread it out into an even layer.
4. Put the baking sheet in the freezer for at least 25 minutes until firm.
5. Remove from the freezer and break the granola into large chunks before serving.

Per Serving
Calories: 764 | fat: 51.7g | carbs: 47.8g | protein: 27.0g | fiber: 16.0g

Tropical Spinach Smoothie

Prep time: 5 minutes | Cook time: 0 minutes | Serves 2

2 bananas
2 cups frozen spinach
1 cup frozen mango
chunks
1 cup unsweetened
nondairy milk, plus
more as needed
1 large navel orange,
peeled and segment-

ed
2 tablespoons cashew
butter or almond but-
ter
2 celery stalks, bro-
ken into pieces
1 tablespoon ground
flaxseed

1. Place all the ingredients in a food processor or blender and pulse until creamy, adding more milk to thin the smoothie if too thick.
2. Serve immediately.

Per Serving
Calories: 389 | fat: 11.8g | carbs: 68.1g | protein: 13.2g | fiber: 13.1g

Cinnamon Applesauce Pancakes

Prep time: 5 minutes | Cook time: 16 minutes | Makes 8 pancakes

1 cup whole-wheat
flour
1 teaspoon baking
powder
½ teaspoon ground
cinnamon
1 cup unsweetened

almond milk
¼ cup maple syrup
½ cup unsweetened
applesauce
1 teaspoon vanilla ex-
tract

1. Mix together the flour, baking powder, and cinnamon in a large bowl.
2. Add the almond milk, maple syrup, applesauce, and vanilla to the bowl. Stir with a fork until the ingredients are well combined and a smooth batter form.
3. Heat a large nonstick skillet over medium heat until hot.
4. Make the pancakes: Pour ¼ cup of batter into the skillet and swirl the pan so the batter covers the bottom evenly. Cook for 1 to 2 minutes until bubbles form on the surface. Flip the pancake and cook for 1 minutes more, or until the pancake is browned around the edges and cooked through. Repeat with the remaining batter.
5. Transfer the pancakes to a plate and serve warm.

Per Serving (2 PANCAKES)
Calories: 212 | fat: 12.2g | carbs: 4.1g | protein: 5.1g | fiber: 5.2g

Vegan Dairy Free Breakfast Bowl

Prep time: 20 minutes | Cook time: 0 minutes | Makes 2 cups

½ cup strawberries
½ cup blueberries
½ cup blackberries
½ cup raspberries
1 grapefruit, peeled
and segmented
3 tablespoons fresh

orange juice (from 1
orange)
1 tablespoon pure
maple syrup
¼ cup chopped fresh
mint
¼ cup sliced almonds

1. In a serving bowl, combine the berries and grapefruit.
2. In a small bowl, stir together the orange juice and maple syrup.
3. Pour the syrup mixture over the fruit. Sprinkle with the mint and almonds. Serve immediately

Rinsed cannellini beans and Carrot Soup Bowl

Prep time: 10 minutes | Cook time: 20 minutes | Makes 3 to 4 large bowls

1 teaspoon olive oil
1 cup chopped onion
1 tablespoon minced fresh ginger
4 large carrots, peeled, or scrubbed and chopped (about 2 cups)
1 cup cooked, or
canned and rinsed cannellini beans, or other soft white beans
½ cup vegetable broth, or water and a bit extra salt
2 cups water
¼ teaspoon sea salt

1. In a large pot, warm the olive oil, then sauté the onion and ginger for 2 or 3 minutes. Add the carrots and cook to soften, about 3 minutes.
2. Add the beans, vegetable broth, water, and salt, and simmer for 20 minutes.
3. Transfer the soup to a blender or use an immersion blender to purée. Serve warm.

Per Serving (1 bowl)
Calories: 141| Total fat: 12g| Carbs: 6g| Fiber: 7g| Protein: 7g

Watercress Mint Creamy Soup

Prep time: 10 minutes | Cook time: 20 minutes | Makes 4 bowls

1 teaspoon coconut oil
1 onion, diced
2 cups fresh or frozen peas
4 cups water or vegetable stock
1 cup fresh water-
cress, chopped
1 tablespoon fresh mint, chopped
Pinch sea salt
Pinch freshly ground black pepper
¾ cup coconut milk

1. Melt the coconut oil in a large pot over medium-high heat. Add the onion and cook until soft, about 5 minutes, then add the peas and the water.
2. Bring to a boil, then lower the heat and add the watercress, mint, salt, and pepper. Cover and simmer for 5 minutes.
3. Stir in the coconut milk and purée the soup until smooth in a blender or with an immersion blender.

Per Serving
Calories: 178| Total fat: 10g| Carbs: 8g| Fiber: 5g| Protein: 6g

Healthy Lettuce Sandwich

Prep time: 5 minutes | Cook time: 10 minutes | Makes 1

¼ cup Classic Hummus
2 slices whole-grain bread
¼ avocado, sliced
½ cup lettuce, chopped
½ tomato, sliced
Pinch sea salt
Pinch freshly ground black pepper
1 teaspoon olive oil, divided

1. Spread some hummus on each slice of bread. Then layer the avocado, lettuce, and tomato on one slice, sprinkle with salt and pepper, and top with the other slice.
2. Heat a skillet to medium heat, and drizzle ½ teaspoon of the olive oil just before putting the sandwich in the skillet.
3. Cook for 3 to 5 minutes, then lift the sandwich with a spatula, drizzle the remaining ½ teaspoon olive oil into the skillet, and flip the sandwich to grill the other side for 3 to 5 minutes.
4. Press it down with the spatula to seal the vegetables inside. Once done, remove from the skillet and slice in half to serve.

Per Serving
Calories: 322| Total fat: 14g| Carbs: 5g| Fiber: 11g| Protein: 12g

Banana Chai Smoothie with Vanilla

Prep time: 5 minutes | Cook time: 10 minutes | Makes 1

1Banana, frozen
1 ½ cup Almond Milk, vanilla, unsweetened
1 tablespoon Almond Butter, no added salt
1 teaspoon Flax Seeds
1/4 Teaspoon Cinnamon, ground
1/4 Teaspoon Clove, ground
1/4 Teaspoon Ginger Root, ground

1. Add ingredients in the order listed and blend until smooth.

Per Serving
Calories: 266.7| Total fat: 15.2g| Carbs: 29.9g| Fiber: 7.1g| Protein: 6.6g

Vanilla Buckwheat Breakfast Bowl

Prep time: 5 minutes | Cook time: 25 minutes | Serves 4

3 cups water
1 cup raw buckwheat groats
1 banana, sliced
1 teaspoon ground cinnamon
¼ cup dried currants
¼ cup sunflower seeds
¼ cup golden raisins
2 tablespoons chia seeds
1 tablespoon sesame seeds, toasted
1 tablespoon hemp seeds
1 tablespoon pure maple syrup (optional)
½ cup unsweetened coconut milk
1 teaspoon vanilla extract

1. Heat the water in a large pot over high heat until boiling. Fold in the buckwheat, banana, and cinnamon and stir well. Bring the pot back to a boil, stirring occasionally.
2. Turn the heat to medium-low and continue to cook, covered, for 15 minutes, or until the buckwheat is softened. Remove from the heat.
3. Add the currants, sunflower seeds, raisins, chia seeds, sesame seeds, hemp seeds, maple syrup (if desired), milk, and vanilla and stir until well mixed.
4. Cover and let stand for 10 minutes.
5. Ladle the porridge into bowls and serve hot.

Per Serving
Calories: 352 | fat: 10.6g | carbs: 60.5g | protein: 10.2g | fiber: 10.0g

Cashew-Date Waffles

Prep time: 20 minutes | Cook time: 10 minutes | Serves 2

1 ounce (28 g) raw, unsalted cashews (about ¼ cup)
1 ounce (28 g) pitted dates, chopped
2 cups unsweetened coconut milk
1½ cups old-fashioned rolled oats
½ cup cornmeal
2 teaspoons baking powder
½ teaspoon cinnamon

1. In a small bowl, add the cashews, dates, and coconut milk. Let the nuts and dates soak in the milk for at least 15 minutes.
2. Grind the rolled oats in a blender, or until it has reached a powdery consistency.
3. Place the oats in a medium bowl, along with the cornmeal, baking powder, and cinnamon. Stir well and set aside.
4. Preheat the waffle iron to medium-high heat.
5. Blend the cashews, dates, and coconut milk in a blender until completely mixed. Pour the mixture into the bowl of dry ingredients and whisk to combine. Let the batter sit for 1 minute.
6. Slowly pour ½ to ¾ cup of the batter into the preheated waffle iron and cook for 3 to 4 minutes until golden brown. Repeat with the remaining batter.
7. Divide the waffles between two plates and serve warm.

Per Serving
Calories: 849 | fat: 13.5g | carbs: 66.4g | protein: 16.8g | fiber: 10.1g

Morning Carrot Oatmeal with Pecans

Prep time: 10 minutes | Cook time: 15 minutes | Serves 2

¼ cup pecans
1 cup finely shredded carrot
1¼ cups unsweetened nondairy milk
½ cup old-fashioned oats
1 tablespoon pure maple syrup (optional)
1 teaspoon ground ginger
1 teaspoon ground cinnamon
¼ teaspoon ground nutmeg
2 tablespoons chia seeds

1. In a small skillet over medium-high heat, toast the pecans for 3 to 4 minutes, stirring often, or until the pecans are browned and fragrant.
2. Transfer the pecans onto a cutting board and coarsely chop them. Set aside.
3. Mix together the carrot, milk, oats, maple syrup (if desired), ginger, cinnamon, and nutmeg in a pot over medium-high heat. Bring the mixture to a boil.
4. Reduce the heat to medium-low and cook uncovered for 10 minutes, stirring occasionally.
5. Add the toasted pecans and chia seeds and stir well. Serve warm.

Per Serving
Calories: 308 | fat: 17.1g | carbs: 35.0g | protein: 7.2g | fiber: 11.0g

Baked Blueberry and Chia Seed Oatmeal

Prep time: 10 minutes | Cook time: 35 to 40 minutes | Serves 4

2 cups unsweetened almond milk
2 tablespoons chia seeds
1½ cups gluten-free rolled oats
2 tablespoons water
2 tablespoons maple syrup
½ teaspoon vanilla extract
1 teaspoon ground cinnamon
¼ teaspoon sea salt (optional)
1 ripe banana, sliced
1 cup blueberries, divided
½ cup chopped walnuts

1. Preheat the oven to 350ºF (180ºC).
2. Whisk together the almond milk and chia seeds in a small bowl. Let the chia seeds absorb the milk for about 5 minutes.
3. Meanwhile, combine the oats, water, maple syrup, vanilla, cinnamon, and salt (if desired) in a medium bowl, and whisk well. Stir in the chia seed mixture.
4. Spread out the banana slices on a baking dish in an even layer. Scatter the top with half of the blueberries and pour over the oat mixture.
5. Place the remaining blueberries and walnuts on top of the oats.
6. Bake in the preheated oven for about 35 to 40 minutes, or until the top is golden brown.
7. Remove from the oven and cool for 5 minutes before serving.

Per Serving
Calories: 461 | fat: 22.1g | carbs: 52.8g | protein: 13.2g | fiber: 10.5g

Veggie and Tofu Scramble

Prep time: 5 minutes | Cook time: 15 minutes | Serves 2

1 (14-ounce / 397-g) package firm or extra-firm tofu, drained
4 ounces (113 g) mushrooms, sliced
½ bell pepper, diced
2 tablespoons nutritional yeast
½ teaspoon onion powder
½ teaspoon garlic powder
1 tablespoon low-sodium vegetable broth
⅛ Teaspoon freshly ground black pepper
1 cup fresh spinach

1. Heat a large skillet over medium-low heat.
2. Add the tofu to the skillet and mash it down with a fork or the back of a spoon.

3. Fold in the sliced mushrooms, bell peppers, nutritional yeast, onion powder, garlic powder, vegetable broth, and black pepper, and stir well.
4. Cook, covered, for 10 minutes, stirring halfway through, or until the tofu is lightly browned and the veggies are softened.
5. Stir in the spinach and cook, uncovered, for 5 minutes.
6. Remove from the heat and serve warm.

Per Serving
Calories: 233 | fat: 10.2g | carbs: 6.1g | protein: 27.2g | fiber: 7.1g

Flaxseed Pancakes

Prep time: 10 minutes | Cook time: 20 minutes | Serves 4

6 tablespoons warm water
3 tablespoons ground flaxseed
1½ cups whole wheat pastry flour
½ cup rye flour
2 tablespoons baking powder
½ teaspoon ground ginger
1 teaspoon ground cinnamon
1½ cups unsweetened nondairy milk
3 tablespoons pure maple syrup (optional)
1 teaspoon vanilla extract

1. Combine the warm water and flaxseed in a small bowl and stir to mix well. Set aside for at least 5 minutes.
2. Mix together the pastry and rye flours, baking powder, ginger, and cinnamon in a large bowl.
3. Whisk the milk, maple syrup (if desired), and vanilla together in a glass measuring cup. Add the wet ingredients into the dry ingredients and stir with a spatula until incorporated. Fold in the soaked flaxseed and mix well.
4. Heat a large skillet over medium-high heat.
5. Working in batches, 3 to 4 pancakes at a time, pour ¼-cup portions of batter into the hot skillet. Cook each side for 3 to 4 minutes, or until golden brown. Repeat with the remaining batter.
6. Remove from the heat and serve on a plate.

Per Serving
Calories: 304 | fat: 4.1g | carbs: 57.2g | protein: 10.2g | fiber: 10.1g

Hot & Healthy Breakfast Bowl with Nuts

Prep time: 5 minutes | Cook time: 0 minutes | Serves 1

½ cup rolled oats, or quinoa flakes for gluten-free	tablespoon pumpkin seeds
1 tablespoon ground flaxseed, or chia seeds, or hemp hearts	1 pear, chopped and
	1 tablespoon cashews
	1 cup sliced grapes and 1 tablespoon sunflower seeds
1 tablespoon maple syrup or coconut sugar (optional)	1 banana, sliced, and 1 tablespoon peanut butter
¼ teaspoon ground cinnamon (optional)	2 tablespoons raisins and 1 tablespoon hazelnuts
1 apple, chopped and 1 tablespoon walnuts	1 cup berries and 1 tablespoon unsweetened coconut flakes
2 tablespoons dried cranberries and 1	

1. Mix the oats, flax, maple syrup, and cinnamon (if using) together in a bowl or to-go container (a travel mug or short thermos works beautifully).
2. Pour enough cool water over the oats to submerge them, and stir to combine. Leave to soak for a minimum of half an hour, or overnight.
3. Add your choice of toppings.
4. Boil about ½ cup water and pour over the oats. Let them soak about 5 minutes before eating.

Per Serving
Calories: 244| Total fat: 16g| Carbs: 10g| Fiber: 6g| Protein: 7g

Banana Blueberry Pancakes

Prep time: 5 minutes | Cook time: 20 minutes | Serves 4

3 ripe bananas	1 cup arrowroot powder
¼ cup pure maple syrup, plus additional for serving (optional)	2 cups almond flour
	¼ cup ground flaxseed
¾ cup water	1 to 2 tablespoons coconut oil (optional)
2 teaspoons baking powder	½ cup wild blueberries (fresh or frozen)
¼ teaspoon salt (optional)	

1. Process the bananas, maple syrup (if desired), water, baking powder, and salt (if desired) in a food processor until smooth and creamy.

2. Add the almond flour, arrowroot powder, and flaxseed and pulse until completely mixed.
3. Melt ½ teaspoon of coconut oil (if desired) in a large, nonstick skillet over medium heat.
4. Pour the batter into the hot skillet to create several 4-inch pancakes. Scatter a few blueberries on top of each pancake. Cook for about 3 minutes, or until the pancake bottoms are slightly browned. Flip the pancakes and cook for an additional 1 to 2 minutes. Repeat with the remaining coconut oil and batter.
5. Serve the pancakes hot with a drizzle of maple syrup, if desired.

Per Serving
Calories: 338 | fat: 14.1g | carbs: 73.1g | protein: 5.2g | fiber: 7.1g

Lentil Tomato Sauce

Prep time: 10 minutes | Cook time: 30 minutes | Serves 6

2 cups brown lentils (or green lentils)	and cilantro
	2 ½ teaspoons cumin
2 or 3 large, ripe tomatoes (grated)	2 ½ teaspoons paprika
1 medium onion (chopped)	1 ½ teaspoons ginger
	½ teaspoon pepper
3 to 5 cloves of garlic (finely chopped or pressed)	Optional: cayenne pepper (to taste)
	2 teaspoons salt (or to taste)
4 tablespoons chopped fresh parsley	

1. Mix all ingredients in a pressure cooker.
2. Add 2 liters (about 2 quarts) of water, and bring to a simmer.
3. Cover, and cook on pressure over medium heat for 35 to 40 minutes, or until the lentils are tender.
4. If the lentils are still submerged in sauce, you must reduce the liquids so that the sauce is ample, but not watery. Adjust the seasoning if desired.
5. Portion into bowls and garnish with some fresh parsley.

Per Serving
Calories: 357| Total fat: 3.94g| Carbs: 74.86g| Protein: 22.4g

Dried Cranberry Almond Bowl

Prep time: 10 minutes | Cook time: 0 minutes | Makes about 5 cups

MUESLI
1 cup rolled oats
1 cup spelt flakes, or quinoa flakes, or more rolled oats
2 cups puffed cereal
¼ cup sunflower seeds
¼ cup almonds
¼ cup raisins
¼ cup dried cranberries
¼ cup chopped dried

figs
¼ cup unsweetened shredded coconut
¼ cup non-dairy chocolate chips
1 to 3 Teaspoons ground cinnamon
BOWL
½ cup non-dairy milk, or unsweetened applesauce
¾ cup muesli
½ cup berries

1. Put the muesli ingredients in a container or bag and shake.
2. Combine the muesli and bowl ingredients in a bowl or to-go container.

Per Serving (1 bowl) :
Calories: 441| Total fat: 20g| Carbs: 13g| Fiber: 13g| Protein: 10g

Grilled Eggplant and Fresh Basil Vegetarian Pizza

Prep time: 10 minutes | Cook time: 10 minutes | Serves 8

1/4 cup olive oil (for brushing eggplant)
1 small eggplant
1 batch prepared pizza dough
12 leaves basil

1/3 cup prepared pizza sauce
2/3 cup mozzarella cheese (grated or thinly sliced)

1. Set oven to broil or heat grill to medium-high heat (about 500 F).
2. Slice eggplant into rounds about 1/3-inch thick.
3. Brush with the eggplant with olive oil.
4. Grill for a few minutes on a grill pan or on the barbecue for about 2 to 3 minutes on each side or just until tender. Set aside. If you don't have a grill handy, you could also roast them in the oven for about 10 minutes at 300 F on a baking sheet.
5. On top of the sauce, arrange the grilled eggplant slices in a single layer and tuck a whole basil leaf under each slice.

6. Depending on the size of your eggplant, you may have some leftover. Dip it in the sauce and eat it as an appetizer while you're waiting for your pizza to cook!
7. Chop 3 to 4 whole basil leaves coarsely, and then sprinkle them on top of the pizza, followed by a layer of grated mozzarella cheese.
8. Bake your vegetarian eggplant pizza in the oven for 10 to 15 minutes, or until cheese is just bubbly and crust is lightly golden brown.

Per Serving
Calories: 908 | Total fat: 71.1g| Carbs: 42.33g| Fiber: 7.1g| Protein: 31.68g

Fresh mint and coconut Fruit Salad

Prep time: 5 minutes | Cook time: 5 minutes | Serves 1

1 orange, zested and juiced
¼ cup whole-wheat couscous, or corn couscous
1 cup assorted berries (strawberries, blackberries, blueberries)
½ cup cubed or balled melon (cantaloupe or

honeydew)
1 tablespoon maple syrup or coconut sugar (optional)
1 tablespoon fresh mint, minced (optional)
1 tablespoon unsweetened coconut flakes

1. Put the orange juice in a small pot, add half the zest, and bring to a boil.
2. Put the dry couscous in a small bowl and pour the boiling orange juice over it. If there isn't enough juice to fully submerge the couscous, add just enough boiling water to do so.
3. Cover the bowl with a plate or seal with wrap, and let steep for 5 minutes.
4. In a medium bowl, toss the berries and melon with the maple syrup (if using) and the rest of the zest. You can either keep the fruit cool, or heat it lightly in the small pot you used for the orange juice.
5. When the couscous is soft, remove the cover and fluff it with a fork. Top with the fruit, fresh mint, and coconut.

Per Serving:
Calories: 496| Total fat: 22g| Carbs: 7g| Fiber: 14g| Protein: 11g

Peppery Mushroom Tomato Bowl

Prep time: 5 minutes | Cook time: 15 minutes | Serves 1

1 teaspoon olive oil, or 1 tablespoon vegetable broth or water
½ cup mushrooms, sliced
Pinch sea salt
½ cup chopped zucchini
½ cup chickpeas (cooked or canned)
1 teaspoon smoked paprika, or regular paprika
1 teaspoon turmeric
1 tablespoon nutritional yeast (optional)
Freshly ground black pepper
½ cup cherry tomatoes, chopped
¼ cup fresh parsley, chopped

1. Heat a large skillet to medium-high. Once the skillet is hot, add the olive oil and mushrooms, along with the sea salt to help them soften, and sauté, stirring occasionally, 7 to 8 minutes.
2. Add the zucchini to the skillet.
3. If you're using canned chickpeas, rinse and drain them. Mash the chickpeas with a potato masher, fork, or your fingers. Add them to the skillet and cook until they are heated through.
4. Sprinkle the paprika, turmeric, and nutritional yeast over the chickpeas, and stir to combine.
5. Toss in the black pepper, cherry tomatoes and fresh parsley at the end, just to warm, reserving a small bit of parsley to use as garnish.

Per Serving:
Calories: 265| Total fat: 18g| Carbs: 7g| Fiber: 12g| Protein: 16g

Healthy Chocolaty Oats Bites

Prep time: 15 minutes | Cook time: 12 minutes | Makes 5 big cookies

1 tablespoon ground flaxseed
2 tablespoons almond butter or sunflower seed butter
2 tablespoons maple syrup
1 banana, mashed
1 teaspoon ground cinnamon
¼ teaspoon ground nutmeg (optional)
Pinch sea salt
½ cup rolled oats
¼ cup raisins, or dark chocolate chips

1. Preheat the oven to 350°F. Line a large baking sheet with parchment paper. Mix the ground flax with just enough water to cover it in a small dish, and leave it to sit.
2. In a large bowl, mix together the almond butter and maple syrup until creamy, then add the banana. Add the flax-water mixture.
3. Sift the cinnamon, nutmeg, and salt into a separate medium bowl, then stir into the wet mixture. Add the oats and raisins, and fold in.
4. From 3 to 4 tablespoons batter into a ball and press lightly to flatten onto the baking sheet. Repeat, spacing the cookies 2 to 3 inches apart. Bake for 12 minutes, or until golden brown.
5. Store the cookies in an airtight container in the fridge.

Per Serving (1 cookie):
Calories: 192| Total fat: 16g| Carbs: 4g| Fiber: 4g| Protein: 4g

Apple Toasted Sweet Sandwich

Prep time: 5 minutes | Cook time: 20 minutes | Makes 2 slices

1 to 2 teaspoons coconut oil
½ teaspoon ground cinnamon
1 tablespoon maple syrup or coconut sugar
1 apple, cored and thinly sliced
2 slices whole-grain bread

1. In a large bowl, mix the coconut oil, cinnamon, and maple syrup together.
2. Add the apple slices and toss with your hands to coat them.
3. To panfry the toast, place the apple slices in a medium skillet on medium-high and cook for about 5 minutes, or until slightly soft, then transfer to a plate.
4. Cook the bread in the same skillet for 2 to 3 minutes on each side. Top the toast with the apples. Alternately, you can bake the toast.
5. Use your hands to rub each slice of bread with some of the coconut oil mixture on both sides.
6. Lay them on a small baking sheet, top with the coated apples, and put in the oven or toaster oven at 350°F (180°C) for 15 to 20 minutes, or until the apples have softened.

Per Serving (1 slice):
Calories: 187| Total fat: 18g| Carbs: 7g| Fiber: 4g| Protein: 4g

Nutty Fruity Breakfast Bowl

Prep time: 15 minutes | Cook time: 30 minutes | Makes 5 cups

2 cups rolled oats
¾ cup whole-grain flour
1 tablespoon ground cinnamon
1 teaspoon ground ginger (optional)
½ cup sunflower seeds, or walnuts, chopped
½ cup almonds, chopped
½ cup pumpkin seeds
½ cup unsweetened shredded coconut
1¼ cups pure fruit juice (cranberry, apple, or something similar)
½ cup raisins, or dried cranberries
½ cup goji berries (optional)

1. Preheat the oven to 350°F.
2. Mix together the oats, flour, cinnamon, ginger, sunflower seeds, almonds, pumpkin seeds, and coconut in a large bowl.
3. Sprinkle the juice over the mixture, and stir until it's just moistened. You might need a bit more or a bit less liquid, depending on how much your oats and flour absorb.
4. Spread the granola on a large baking sheet (the more spread out it is the better), and put it in the oven. After about 15 minutes, use a spatula to turn the granola so that the middle gets dried out. Let the granola bake until it's as crunchy as you want it, about 30 minutes more.
5. Take the granola out of the oven and stir in the raisins and goji berries (if using).
6. Store leftovers in an airtight container for up to 2 weeks.

Per Serving (½ cup)
Calories: 398| Total fat: 25g| Carbs: 9g| Fiber: 8g| Protein: 10g

Grilled Cauliflower Steaks with Fresh Herb Sauce

Prep time: 10 minutes | Cook time: 10 minutes | Serves 2

1 large head cauliflower
1 tablespoon canola or grape seed oil
1 teaspoon ground cumin
1 teaspoon ground turmeric
Salt and pepper
2 tablespoons packed (finely chopped fresh parsley)
1 tablespoon packed (finely chopped fresh mint)
½ small lemon (zested and juiced)
1 teaspoon olive oil
1 garlic clove (finely minced)
1 large pinch red pepper flakes
Steps to Make It
Preheat your grill at medium-high heat.

1. Trim the leaves off of the cauliflower and remove the end of the stalk.
2. Set it on your cutting board and cut into thick steaks from top to bottom (so that they look like the photo).
3. You will get two to four whole steaks. Save the remaining loose cauliflower florets for another use.
4. Brush both sides of the steaks with oil. Dust with the cumin and turmeric and season with salt and pepper on both sides.
5. Grill the steaks for about five minutes per side, or until they have reached the desired doneness.
6. Combine the parsley, mint, lemon zest and juice, olive oil, garlic and pepper flakes in a small bowl. Season with salt and pepper.
7. Serve the sauce drizzled over the top and more on the side.

Per Serving
Calories: 300| Total fat: 22.02g| Carbs: 28.34g| Protein: 8.62g

Homemade Nutty Fruity Muffins

Prep time: 15 minutes | Cook time: 30 minutes | Makes 6 muffins

1 teaspoon coconut oil, for greasing muffin tins (optional)
2 tablespoons almond butter, or sunflower seed butter
¼ cup non-dairy milk
1 orange, peeled
1 carrot, coarsely chopped
2 tablespoons chopped dried apricots, or other dried fruit
3 tablespoons molasses
2 tablespoons ground flaxseed
1 teaspoon apple cider vinegar
1 teaspoon pure vanilla extract
½ teaspoon ground cinnamon
½ teaspoon ground ginger (optional)
¼ teaspoon ground nutmeg (optional)
¼ teaspoon allspice (optional)
¾ cup rolled oats, or whole-grain flour
1 teaspoon baking powder
½ teaspoon baking soda
MIX-INS (OPTIONAL)
½ cup rolled oats
2 tablespoons raisins, or other chopped dried fruit
2 tablespoons sunflower seeds

1. Preheat the oven to 350°F. Prepare a 6-cup muffin tin by rubbing the insides of the cups with coconut oil or using silicone or paper muffin cups.
2. Purée the nut butter, milk, orange, carrot, apricots, molasses, flaxseed, vinegar, vanilla, cinnamon, ginger, nutmeg, and allspice in a food processor or blender until somewhat smooth.
3. Grind the oats in a clean coffee grinder until they're the consistency of flour (or use whole-grain flour). In a large bowl, mix the oats with the baking powder and baking soda.
4. Mix the wet ingredients into the dry ingredients until just combined. Fold in the mix-ins (if using).
5. Spoon about ¼ cup batter into each muffin cup and bake for 30 minutes, or until a toothpick inserted into the center comes out clean.

Per Serving (1 muffin) :
Calories: 287| Total fat: 23g| Carbs: 11g| Fiber: 6g| Protein: 8g

Vanilla Flavoured Whole Grain Muffins

Prep time: 15 minutes | Cook time: 20 minutes | Makes 12 muffins

1 teaspoon coconut oil, for greasing muffin tins (optional)
2 tablespoons nut butter or seed butter
1½ cups unsweetened applesauce
⅓ cup coconut sugar
½ cup non-dairy milk
2 tablespoons ground flaxseed
1 teaspoon apple cider vinegar
1 teaspoon pure vanilla extract
2 cups whole-grain flour
1 teaspoon baking soda
½ teaspoon baking powder
1 teaspoon ground cinnamon
Pinch sea salt
½ cup walnuts, chopped
TOPPINGS (OPTIONAL)
¼ cup walnuts
¼ cup coconut sugar
½ teaspoon ground cinnamon

1. Preheat the oven to 350°F. Prepare two 6-cup muffin tins by rubbing the insides of the cups with coconut oil, or using silicone or paper muffin cups.
2. In a large bowl, mix the nut butter, applesauce, coconut sugar, milk, flaxseed, vinegar, and vanilla until thoroughly combined, or purée in a food processor or blender.
3. In another large bowl, sift together the flour, baking soda, baking powder, cinnamon, salt, and chopped walnuts.
4. Mix the dry ingredients into the wet ingredients until just combined.
5. Spoon about ¼ cup batter into each muffin cup and sprinkle with the topping of your choice (if using).
6. Bake for 15 to 20 minutes, or until a toothpick inserted into the center comes out clean. The applesauce creates a very moist base, so the muffins may take longer, depending on how heavy your muffin tins are.

Per Serving (1 muffin):
Calories: 287| Total fat: 12g| Carbs: 8g| Fiber: 6g| Protein: 8g

Coconut Banana Sandwich with Raspberry Spread

Prep time: 10minutes | Cook time: 30 minutes | Makes 8 slices

FRENCH TOAST
1 banana
1 cup coconut milk
1 teaspoon pure vanilla extract
¼ teaspoon ground nutmeg
½ teaspoon ground cinnamon
1½ Teaspoons arrowroot powder or flour
Pinch sea salt

8 slices whole-grain bread
RASPBERRY SYRUP
1 cup fresh or frozen raspberries or other berries
2 tablespoons water or pure fruit juice
1 to 2 tablespoons maple syrup or coconut sugar (optional)

1. Preheat the oven to 350ºF.
2. In a shallow bowl, purée or mash the banana well. Mix in the coconut milk, vanilla, nutmeg, cinnamon, arrowroot, and salt.
3. Dip the slices of bread in the banana mixture, and then lay them out in a 13-by-9-inch baking dish. They should cover the bottom of the dish and can overlap a bit but shouldn't be stacked on top of each other.
4. Pour any leftover banana mixture over the bread, and put the dish in the oven. Bake about 30 minutes, or until the tops are lightly browned.
5. Serve topped with raspberry syrup.
6. Heat the raspberries in a small pot with the water and the maple syrup (if using) on medium heat.
7. Leave to simmer, stirring occasionally and breaking up the berries, for 15 to 20 minutes, until the liquid has reduced.

Per Serving (1 slice with syrup)
Calories: 166| Total fat: 15g| Carbs: 7g| Fiber: 4g| Protein: 5g

Pumpkin Spice Muffins

Prep time: 10 minutes | Cook time: 18 to 20 minutes | Makes 12 muffins

2 tablespoons ground flaxseed
¼ cup water
1¾ cups whole wheat flour
1½ Teaspoons ground cinnamon
2 teaspoons baking powder
½ teaspoon baking soda
½ teaspoon ground ginger

¼ teaspoon ground nutmeg
⅛ Teaspoon ground cloves
1 cup pumpkin purée
½ cup pure maple syrup (optional)
¼ cup unsweetened nondairy milk
¼ cup unsweetened applesauce
1½ Teaspoons vanilla extract

1. Preheat the oven to 350ºF (180ºC). Line a 12-cup metal muffin pan with paper liners.
2. Whisk the flaxseed and water together in a small bowl. Set aside for at least 5 minutes.
3. Mix together the flour, cinnamon, baking powder, baking soda, ginger, nutmeg, and cloves in a large bowl.
4. Whisk together the remaining ingredients to combine in a medium bowl.
5. Add the wet ingredients to the dry ingredients and stir until just incorporated. Fold in the soaked flaxseed and stir well.
6. Spoon about ¼ cup of batter per muffin into the prepared muffin pan.
7. Bake in the preheated oven for 18 to 20 minutes, or until a toothpick inserted into the center of a muffin comes out clean.
8. Remove from the oven and place on a wire rack to cool. Serve warm.

Per Serving (1 muffin)
Calories: 118 | fat: 1.1g | carbs: 25.1g | protein: 3.2g | fiber: 3.3g

Vegetable Hash Breakfast

Prep time: 15 minutes | Cook time: 25 minutes | Serves 4

2 rosemary sprigs, leaves removed and minced
1 tablespoon dried thyme
1 teaspoon Hungarian paprika
½ teaspoon freshly ground black pepper
4 large carrots cut into ½-inch cubes
2 large sweet potatoes cut into ½-inch cubes
2 Yukon Gold pota-toes, cut into ½-inch cubes
2 parsnips, cut into ½-inch cubes
1 rutabaga, cut into ½-inch cubes
3 garlic cloves, minced
1 large onion, diced
1 (15-ounce / 425-g) can chickpeas, drained and rinsed
1 (15-ounce / 425-g) can red kidney beans, drained and rinsed

1. Preheat the oven to 375ºF (190ºC). Line a sheet pan with parchment paper.
2. Combine the rosemary, thyme, paprika, and pepper in a small bowl. Set aside.
3. Bring a large pot of water to a boil over high heat.
4. Add the carrots, sweet potatoes, Yukon Gold potatoes, parsnips, and rutabaga. Parboil for 2 minutes. Drain well but don't rinse.
5. Transfer the vegetables to a large bowl.
6. Add the rosemary mixture and toss until evenly coated. Spread out the parboiled vegetables on the prepared sheet pan and sprinkle with the garlic and onion.
7. Bake in the preheated oven for 20 minutes, or until the vegetables are crisp-tender.
8. Meanwhile, stir together the chickpeas and kidney beans in a medium bowl.
9. Serve with the baked vegetable hash.

Per Serving
Calories: 459 | fat: 3.1g | carbs: 95.0g | protein: 17.2g | fiber: 20.1g

Lemony Oat Pancakes with Dates

Prep time: 20 minutes | Cook time: 12 to 24 minutes | Makes about 6 pancakes

2 ounces (57 g) pit-ted dates, chopped
2 cups unsweetened almond milk
1½ cups old-fash-ioned rolled oats
½ cup cornmeal
½ teaspoon baking soda
1½ Teaspoons baking
powder
½ teaspoon cinnamon
3 tablespoons lemon juice
1 tablespoon lemon zest
Finely chopped wal-nuts, for topping (optional)

1. In a small bowl, put the dates and almond milk. Let the dates soak for 15 minutes until softened.
2. Meanwhile, grind the rolled oats in a blender, or until they are ground into a powder-like consistency.
3. Transfer the ground oats to a medium bowl and fold in the cornmeal, baking soda, baking powder, and cinnamon. Whisk well to combine.
4. Put the dates and milk into the blender and blend until finely smooth.
5. Pour the date and milk mixture into the bowl of dry ingredients. Add the lemon juice and lemon zest and stir until the batter is smooth.
6. Heat a large nonstick skillet over medium heat.
7. Make the pancakes: Using a measuring cup, add ¼ to ½ cup of the batter to the skillet, tilting the pan to spread it evenly. Cook for 1 to 2 minutes until bubbles form on the surface. Flip the pancake and cook for 1 to 2 minutes more, or until the pancake turns golden brown around the edges. Repeat with the remaining batter.
8. Scatter the chopped walnuts on top, if desired. Serve immediately.

Per Serving
Calories: 340 | fat: 6.9g | carbs: 57.8g | protein: 11.7g | fiber: 7.6g

Roasted Beets & Carrot with Avocado Dip

Prep time: 10 minutes | Cook time: 30 minutes | Serves 2

Avocado Dip:
1 avocado
1 tablespoon apple cider vinegar
¼ to ½ cup water
2 tablespoons nutritional yeast
1 teaspoon dried dill, or 1 tablespoon fresh dill
Pinch sea salt
Roasted Veg:
1 small sweet potato, peeled and cubed
2 small beets, peeled and cubed
2 small carrots, peeled and cubed
1 teaspoon sea salt
1 teaspoon dried oregano
¼ teaspoon cayenne pepper
Pinch freshly ground black pepper

1. In a blender, purée the avocado with the other dip ingredients, using just enough water to get a smooth, creamy texture.
2. Alternately, you can mash the avocado thoroughly in a large bowl, then stir in the rest of the dip ingredients.
3. Preheat the oven to 350°F.
4. Put the sweet potato, beets, and carrots in a large pot with a small amount of water, and bring to a boil over high heat. Boil for 15 minutes, until they're just barely soft, and then drain.
5. Sprinkle the salt, oregano, cayenne, and pepper over them and stir gently to combine. (Use more or less cayenne depending on your taste.)
6. Spread the vegetables on a large baking sheet and roast them in the oven 10 to 15 minutes, until they've browned around the edges.
7. Serve the veg with the avocado dip on the side.

Per Serving
Calories: 335 | fat: 32g | carbs: 11g | protein: 11g | fiber: 16g

Mom's Special Legume Burgers

Prep time: 30 minutes | Cook time: 30 minutes | Serves 12

1 cup lentils
2½ to 3 cups water
3 carrots, grated
1 small onion, diced
¾ cup whole-grain flour
1½ to 2 teaspoons curry powder
½ teaspoon sea salt
Pinch freshly ground black pepper

1. Put the lentils in a medium pot with the water. Bring to a boil and then simmer for about 30 minutes, until soft.
2. While the lentils are cooking, put the carrots and onion in a large bowl. Toss them with the flour, curry powder, salt, and pepper.
3. When the lentils are cooked, drain off any excess water, then add them to the bowl with the veggies. Use a potato masher or a large spoon to mash them slightly, and add more flour if you need to get the mixture to stick together.
4. The amount of flour depends on how much water the lentils absorbed, and on the texture of the flour, so use more or less until the mixture sticks when you form it into a ball. Scoop up ¼-cup portions and form into 12 patties.
5. You can either panfry or bake the burgers. To panfry, heat a large skillet to medium, add a tiny bit of oil, and cook the burgers about 10 minutes on the first side.
6. Flip, and cook another 5 to 7 minutes. To bake them, put them on a baking sheet lined with parchment paper and bake at 350°F (180°C) for 30 minutes.

Per Serving (1 burger):
Calories: 114| Total fat: 11g| Carbs: 2g| Fiber: 7g| Protein: 6g

Chapter 4 Lunch Recipes

Grains and Spinach Salad

Prep time: 10 minutes | Cook time: 0 minutes | Serves 2

½ tablespoon barbecue sauce
½ tablespoon balsamic vinegar
½ teaspoon smoked paprika
¼ teaspoon red pepper flakes
8 ounces (227 g)
fresh spinach
½ cup brown rice, cooked
½ cup black beans, cooked
½ cup corn
½ tablespoon sesame seeds

1. Stir together the BBQ sauce, vinegar, paprika and red pepper flakes in a large bowl.
2. Add the spinach, brown rice, black beans and corn to the bowl and combine until well mixed.
3. Sprinkle with sesame seeds and serve.

Per Serving
Calories: 196 | fat: 3.9g | carbs: 33.8g | protein: 10.9g | fiber: 10.2g

Chickpea and Heart of Palm Salad

Prep time: 10 minutes | Cook time: 0 minutes | Serves 4

1 (15½-ounce / 439-g) can chickpeas, drained and rinsed
1 (14-ounce / 397-g) can hearts of palm, drained and chopped
½ cup diced celery
½ cup chopped white onion
¼ cup almond butter
½ teaspoon sea salt (optional)
¼ teaspoon freshly ground black pepper

1. Place the chickpeas in a large bowl and mash them into a chunky paste with a hand masher.
2. Make the salad: Add the remaining ingredients to the bowl and toss to combine well.
3. Divide the salad among 4 bowls and serve immediately.

Per Serving
Calories: 212 | fat: 5.7g | carbs: 34.8g | protein: 8.8g | fiber: 8.1g

Grapefruit and Fennel Salad

Prep time: 15 minutes | Cook time: 0 minutes | Serves 2 to 4

2 grapefruits, supremed and juice reserved
2 small fennel bulbs, cored and thinly sliced
1 red or orange bell pepper, thinly sliced
2 cups shredded red cabbage
1 tablespoon fresh lime juice
Sea salt, to taste (optional)
Black pepper, to taste
½ cup chopped cilantro
1 avocado, diced or sliced
¼ cup walnut pieces

1. In a large bowl, toss together the grapefruit segments and juice, fennel, bell pepper, cabbage and lime juice to well coated. Sprinkle with sea salt (if desired), pepper and chopped cilantro. Toss again to mix well.
2. Transfer the salad to bowls and top with avocado slices and walnut pieces. Serve immediately.

Per Serving
Calories: 432 | fat: 22.3g | carbs: 60.1g | protein: 10.4g | fiber: 20.1g

Citrus and Grapefruit Salad

Prep time: 15 minutes | Cook time: 0 minutes | Serves 2

2 large oranges, peeled, pith removed, and segmented
1 large grapefruit, peeled, pith removed and segmented
Zest and juice of 1 lime
1 teaspoon pure maple syrup (optional)
1 tablespoon minced fresh mint

1. In a large bowl, combine all the ingredients, except for the fresh mint, until well coated.
2. Transfer the salad to the serving dishes and top with the fresh mint. Serve immediately.

Per Serving
Calories: 154 | fat: 0.4g | carbs: 39.2g | protein: 2.9g | fiber: 6.4g

Chickpea and Avocado Salad

Prep time: 10 minutes | Cook time: 0 minutes | Serves 2

1 (15-ounce / 425-g) can chickpeas, drained and rinsed
1 cup arugula
1 cup chopped romaine lettuce
1 cup halved cherry tomatoes
1 cup diced English cucumber
1 large avocado, halved, pitted, and diced
1 teaspoon dried parsley
½ teaspoon dried thyme
Freshly ground black pepper, to taste
3 tablespoons apple cider vinegar

1. Toss all the ingredients except the black pepper and vinegar in a large bowl until combined. Season to taste with black pepper.
2. Drizzle with the vinegar and toss until well coated. Serve immediately.

Per Serving
Calories: 381 | fat: 19.1g | carbs: 45.5g | protein: 12.8g | fiber: 18.1g

Bulgur Tabbouleh

Prep time: 20 minutes | Cook time: 0 minutes | Serves 4

½ cup bulgur
2 Roma tomatoes, diced
2 bunches fresh parsley, finely chopped
1 cup diced English cucumber
½ cup finely chopped scallions, green parts only
¼ cup freshly squeezed lemon juice
¼ cup pitted and coarsely chopped green olives
¼ cup chopped fresh mint
1 small red bell pepper, diced
1 garlic clove, minced

1. Wash the bulgur and soak it in water for 5 to 7 minutes. Drain well.
2. In a large bowl, combine the bulgur with all the other ingredients and stir to mix well.
3. Let sit for 15 minutes before serving.

Per Serving
Calories: 108 | fat: 2.4g | carbs: 22.1g | protein: 4.2g | fiber: 5.0g

Couscous Tabbouleh Salad

Prep time: 10 minutes | Cook time: 0 minutes | Serves 4

1 cup couscous
1 cup boiling water
½ cucumber, diced
1 tomato, diced
4 tablespoons sunflower seeds
1 cup fresh parsley, chopped
2 scallions, chopped
¼ cup chopped fresh mint
Zest and juice of 1 lemon
1 garlic clove, pressed
1 tablespoon avocado oil (optional)
Pinch sea salt (optional)

1. Pour the couscous in a large bowl, then pour the boiling water over and cover the bowl. Let it sit for 5 minutes or until the couscous is tender.
2. Drain the couscous and add the remaining ingredients. Toss to combine well.
3. Serve immediately.

Per Serving
Calories: 304 | fat: 11.0g | carbs: 4.0g | protein: 10.0g | fiber: 6.0g

Ritzy Southwest Beans Salad

Prep time: 10 minutes | Cook time: 0 minutes | Serves 2

½ cup cooked chickpeas
½ cup cooked black beans
1 medium avocado, peeled, pitted, and cubed
1 cup canned unsweetened kernel corn
4 cups chopped fresh lettuce
1 cup halved cherry tomatoes
1 red bell pepper, sliced
1/3 cup onion, diced
½ teaspoon chili powder
¼ teaspoon cumin
1 tablespoon apple cider vinegar
2 teaspoons avocado oil (optional)
Salt and ground black pepper, to taste (optional)

1. Combine all the ingredients in a large bowl. Toss to mix well.
2. Serve immediately.

Per Serving
Calories: 397 | fat: 16.8g | carbs: 51.0g | protein: 11.2g | fiber: 13.2g

Potato, Asparagus, and Bean Salad

Prep time: 15 minutes | Cook time: 10 minutes | Serves 4

1 pound (454 g) red-skin potatoes, scrubbed and cut into ½-inch dices
½ pound (227 g) asparagus, trimmed and cut into ½-inch pieces
2 tablespoons Dijon mustard
2 tablespoons brown rice vinegar
2 cloves garlic, peeled and minced
Salt, to taste (optional)
Freshly ground black pepper, to taste
2 cups cooked navy beans, or 1 (15-ounce / 425-g) can, drained and rinsed
8 green onions (white and green parts), thinly sliced
3 tablespoons minced chives

1. Steam the potatoes in a double boiler or steamer basket for 10 minutes until softened, adding the asparagus during the last 3 minutes.
2. In a large bowl, whisk together the mustard, vinegar, garlic, salt (if desired), and pepper to combine.
3. Add the warm potatoes and asparagus along with the beans, green onions, and chives and toss well. Serve immediately.

Per Serving
Calories: 250 | fat: 1.1g | carbs: 48.5g | protein: 11.9g | fiber: 13.9g

Brown Basmati and Currant Salad

Prep time: 50 minutes | Cook time: 0 minutes | Serves 4

2 cups cooked brown basmati
¼ cup maple syrup
¼ cup chopped cilantro
¼ cup brown rice vinegar
½ cup dried currants
½ small red onion, peeled and minced
1 tablespoon curry
powder
1 jalapeño pepper, minced
6 green onions, finely chopped
Zest and juice of 2 limes
Salt, to taste (optional)
Ground black pepper, to taste

1. Combine all the ingredients in a large serving bowl. Toss to combine well, then serve immediately.

Per Serving
Calories: 437 | fat: 3.5g | carbs: 93.9g | protein: 9.1g | fiber: 7.2g

Ritzy Summer Salad

Prep time: 10 minutes | Cook time: 0 minutes | Serves 2

Dressing:
1 medium avocado, halved, diced, use half for the salad
1 teaspoon lemon juice
¼ cup water
¼ cup chopped basil
Salt, to taste (optional)
Salad:
¼ cup dried chickpeas
¼ cup dried red kidney beans
2 radishes, thinly sliced
2 cups shredded Brussels sprouts
4 cups shredded raw kale
1 tablespoon chopped walnuts
1 teaspoon flaxseeds
Salt, to taste (optional)
Ground black pepper, to taste

1. Combine half of the diced avocado with the remaining ingredients for dressing in a food processor. Pulse until smooth and creamy. Keep adding a small amount of water during the pulsing. Pour the dressing in a bowl and set aside until ready to serve.
2. Combine the remaining half of the avocado with all the ingredients for the salad in a large serving bowl. Top the salad with dressing and serve.

Per Serving
Calories: 371 | fat: 20.8g | carbs: 33.3g | protein: 12.3g | fiber: 18.7g

Endive and Green Lentil Salad

Prep time: 10 minutes | Cook time: 0 minutes | Serves 2

½ cup chopped fresh endive, rinsed
2 cups cooked green lentils
¼ cup lemon juice
2 tablespoons dried oregano
1 tablespoon ground black pepper

1. Combine all the ingredients in a large serving bowl. Toss to combine well, then serve immediately.

Per Serving
Calories: 261 | fat: 1.2g | carbs: 48.3g | protein: 19.0g | fiber: 19.3g

Quinoa and Chickpea Tabbouleh

Prep time: 10 minutes | Cook time: 0 minutes | Serves 4

2½ cups cooked quinoa
1 cup chopped parsley
1 cucumber, peeled, halved, seeded, and diced
2 cups cooked chickpeas
3 Roma tomatoes, diced

3 tablespoons chopped mint
8 green onions, white and green parts, thinly sliced
Zest of 1 lemon and juice of 2 lemons
Salt, to taste (optional)
Ground black pepper, to taste

1. Put all the ingredients in a large serving bowl. Toss to combine well.
2. Refrigerate for an hour and serve.

Per Serving
Calories: 323 | fat: 4.9g | carbs: 58.8g | protein: 14.8g | fiber: 12.7g

Asian Flavor Quinoa and Spinach Salad

Prep time: 15 minutes | Cook time: 0 minutes | Serves 4

Dressing:
¼ cup plus 2 tablespoons brown rice vinegar
1½ tablespoons grated ginger
1½ Teaspoons crushed red pepper flakes
4 cloves garlic, peeled and minced
Zest and juice of 2 limes
Salad:

½ cup finely chopped cilantro
¾ cup mung bean sprouts
2 cups cooked adzuki beans
4 cups cooked quinoa
4 cups spinach
6 green onions, white and green parts, thinly sliced
Salt, to taste (optional)

1. Combine all the ingredients for the dressing in a large bowl. Stir to mix well.
2. Add all the ingredients for the salad to the dressing and toss to combine well.
3. Refrigerate for half an hour and serve.

Per Serving
Calories: 407 | fat: 4.0g | carbs: 75.6g | protein: 19.1g | fiber: 15.6g

Lemony Millet and Fruit Salad

Prep time: 10 minutes | Cook time: 15 minutes | Serves 4

Dressing:
3 tablespoons maple syrup
Juice of 1 lemon
Zest and juice of 1 orange
Salad:
1 cup cooked millet
½ cup golden raisins
½ cup dried currants

½ cup dried unsulfured apricots, chopped
1 Gala apple, cored and diced
2 tablespoons finely chopped mint
Salt, to taste (optional)

1. Combine all the ingredients for the dressing in a large bowl. Stir to mix well.
2. Add all the ingredients for the salad to the dressing and toss to combine well.
3. Refrigerate for half an hour and serve.

Per Serving
Calories: 328 | fat: 2.4g | carbs: 72.6g | protein: 6.8g | fiber: 7.2g

White Bean and Carrot Salad

Prep time: 10 minutes | Cook time: 0 minutes | Serves 2

Dressing:
2 tablespoons balsamic vinegar
1 tablespoon olive oil (optional)
1 tablespoon fresh rosemary, chopped
1 tablespoon fresh oregano, chopped
1 teaspoon minced fresh chives
1 garlic clove, minced

Pinch sea salt (optional)
Salad:
1 (14-ounce / 397-g) can cannellini beans, drained and rinsed
2 carrots, diced
6 mushrooms, thinly sliced
1 zucchini, diced
2 tablespoons fresh basil, chopped

1. In a large bowl, stir together all the ingredients for the dressing.
2. Add all the ingredients for the salad to the bowl and toss to combine well.
3. Divide the salad between 2 bowls and serve immediately.

Per Serving
Calories: 359 | fat: 17.9g | carbs: 7.8g | protein: 18.1g | fiber: 15.2g

Pinto Bean and Avocado Salad

Prep time: 10 minutes | Cook time: 0 minutes | Serves 2

2 cups cooked pinto beans
1 small Hass avocado, peeled, cored, and cubed
10 cherry tomatoes, halved
¼ cup corn kernels
¼ cup lime juice
¼ cup fresh cilantro, chopped
1 jalapeño, sliced
Half of 1 red onion

1. Combine all the ingredients in a large serving bowl. Toss to combine well, then serve immediately.

Per Serving
Calories: 399 | fat: 10.3g | carbs: 56.7g | protein: 19.8g | fiber: 22.2g

Ancient Grain Salad with Fruits

Prep time: 10 minutes | Cook time: 50 minutes | Serves 6

¼ cup farro
¼ cup raw rye berries
2 celery stalks, coarsely chopped
2 ripe pears, cored and coarsely chopped
1 green apple, cored and coarsely chopped
¼ cup golden raisins
½ cup chopped fresh parsley
3 tablespoons freshly squeezed lemon juice
¼ teaspoon ground cumin
Pinch cayenne pepper

1. In a large pot, combine the farro, rye berries, and enough water to cover by 3 inches, then bring to a boil over high heat.
2. When it comes to boil, reduce the heat to medium-low, cover, and cook for 45 to 50 minutes, or until the grains are firm and chewy but not hard.
3. Remove from the heat, drain, and set aside to cool.
4. Once cooled, stir together the cooked grains, celery, pears, apple, raisins, parsley, lemon juice, cumin, and cayenne pepper in a large bowl. Serve immediately.

Per Serving
Calories: 128 | fat: 1.1g | carbs: 30.8g | protein: 3.4g | fiber: 5.3g

Carrot Salad with Dates and Walnuts

Prep time: 15 minutes | Cook time: 0 minutes | Serves 4 to 6

Dressing:
¼ cup water
2 tablespoons apple cider vinegar
1 tablespoon lemon zest
1 tablespoon pure maple syrup (optional)
1 teaspoon Dijon mustard
½ teaspoon cayenne
pepper
¼ teaspoon freshly ground black pepper
Salad:
10 carrots
1 small red onion
4 dates, finely chopped
½ cup chopped walnuts
¼ cup golden raisins

1. In a small bowl, whisk together all the dressing ingredients to combine. Set aside.
2. Using a mandoline, cut the carrots and red onion with the julienne blade. Transfer them to a large bowl and add the dates, walnuts, and raisins. Toss well to combine.
3. Pour over the dressing and toss until well incorporated. Serve immediately.

Per Serving
Calories: 228 | fat: 9.4g | carbs: 35.1g | protein: 4.2g | fiber: 6.1g

Lemony Quinoa and Arugula Salad

Prep time: 20 minutes | Cook time: 0 minutes | Serves 4

1½ cups cooked quinoa
4 cups arugula
¼ cup brown rice vinegar
1 small red onion, peeled and thinly sliced
1 red bell pepper, seeded and cut into ½-inch cubes
2 tablespoons toasted pine nuts
Zest and juice of 1 lime
Zest and juice of 2 oranges
Salt, to taste (optional)
Ground black pepper, to taste

1. Combine all the ingredients in a large serving bowl. Toss to combine well, then serve immediately.

Per Serving
Calories: 282 | fat: 4.3g | carbs: 50.6g | protein: 10.4g | fiber: 5.8g

Cannellini Bean Gazpacho

Prep time: 1 hour | Cook time: 0 minutes | Serves 4

6 large ripe tomatoes (about 4 pounds / 1.8 kg), chopped, divided
2 cups cooked cannellini beans
1 medium Vidalia onion, peeled and diced small
1 large red bell pepper, deseeded and diced small

2 large cucumbers, peeled, halved, deseeded, and diced
½ cup chopped basil
¼ cup red wine vinegar
Zest of 1 lemon
Salt, to taste (optional)
Ground black pepper, to taste

1. Purée 2 of the chopped tomatoes in a food processor, then pour the tomato purée in a large bowl.
2. Add the remaining ingredients to the bowl and stir to combine well.
3. Refrigerate for 1 hour before serving.

Per Serving
Calories: 220 | fat: 1.3g | carbs: 42.1g | protein: 12.8g | fiber: 11.3g

Sumptuous Gazpacho

Prep time: 20 to 40 minutes | Chill time: 3 to 4 hours | Serves 10

1 cup chopped cucumber
¼ cup chopped zucchini
¼ cup chopped mild green chilies
½ cup fresh corn kernels
2 cups peeled, deseeded, and chopped tomatoes
½ cup chopped green bell pepper

½ cup chopped celery
¼ cup chopped fresh parsley
1 clove garlic, minced
½ cup chopped red onion
¼ cup chopped scallion
4 cups tomato juice
2 tablespoons red wine vinegar
2 tablespoons fresh lime juice

1. Combine all the ingredients in a large bowl. Stir to mix well.
2. Cover and chill for 3 to 4 hours before serving.

Per Serving
Calories: 39 | fat: 0.4g | carbs: 8.7g | protein: 1.7g | fiber: 3.1g

Asparagus Soup

Prep time: 10 minutes | Cook time: 20 minutes | Serves 6

1 large yellow onion, peeled and diced
2 pounds (907 g) fresh asparagus, trimmed and cut into ½-inch pieces
1 tablespoon minced tarragon

2 teaspoons thyme
4 cups low-sodium vegetable broth
Salt, to taste (optional)
Ground black pepper, to taste

1. Heat a saucepan over medium heat, then add the onion and sauté for 6 minutes or until lightly caramelized. Add a dash of water during the sautéing.
2. Add the asparagus, tarragon, thyme, and vegetable broth to the pan and cook over medium-low heat for 20 minutes or until soft. Give them a stir for every 5 minutes.
3. Allow to cool for 10 minutes, then pour the soup in a blender. Pulse to purée the soup until smooth. Sprinkle with salt (if desired) and pepper before serving.

Per Serving
Calories: 151 | fat: 1.7g | carbs: 28.8g | protein: 7.4g | fiber: 7.2g

Butternut Squash Soup

Prep time: 30 minutes | Cook time: 45 minutes | Serves 8

1 large butternut squash, peeled and cut into cubes
1½ cups peeled and chopped apple

1½ cups sliced onion
5 cups water
1 cup chopped carrot
2 to 3 Teaspoons minced fresh ginger

1. In a large soup pot, simmer all the ingredients over medium-low heat for 45 minutes until the fruit and veggies are softened, stir periodically.
2. Working in batches, transfer the soup to a blender or food processor and purée until the soup is vibrant orange and creamy.
3. Divide the soup among bowls and serve hot.

Per Serving
Calories: 102 | fat: 0.3g | carbs: 26.1g | protein: 2.1g | fiber: 4.7g

Super Easy and Ritzy Borscht

Prep time: 30 minutes | Cook time: 45 minutes | Serves 8

4 cups shredded red cabbage
2 large potatoes, peeled and chopped
1 cup peeled julienned beets
¼ cup chopped fresh parsley
2 cloves garlic, crushed
¼ cup red-wine vinegar
1 onion, chopped
2 teaspoons chopped fresh dill
2 tablespoons maple syrup (optional)
1 teaspoon paprika
Freshly ground pepper, to taste
6 cups water
Fresh dill, for garnish

1. Combine all the ingredients in a large pot, except the dill.
2. Bring to a boil, cover, reduce the heat, and cook over medium heat for 45 minutes.
3. Garnish with fresh dill and serve.

Per Serving
Calories: 127 | fat: 0.3g | carbs: 29.5g | protein: 3.1g | fiber: 4.2g

Miso Tofu Soup

Prep time: 10 minutes | Cook time: 5 minutes | Serves 4

4 cups water
¼ cup mellow white miso
1 tablespoons soy
sauce
¼ cup chopped scallion
½ cup diced firm tofu

1. Pour the water in a saucepan and bring to a boil.
2. Put the miso in a small bowl. Add about ½ cup of the boiling water to the miso and mix well.
3. Pour into the saucepan. Add 1 tablespoon of soy sauce, scallion, and tofu. Cook over medium heat for 1 to 2 minutes or until the vegetables and tofu are well distributed. Keep stirring during the cooking.
4. Serve hot.

Per Serving
Calories: 90 | fat: 4.4g | carbs: 6.4g | protein: 8.1g | fiber: 1.3g

Rice and Bean Salad

Prep time: 20 minutes | Cook time: 0 minutes | Serves 6 to 8

3 cups cooked brown rice
1 (15-ounce / 425-g) can pinto beans, rinsed and drained
1 (15-ounce / 425-g) can black beans, rinsed and drained
1 (10-ounce / 284-g) package frozen green peas, thawed
1 cup sliced celery
1 medium red onion, chopped
1 (7-ounce / 198-g) can chopped green chilies
¼ cup chopped fresh cilantro
1 (8-ounce / 227-g) jar oil-free Italian dressing

1. In a large bowl, toss together all the ingredients until well blended. Wrap the bowl in plastic and set in the refrigerator for more than 2 hours before serving.

Per Serving
Calories: 224 | fat: 3.1g | carbs: 40.4g | protein: 9.6g | fiber: 8.4g

Rice, Chickpea, Fennel, and Orange Salad

Prep time: 1 hour 10 minutes | Cook time: 45 to 50 minutes | Serves 4

1½ cups brown basmati, rinsed
3 cups water
2 cups chickpeas, soaked in water overnight, cooked
1 fennel bulb, trimmed and diced
Zest and segments of
1 orange
¼ cup parsley, finely chopped
¼ cup plus 2 tablespoons white wine vinegar
½ teaspoon red pepper flakes

1. Put the brown basmati in a pot, then pour in the water. Bring to a boil over high heat. Reduce the heat to medium, then simmer for 15 to 50 minutes or until the water is absorbed.
2. Combine the cooked basmati with remaining ingredients in a large serving bowl. Toss to combine well, then serve immediately.

Per Serving
Calories: 438 | fat: 4.4g | carbs: 86.3g | protein: 14.1g | fiber: 11.8g

Easy Zucchini Soup

Prep time: 15 minutes | Cook time: 15 minutes | Serves 6

6 medium zucchini, chopped
2 cloves garlic
1 small onion, chopped
5 cups water
4 bay leaves
½ cup soy milk
3 tablespoons vegetable seasoning

1. Put the zucchini, garlic, onion, water, and bay leaves in a saucepan and cook over medium heat until the vegetables are tender, about 15 minutes.
2. Remove the bay leaves. Add the remaining ingredients. Blend the soup in a food processor until smooth.
3. Serve immediately.

Per Serving
Calories: 59 | fat: 1.0g | carbs: 10.7g | protein: 3.7g | fiber: 2.6g

Lemony Red Lentil Soup

Prep time: 5 minutes | Cook time: 34 to 36 minutes | Serves 6

1 medium onion, finely diced
3 cloves garlic, minced
8 cups low-sodium vegetable soup
2 cups dried red lentils
Zest and juice of 1 lemon
1 tablespoon dried mint
Sea salt, to taste (optional)
Pinch cayenne pepper

1. Heat a saucepan over medium heat. Add the onion to the saucepan and sauté for 8 to 10 minutes, or until translucent and soft. Add the garlic to the saucepan and sauté for 1 minute.
2. Pour the vegetable soup into the saucepan and add the lentils. Increase the heat to high and bring to a boil. Reduce the heat back to medium. Cover and cook for 25 minutes, or until the lentils are soft and fall apart.
3. Add the lemon zest and juice and mint to the soup and season with sea salt (if desired) and cayenne pepper.
4. Remove the saucepan from the heat. Rest for 5 minutes before serving.

Per Serving
Calories: 459 | fat: 4.5g | carbs: 83.9g | protein: 23.0g | fiber: 14.4g

Chilean Squash and Bean Stew

Prep time: 15 minutes | Cook time: 35 minutes | Serves 4

1 large yellow onion, peeled and diced small
1 medium butternut squash (about 1 pound / 454 g), peeled, halved, deseeded, and cut into ½-inch pieces
2 cups cooked pinto beans, drained and rinsed
6 ears corn, kernels removed (about 3½ cups)
4 cloves garlic, peeled and minced
2 cups water
Salt and freshly ground black pepper, to taste (optional)
1 cup finely chopped basil

1. Put the onion in a large saucepan and sauté over medium heat for 10 minutes.
2. Add the squash, beans, corn, garlic, and water and cook for 25 minutes, or until the squash is tender.
3. Season with salt (if desired) and pepper and stir in the basil before serving.

Per Serving
Calories: 335 | fat: 3.3g | carbs: 69.5g | protein: 16.0g | fiber: 14.8g

Chili Vegetable Stew

Prep time: 20 minutes | Cook time: 1 hour | Serves 6

3 potatoes, peeled and chopped
2 carrots, scrubbed and sliced
1 zucchini, sliced
1 cup cauliflower florets
1 onion, sliced
1 cup frozen corn kernels
1 green bell pepper,
chopped into large pieces
2 cups water
2 (4-ounce / 113-g) cans chopped green chilies
1 (16-ounce / 454-g) can whole tomatoes, chopped, with liquid
1 tablespoon diced jalapeño pepper

1. Stir together all the ingredients in a large soup pot and simmer over low heat for about 1 hour, or until the vegetables are softened.
2. Serve warm.

Per Serving
Calories: 253 | fat: 2.3g | carbs: 50.8g | protein: 7.5g | fiber: 11.1g

Cajun Stewed Black-Eyed Peas

Prep time: 15 minutes | Cook time: 1 hour | Serves 2

½ cup black-eyed peas, soaked overnight and drained
1 (14-ounce / 397-g) can Cajun-style stewed tomatoes
3 tablespoons ketchup
¾ cup water
1 onion, sliced
2 tablespoons low-sodium soy sauce
2 cloves garlic, chopped
2 teaspoons Cajun Seasoning
⅛ Teaspoon hot sauce

1. Combine all the ingredients in a medium saucepan and cook for about 1 hour until the peas are tender.
2. Cool for 5 minutes and serve warm.

Per Serving
Calories: 198 | fat: 3.8g | carbs: 34.3g | protein: 6.6g | fiber: 3.9g

Lentils and Mushroom Soup

Prep time: 10 minutes | Cook time: 35 minutes | Serves 4

²/₃ cup dried green lentils
4 cups low-sodium vegetable broth
2 cups sliced button mushrooms
¼ cup dried thyme
1 red bell pepper,
remove the steam, deseeded, diced
4 pieces sun-dried tomatoes, diced
Salt, taste (optional)
Ground black pepper, to taste

1. Add the green lentils and vegetable broth to a large saucepan. Bring to a boil over medium-high heat. Reduce the heat to medium and simmer for 15 minutes. Stir periodically.
2. Add the mushrooms and thyme to the pan and simmer for 10 more minutes. Stir periodically.
3. Add the bell pepper to the pan and simmer for an additional 5 minutes.
4. Allow to cool for 5 minutes and serve with sun-dried tomatoes, salt (if desired), and black pepper on top.

Per Serving
Calories: 146 | fat: 0.7g | carbs: 24.9g | protein: 10.1g | fiber: 12.4g

Black Bean Chili

Prep time: 40 minutes | Cook time: 45 minutes | Serves 8 to 10

1 medium eggplant, cut into ½-inch cubes
1 cup low-sodium vegetable broth or water
4 cloves garlic, minced
2 medium onions, chopped
1 yellow bell pepper, diced
1 red bell pepper, diced
2 zucchini, chopped
1 (28-ounce / 794-g) can Italian plum tomatoes, with juice
4 large ripe plum tomatoes, diced
½ cup slivered fresh basil leaves
½ cup chopped fresh parsley or cilantro
2 tablespoons chili powder
2 teaspoons dried oregano
1 tablespoon ground cumin
1 teaspoon freshly ground black pepper
¼ teaspoon crushed red pepper flakes
2 cups cooked black beans
1½ cups frozen corn kernels, thawed
¼ cup fresh lemon juice
½ cup chopped fresh dill

1. Preheat the broiler to High.
2. Arrange the eggplant on a nonstick baking sheet and broil 8 inches from the heat source for about 5 minutes until tender and browned.
3. Remove from the broiler and set aside to cool.
4. Pour the broth into a large soup pot over medium heat. Add the garlic, onions, peppers, and zucchini and cook for 10 minutes, stirring occasionally.
5. On your cutting board, coarsely chop the canned tomatoes and add them to the soup pot, along with their juice. Stir in the fresh tomatoes, basil, parsley, chili powder, oregano, cumin, black pepper, and red pepper flakes. Add the broiled eggplant and simmer covered over low heat for 20 minutes, or until the tomatoes are tender.
6. Add the beans, corn kernels, lemon juice, dill, and mix well. Cook for an additional 10 minutes until heated through.
7. Allow to cool for 5 minutes and serve warm.

Per Serving
Calories: 127 | fat: 1.1g | carbs: 23.8g | protein: 5.6g | fiber: 7.1g

Lush Green Salad

Prep time: 10 minutes | Cook time: 0 minutes | Serves 2

1 cup kale, stems removed and chopped
3 Teaspoons low-sodium soy sauce, divided
1 cup spinach, chopped
2 tablespoons chives
¼ teaspoon salt (optional)
⅛ Teaspoon freshly ground black pepper

¼ avocado, mashed
2 tablespoons almond butter
2 tablespoons walnuts, roughly chopped
¼ cup chopped scallions, green parts only
½ stalk celery, chopped

1. Massage the kale with 1 teaspoon of soy sauce in a large bowl with your hands to break the kale. Add the spinach ,chives, salt (if desired), and ground black pepper. Toss to combine well.
2. Put the avocado in a food processor, then add the almond butter and sprinkle with remaining soy sauce. Pulse to mash the avocado.
3. Pour the avocado mixture over the kale and spinach mix, then add the remaining ingredients and toss to serve.

Per Serving
Calories: 202 | fat: 17.4g | carbs: 8.4g | protein: 7.4g | fiber: 4.9g

Spinach and Eggplant Salad

Prep time: 15 minutes | Cook time: 17 minutes | Serves 2

1 teaspoon olive oil (optional)
1 eggplant, diced
½ teaspoon ground ginger
½ teaspoon ground cumin
¼ teaspoon ground nutmeg
¼ teaspoon turmeric
Pinch sea salt (optional)

1 lemon, half zested and juiced, half cut into wedges
2 tablespoons capers
1 garlic clove, pressed
1 tablespoon chopped green olives
Handful fresh mint, finely chopped
2 cups chopped spinach

1. Heat the olive oil (if desired) in a large skillet over medium heat until it shimmers.
2. Add the eggplant and sauté for about 5 minutes until slightly softened.
3. Stir in the ginger, cumin, nutmeg, turmeric, and salt (if desired). Continue to cook for about 10 minutes, or until the eggplant is very soft.
4. Add the lemon zest and juice, capers, garlic, olives, and mint. Sauté for an additional 1 to 2 minutes to blend the flavors.
5. Arrange a handful of spinach on each plate and top with the cooked eggplant mixture. Serve with a wedge of lemon, to squeeze the fresh juice over the greens.

Per Serving
Calories: 98 | fat: 4.3g | carbs: 1.1g | protein: 3.8g | fiber: 7.6g

Barley and Strawberry Salad

Prep time: 15 minutes | Cook time: 0 minutes | Serves 4

¼ cup orange juice
2 tablespoons fresh lime juice
1 tablespoon olive oil (optional)
¼ teaspoon sea salt, plus more to taste (optional)
⅛ Teaspoon black pepper, plus more to taste
½ small red onion, sliced
2 cups cooked barley, cooled

2 cups strawberries, hulled and chopped
1½ cups cooked cannellini beans
½ cup chopped cilantro
5 ounces (142 g) mixed baby greens
½ cup roasted pistachios, shelled and chopped
½ avocado, diced
1 teaspoon balsamic vinegar

1. In a large bowl, combine the orange juice, lime juice, olive oil (if desired), ¼ teaspoon sea salt (if desired) and ⅛ Teaspoon pepper.
2. Make the salad: Add the onion slices, barley, strawberries, cannellini beans, cilantro and mixed baby greens to the bowl. Toss until well blended. Sprinkle with sea salt (if desired) and pepper to taste.
3. Divide the salad into bowls. Spread the roasted pistachios and avocado on top and drizzle with the balsamic vinegar. Serve immediately.

Per Serving
Calories: 311 | fat: 15.1g | carbs: 41.2g | protein: 7.9g | fiber: 10.0g

Citrus Kale and Carrot Salad

Prep time: 15 minutes | Cook time: 0 minutes | Serves 3

Dressing:
¼ cup orange juice
½ tablespoon maple syrup (optional)
½ tablespoon sesame oil (optional)
1 teaspoon lime juice
½ teaspoon ginger, finely minced
Salad:
4 cups fresh kale, chopped
2 cups carrots, shred-
ded
1 cup edamame, shelled
½ cup cooked green lentils
1 tablespoon roasted sesame seeds
2 teaspoons mint, chopped
1 small avocado, peeled, pitted and diced

1. Make the dressing: In a small bowl, stir together the orange juice, maple syrup (if desired), sesame oil (if desired), lime juices and ginger.
2. Make the salad: In a large bowl, toss together the fresh kale, carrots, edamame, cooked lentils, sesame seeds and mint until well combined.
3. Spread the dressing over the salad and toss to coat well.
4. Divide the salad among 3 bowls. Top with avocado and serve immediately.

Per Serving
Calories: 315 | fat: 11.3g | carbs: 38.8g | protein: 14.5g | fiber: 15.5g

Green Salad with Orange Dressing

Prep time: 15 minutes | Cook time: 0 minutes | Serves 2

Salad:
4 cups chopped lettuce
½ cup chickpeas, cooked
½ cup pickled beets
¼ cup sunflower seeds
1 medium carrot, shredded
10 cherry tomatoes, sliced
Handful broccoli sprouts
Dressing:
¼ cup freshly squeezed orange juice
2 tablespoons apple cider vinegar
2 tablespoons tahini
¼ teaspoon sea salt, plus more to taste (optional)
¼ teaspoon freshly ground black pepper, plus more to taste

1. Add all the ingredients for the salad to a large bowl. Toss until well blended. Set the salad aside.
2. Stir together all the ingredients for the dressing in a different bowl. Stir in water, 1 tablespoon at a time, until it reaches a pourable consistency. Season with more sea salt (if desired) and pepper, if desired.
3. Divide the salad between 2 bowls and drizzle ¼ cup dressing in each bowl. Toss to coat well and serve.

Per Serving
Calories: 479 | fat: 20.7g | carbs: 59.8g | protein: 19.8g | fiber: 13.9g

Potato in Creamy Avocado Salad

Prep time: 1 hour | Cook time: 10 minutes | Serves 4

5 large potatoes, cut into 1-inch cubes
1 large avocado, chopped
¼ cup chopped fresh chives
½ tablespoon freshly squeezed lemon juice
2 tablespoons Dijon
mustard
½ teaspoon onion powder
½ teaspoon garlic powder
½ teaspoon dried dill
¼ teaspoon freshly ground black pepper

1. Put the potatoes in a pot, then pour in enough water to cover. Bring to a boil. Cook for 10 more minutes or until the potatoes are soft.
2. Allow the potatoes to cool for 10 minutes, then put the potatoes in a colander and rinse under running water. Pat dry with paper towels and transfer to a large bowl. Refrigerate for at least 20 minutes.
3. Meanwhile, combine the avocado with chives, lemon juice, and mustard in a food processor. Sprinkle with onion powder, garlic powder, dill, and pepper. Pulse to mash the avocado until creamy and well combined.
4. Pour the creamy avocado in the bowl of potatoes, then toss to coat the potato cubes well. Refrigerate for 30 minutes before serving.

Per Serving
Calories: 341 | fat: 21.0g | carbs: 14.0g | protein: 10.0g | fiber: 12.0g

Kidney bean and Tomato Chili

Prep time: 10 minutes | Cook time: 10 to 20 minutes | Makes 4 bowls

2 to 3 garlic cloves, minced
1 onion, diced
1 to 2 tablespoons water, vegetable broth, or red wine
¼ cup tomato paste or crushed tomatoes
1 (28-ounce / 794-g) can tomatoes

2 to 3 Teaspoons chili powder
1 (14-ounce / 397-g) can kidney beans, rinsed and drained, or 1½ cups cooked
¼ teaspoon sea salt (optional)
¼ cup fresh cilantro or parsley leaves

1. Add the garlic, onion, and water in a large pot and sauté for about 5 minutes until the vegetables are softened. Mix in the tomato paste, tomatoes, chili powder, and beans. Sprinkle with the salt, if desired.
2. Bring the mixture to a simmer for at least 10 minutes, or until cooked to your preferred doneness, stirring occasionally.
3. Divide the chili among bowls and serve garnished with cilantro.

Per Serving (1 bowl)
Calories: 179 | fat: 12.5g | carbs: 8.6g | protein: 8.0g | fiber: 7.1g

Navy Bean Chili

Prep time: 15 minutes | Cook time: 35 minutes | Serves 6

1 large green pepper, deseeded and diced
1 large yellow onion, peeled and diced
3 jalapeño peppers, deseeded and minced
6 cloves garlic, peeled and minced
2 tablespoons ground cumin seeds, toasted
4 cups cooked navy beans, drained and

rinsed
1 (28-ounce / 794-g) can diced tomatoes
3 cups low-sodium vegetable broth
Zest of 1 lime and juice of 2 limes
1 cup finely chopped cilantro
Salt, to taste (optional)

1. Put the green pepper, onion, and jalapeño peppers in a large saucepan and sauté over medium cook for 8 minutes.
2. Add the garlic and cumin and cook for 2 minutes. Add the beans, tomatoes, and vegetable broth and bring to a boil over high heat.

3. Reduce the heat to medium and cook, covered, for 25 minutes. Add the lime zest and juice and cilantro and season with salt, if desired.
4. Serve immediately.

Per Serving
Calories: 373 | fat: 8.9g | carbs: 61.1g | protein: 15.4g | fiber: 20.1g

Ritzy Grain Salad

Prep time: 25 minutes | Cook time: 25 minutes | Serves 8

1½ cups quinoa, rinsed and drained
2¼ cups water
Salt and ground black pepper, to taste (optional)
½ jalapeño, stemmed, deseeded, and chopped
5 tablespoons lime juice (about 3 limes)
¾ teaspoon ground cumin
$1/3$ cup fresh cilantro leaves

1 (15-ounce / 425-g) can black beans, rinsed
1 avocado, halved, pitted, and sliced thin
1 mango, peeled, pitted, and cut into ¼-inch pieces
1 red bell pepper, stemmed, deseeded, and chopped
2 scallions, sliced
½ cup avocado oil (optional)

1. Pour the quinoa in a saucepan and cook over medium-high heat for 6 minutes or until soft.
2. Pour in the water and sprinkle with salt (if desired). Bring to a boil. Reduce the heat to low. Cover and simmer for 15 minutes, or until most of the liquid is absorbed.
3. Transfer the quinoa in a bowl and allow to cool for 15 minutes, then fluff with a fork.
4. Meanwhile, put the jalapeño in a food processor, then drizzle with lime juice and sprinkle with cumin and salt (if desired). Pulse to chop the jalapeño well until the mixture is creamy and smooth. Fold in the cilantro while pulsing.
5. Add the chopped jalapeño with remaining ingredients to the bowl of quinoa. Toss to combine well. Sprinkle with salt (if desired) and pepper and serve immediately.

Per Serving
Calories: 465 | fat: 20.1g | carbs: 59.0g | protein: 15.4g | fiber: 11.9g

Spicy Lentil Chili

Prep time: 15 minutes | Cook time: 30 to 35 minutes | Serves 6 to 8

1 pound (454 g) lentils
8 cups water or low-sodium vegetable broth, plus more as needed
2 cups diced onion
1 cup crushed tomatoes
¼ cup tomato paste
2 tablespoons chopped garlic

2 tablespoons balsamic vinegar
2 tablespoons fresh lime juice
1 tablespoon ground cumin
2 tablespoons chili powder
1 teaspoon cayenne (use less if you don't like your chili spicy)

1. In a large pot, add all the ingredients and bring to a boil over high heat.
2. Reduce the heat to medium-low and let simmer covered for 30 to 35 minutes, or until the lentils are softened, adding more water or broth if needed for desired chili consistency.
3. Remove from the heat and serve.

Per Serving
Calories: 145 | fat: 1.0g | carbs: 26.7g | protein: 7.3g | fiber: 3.4g

Navy Bean and Green Salad

Prep time: 20 minutes | Cook time: 10 minutes | Serves 2

2 tablespoons avocado oil (optional)
3 cups cabbage, chopped
1 green onion, chopped
2 teaspoons garlic, minced
4 cups kale, chopped

Salt and ground black pepper, to taste (optional)
2 cups cooked navy beans
½ cup cooked quinoa
1 cup carrot, chopped
1 teaspoon lemon juice

1. Heat 1 tablespoon of the avocado oil (if desired) in a skillet over medium heat.
2. Add the cabbage, green onion, and garlic to the skillet and sauté for 3 minutes or until soft.
3. Add the kale and remaining oil (if desired) to the skillet. Sprinkle with salt (if desired). Reduce the heat and cover. Cook for 5 minutes or until the cabbage is wilted. Turn off the heat. Transfer the cabbage and kale to a large serving bowl.

4. Add the remaining ingredients to the bowl and sprinkle with salt (if desired) and pepper. Toss the combine well and serve immediately.

Per Serving
Calories: 487 | fat: 15.5g | carbs: 64.8g | protein: 22.3g | fiber: 17.4g

Wheat Berry Salad with Chickpeas

Prep time: 25 minutes | Cook time: 1 hour to 1 hour 10 minutes | Serves 4 to 6

1½ cups wheat berries
16 cups water
2 teaspoons sea salt (optional)
¼ teaspoon ground black pepper
4 Teaspoons sherry vinegar
2 teaspoons Dijon mustard
1 garlic clove, minced
¾ teaspoon smoked paprika

3 tablespoons extra-virgin olive oil (optional)
1 (15-ounce / 425-g) can chickpeas, rinsed
3 ounces (85 g) baby spinach, chopped
1 small red onion, thinly sliced
3 oranges, peeled, pitted and thinly sliced
¼ cup minced fresh mint

1. Pour the water in a pot over medium heat and bring to a boil. Add the wheat berries and 1½ Teaspoons salt (if desired) to the pot and bring to a boil. Reduce the heat to low and simmer for 1 hour to 1 hour 10 minutes, or until the wheat berries become just tender and still chewy. Drain the wheat berries and place on a baking pan to let rest for 15 minutes until completely cool.
2. In a large bowl, stir together the sherry vinegar, Dijon mustard, garlic, smoked paprika, ½ teaspoon salt (if desired), ¼ teaspoon pepper and the olive oil (if desired).
3. Combine the cooled wheat berries, chickpeas, spinach, onion, oranges and mint to the bowl. Toss to blend well.
4. Transfer to bowls and serve immediately.

Per Serving
Calories: 327 | fat: 9.3g | carbs: 54.7g | protein: 10.7g | fiber: 4.9g

Basmati, Navy, and Spinach Bean Salad

Prep time: 50 minutes | Cook time: 40 minutes | Serves 4

2 cups navy beans	green onion, white
1½ cups cooked bas-mati	and green parts
	2 tablespoons minced
4 cups baby spinach	tarragon
¼ cup maple syrup	Zest and juice of 1
¼ cup minced basil	lemon
¼ cup plus 2	Salt, to taste (option-
tablespoons balsamic	al)
vinegar	Ground black pepper,
1 cup thinly sliced	to taste

1. Put the navy beans in a pot, then pour in the water to cover the beans by about 1 inch. Bring to a boil over medium heat. Reduce the heat to low and simmer for 40 minutes or until the water is absorbed.
2. Meanwhile, toast the brown basmati in a nonstick skillet over low heat for 2 to 3 minutes.
3. Combine the navy beans, toasted basmati, and remaining ingredients in a large serving bowl. Toss to combine well, then serve immediately.

Per Serving
Calories: 269 | fat: 1.5g | carbs: 54.5g | protein: 10.7g | fiber: 12.2g

Jicama Salad with Creamy Mango Dressing

Prep time: 1 hour 10 minutes | Cook time: 0 minutes | Serves 6

1 jicama, peeled and	chopped
grated	⅛ Teaspoon sea salt
1 mango, peeled and	(optional)
sliced	1½ tablespoons tahini
¼ cup unsweetened	6 medium lettuce
almond milk	leaves
2 tablespoons	½ cup roasted
chopped fresh basil	cashews, chopped
1 large scallion,	

1. Put the mango in a food processor, then pulse to purée. Fold in the milk and tahini, then sprinkle with scallions, basil, and salt (if desired). Pulse for a few more times until combined well and becomes thick and creamy.

2. Pour the mango mixture in a large bowl, then put in the jicama. Toss to mix well. Wrap the bowl in plastic and refrigerate to marinate for an hour.
3. Unfold the lettuce leaves on 6 plates, then top the lettuce leaves with the jicama and mango mixture. Spread with chopped cashews and serve.

Per Serving
Calories: 76 | fat: 6.0g | carbs: 6.0g | protein: 1.0g | fiber: 1.0g

Dill Potato and Zucchini Salad

Prep time: 15 minutes | Cook time: 20 minutes | Serves 4

6 medium pota-toes, scrubbed and chopped into bite-size pieces	(optional)
	Freshly ground black
	pepper, to taste
	1 tablespoon nutri-
1 zucchini, chopped	tional yeast (optional)
(same size pieces as	3 celery stalks,
the potatoes)	chopped
¼ cup chopped fresh	1 green or red bell
dill	pepper, seeded and
1 to 2 teaspoons Di-	chopped
jon mustard	1 tablespoon chopped
⅛ Teaspoon sea salt	chives, or scallions

1. Fill a large pot about a quarter of the way with water and bring to a boil. Add the potatoes and let boil for 10 minutes.
2. Add the zucchini to the pot and boil for another 10 minutes.
3. Remove the pot from the heat and drain the water, reserving about 1 cup cooking liquid. Set the cooked vegetables aside in a large bowl to cool.
4. Place ½ cup of cooked potatoes into a blender or food processor, along with the reserved cooking liquid and the dill, mustard, salt (if desired), pepper, and nutritional yeast (if using). Purée until smooth. You can add a little water to get your desired consistency.
5. In a large mixing bowl, toss the celery, bell pepper, and chives with the cooked potatoes and zucchini. Pour the dressing over them and toss to coat, then serve.

Per Serving
Calories: 248 | fat: 11.2g | carbs: 5.6g | protein: 8.2g | fiber: 6.9g

Luxury Thai Style Salad

Prep time: 15 minutes | Cook time: 0 minutes | Serves 4 to 6

Dressing:
3 tablespoons fresh lime juice
½-inch piece of fresh ginger, peeled and finely grated
Sriracha sauce, to taste
1 tablespoon maple syrup (optional)
1 clove garlic, finely grated
¼ cup plus 1 tablespoon grapeseed oil (optional)
Salt and ground black pepper, to taste (optional)
Salad:
½ head cabbage, shredded (about 5 cups)

1 ripe mango, peeled, shredded
1 red bell pepper, stem removed, de-seeded, shredded
3 green onions, thinly sliced
1 large carrot, shredded
¼ cup fresh basil leaves
¼ cup fresh cilantro leaves
¼ cup fresh mint leaves
Salt and ground black pepper, to taste (optional)
½ cup roasted cashews, chopped, for garnish

1. Combine the ingredients for the dressing in a small bowl. Stir to mix well.
2. Combine the ingredients for the salad in a large serving bowl. Spread the dressing on top and toss to serve.

Per Serving
Calories: 402 | fat: 26.8g | carbs: 38.8g | protein: 8.3g | fiber: 6.2g

Bulgur Salad with Cucumber and Tomato

Prep time: 20 minutes | Cook time: 5 minutes | Serves 4

3 cups water
1½ cups bulgur
1 medium cucumber, halved, seeded, and diced
1 cup halved cherry tomatoes
4 green onions (white and green parts), sliced
3 cloves garlic, peeled and minced
Zest and juice of 2

lemons
¼ cup minced tarragon
2 tablespoons red wine vinegar
1 teaspoon crushed red pepper flakes, or more to taste
Salt, to taste (optional)
Freshly ground black pepper, to taste

1. Bring the water to a boil in a medium pot and add the bulgur.
2. Remove the pot from the heat, cover, and allow to sit for about 15 minutes, or until the water is absorbed and the bulgur is tender.
3. Spread the bulgur on a baking sheet and let cool to room temperature. Transfer the cooled bulgur to a large bowl, along with the remaining ingredients, and stir until well incorporated.
4. Chill for 1 hour before serving.

Per Serving
Calories: 216 | fat: 0.9g | carbs: 45.6g | protein: 7.4g | fiber: 7.6g

Creamy Potato Soup

Prep time: 10 minutes | Cook time: 28 to 40 minutes | Serves 6

5 cups water
1 medium white onion, chopped
2 pounds (907 g) white potatoes, peeled and cut into chunks
2 teaspoons dried basil
1½ Teaspoons granu-

lated garlic
1 teaspoon ground coriander
1 teaspoon dried dill
½ cup unsweetened coconut milk, at room temperature
3 cups coarsely chopped Swiss chard

1. Warm 1 tablespoon of water in a soup pot over medium-high heat. Add the onion and sauté for 3 to 5 minutes.
2. Add the water, potatoes, basil, garlic, coriander and dill to the pot. Bring the mixture to a boil, uncovered. Reduce the heat to medium and simmer for 20 to 25 minutes, or until the potatoes become softened, stirring constantly.
3. Reduce the heat to low. Pour the milk into the pot and stir until well blended.
4. Pour the soup mixture into a blender. Pulse until smooth and creamy.
5. Transfer the soup back to the pot and add the Swiss chard. Simmer over low heat for another 5 to 10 minutes, or until the Swiss chard becomes wilted.
6. Pour the soup into bowls and serve warm.

Per Serving
Calories: 202 | fat: 5.1g | carbs: 35.9g | protein: 4.3g | fiber: 4.4g

Mushroom, Chickpea, and Tomato Soup

Prep time: 15 minutes | Cook time: 20 minutes | Serves 2

2 tablespoons low-sodium vegetable broth
1 cup chopped mushrooms
½ cup chopped onion
3 garlic cloves, minced
½ cups cooked chickpeas
19 ounces (539 g) tomatoes, diced
1 to 2 cups chopped kale
½ tablespoon dried oregano
1 tablespoon dried basil
⅛ to ¼ teaspoon sea salt (optional)
1 to 2 tablespoons balsamic vinegar
2 cups water
1 tablespoon toasted walnuts
1 teaspoon nutritional yeast

1. Heat the vegetable broth in a saucepan over medium heat. Add the mushrooms, onion, and garlic to the pan and sauté for 7 to 8 minutes or until the mushrooms are tender and the onion is translucent.
2. Add the chickpeas, tomatoes, and kale. Sprinkle with dried oregano, basil, and salt (if desired). Drizzle with balsamic vinegar, then pour in the water. Stir to combine well.
3. Put the pan lid on and simmer for 10 minutes or until the vegetables are tender and chickpeas are soft.
4. Allow to cool, then pour the soup in a large bowl. Sprinkle with walnuts and yeast before serving.

Per Serving (1 bowl)
Calories: 343 | fat: 19.0g | carbs: 21.0g | protein: 17.0g | fiber: 15.0g

Simple Broccoli and Potato Soup

Prep time: 10 minutes | Cook time: 18 to 25 minutes | Serves 6 to 8

1½ pounds (680 g) white potatoes, peeled and chopped
6 cups water
1 medium white onion, chopped
2 teaspoons granulated garlic
2 teaspoons ground coriander
1 teaspoon onion powder
1 teaspoon salt-free poultry seasoning
1½ pounds (680 g) broccoli, cut into small florets
4 cups coarsely chopped Swiss chard

1. Combine all the ingredients, except for the broccoli and Swiss chard, in a soup pot over medium-high heat and bring to a boil, uncovered.
2. Reduce the heat to medium and add the broccoli florets. Cover and cook for 15 to 20 minutes, or until the vegetables become tender. Stir in the Swiss chard and cook for another 3 to 5 minutes, or until soft.
3. Pour the soup mixture into a blender. Pulse until smooth and creamy.
4. Transfer the soup to bowls and serve warm.

Per Serving
Calories: 147 | fat: 0.8g | carbs: 30.5g | protein: 6.7g | fiber: 6.3g

Mushroom Soup with Spinach

Prep time: 15 minutes | Cook time: 20 minutes | Serves 6

1½ pounds (680 g) mushrooms, thinly sliced
¼ cup white wine
1 large onion, thinly sliced
1 (3.5-ounce / 99-g) package enoki mushrooms
4 cups water or
low-sodium vegetable soup
2 tablespoons low-sodium soy sauce
4 cups packed spinach leaves, rinsed and cut into thin strips
Freshly ground black pepper, to taste

1. In a large saucepan, combine the mushrooms, wine, and onion. Gently sauté over low heat for about 10 minutes or until the vegetables are softened.
2. Gradually stir in the enoki mushrooms, water or vegetable soup, and the soy sauce. Cook for another 10 minutes, or until the mushrooms start to brown.
3. Fold in the spinach and sprinkle with the pepper.
4. Remove from the heat and divide the soup into bowls as soon as the spinach is wilted.

Per Serving
Calories: 409 | fat: 2.0g | carbs: 99.2g | protein: 14.1g | fiber: 15.8g

Cannellini Bean and Carrot Soup

Prep time: 10 minutes | Cook time: 20 minutes | Makes 3 to 4 Large Bowls

½ cup low-sodium vegetable broth, plus more as needed for sautéing
1 cup chopped onion
4 large carrots, peeled and chopped (about 2 cups)
1 cup cooked cannellini beans
1 tablespoon minced fresh ginger
¼ teaspoon sea salt (optional)
2 cups water

1. Warm a large pot over medium heat. Add 1 tablespoon of vegetable broth, then sauté the onion and ginger for 2 or 3 minutes until fragrant.
2. Add 1 tablespoon of vegetable broth, then add the carrots and sauté for 3 minutes or until tender.
3. Add the remaining ingredients to the pot and simmer for 20 minutes or until the beans are soft. Stir the soup once or twice during the simmering.
4. Allow to cool for 10 minutes. Pour them in a blender to purée until creamy and smooth. Serve warm.

Per Serving (1 bowl)
Calories: 141 | fat: 12.0g | carbs: 13.0g | protein: 7.0g | fiber: 7.0g

Spicy Potato and Carrot Stew

Prep time: 25 minutes | Cook time: 35 minutes | Serves 8 to 10

1½ cups low-sodium vegetable broth or water
2 medium sweet potatoes, peeled and cubed
2 medium carrots, scrubbed, quartered and chopped into 1-inch chunks
2 cups celery, sliced on the diagonal
1 (16-ounce / 454-g) can whole tomatoes, chopped
1 large onion, coarse-
ly chopped
1 green bell pepper, coarsely chopped
1 to 2 tablespoons low-sodium soy sauce
1 (3-inch) piece stick cinnamon
Freshly ground black pepper, to taste
Pinch cayenne
2 tablespoons cornstarch, dissolved in 2 tablespoons cold water
¼ cup chopped fresh parsley, for garnish

1. Combine all the ingredients except the cornstarch mixture and parsley in a large soup pot. Cover and cook over medium-low heat for 30 minutes, or until the vegetables are softened, stirring occasionally.
2. Add the cornstarch mixture and stir until thickened.
3. Taste and adjust the seasoning to taste. Serve garnished with the chopped parsley.

Per Serving
Calories: 58.2 | fat: 0.2g | carbs: 12.7g | protein: 1.4g | fiber: 2.7g

Thai Spicy Stew

Prep time: 20 minutes | Cook time: 40 minutes | Serves 6

2 celery stalks, diced
2 large yellow onions, peeled and diced
2 medium carrots, peeled and diced
2 Serrano chiles, deseeded and minced
3 tablespoons Thai red chili paste
1 tablespoon ground coriander
2 teaspoons grated ginger
4 cloves garlic, peeled and minced
½ cup water
6 cups low-sodium vegetable broth
4 large sweet potatoes, peeled and cut into ½-inch pieces (about 8 cups)
Zest of 1 lime and juice of 2 limes
Salt and freshly ground black pepper, to taste (optional)
½ cup chopped cilantro

1. Put the celery, onions, and carrots in a large saucepan and sauté over medium heat for 10 minutes.
2. Add the serrano chiles, red chili paste, coriander, ginger, garlic, and water. Whisk to combine well and cook 4 minutes.
3. Add the vegetable broth and sweet potatoes and bring to a boil over high heat.
4. Reduce the heat to medium and cook, covered, for 25 minutes, or until the potatoes are tender.
5. Stir in the lime zest and juice. Season with salt (if desired) and pepper and serve garnished with cilantro.

Per Serving
Calories: 46 | fat: 3.0g | carbs: 50.3g | protein: 8.3g | fiber: 10.0g

Simple Potato and Leek Soup

Prep time: 20 minutes | Cook time: 30 to 40 minutes | Serves 4 to 6

4 cups peeled and chunked potatoes
4 cups water
2 leeks, white parts only, washed well and sliced

¼ teaspoon garlic powder
½ teaspoon onion powder
⅛ Teaspoon freshly ground white pepper

1. Put the potatoes, water, and leeks in a pot. Bring to a boil, reduce the heat, cover, and cook until the potatoes are tender, about 30 minutes.
2. Transfer to a food processor and process until smooth.
3. Return to the pot and stir to mix. Add the remaining ingredients.
4. Cook for 2 minutes or until heated through. Serve immediately.

Per Serving
Calories: 96 | fat: 0.2g | carbs: 22.0g | protein: 2.1g | fiber: 2.8g

Kale Slaw with Curried Dressing

Prep time: 10 minutes | Cook time: 0 minutes | Serves 4

Dressing:
⅔ cup water
2 tablespoons pure maple syrup (optional)
2 tablespoons apple cider vinegar
1 garlic clove, minced
1 teaspoon Dijon mustard
1 teaspoon grated peeled fresh ginger
½ teaspoon curry powder

Freshly ground black pepper, to taste
Slaw:
1 apple, shredded
1 tablespoon freshly squeezed lemon juice
3 cups thinly sliced kale
1 cup shredded fennel
1 carrot, shredded
¼ cup golden raisins
¼ cup sliced almonds, plus more for garnish

Make the Dressing
1. In a blender, combine the water, maple syrup (optional), vinegar, garlic, mustard, ginger, and curry powder. Season to taste with pepper. Purée until smooth. Set aside.

Make the Slaw
2. Toss together the apple and lemon juice in a large bowl.

3. Add the remaining ingredients to the bowl and toss to combine.
4. Pour in about three-quarters of the dressing and toss to coat. Taste and add more dressing as needed. Allow to sit for 10 minutes to soften the kale leaves. Toss again and serve garnished with more almonds.

Per Serving
Calories: 148 | fat: 3.9g | carbs: 25.8g | protein: 3.2g | fiber: 4.1g

Lentil Stew

Prep time: 20 minutes | Cook time: 50 minutes | Serves 6 to 8

1 medium yellow or white onion, chopped (about 2 cups)
8 cups water, plus more as needed
2 medium carrots, sliced (about 1½ cups)
1½ pounds (680 g) white potatoes, peeled and chopped (about 4½ cups)

1½ cups uncooked brown lentils, rinsed
3 ribs celery, chopped (about 1 cup)
1 tablespoon dried Italian herb seasoning
½ teaspoon ground cumin
1 teaspoon granulated garlic
3 cups chopped green cabbage

1. Heat 1 tablespoon of water in a soup pot over medium-high heat until sputtering.
2. Add the onion and cook for 3 to 5 minutes, stirring occasionally, adding a little more water as needed.
3. Stir in the 8 cups water, carrots, potatoes, lentils, celery, Italian seasoning, cumin, and granulated garlic and bring to a boil.
4. Reduce the heat to medium-low, cover, and simmer for 30 minutes until the vegetables are softened.
5. Add the chopped cabbage and stir well. Cover and cook for an additional 10 minutes, or until the lentils are tender.
6. Serve warm.

Per Serving
Calories: 139 | fat: 1.5g | carbs: 27.2g | protein: 4.1g | fiber: 3.9g

Pea and Watercress Soup

Prep time: 10 minutes | Cook time: 10 minutes | Makes 4 bowls

1 teaspoon coconut oil (optional)
1 onion, diced
2 cups fresh peas
4 cups low-sodium vegetable soup
1 cup fresh watercress, chopped
1 tablespoon fresh mint, chopped
Pinch sea salt (optional)
Pinch freshly ground black pepper
¾ cup unsweetened coconut milk

1. Heat the coconut oil (if desired) in a saucepan over medium-high heat. Add the onion to the saucepan and sauté for about 5 minutes, or until translucent and soft.
2. Add the peas and vegetable soup and bring to a boil. Reduce the heat to medium-low and add the watercress, mint, sea salt (if desired) and black pepper to the saucepan. Cover and cook for 5 minutes, or until the vegetables are wilted.
3. Pour the coconut milk in the saucepan and stir well. Remove the saucepan from the heat. Pour the soup into a blender and pulse until creamy and smooth.
4. Divide the soup among 4 bowls and serve warm.

Per Serving (1 bowl)
Calories: 177 | fat: 9.8g | carbs: 7.8g | protein: 6.2g | fiber: 5.1g

Hearty Vegetable Stew

Prep time: 25 minutes | Cook time: 1 hour | Serves 6 to 8

3 potatoes, scrubbed and chunked
2 carrots, scrubbed and thickly sliced
½ pound (227) mushrooms, quartered
2 cups water
2 onions, sliced
2 stalks celery, thickly sliced
2 to 3 cloves garlic
1 green bell pepper, cut into strips
¼ cup tomato juice
¼ cup low-sodium soy sauce
½ tablespoon grated fresh ginger
½ teaspoon dried marjoram
½ teaspoon dried thyme
½ teaspoon paprika
3 to 4 tablespoons cornstarch, mixed with ½ cup cold water

1. Combine all the ingredients except the cornstarch mixture in a large soup pot over medium-high heat and bring to a boil.
2. When it starts to boil, reduce the heat, cover, and let simmer for about 1 hour, or until the vegetables are tender.
3. Add the cornstarch mixture to the stew and keep stirring until thickened.
4. Ladle into bowls and serve warm.

Per Serving
Calories: 235 | fat: 0.5g | carbs: 51.2g | protein: 6.5g | fiber: 6.8g

Summer Soup

Prep time: 15 minutes | Cook time: 35 minutes | Serves 6

1 large yellow onion, peeled and chopped
4 cloves garlic, peeled and minced
6 medium tomatoes, chopped
3 medium zucchinis, diced
2 cups corn kernels (about 3 ears corn)
6 cups low-sodium vegetable broth
½ cup finely chopped basil
Zest and juice of 1 lemon
Salt, to taste (optional)
Ground black pepper, to taste

1. Heat a saucepan over medium heat, then add the onion and sauté for 6 minutes or until lightly caramelized. Add a dash of water during the sautéing.
2. Add the garlic to the pan and sauté for 30 seconds or until fragrant.
3. Add the tomatoes to the pan and sauté for 10 minutes or until lightly wilted.
4. Add the zucchini, corn, and vegetable broth to the pan. Bring to a boil over high heat, then reduce the heat to medium and simmer for 15 minutes or until the vegetables are soft. Keep stirring during the boiling and simmering.
5. Pour the soup in a large serving bowl. Sprinkle with lemon zest, basil, salt (if desired), and pepper. Drizzle with lemon juice. Serve warm.

Per Serving
Calories: 418 | fat: 6.8g | carbs: 80.1g | protein: 12.5g | fiber: 11.8g

Miso Adzuki Bean Stew

Prep time: 15 minutes | Cook time: 58 minutes | Serves 4

1 large yellow on-
ion, peeled and diced
small
1 large carrot, peeled
and diced small
3 cloves garlic, peeled
and minced
2 tablespoons ground
coriander
2½ cups adzuki
beans, soaked over-

night
8 cups water
2 tablespoons mellow
white miso
1 cup chopped cilan-
tro
1 teaspoon crushed
red pepper flakes
Salt, to taste (option-
al)

1. Put the onion and carrot in a large pot
   and sauté for 8 minutes over medium
   heat. Add the garlic and coriander and
   sauté for 1 more minute.
2. Add the beans and water and bring to a
   boil over high heat. Reduce the heat to
   medium, cover, and cook until the beans
   are tender, about 50 minutes.
3. Transfer 1 cup of the cooking liquid to a
   small bowl and mix in the miso.
4. Add the miso mixture to the pot. Add the
   cilantro and crushed red pepper flakes
   and season with salt, if desired.
5. Serve immediately.

Per Serving
Calories: 450 | fat: 1.4g | carbs: 86.1g | pro-
tein: 26.3g | fiber: 17.5g

Thai Water Chestnut Stew

Prep time: 15 minutes | Cook time: 20 minutes | Serves 4

1 medium yellow on-
ion, peeled and diced
small
2 teaspoons Thai red
chili paste
2 teaspoons grated
ginger
2 cloves garlic, peeled
and minced
Zest and juice of 1
lime
1 Serrano chile,
minced

1 (14-ounce / 397-g)
can lite coconut milk
1 cup low-sodium
vegetable broth
2 tablespoons low-so-
dium soy sauce
3 cups water chest-
nuts
½ cup chopped
cilantro
2 tablespoons minced
mint

1. Put the onion in a large saucepan and
   sauté over medium-high heat for 8 minutes, or until the onion is tender and
   lightly browned.
2. Add the chili paste, ginger, garlic, lime
   zest and juice, and serrano chile and
   cook for 30 seconds.
3. Add the coconut milk, vegetable broth,
   soy sauce, and water chestnuts, reduce
   the heat to medium, and cook for 10
   minutes, or until the vegetables are tender.
4. Stir in the cilantro and mint and serve.

Per Serving
Calories: 518 | fat: 28.3g | carbs: 63.6g |
protein: 7.4g | fiber: 12.9g

Bean and Mushroom Chili

Prep time: 15 minutes | Cook time: 38 minutes | Serves 6

1 large onion, peeled
and chopped
1 pound (454 g)
button mushrooms,
chopped
6 cloves garlic, peeled
and minced
1 tablespoon ground
cumin
4 Teaspoons ground
fennel
1 tablespoon ancho
chile powder

½ teaspoon cayenne
pepper
1 tablespoon un-
sweetened cocoa
powder
4 cups cooked pinto
beans, drained and
rinsed
1 (28-ounce / 794-g)
can diced tomatoes
Salt, to taste (option-
al)

1. Put the mushrooms and onion in a saucepan and sauté over medium heat for 10
   minutes.
2. Add the garlic, cumin, fennel, chile powder, cayenne pepper, and cocoa powder
   and cook for 3 minutes.
3. Add the beans, tomatoes, and 2 cups of
   water and simmer, covered, for 25 minutes. Season with salt, if desired.
4. Serve immediately.

Per Serving
Calories: 436 | fat: 2.5g | carbs: 97.1g | pro-
tein: 19.7g | fiber: 23.2g

Indian Tomato and Bean Zuppa

Prep time: 10 minutes | Cook time: 18 minutes | Serves 4

½ cup uncooked quinoa
1½ cups cooked fava beans
Pinch fenugreek seeds
4½ cups water, divided
½ cup leeks, white and light green parts, finely chopped and rinsed
½ clove garlic, peeled and minced
2 medium tomatoes, chopped
¼ teaspoon ground cumin
⅛ Teaspoon turmeric
¼ teaspoon salt (optional)
½ cup spinach
Freshly ground black pepper, to taste

1. Add the quinoa, fava beans, and fenugreek seeds to a pot. Pour in 3 cups of the water and bring to a boil over high heat.
2. Add the leeks and garlic and cook on medium heat for 12 minutes. Add 1½ cups of water, the tomatoes, cumin, turmeric, and salt (if desired) and cook for another 6 minutes on medium heat, or until the quinoa and fava beans are tender.
3. Add the spinach and season with black pepper. Serve hot.

Per Serving
Calories: 143 | fat: 1.9g | carbs: 26.9g | protein: 7.8g | fiber: 6.3g

Vegetable Gnocchi Soup

Prep time: 15 minutes | Cook time: 25 minutes | Serves 4

1 small onion, chopped
¼ cup chopped scallion
6 cups water
6 cups finely chopped mustard greens
1 medium chayote, peeled and chopped
½ pound (227 g) gnocchi
Freshly ground pepper, for garnish

1. Sauté the onion, scallion, and ½ cup of the water in a large soup pot for about 4 minutes, or until the onion is softened.
2. Stir in the mustard greens, cover and cook over low heat for about 4 minutes or until the vegetables are tender. Add the chayote and the remaining 5½ cups of water. Bring to a boil over medium heat, cover, and simmer for about 15 minutes, or until the chayote is soft.

3. Transfer batches of the hot soup to a blender or food processor and blitz until smooth. Pour the soup into a saucepan and keep warm over low heat.
4. Meanwhile, make the gnocchi: Bring a large pot of salted water to a boil. Add the gnocchi and cook them for 2 to 3 minutes, or until they float to the surface.
5. Drain the gnocchi and add to the puréed soup.
6. Serve hot sprinkled with freshly ground pepper.

Per Serving
Calories: 117 | fat: 4.0g | carbs: 18.0g | protein: 4.5g | fiber: 4.6g

Sumptuous Pea, Yam, and Potato Soup

Prep time: 15 minutes | Cook time: 55 minutes | Serves 6 to 8

2 cups dry split peas
8½ cups water
1 medium yam, peeled and chopped (about 1½ cups)
2 ribs celery, sliced (about ⅔ cup)
1 medium yellow or white onion, chopped (about 2 cups)
1 medium white potato, peeled and
chopped (about 1½ cups)
1 teaspoon granulated garlic
½ teaspoon ground cumin
¼ teaspoon ground celery seed
1½ Teaspoons dried oregano
5 cups coarsely chopped Swiss chard

1. Put the peas in a pot, then pour in the water. Bring to a boil over medium-high heat.
2. Cover the pot and reduce the heat to medium-low. Simmer for 30 more minutes. Stir periodically.
3. When the simmering is complete, fold in the yams, celery, onion, potatoes, garlic, cumin, celery seed, and oregano. Bring to a boil over medium-high heat.
4. Uncovered, reduce the heat to medium-low and cook for an additional 20 minutes or until the vegetables are tender. Stir constantly.
5. Mix in the Swiss chard and cook for another 5 minutes or until the chard is soft.
6. Serve immediately.

Per Serving
Calories: 349 | fat: 4.2g | carbs: 62.4g | protein: 17.8g | fiber: 20.5g

Millet and Corn Salad

Prep time: 20 minutes | Cook time: 25 minutes | Serves 4

½ cup millet, rinsed
1 cup water
1 teaspoon avocado oil (optional)
Corn of 4 cobs
1 teaspoon chili powder
Salt and ground black pepper, to taste (optional)
1 tablespoon fresh lime juice
1 poblano pepper
1 red bell pepper
½ cup cherry tomatoes, halved
1/3 cup chopped fresh cilantro leaves

2 green onions, sliced
Garlic Dressing:
2 cloves garlic, finely grated
2 teaspoons Dijon mustard
3 tablespoons fresh lemon juice
¼ cup raw cashew butter
¼ cup plus 2 tablespoons avocado oil (optional)
¼ cup water
Salt and ground black pepper, to taste (optional)

1. Pour the millet and water in a pot. Bring to a boil, then reduce the heat to low and simmer for 15 more minutes or until the water is almost absorbed. Turn off the heat and allow to cool for 5 minutes. Fluff the millet with a fork. Set aside.
2. Meanwhile, heat the avocado oil (if desired) in a skillet over medium-high heat.
3. Add the corn to the skillet and sauté for 2 minutes or until the corn is lightly browned. Sprinkle with chili powder, salt (if desired), and ground black pepper. Drizzle with lime juice. Turn off the heat and transfer the corn on a plate and set aside.
4. Add the poblano pepper and red bell pepper to the cleaned skillet and sauté over medium-high heat for 5 minutes or until wilted and charred.
5. Transfer the peppers in a bowl, then wrap the bowl in plastic and let sit to steam for 8 minutes.
6. Meanwhile, combine the ingredients for the garlic dressing in a small bowl. Stir to mix well until creamy and smooth.
7. Remove the seeds, stems, and skins of the steamed peppers, then cut them into strips. Transfer the peppers to the plate with corn.
8. Add the cooked millet, cherry tomatoes, cilantro, and green onions to the plate with peppers and corn. Dress with the garlic dressing and serve immediately.

Per Serving
Calories: 473 | fat: 25.7g | carbs: 58.5g | protein: 9.9g | fiber: 7.7g

Edamame and Black Rice Salad

Prep time: 10 minutes | Cook time: 45 to 50 minutes | Serves 4

Salad:
1 cup black rice
2 cups water
Pinch sea salt (optional)
1 large sweet potato, peeled and diced
1 teaspoon olive oil (optional)
1 cup shelled frozen edamame, thawed
4 scallions, chopped
1 red bell pepper, deseeded and chopped
½ head broccoli,

chopped
¼ cup chopped fresh cilantro
1 teaspoon sesame seeds
Dressing:
Juice of ½ orange
1 tablespoon low-sodium soy sauce
1 tablespoon rice vinegar
2 teaspoons maple syrup (optional)
2 teaspoons sesame oil (optional)

1. Preheat the oven to 400ºF (205ºC). Line a baking pan with the parchment paper.
2. Pour the water in a pot and add the black rice and salt (if desired) to the pot over high heat. Bring to a boil. Reduce the heat to medium. Cover and cook for 30 minutes, or until the water is absorbed and the rice is tender. Set aside and let cool.
3. In a medium bowl, toss together the potato and olive oil (if desired) until well coated. Spread the coated potato in the prepared pan and roast for 15 to 20 minutes, or until softened. Set aside and let cool.
4. In a small bowl, whisk together all the ingredients for the dressing.
5. Add the cooked black rice, roasted potato edamame, scallions, bell pepper and broccoli to a large bowl. Spread the dressing and toss to combine well. Sprinkle the cilantro and sesame seeds on top.
6. Divide the salad among 4 dishes and serve immediately.

Per Serving
Calories: 444 | fat: 11.1g | carbs: 7.2g | protein: 14.8g | fiber: 10.9g

Farro Salad with White Beans

Prep time: 30 minutes | Cook time: 17 to 32 minutes | Serves 4 to 6

12 ounces (340 g) sugar snap peas, strings removed and cut into 1-inch lengths
3¼ teaspoon sea salt, plus more to taste, divided (optional)
1½ cups whole farro
3 tablespoons extra-virgin olive oil (optional)
2 tablespoons lemon juice
2 tablespoons minced shallot
1 teaspoon Dijon mustard
¼ teaspoon black pepper, plus more to taste, divided
1 (15-ounce / 425-g) can cannellini beans, rinsed
6 ounces (170 g) cherry tomatoes, halved
1/3 cup chopped pitted kalamata olives
2 tablespoons chopped fresh dill

1. Pour the water in a pot over medium heat and bring to a boil. Add the snap peas and 3 Teaspoon sea salt (if desired) to the pot and cook for 2 minutes, or until tender-crisp. Drain the snap peas and transfer to a bowl. Let rest for 15 minutes to cool completely.
2. Pour the water in the pot over medium heat. Add the farro to the pot and bring to a boil. Cover and cook for 15 to 30 minutes, or until tender. Drain the farro and spread evenly on a baking pan. Let rest for 15 minutes to cool completely.
3. In a large bowl, stir together the olive oil (if desired), lemon juice, shallot, Dijon mustard ¼ teaspoon sea salt (if desired) and ¼ teaspoon black pepper. Add the cooled snap peas, cooled farro, cannellini beans, tomatoes, olives, and dill to the bowl. Toss until well blended. Sprinkle with sea salt (if desired) and pepper to taste.
4. Transfer the salad to 4 to 6 bowls and serve immediately.

Per Serving
Calories: 501 | fat: 14.9g | carbs: 81.6g | protein: 16.6g | fiber: 7.3g

Lentil and Swiss Chard Salad

Prep time: 10 minutes | Cook time: 50 minutes | Serves 4

1 teaspoon plus ¼ cup avocado oil, divided (optional)
1 garlic clove, minced
1 small onion, diced
1 carrot, diced
1 cup lentils
1 tablespoon dried oregano
1 tablespoon dried basil
1 tablespoon low-so-
dium balsamic vinegar
2 cups water
¼ cup red wine vinegar
1 teaspoon sea salt (optional)
2 cups chopped Swiss chard
2 cups torn red leaf lettuce

1. Heat 1 teaspoon of avocado oil (if desired) in a saucepan over medium heat.
2. Add the garlic and onion and sauté for 5 minutes or until fragrant and the onion is soft.
3. Add the carrot and sauté for 3 minutes or until the carrot is tender.
4. Add the lentils and sprinkle with oregano and basil. Drizzle with balsamic vinegar. Pour in the water and bring to a boil over high heat.
5. Reduce the heat to low and simmer for 20 minutes or until the lentils are tender and hold together. Stir constantly.
6. Meanwhile, combine the red wine vinegar with remaining avocado oil (if desired) and salt (if desired) in a small bowl. Stir to mix well.
7. When the simmering is complete, pour in half of the red wine vinegar mixture and stir in the Swiss chard. Cook on low heat for another 10 minutes. Stir constantly.
8. Toss the lettuce with remaining red wine vinegar mixture and place on 4 serving plate. Top the lettuce with the lentil mixture and serve immediately.

Per Serving
Calories: 387 | fat: 17.0g | carbs: 23.0g | protein: 18.0g | fiber: 19.0g

Smoky Potato and Almond Salad

Prep time: 20 minutes | Cook time: 10 minutes | Serves 4 to 6

2 pounds (907 g) waxy potatoes
¼ cup apple cider vinegar
1 teaspoon low-sodium tomato paste
2 scallions, white and light green parts, sliced
½ teaspoon Dijon mustard
½ teaspoon smoked paprika
1 teaspoon maple syrup (optional)
2 drops liquid smoke
2 tablespoons avocado oil (optional)
½ teaspoon salt (optional)
¼ teaspoon ground black pepper
¼ cup roasted almonds, chopped
12 ounces (340 g) baby broccoli, chopped

1. Put the potatoes in a pot, then pour in enough water to cover. Bring to a boil over medium-high heat, then cook for 10 more minutes or until soft.
2. Allow the potatoes to cool for 5 minutes, then put the potatoes in a colander and rinse under running water. Pat dry with paper towels.
3. Meanwhile, combine the cider vinegar, tomato paste, scallions, mustard, paprika, maple syrup (if desired), liquid smoke, avocado oil (if desired), salt (if desired), and black pepper in a small bowl. Stir to mix well.
4. On a clean work surface, chop the cooked potatoes into bite-size pieces, then transfer the potato pieces to the vinegar mixture. Add the almonds and baby broccoli. Toss to serve.

Per Serving
Calories: 201 | fat: 7.1g | carbs: 30.4g | protein: 5.9g | fiber: 5.6g

Brussels Sprouts and Avocado Salad

Prep time: 20 minutes | Cook time: 20 minutes | Serves 4

Dressing:
2 teaspoons miso
1 teaspoon Dijon mustard
½ teaspoon lime zest
1½ tablespoons fresh lime juice
1 teaspoon maple syrup (optional)
2 tablespoons avocado oil (optional)
Salt and ground black pepper, to taste (optional)
Salad:
1 pound (454 g) Brussels sprouts, trimmed and quartered
½ teaspoon dried chili flakes
2 teaspoons avocado oil (optional)
Salt and ground black pepper, to taste (optional)
1 small ripe avocado, peeled, pitted, diced
Garnish:
¼ cup toasted sunflower seeds
¼ cup chopped fresh basil leaves
¼ cup chopped fresh mint leaves

1. Preheat the oven to 400°F (205°C). Line a baking pan with parchment paper.
2. Combine the ingredients for the dressing in a small bowl. Stir to mix well. Set aside until ready to use.
3. Toss the Brussels sprouts with chili flakes, avocado oil (if desired), salt (if desired), and black pepper in a large bowl to coat well. Set to the prepared baking pan.
4. Roast the Brussels sprouts in the preheated oven for 20 minutes or charred and wilted. Flip the Brussels sprouts halfway through.
5. Put the Brussels sprouts back to the bowl, then pour half of the dressing over and toss to coat well.
6. Top the Brussels sprouts with the avocado, then pour the remaining dressing over. Toss with the remaining ingredients before serving.

Per Serving
Calories: 321 | fat: 24.0g | carbs: 26.9g | protein: 9.3g | fiber: 14.4g

Brussels Sprout and Sweet Potato Salad

Prep time: 20 minutes | Cook time: 30 minutes | Serves 4

3 sweet potatoes, peeled, cut into ¼-inch dices, and rinsed
1 teaspoon garlic powder
1 teaspoon dried thyme
½ teaspoon onion powder
1 pound (454 g)
Brussels sprouts, outer leaves removed and halved lengthwise
1 cup chopped walnuts
¼ cup reduced-sugar dried cranberries
2 tablespoons balsamic vinegar
Freshly ground black pepper, to taste

1. Preheat the oven to 450ºF (235ºC). Line a baking sheet with parchment paper.
2. In a large bowl, sprinkle the sweet potatoes with the thyme, garlic powder, and onion powder. Toss to coat well.
3. Spread out the sweet potatoes onto the prepared baking sheet in a single layer.
4. Bake in the preheated oven for 20 minutes. Flip the sweet potatoes and bake for another 10 minutes until fork-tender.
5. Meanwhile, place the Brussels sprouts, cut side down, on your cutting board and thinly slice the sprouts crosswise into thin shreds. Discard the root end and loosen the shreds.
6. Toss together the Brussels sprouts, cooked sweet potatoes, walnuts, and cranberries in a salad bowl. Drizzle the vinegar all over the vegetables and sprinkle with the pepper. Toss again and serve immediately.

Per Serving
Calories: 368 | fat: 21.1g | carbs: 44.3g | protein: 10.6g | fiber: 12.3g

Potato and Corn Chowder

Prep time: 20 minutes | Cook time: 30 minutes | Serves 4

2 tablespoons low-sodium vegetables broth
1 medium yellow onion, diced
1 stalk celery, diced
1 small red bell pepper, diced
2 teaspoons minced fresh thyme leaves (about 4 sprigs)
½ teaspoon smoked paprika
½ teaspoon no-salt-added Old Bay seasoning
1 jalapeño pepper,
deseeded and minced
1 clove garlic, minced
1 pound (454 g) new potatoes, diced
3 cups fresh corn kernels (about 4 fresh cobs)
Salt, to taste (optional)
Ground black or white pepper, to taste
4 cup low-sodium vegetable broth
2 teaspoons white wine vinegar
Chopped chives, for garnish

1. Heat the vegetables broth in a large pot over medium heat. Add the onions and sauté for 4 minutes or until translucent.
2. Add the red bell pepper, celery, paprika, thyme, jalapeño, and Old Bay seasoning. Sauté for 1 minutes or until the vegetables are tender.
3. Add the garlic and sauté for another 1 minutes or until fragrant.
4. Add the corn, potatoes, vegetable broth, salt (if desired), and pepper. Stir to mix well. Bring to a boil, then reduce the heat to low and simmer for 25 minutes or until the potatoes are soft.
5. Pour half of the soup in a blender, then process until the soup is creamy and smooth. Pour the puréed soup back to the pot and add the white wine vinegar. Stir to mix well.
6. Spread the chopped chives on top and serve.

Per Serving
Calories: 733 | fat: 8.5g | carbs: 148.5g | protein: 20.4g | fiber: 18.3g

Mexican Fiesta Soup

Prep time: 20 minutes | Cook time: 26 minutes | Serves 6

1 tablespoon avocado oil (optional)
1 red bell pepper, diced
1 yellow onion, diced
3 garlic cloves, minced
1 zucchini, diced
2 tablespoons taco seasoning
4 cups low-sodium vegetable soup
1 (15-ounce / 425-g) can organic diced tomatoes, undrained
1 (15-ounce / 425-g) can pinto beans, drained and rinsed
1 (15-ounce / 425-g) can black beans, drained and rinsed
1 (7-ounce / 198-g) can diced green chiles
1 cup organic frozen corn, thawed
¼ cup fresh cilantro, chopped
2 tablespoons fresh lime juice (from 1 lime)
Sea salt and ground black pepper, to taste (optional)
Serving:
½ cup organic corn tortilla strips
3 ripe avocados, diced
½ cup fresh cilantro, roughly chopped
1 lime, cut into wedges

1. Heat the oil (if desired) in a large pot over medium-high heat for 30 seconds. Add the bell pepper and onion and sauté for 5 minutes, or until the bell peppers are lightly browned and the onions are translucent.
2. Stir in the garlic and zucchini and sauté for another 1 minute or until fragrant. Sprinkle with the taco seasoning and continue to sauté until the spices are toasted.
3. Fold in the stock, tomatoes, beans, and chiles and stir to combine. Bring to a boil, reduce the heat to low, and simmer for 20 minutes, or until the vegetables are softened and the flavors are blended.
4. Add the corn, cilantro, and lime juice and stir well. Sprinkle with salt (if desired) and pepper.
5. Turn off the heat. Divide the hot soup among bowls.
6. Spread the tortilla strips, avocado, and cilantro on top and squeeze the lime wedges over.

Per Serving
Calories: 469 | fat: 20.5g | carbs: 62.9g | protein: 13.7g | fiber: 17.7g

Mushroom and Potato Soup

Prep time: 35 minutes | Cook time: 35 minutes | Serves 6 to 8

1 medium yellow or white onion, chopped (about 2 cups)
5 cups water, plus more as needed
6 medium cremini or white mushrooms, sliced (about 2½ cups)
1½ pounds (680 g) white potatoes, peeled and chopped (about 4½ cups)
1 small yam or sweet potato, peeled and chopped (about 2 cups)
2 ribs celery, sliced
(about ²/₃ cup)
2 teaspoons dried Italian herb seasoning
1 teaspoon granulated garlic
1 teaspoon paprika
½ teaspoon ground nutmeg
½ teaspoon granulated onion
12 medium cremini or white mushrooms, thinly sliced (4 to 5 cups)
1 cup unsweetened almond milk, at room temperature

1. Heat 1 tablespoon of water in a soup pot over medium-high heat until sputtering. Add the onion and sauté for 3 to 5 minutes, stirring occasionally. Add 1 to 2 tablespoons of water to keep it from sticking to the bottom of the pot, if needed.
2. Add 4 cups water, 6 sliced mushrooms, potatoes, yams, celery, Italian seasoning, granulated garlic, paprika, nutmeg, and onion. Stir to mix well. Reduce the heat to medium and simmer for about 10 to 15 minutes, or until the vegetables are softened.
3. Pour in the remaining 1 cup of water. Using an immersion blender, blend the soup until mostly smooth.
4. Fold in the 12 sliced mushrooms and cook over low heat for 15 to 20 minutes until tender, stirring occasionally.
5. Turn off the heat and stir in the almond milk.
6. Divide the soup among the bowls and serve hot.

Per Serving
Calories: 195 | fat: 3.8g | carbs: 34.5g | protein: 7.2g | fiber: 4.6g

Ritzy Lasagna Soup

Prep time: 30 minutes | Cook time: 30 minutes | Serves 6 to 8

2 tablespoons low-sodium vegetable broth
1 cup finely chopped onion (about 1 onion)
1 teaspoon dried oregano
3 garlic cloves, minced
1 bay leaf
¼ teaspoon red pepper flakes
1 teaspoon sea salt (optional)
1 teaspoon ground pepper
4 cups sliced cremini mushrooms (about 10 ounces / 284 g)
28 ounces (794 g) tomatoes, crushed
3 cups diced zucchini
(about 1 large zucchini)
½ cup finely chopped fresh flat-leaf parsley
2 teaspoons date sugar
½ cup finely chopped fresh basil
2 tablespoons balsamic vinegar
¼ cup tomato paste
6 cups low-sodium vegetable broth
2 cups water
12 lasagna, break into small pieces
6 cups baby spinach leaves
Vegan Mozzarella shreds, for garnish

1. Heat 2 tablespoons of vegetable broth in a large pot over medium heat.
2. Add the onion to the pan and sauté for 2 minutes or until translucent.
3. Add the oregano, garlic, bay leaf, red pepper flakes, salt (if desired), and pepper to the pot and sauté for 2 minutes or until aromatic.
4. Add the mushrooms, tomatoes, and zucchini to the pot and sauté for 6 minutes or until the vegetables are soft and wilted.
5. Add the parsley, date sugar, basil, vinegar, and tomato paste to the pot and sauté for 2 minutes.
6. Pour in the vegetable broth and water, then add the lasagna. Stir to mix well. Bring to a boil, then simmer for 8 minutes. Keep stirring during the simmering.
7. Add the spinach to the pot and simmer for an additional 2 to 4 minutes or until the lasagna is al dente.
8. Discard the bay leaf. Spread the vegan Mozzarella shreds on top and serve warm.

Per Serving
Calories: 407 | fat: 2.8g | carbs: 85.1g | protein: 15.2g | fiber: 4.8g

Sumptuous Minestrone Soup

Prep time: 15 minutes | Cook time: 35 to 39 minutes | Serves 6 to 8

6 cups water
1 medium white onion, chopped
¾ cup chopped fresh fennel
1 tablespoon finely chopped garlic
1 teaspoon whole fennel seeds
¼ to ½ teaspoon crushed red pepper flakes (optional)
1½ pounds (680 g) white potatoes, peeled and chopped
1 (15-ounce / 425-g) can cooked red kidney beans, drained
and rinsed
2 (14.5-ounce / 411-g) cans diced tomatoes, undrained
2 medium carrots, sliced
1 medium zucchini, sliced
6 medium white or cremini mushrooms, sliced
2 cups cooked small-shell pasta
½ cup chopped fresh basil
½ cup chopped fresh parsley

1. Warm 1 tablespoon of water in a soup pot over medium-high heat. Add the onion and fresh fennel and sauté for 3 to 5 minutes.
2. Add the garlic, fennel seeds, and red pepper flakes to the pot and sauté for 1 to 2 minutes.
3. Add the water, potatoes, kidney beans, tomatoes and carrots to the pot. Bring the mixture to a boil, uncovered. Reduce the heat to medium-low and simmer for 25 minutes, stirring constantly.
4. Add the zucchini and mushrooms and cook for 5 minutes, or until the potatoes and carrots become softened.
5. Add the cooked pasta, basil and parsley and cook for another 1 to 2 minutes.
6. Pour the soup into the bowls and serve hot.

Per Serving
Calories: 253 | fat: 3.6g | carbs: 50.2g | protein: 7.6g | fiber: 9.3g

Vegetable Soup

Prep time: 15 minutes | Cook time: 35 to 40 minutes | Serves 6

1 tablespoon avocado oil (optional)
1 yellow onion, diced
Sea salt, to taste (optional)
2 ribs celery, chopped
3 carrots, peeled and sliced
3 garlic cloves, minced
1 zucchini, sliced
1 can (28 ounces / 794 g) organic diced tomatoes, undrained
4 cups vegetable stock
2 teaspoons Italian seasoning
Ground black pepper, to taste

1. Heat the oil (if desired) in a large saucepan over medium-high heat. Add the onion and lightly season with salt (if desired). Cook for 7 minutes, or until the onion turns translucent, stirring frequently.
2. Mix in the celery and carrots and cook for 5 minutes, stirring occasionally. Fold in the garlic and cook for 1 minute until fragrant. Add the zucchini and sauté for 5 to 7 minutes, or until the zucchini begins to soften.
3. Stir in the tomatoes, stock, and Italian seasoning and bring the mixture to just a boil. Reduce the heat to low and let simmer for 20 minutes, or until the vegetables are tender.
4. Purée the soup with an immersion blender until smooth. Sprinkle with salt (if desired) and pepper.
5. Divide the soup among bowls and serve hot.

Per Serving
Calories: 181 | fat: 4.3g | carbs: 31.6g | protein: 5.6g | fiber: 7.8g

Classic Vichyssoise

Prep time: 15 minutes | Cook time: 25 to 30 minutes | Serves 6 to 8

2 large leeks, white and light green parts, rinsed and diced
1 bay leaf
1 tablespoon chopped dill
1½ pounds (680 g) russet potatoes (about 4 to 5 medium), peeled and diced
5 cups low-sodium vegetable broth
½ pound (227 g) spinach, chopped
Zest of 1 lemon
Salt, to taste (optional)
Ground black pepper, to taste
1 cup unsweetened almond milk

1. Heat a saucepan over medium heat, then add the leeks and sauté for 5 minutes or until soft. Add a dash of water until the sautéing.
2. Add the bay leaf and dill to the pan and sauté for 1 minutes or until aromatic.
3. Add the potatoes and vegetable broth to the pan and stir to mix well. Bring to a boil, then cook for 15 to 20 minutes or until the potatoes are soft.
4. Add the spinach, lemon zest, salt (if desired), and pepper to the pan and cook for 5 minutes or until the spinach is tender.
5. Allow the soup to cool for 10 minutes and discard the bay leaf, then pour the soup in a food processor. Pulse to purée the soup until creamy and smooth.
6. Pour the soup in a large bowl, then add the almond milk. Stir to mix well before serving.

Per Serving
Calories: 209 | fat: 1.9g | carbs: 40.2g | protein: 9.5g | fiber: 5.7g

Chapter 5 Vegetarian Mains

Mushrooms and Chilies McDougall

Prep time: 10 minutes | Cook time: 11 to 14 minutes | Serves 6 to 8

1½ pounds (680 g) mushrooms, sliced
1 (4-ounce / 113-g) can chopped green chilies
2 cloves garlic, minced
1 bunch scallions, chopped
¼ cup sherry
¼ cup water
2 tablespoons fresh lemon juice
½ teaspoon Worcestershire sauce
Freshly ground pepper, to taste

1. Pour the water in a large pan over medium heat and bring to a boil. Stir in the mushrooms, chilies, garlic and scallions. Sauté for 1 to 2 minutes and add the remaining ingredients.
2. Continue to cook for 10 to 12 minutes, stirring constantly, or until all the liquid has been absorbed.
3. Serve immediately.

Per Serving
Calories: 270 | fat: 0.9g | carbs: 67.1g | protein: 8.7g | fiber: 10.3g

Simple Cauliflower Florets

Prep time: 5 minutes | Cook time: 10 minutes | Serves 2

1 cup water
1 large head cauliflower, cut into florets
½ teaspoon salt (op-
tional)
1 teaspoon red pepper flakes

1. Put the water and cauliflower florets in a large saucepan over medium heat. Sprinkle with the salt, if desired. Allow to boil for about 4 to 5 minutes until fork-tender.
2. Drain the cauliflower well and dry with paper towels, then transfer to a bowl.
3. Add the red pepper flakes to the bowl of cauliflower and toss well. Serve immediately.

Per Serving
Calories: 39 | fat: 0.3g | carbs: 6.6g | protein: 2.5g | fiber: 2.7g

Spicy Braise Vegetables

Prep time: 10 minutes | Cook time: 4 hours | Serves 8

6 large carrots, cut into ½-inch rounds
6 medium white potatoes, cut into 1-inch cubes
3 sweet onions, cut into ½-inch cubes
12 ounces (340 g) fresh green beans
8 ounces (227 g)
mushrooms, sliced
4 cups low-sodium vegetable broth
1 teaspoon garlic powder
1 teaspoon onion powder
1 teaspoon freshly ground black pepper

1. Combine all the ingredients in a slow cooker. Stir together so the spices are well distributed.
2. Cook for 4 hours on high or 6 to 8 hours on low.
3. Remove the lid and stir before serving.

Per Serving
Calories: 189 | fat: 20.8g | carbs: 12.9g | protein: 8.2g | fiber: 8.1g

Smoky Chipotle Coleslaw

Prep time: 10 minutes | Cook time: 0 minutes | Serves 4

1 pound (454 g) shredded cabbage
$1/_3$ cup vegan mayonnaise
¼ cup unseasoned rice vinegar
3 tablespoons unsweetened soy milk
1 tablespoon date
sugar
½ teaspoon salt (optional)
¼ teaspoon freshly ground black pepper
¼ teaspoon chipotle powder
¼ teaspoon smoked paprika

1. In a large bowl, add the shredded cabbage. In a medium bowl, stir together the mayo, rice vinegar, soy milk, date sugar, salt (if desired), black pepper, chipotle powder, and paprika until completely mixed.
2. Pour the mayo mixture over the shredded cabbage and toss to incorporate. Serve immediately.

Per Serving
Calories: 74 | fat: 4.1g | carbs: 8.2g | protein: 1.1g | fiber: 2.1g

Broccoli Cashew Stir-Fry

Prep time: 10 minutes | Cook time: 7 to 8 minutes | Serves 2

1 large head broccoli, cut into florets
1 medium yellow onion, peeled and cut into ½-inch slices
1 (6-ounce / 170-g) can sliced water chestnuts, drained
Water, as needed
1 cup snow peas, trimmed
¼ cup plus 2 tablespoons Chinese brown gravy sauce
¼ cup cashews, toasted

1. Heat a large skillet over high heat. Add the broccoli, onion, water chestnuts, and snow peas and stir-fry for 4 to 5 minutes until the broccoli is tender but still crisp. Add water, 1 to 2 tablespoons at a time, to prevent sticking.
2. Stir in the sauce and cook for about 3 minutes until the sauce starts to thicken.
3. Serve scattered with the toasted cashews on top.

Per Serving
Calories: 386 | fat: 18.8g | carbs: 50.5g | protein: 9.8g | fiber: 10.1g

Broccoli Stir-Fry with Sesame Seeds

Prep time: 10 minutes | Cook time: 8 minutes | Serves 4

2 tablespoons extra-virgin olive oil (optional)
1 tablespoon grated fresh ginger
4 cups broccoli florets
¼ Teaspoon sea salt (optional)
2 garlic cloves, minced
2 tablespoons toasted sesame seeds

1. Heat the olive oil (if desired) in a large nonstick skillet over medium-high heat until shimmering.
2. Fold in the ginger, broccoli, and sea salt (if desired) and stir-fry for 5 to 7 minutes, or until the broccoli is browned.
3. Add the garlic and cook until tender, about 30 seconds.
4. Sprinkle with the sesame seeds and serve warm.

Per Serving
Calories: 135 | fat: 10.9g | carbs: 9.7g | protein: 4.1g | fiber: 3.3g

Sweet Potato and Mushroom Skillet

Prep time: 5 minutes | Cook time: 15 minutes | Serves 4

1 cup low-sodium vegetable broth
8 ounces (227 g) mushrooms, sliced
4 medium sweet potatoes, cut into ½-inch dice
1 sweet onion, diced
1 bell pepper, diced
1 teaspoon garlic powder
½ teaspoon chili powder
½ teaspoon ground cumin
⅛ Teaspoon freshly ground black pepper

1. Heat a large skillet over medium-low heat. Stir in all the ingredients. Cover and cook for 10 minutes, or until the sweet potatoes are easily pierced with a fork.
2. Uncover and give the mixture a good stir. Cook, uncovered, for an additional 5 minutes, stirring once halfway through.
3. Serve hot.

Per Serving
Calories: 159 | fat: 1.2g | carbs: 33.9g | protein: 6.2g | fiber: 5.9g

Sautéed Collard Greens

Prep time: 10 minutes | Cook time: 25 minutes | Serves 4

1½ pounds (680 g) collard greens
1 cup low-sodium vegetable broth
½ teaspoon onion
powder
½ teaspoon garlic powder
⅛ Teaspoon freshly ground black pepper

1. Remove the hard middle stems from the greens and roughly chop the leaves into 2-inch pieces.
2. In a large saucepan over medium-high heat, combine all the ingredients, except for the collard greens. Bring to a boil, then add the chopped greens. Reduce the heat to low and cover.
3. Cook for 20 minutes, stirring constantly.
4. Serve warm.

Per Serving
Calories: 528 | fat: 55.1g | carbs: 8.8g | protein: 3.2g | fiber: 2.3g

Tomato and Green Pepper Teriyaki

Prep time: 10 minutes | Cook time: 22 minutes | Serves 4

1½ cups chopped onion
2 cloves garlic, minced
1½ cups quartered mushrooms
1 cup sliced celery
¼ cup soy sauce
¼ cup unsweetened pineapple juice
¼ cup cornstarch
1½ Teaspoons maple

syrup (optional)
½ teaspoon grated fresh ginger
⅛ Teaspoon crushed red pepper flakes
1½ cups green bell pepper strips
2 cups tomato wedges
1¾ cups water, divided

1. Pour ¾ cup of the water in a large pot over medium heat. Add the onion and garlic and sauté for 5 minutes, stirring frequently. Add the mushrooms and celery to the pot and sauté for 10 minutes.
2. In a bowl, whisk together the remaining 1 cup of the water, soy sauce, pineapple juice, cornstarch, maple syrup (if desired), ginger and red pepper. Add to the pot. Cook for 2 more minutes, stirring constantly, or until thickened.
3. Add the green bell pepper and tomato wedges to the pot. Cook over low heat for 5 minutes, stirring occasionally. Serve warm.

Per Serving
Calories: 100 | fat: 0.2g | carbs: 11.3g | protein: 3.2g | fiber: 1.5g

Garlic Zoodles with Herbs

Prep time: 5 to 10 minutes | Cook time: 2 minutes | Serves 4

1 teaspoon minced garlic clove
4 medium zucchinis, spiralized
2 tablespoons low-sodium vegetable broth
½ teaspoon dried oregano
½ teaspoon dried ba-

sil
¼ to ½ teaspoon red pepper flakes, to taste
¼ teaspoon freshly ground black pepper
¼ teaspoon salt (optional)

1. Heat a large skillet over medium-high heat. Add the garlic and zucchini to the hot skillet and sauté for 1 minute.

2. Add the vegetable broth and sprinkle with the oregano, basil, red pepper flakes, black pepper, and salt (if desired). Stir to combine and continue cooking for about 4 minutes, stirring frequently, or until the zucchini is barely tender.
3. Remove from the heat to four plates and serve warm.

Per Serving
Calories: 45 | fat: 2.2g | carbs: 7.1g | protein: 3.2g | fiber: 2.0g

Vegetable Pie

Prep time: 10 minutes | Cook time: 45 minutes | Makes 1 (8-inch) pie

2 small carrots, scrubbed and finely chopped
1 small green bell pepper, finely chopped
1 onion, finely chopped
2 (10-ounce / 284-g) packages firm tofu, divided
1 tablespoon soy sauce

1 tablespoon Worcestershire sauce
2 teaspoons maple syrup (optional)
1 teaspoon mustard
2 ounces (57 g) vegan Cheddar cheese, grated, divided
½ cup frozen green peas
1 zucchini, finely chopped

1. Preheat the oven to 350ºF (180ºC).
2. Combine the onion, green pepper, and carrots in a large bowl. Place 1 package of the tofu in a blender and add all the seasonings and half of the cheese. Blend until smooth. Add to the vegetable mixture in the bowl and mix well.
3. Mash the remaining 1 package of the tofu with a potato masher and add to the vegetable mixture. Stir in the peas and zucchini.
4. Pour the mixture into a nonstick 8-inch pie plate. Sprinkle the top with the remaining half of the cheese. Place the pie plate into the oven and bake for 45 minutes, or until firmly set.
5. Let rest for 5 minutes before serving.

Per Serving (1 pie)
Calories: 1291 | fat: 61.1g | carbs: 94.4g | protein: 117.8g | fiber: 24.4g

Rice and Tempeh Stuffed Peppers

Prep time: 20 minutes | Cook time: 45 minutes | Serves 4

1 cup cooked brown rice
1 (8-ounce / 227-g) package tempeh, either plain or with quinoa, crumbled
1 (8- to 10-ounce / 227- to 284-g) jar salsa, divided

2 ounces (57 g) grated vegan Cheddar cheese, divided
1 (4-ounce / 113-g) can chopped green chilies
4 green or red bell peppers, cleaned and tops removed

1. Preheat the oven to 350ºF (180ºC).
2. In a bowl, stir together the rice, tempeh, half of the salsa, half of the cheese, and chilies. Stuff the bell peppers evenly with the rice mixture.
3. Drizzle the remaining salsa on top of the peppers and scatter with the remaining cheese.
4. Arrange the peppers in a casserole dish and bake for about 45 minutes until cooked through.
5. Allow to cool to room temperature and serve.

Per Serving
Calories: 253 | fat: 7.3g | carbs: 30.4g | protein: 17.0g | fiber: 7.7g

Harvest Vegetable Sauté

Prep time: 10 minutes | Cook time: 14 minutes | Serves 4

2 cloves garlic, pressed
2 tablespoons soy sauce
1 teaspoon grated fresh ginger
Dash of sesame oil (optional)
1 small onion, coarsely chopped
¼ pound (113 g) mushrooms, sliced

2 small zucchini, sliced
1 small yellow crookneck squash, cut in half and sliced
1 cup small cauliflower florets
1 cup small broccoli florets
Freshly ground black pepper, to taste
1 cup water, divided

1. In a pan over medium heat, combine the garlic, soy sauce, ginger, sesame oil (if desired) and ¼ cup of the water. Bring to a boil.

2. Add the onion and cook for 2 minutes, or until softened, stirring constantly.
3. Stir in the remaining vegetables. Cook for 5 minutes, stirring constantly, or until the vegetables are coated with sauce. Pour in the remaining ¾ cup of the water, cover and steam for 5 minutes. Uncover and cook for 2 more minutes, or until all the liquid has been absorbed, stirring constantly.
4. Season with pepper and serve.

Per Serving
Calories: 192 | fat: 2.0g | carbs: 33.6g | protein: 15.8g | fiber: 5.6g

Sour and Sweet Vegetables

Prep time: 10 minutes | Cook time: 12 minutes | Serves 6

1 large green bell pepper, cut into 1-inch pieces
1 bunch scallions, cut into 1-inch pieces
1 onion, cut in wedges
1 cup sliced carrots
2 cloves garlic, crushed
1 teaspoon grated fresh ginger
4 cups chopped broccoli

1 cup water, divided
1 (20-ounces / 567-g) can pineapple chunks, drained and juice reserved
Sauce:
1 cup unsweetened pineapple juice
$1/3$ cup date sugar
¼ cup cider vinegar
2½ tablespoons soy sauce
2 tablespoons cornstarch

1. In a bowl, whisk together all the ingredients for the sauce. Set aside.
2. In a large pot, heat ½ cup of the water. Add the green bell pepper, scallions, onion, carrots, garlic and ginger. Sauté for 5 minutes. Stir in the broccoli and the remaining ½ cup of the water. Cover and cook over low heat for 5 minutes.
3. Stir in the sauce and pineapple chunks along with the juice. Cook for 2 minutes, stirring constantly, or until thickened. Serve warm.

Per Serving
Calories: 209 | fat: 0.7g | carbs: 42.2g | protein: 11.7g | fiber: 3.0g

Cabbage and Tomato Macaroni

Prep time: 10 minutes | Cook time: 1 hour | Serves 6

12 ounces (340 g) whole-wheat macaroni
1 cup water
1 medium onion, chopped
1 small head cabbage,

coarsely chopped
28 ounces (794 g) tomatoes, coarsely chopped
8 ounces (227 g) unsweetened tomato purée

1. Preheat the oven to 350ºF (180ºC).
2. Place the macaroni into a large pot of boiling water and cook for 8 to 10 minutes, or until al dente. Drain the macaroni and transfer to a bowl.
3. In a saucepan over medium heat, sauté the onion in the water for 5 minutes, or until transparent. Add the cabbage and sauté for 5 minutes, or until limp.
4. In a nonstick casserole dish, spread a layer of the cooked macaroni on the bottom, followed by a layer of the cabbage and onion mixture. Repeat until all is used.
5. Spread the chopped tomatoes and tomato purée over the macaroni-cabbage mixture. Cover and bake in the oven for 45 minutes, or until the sauce appears to have thickened slightly.
6. Serve warm

Per Serving
Calories: 142 | fat: 0.8g | carbs: 31.3g | protein: 6.7g | fiber: 5.8g

Provençal Summer Vegetables

Prep time: 15 minutes | Cook time: 15 minutes | Serves 6

2 small zucchinis
2 ripe tomatoes
2 small thin eggplants
1 medium green bell pepper
1 small red onion
¼ pound (113 g) mushrooms
$1/_3$ cup water
1 clove garlic, minced
1 tablespoon unsweetened tomato

purée
Freshly ground pepper, to taste
¼ cup chopped fresh basil
¼ cup chopped fresh parsley
1 teaspoon minced fresh thyme
½ teaspoon minced fresh rosemary

1. Wash and trim all the vegetables and cut into ½-inch cubes.
2. Place the water in a large, heavy pot. Add the garlic and tomato purée. Heat, stirring, until well mixed.
3. Add all the vegetables. Cover and cook over low heat for about 15 minutes, or until the vegetables are softened but not mushy. Season with freshly ground pepper.
4. Stir in the basil, parsley, thyme and rosemary.Serve warm or cold.

Per Serving
Calories: 121 | fat: 0.7g | carbs: 29.1g | protein: 4.5g | fiber: 8.7g

Spiced Yams and Green Peas

Prep time: 10 minutes | Cook time: 12 to 20 minutes | Serves 4

3 medium white yams, cut into ½-inch dice
1 cup plus 2 tablespoons water, divided
½ cup green peas
¾ teaspoon toasted cumin seeds
¼ teaspoon garam masala
¼ teaspoon cayenne

pepper
½ teaspoon ground cumin
½ teaspoon ground coriander
½ teaspoon salt (optional)
½ tablespoon fresh lime juice
½ tablespoon finely chopped cilantro

1. Steam the yams in a double boiler for 5 to 7 minutes, or until tender. Set aside.
2. In a saucepan over medium heat, bring 1 cup of the water to a boil. Add the peas and cook for 5 to 10 minutes, or until tender. Drain the peas and set aside.
3. In a large skillet over medium heat, place the steamed white yams, cooked peas, cumin seeds, garam masala, cayenne pepper, cumin, coriander and salt, if desired. Stir in the remaining 2 tablespoons of the water and cook for another 2 to 3 minutes, or until the water has evaporated. Stir in the lime juice and mix well.
4. Serve garnished with the cilantro.

Per Serving
Calories: 207 | fat: 0.5g | carbs: 47.7g | protein: 3.6g | fiber: 7.6g

Garlicky Brussels Sprouts

Prep time: 10 minutes | Cook time: 35 to 40 minutes | Serves 4

1 pound (454 g) Brussels sprouts, trimmed and halved
4 Teaspoons minced garlic (about 4 cloves)
2 teaspoons low-sodium vegetable broth
1 teaspoon dried oregano
½ teaspoon salt (optional)
½ teaspoon dried rosemary
¼ teaspoon freshly ground black pepper
1 tablespoon balsamic vinegar

1. Preheat the oven to 400ºF (205ºC). Line a rimmed baking sheet with parchment paper and set aside.
2. In a large bowl, toss the Brussels sprouts with the garlic, vegetable broth, oregano, salt (if desired), rosemary, and black pepper, or until the Brussels sprouts are evenly coated.
3. Transfer the Brussels sprouts to the parchment-lined baking sheet. Bake in the preheated oven for 35 to 40 minutes until the Brussels sprouts have a perfectly crispy outside, giving a good stir or shaking the pan halfway through.
4. Remove the Brussels sprouts from the oven to a serving bowl. Drizzle with the balsamic vinegar and stir well, then serve.

Per Serving
Calories: 78 | fat: 3.2g | carbs: 12.3g | protein: 4.1g | fiber: 5.1g

Baked Potato Patties

Prep time: 20 minutes | Cook time: 30 minutes | Serves 4

6 medium potatoes, scrubbed and coarsely shredded
2 tablespoons minced onion
2 tablespoons whole-wheat pastry flour
1 tablespoon chopped fresh parsley
$1/_8$ Teaspoon freshly ground black pepper

1. Preheat the oven to 375ºF (190ºC).
2. Place the shredded potatoes in a large bowl. Add the onion, flour, parsley, and black pepper and stir until well combined. Divide the mixture into four equal portions and shape into patties with your hands.
3. Arrange them on a nonstick baking sheet and bake until nicely browned, about 30 minutes.
4. Let the potato patties rest for 5 minutes before serving.

Per Serving
Calories: 412 | fat: 0.6g | carbs: 90.2g | protein: 11.7g | fiber: 12.6g

Sweet Potato Chili

Prep time: 10 minutes | Cook time: 25 to 30 minutes | Serves 4

1 small sweet onion, diced
2 garlic cloves, minced
½ cup plus 2 tablespoons water, divided
½ green bell pepper
½ red bell pepper
2 medium sweet potatoes, cubed
1 (14-ounce / 397-g) block extra firm tofu, drained and cubed
1 (10-ounce / 283-g) can diced tomatoes with green chilies
1 tablespoon chili powder
1 teaspoon cumin
½ teaspoon cayenne
½ teaspoon paprika
Salt, to taste (optional)
Pepper, to taste
¼ cup parsley, chopped

1. Heat a medium saucepan over medium-high heat. Add the diced onions and garlic and sauté for about 5 minutes until tender. Add 1 to 2 tablespoons water to keep them from sticking to the pan.
2. Stir in the bell peppers and cook for 5 minutes more until softened.
3. Reduce the heat to low, add the remaining ingredients except for the parsley to the pan, and stir to combine. Bring the mixture to a gentle simmer. Cover and continue cooking for 15 to 20 minutes, stirring frequently, or until the liquid is thickened and the potatoes are easily pierced with a fork.
4. Transfer the sweet potato chill to a bowl and garnish with the chopped parsley. Serve immediately.

Per Serving
Calories: 174 | fat: 8.7g | carbs: 15.6g | protein: 8.5g | fiber: 5.2g

Yam and Carrot Casserole

Prep time: 5 minutes | Cook time: 55 minutes | Serves 6 to 8

6 medium yams, peeled and coarsely chopped
1 pound (454 g) carrots, scrubbed and sliced 1-inch thick
¾ cup pitted prunes
1 cup freshly squeezed orange juice
½ cup maple syrup (optional)
½ teaspoon ground cinnamon

1. Preheat the oven to 350ºF (180ºC).
2. Place the yams and carrots in a large pot and cover with water. Cook over medium heat for about 15 minutes, or until tender but still firm. Remove from the heat and drain.
3. Place the vegetables in a covered casserole dish. Stir in the prunes.
4. Whisk together the orange juice, maple syrup (if desired) and cinnamon in a bowl. Spread over the vegetables and fruit. Cover and bake in the oven for 30 minutes. Uncover, stir gently, and continue to bake, uncovered, for another 10 minutes.
5. Serve hot.

Per Serving
Calories: 317 | fat: 0.5g | carbs: 77.1g | protein: 3.6g | fiber: 8.4g

Roasted Asparagus and Broccoli

Prep time: 5 minutes | Cook time: 20 to 25 minutes | Serves 2

1 cup chopped asparagus, woody ends removed
1 cup chopped broccoli florets
1 green bell pepper, chopped
2 tablespoons low-sodium vegetable broth
Pinch salt (optional)
Pinch freshly ground black pepper

1. Preheat the oven to 400ºF (205ºC).
2. In a large bowl, toss the asparagus, broccoli florets, and bell pepper with the vegetable broth, salt (if desired), and pepper until completely coated.
3. Arrange the vegetables on a rimmed baking sheet in a single layer. Roast in the preheated oven for 20 to 25 minutes until the vegetables are tender.

4. Remove from the heat and cool for 5 minutes before serving.

Per Serving
Calories: 38 | fat: 0.3g | carbs: 6.2g | protein: 2.7g | fiber: 2.5g

Spiced Winter Vegetables

Prep time: 15 minutes | Cook time: 17 to 22 minutes | Serves 4 to 6

2 carrots, peeled and sliced
1 medium potato, chopped
1 cup green beans, trimmed, cut into ¼-inch pieces
1 cup cauliflower florets
1 small yellow onion, peeled and finely chopped
1 clove garlic, peeled and minced
3 tablespoons toasted white poppy seeds
½ teaspoon toasted cumin seeds
½ teaspoon turmeric
½ teaspoon grated
ginger
¼ teaspoon freshly ground black pepper
⅛ Teaspoon ground cinnamon
⅛ Teaspoon ground cloves
Pinch of ground cardamom
1 medium tomato, chopped
1 teaspoon salt (optional)
2 tablespoons finely ground raw cashews
½ tablespoon fresh lime juice
1½ cups water
1 tablespoon chopped cilantro

1. Steam the carrot, potato, green beans and cauliflower in a double boiler for 8 to 10 minutes, or until tender. Set aside.
2. Combine the onion, garlic, toasted seeds, turmeric, ginger, pepper, cinnamon, cloves and cardamom in a blender and process into a thick paste. Add the paste to a large skillet over medium heat and cook for 5 to 7 minutes.
3. Add the tomato to the blender and pulse until smooth. Add the tomato purée and salt (if desired) to the onion paste in the skillet and cook for another 2 to 3 minutes.
4. Add the cashew powder and cook for 2 minutes. Add the steamed vegetables, lime juice and water, and bring to a boil. Remove the pan from the heat and serve garnished with the cilantro.

Per Serving
Calories: 109 | fat: 4.3g | carbs: 16.0g | protein: 3.7g | fiber: 4.0g

Roasted Root Vegetables

Prep time: 10 minutes | Cook time: 45 minutes | Serves 4

2 cups cubed sweet potatoes
6 large radishes, chopped
2 parsnips, chopped
3 tablespoons low-sodium vegetable broth
½ teaspoon salt (optional)
½ teaspoon freshly ground pepper

1. Preheat the oven to 425ºF (220ºC).
2. In a large bowl, combine the sweet potatoes, radishes, parsnips, vegetable broth, salt (if desired), and pepper, and toss to coat.
3. Place the root vegetables on a rimmed baking sheet in a single layer and cover with aluminum foil. You may need to work in batches to avoid overcrowding.
4. Roast in the preheated oven for 45 minutes, stirring the vegetables once during cooking, or lightly browned around the edges.
5. Remove from the oven and serve on plates while warm.

Per Serving
Calories: 75 | fat: 0.3g | carbs: 16.8g | protein: 1.5g | fiber: 5.2g

Grilled Portobello Mushrooms

Prep time: 10 minutes | Cook time: 8 minutes | Serves 4

3 tablespoons maple syrup
3 tablespoons low-sodium soy sauce
3 cloves garlic, peeled and minced
1 tablespoon grated ginger
Freshly ground black pepper, to taste
4 large portobello mushrooms, stemmed

1. Make the marinade: In a small bowl, whisk together the maple syrup, soy sauce, garlic, ginger, and pepper.
2. Arrange the mushrooms on a baking dish, stem-side up. Evenly pour the prepared marinade over the mushrooms and set aside to marinate for 1 hour.
3. Preheat the grill to medium-high heat.
4. Transfer the marinated mushrooms to the preheated grill and reserve the marinade.

5. Grill for 4 minutes per side, brushing the mushrooms periodically with the remaining marinade, or until the mushrooms are tender.
6. Let the mushrooms cool for 5 minutes before serving.

Per Serving
Calories: 86 | fat: 0.6g | carbs: 16.0g | protein: 4.3g | fiber: 2.3g

Stir-Fried Veggies with Miso and Sake

Prep time: 10 minutes | Cook time: 8 to 9 minutes | Serves 4

¼ cup mellow white miso
¼ cup sake
½ cup vegetable stock
1 large carrot, peeled, cut in half lengthwise, and then cut into half-moons on the diagonal
1 medium yellow onion, peeled and thinly sliced
1 large head broccoli, cut into florets
1 medium red bell pepper, seeded and cut into ½-inch strips
Water, as needed
½ pound (227 g) snow peas, trimmed
2 cloves garlic, peeled and minced
½ cup chopped cilantro (optional)
Sea salt, to taste (optional)
Freshly ground black pepper, to taste

1. In a small bowl, stir together the miso, sake, and vegetable stock. Set aside.
2. Heat a large skillet over high heat. Add the carrot, onion, broccoli and red pepper and stir-fry for 4 to 5 minutes. Add water, 1 to 2 tablespoons at a time, to prevent sticking.
3. Fold in the snow peas and stir-fry for an additional 4 minutes. Add the garlic and continue to cook for 30 seconds. Pour the miso mixture into the skillet and cook until the veggies are tender.
4. Remove the skillet from the heat and stir in the cilantro, if desired. Sprinkle with salt (if desired) and pepper. Serve warm.

Per Serving
Calories: 110 | fat: 1.6g | carbs: 18.1g | protein: 5.8g | fiber: 5.0g

Vegetable Burritos

Prep time: 10 minutes | Cook time: 7 to 8 minutes | Serves 4

1 bunch scallions, cut into 1-inch pieces
1 red bell pepper, sliced into strips
1 green bell pepper, sliced into strips
½ cup water
1 cup frozen corn kernels, thawed
1 cup salsa
2 teaspoons cornstarch
12 cherry tomatoes, cut in half
4 large whole-wheat tortillas
Fresh cilantro sprigs (optional)

1. In a pan over medium heat, sauté the scallions and peppers in the water for 2 minutes. Add the corn and cook for another 2 to 3 minutes.
2. Stir together the salsa and cornstarch in a small bowl. Pour over the vegetables. Cook for 2 minutes, stirring, or until thickened. Add the tomatoes and cook for 1 more minute.
3. Place a line of the vegetable mixture down the center of a tortilla, and top with sprigs of cilantro, if desired. Roll up and serve.

Per Serving
Calories: 228 | fat: 4.9g | carbs: 40.2g | protein: 7.7g | fiber: 8.2g

Grilled Vegetable Kabobs

Prep time: 10 minutes | Cook time: 12 to 15 minutes | Serves 6

½ cup balsamic vinegar
3 cloves garlic, peeled and minced
1½ tablespoons minced thyme
1½ tablespoons minced rosemary
Freshly ground black pepper, to taste
Salt, to taste (optional)
1 medium red onion, peeled and cut into
large chunks
1 medium zucchini, cut into 1-inch rounds
1 medium yellow squash, cut into 1-inch rounds
1 pint cherry tomatoes
1 green bell pepper, seeded and cut into 1-inch pieces
1 red bell pepper, seeded and cut into 1-inch pieces

SPECIAL EQUIPMENT:
12 bamboo skewers, soaked in water for at least 30 minutes

1. Prepare the grill to medium heat.
2. Make the marinade: In a small bowl, whisk together the balsamic vinegar, garlic, thyme, rosemary, pepper, and salt (if desired). Set aside.
3. Skewer the vegetables by alternating between red onions, zucchini, squash, cherry tomatoes, and the different colored bell pepper.
4. Arrange the skewers on the preheated grill and cook for 12 to 15 minutes, basting the vegetables with the prepared marinade every 3 to 4 minutes, or until the vegetables are just beginning to char. Flip the skewers a few times during cooking.
5. Let the vegetables cool for 5 minutes and serve hot.

Per Serving
Calories: 48 | fat: 0.2g | carbs: 10.4g | protein: 1.2g | fiber: 1.3g

Bok Choy Stir-Fry

Prep time: 12 minutes | Cook time: 10 to 13 minutes | Serves 4 to 6

2 tablespoons coconut oil (optional)
1 large onion, finely diced
2 teaspoons ground cumin
1-inch piece fresh ginger, grated
1 teaspoon ground
turmeric
½ teaspoon salt (optional)
12 baby bok choy heads, ends trimmed and sliced lengthwise
Water, as needed
3 cups cooked brown rice

1. Heat the coconut oil (if desired) in a large pan over medium heat.
2. Add the onion and sauté for 5 minutes until translucent.
3. Stir in the cumin, ginger, turmeric, and salt (if desired). Add the bok choy and stir-fry for 5 to 8 minutes, or until the bok choy is tender but still crisp. Add water 1 to 2 tablespoons at a time to keep from sticking to the pan.
4. Remove from the heat and serve over the brown rice.

Per Serving
Calories: 447 | fat: 8.9g | carbs: 75.6g | protein: 29.7g | fiber: 19.1g

Sweet Potato Casserole

Prep time: 15 minutes | Cook time: 30 minutes | Serves 6

8 cooked sweet pota-
toes, skin removed
½ cup low-sodium
vegetable broth
1 teaspoon dried

thyme
1 teaspoon dried
rosemary
1 tablespoon dried
sage

1. Preheat the oven to 375ºF (190ºC).
2. Place the sweet potatoes in a large bowl and mash them with a potato masher or the back of a fork. Add the vegetable broth, thyme, rosemary, and sage, and stir to combine.
3. Scrape the potato mixture into an even layer in a baking dish. Bake in the pre-heated oven for 30 minutes or until golden.
4. Allow to cool for 5 minutes before serving.

Per Serving
Calories: 155 | fat: 10.1g | carbs: 5.1g | protein: 3.2g | fiber: 6.1g

Red Cabbage with Carrots and Beans

Prep time: 10 minutes | Cook time: 37 to 38 minutes | Serves 4

2 large carrots,
peeled and diced
2 celery stalks, diced
1 large yellow onion,
peeled and diced
2 tablespoons water,
plus more as needed
2 tablespoons Dijon
mustard
2 teaspoons thyme
1½ cups red wine
4 cups cooked navy

beans, drained and
rinsed
1 large head red
cabbage, cored and
shredded
2 tart apples, peeled,
cored, and diced
Salt, to taste (option-
al)
Freshly ground black
pepper, to taste

1. Put the carrots, celery, and onion in a large saucepan over medium heat. Sauté for 7 to 8 minutes, or until they start to soften. Add 1 to 2 tablespoons water at a time to help keep them from sticking to the pan.
2. Stir in the Dijon mustard, thyme, and red wine, and continue cooking for about 10 minutes or until the red wine is reduced by half.
3. Add the navy beans, cabbage, and ap-ples, and stir well. Cover and cook for about 20 minutes, stirring occasionally, or until the mixture is heated through.
4. Sprinkle with the salt (if desired) and pepper. Let them cool for 5 minutes, then serve warm.

Per Serving
Calories: 184 | fat: 0.9g | carbs: 38.4g | pro-tein: 5.7g | fiber: 10.3g

Cauliflower and Potato Curry

Prep time: 10 minutes | Cook time: 27 minutes | Serves 4

1 medium yellow on-
ion, peeled and diced
Water, as needed
2 cloves garlic, peeled
and minced
1 tablespoon grated
ginger
½ jalapeño pepper,
deseeded and minced
1 medium head cauli-
flower, cut into florets
2 medium tomatoes,
diced
1 pound (454 g) Yu-
kon Gold potatoes,

cut into ½-inch dices
1 teaspoon ground
coriander
1 teaspoon ground
cumin
1 teaspoon crushed
red pepper flakes
½ teaspoon turmeric
¼ teaspoon ground
cloves
2 bay leaves
1 cup green peas
¼ cup chopped cilan-
tro or mint, for gar-
nish

1. Sauté the onion in a large saucepan over medium heat for 7 to 8 minutes, stirring occasionally. Add water, 1 to 2 table-spoons at a time, to keep it from sticking to the pan.
2. Stir in the garlic, ginger, and jalapeño pepper and sauté for 3 minutes.
3. Add the cauliflower, tomatoes, potatoes, coriander, cumin, crushed red pepper flakes, turmeric, cloves, and bay leaves and stir to combine. Cover and cook for 10 to 12 minutes, or until the vegetables are soft.
4. Mix in the peas and cook for an addition-al 5 minutes.
5. Remove the bay leaves and sprinkle the chopped cilantro on top for garnish. Serve immediately.

Per Serving
Calories: 175 | fat: 0.9g | carbs: 34.9g | pro-tein: 6.7g | fiber: 7.5g

Zucchini and Potato Casserole

Prep time: 10 minutes | Cook time: 40 to 45 minutes | Serves 6

3 medium zucchinis, halved lengthwise and thinly sliced
3 large russet potatoes, halved lengthwise and thinly sliced
¾ cup diced green or red bell pepper
¾ cup diced red, white, or yellow onion
½ cup dry bread crumbs
¼ cup low-sodium vegetable broth
¾ cup nutritional yeast
1½ Teaspoons minced garlic (about 3 small cloves)
Salt, to taste (optional)
Pepper, to taste

1. Preheat the oven to 400ºF (205ºC).
2. Mix together all the ingredients in a large bowl, or until the vegetables are well coated.
3. Layer the vegetables in a large baking dish, alternating with zucchinis and potatoes.
4. Bake in the preheated oven for about 40 to 45 minutes, stirring the mixture halfway through the cooking time, or until the potatoes are easily pierced with a fork.
5. Remove from the oven and serve warm.

Per Serving
Calories: 220 | fat: 0.9g | carbs: 47.2g | protein: 5.8g | fiber: 3.3g

Creamy Mushroom Stroganoff

Prep time: 10 minutes | Cook time: 25 to 26 minutes | Serves 6 to 8

1 large onion, chopped
1 pound (454 g) mushrooms, sliced
1 cup low-sodium vegetable broth
1 cup unsweetened soy milk
2 tablespoons sherry
2 tablespoons soy sauce
Dash of cayenne
2 cups sliced seitan
2 tablespoons corn starch, mixed with ¹/₃ cup cold water

1. In a saucepan over medium, heat a small amount of water. Add the onion and sauté for 2 to 3 minutes.
2. Add the mushrooms and sauté for 3 minutes, or until the mushrooms are slightly limp.
3. Stir in the vegetable broth, soy milk, sherry, soy sauce and cayenne. Mix in the seitan. Cover and cook over low heat for 20 minutes.
4. Add the cornstarch mixture to the pan and stir until thickened.
5. Serve immediately.

Per Serving
Calories: 308 | fat: 3.7g | carbs: 52.4g | protein: 21.2g | fiber: 7.1g

Grilled Veggie Kabobs

Prep time: 15 minutes | Cook time: 12 to 15 minutes | Serves 6

Marinade:
½ cup balsamic vinegar
1½ tablespoons minced thyme
1½ tablespoons minced rosemary
3 cloves garlic, peeled and minced
Sea salt, to taste (optional)
Freshly ground black pepper, to taste
Veggies:
2 cups cherry tomatoes
1 red bell pepper, seeded and cut into 1-inch pieces
1 green bell pepper, seeded and cut into 1-inch pieces
1 medium yellow squash, cut into 1-inch rounds
1 medium zucchini, cut into 1-inch rounds
1 medium red onion, peeled and cut into large chunks

Special Equipment:
12 bamboo skewers, soaked in water for 30 minutes

1. Preheat the grill to medium heat.
2. Make the marinade: In a small bowl, stir together the balsamic vinegar, thyme, rosemary, garlic, salt (if desired), and pepper.
3. Thread veggies onto skewers, alternating between different-colored veggies.
4. Grill the veggies for 12 to 15 minutes until softened and lightly charred, brushing the veggies with the marinade and flipping the skewers every 4 to 5 minutes.
5. Remove from the grill and serve hot.

Per Serving
Calories: 98 | fat: 0.7g | carbs: 19.2g | protein: 3.8g | fiber: 3.4g

Easy Stuffed Bell Peppers

Prep time: 10 minutes | Cook time: 25 minutes | Serves 4

4 green or red bell peppers cut in half lengthwise and seeds removed
2 cups cooked quinoa
1 (15-ounce / 425-g) can no-salt-added black beans, drained and rinsed
1 tablespoon taco seasoning
¼ teaspoon salt (optional)
1 (10-ounce / 284-g) can red enchilada sauce

1. Preheat the oven to 400ºF (205ºC).
2. Arrange the bell peppers on a baking sheet and set aside.
3. Stir together the quinoa, black beans, taco seasoning, and salt (if desired) in a medium bowl until combined.
4. Using a spoon, evenly stuff the bell peppers with the quinoa mixture. Pour the red enchilada sauce over them and cover with aluminum foil.
5. Bake in the preheated oven for 25 minutes, or until the bell peppers are browned.
6. Divide the stuffed bell peppers among four plates and serve.

Per Serving
Calories: 54 | fat: 0.7g | carbs: 10.2g | protein: 1.8g | fiber: 1.6g

Eggplant Stir-Fry

Prep time: 25 minutes | Cook time: 15 minutes | Serves 2 to 4

½ cup chopped red onion
1 tablespoon finely chopped garlic
1 small eggplant (about 8 ounces / 227 g), peeled and cut into ½-inch cubes
1 tablespoon dried Italian herb seasoning
1 teaspoon ground cumin
2 cups green beans, cut into 1-inch pieces
1 medium carrot, sliced
2 ribs celery, sliced
1 cup corn kernels
1 cup water, plus more as needed
2 tablespoons almond butter
2 medium tomatoes, chopped

1. Heat 1 tablespoon of water in a large soup pot over medium-high heat until sputtering.
2. Add the onion and cook for 2 minutes, adding a little more water as needed.
3. Add the garlic, eggplant, Italian seasoning, and cumin and stir-fry for 2 to 3 minutes, adding a little more water as needed.
4. Add the green beans, carrot, celery, corn, and ½ cup of water and mix well. Reduce the heat to medium, cover, and cook for 8 to 10 minutes, stirring occasionally, or until the beans and carrot are softened.
5. Meanwhile, whisk together the almond butter and ½ cup of water in a bowl.
6. Remove the vegetables from the heat and mix in the almond butter mixture and tomatoes. Serve warm.

Per Serving
Calories: 175 | fat: 5.6g | carbs: 25.3g | protein: 5.9g | fiber: 8.7g

Simple Grilled Portobello Mushrooms

Prep time: 5 minutes | Cook time: 8 minutes | Serves 4

3 tablespoons low-sodium soy sauce
1 tablespoon grated ginger
3 cloves garlic, peeled and minced
3 tablespoons brown rice syrup (optional)
Freshly ground black pepper, to taste
4 large portobello mushrooms, stemmed

1. In a small bowl, mix together the soy sauce, ginger, garlic, brown rice syrup (if desired), and pepper and stir to combine.
2. Arrange the mushrooms on a baking dish, stem-side up. Drizzle the marinade over the mushrooms and let stand for 1 hour.
3. Preheat the grill to medium heat.
4. Drain the liquid from the mushrooms and reserve the marinade.
5. Grill the mushrooms until tender, brushing both sides of the mushrooms with the remaining marinade, about 4 minutes per side.
6. Remove from the heat and serve on a plate.

Per Serving
Calories: 17 | fat: 0.1g | carbs: 2.3g | protein: 1.8g | fiber: 0.4g

Braised Carrot and Red Cabbage

Prep time: 10 minutes | Cook time: 37 to 38 minutes | Serves 4

1 large yellow onion, peeled and diced
2 celery stalks, diced
2 large carrots, peeled and diced
Water, as needed
2 tablespoons Dijon mustard
2 teaspoons thyme
1½ cups red wine
4 cups cooked navy beans, or 2 (15-ounce / 425-g) cans, drained and rinsed
1 large head red cabbage, cored and shredded
2 tart apples (such as Granny Smith), peeled, cored, and diced
Salt, to taste (optional)
Freshly ground black pepper, to taste

1. Combine the onion, celery, and carrots in a large saucepan over medium heat and sauté for 7 to 8 minutes, stirring occasionally, or until the carrots are lightly tender. Add water 1 to 2 tablespoons at a time to keep the vegetables from sticking to the pan.
2. Stir in the mustard, thyme, and red wine and cook for about 10 minutes, or until the wine is reduced by half.
3. Add the beans, cabbage, and apples and mix well. Cover and cook for about 20 minutes until the cabbage is tender.
4. Season with salt (if desired) and pepper before serving.

Per Serving
Calories: 404 | fat: 1.9g | carbs: 78.4g | protein: 18.4g | fiber: 26.4g

Vegetable Tortillas

Prep time: 15 minutes | Cook time: 7 minutes | Serves 4

2 zucchinis, cut in half, then sliced ½ inch thick
1 leek, washed and sliced
1 bunch scallions, cut into ½-inch pieces
¼ pound (113 g) mushrooms, sliced
1 cup small broccoli florets
¾ cup water, divided
1 (7 0unce / 190 g) can Mexican green sauce
⅛ cup packed chopped fresh cilantro
1 tablespoon cornstarch, mixed with 2 tablespoons water
8 whole-wheat flour tortillas

1. In a pan over medium heat, sauté the zucchinis, leek, scallions, mushrooms and broccoli florets in ½ cup of the water for 5 minutes, or until tender-crisp.
2. Stir in the remaining ¼ cup of the water, green sauce and cilantro. Pour in the cornstarch mixture. Cook for 2 minutes, stirring constantly, or until thickened.
3. Place a line of the vegetable mixture down the center of a tortilla. Roll up and serve.

Per Serving
Calories: 410 | fat: 9.1g | carbs: 73.1g | protein: 11.2g | fiber: 11.3g

Spiced Eggplant and Tomatoes

Prep time: 10 minutes | Cook time: 25 minutes | Serves 4

1 large red bell pepper, seeded and diced
2 medium onions, peeled and diced
2 tablespoons water, plus more as needed
2 large tomatoes, finely chopped
2 medium eggplants, stemmed, peeled, and cut into ½-inch cubes
3 tablespoons grated ginger
1 teaspoon ground coriander seeds, toasted
2 teaspoons ground cumin seeds, toasted
½ teaspoon crushed red pepper flakes
Pinch cloves
Salt, to taste (optional)
½ bunch cilantro, leaves and tender stems, finely chopped

1. Put the red pepper and onions in a large saucepan over medium heat. Sauté the vegetables for 10 minutes, stirring occasionally, or until the onions are translucent.
2. Add 1 to 2 tablespoons water at a time to help keep them from sticking to the pan.
3. Stir in the tomatoes, eggplants, ginger, coriander, cumin, red pepper flakes, and cloves. Continue cooking for 15 minutes, stirring occasionally, or until the eggplants are cooked through.
4. Season with salt to taste, if desired. Sprinkle the cilantro on top for garnish before serving.

Per Serving
Calories: 138 | fat: 1.1g | carbs: 27.6g | protein: 4.6g | fiber: 10.9g

Tangy and Sweet Vegetables

Prep time: 10 minutes | Cook time: 17 minutes | Serves 6 to 8

2 cups cauliflower florets	1 cup water
2 cups broccoli florets	2 cups sliced mushrooms
1 cup sliced carrots	Sauce:
1 onion, coarsely chopped	1½ cups unsweetened apple juice
2½ tablespoons cornstarch	¼ cup soy sauce
2 teaspoons minced garlic	1 tablespoon maple syrup (optional)
2 teaspoons grated fresh ginger	1 tablespoon cider vinegar

1. In a bowl, whisk together all the ingredients for the sauce. Set aside.
2. In a pot over medium heat, add the remaining ingredients, except for the mushrooms. Cover and cook for 10 minutes. Stir in the mushrooms and cook for 5 minutes. Stir in the sauce and cook for 2 minutes, stirring constantly, or until thickened.
3. Serve warm.

Per Serving
Calories: 531 | fat: 2.1g | carbs: 118.6g | protein: 16.3g | fiber: 11.2g

Ratatouille

Prep time: 20 minutes | Cook time: 25 minutes | Serves 4

1 medium red onion, peeled and diced	diced
Water, as needed	1 medium eggplant, stemmed and diced
4 cloves garlic, peeled and minced	1 large tomato, diced
1 medium red bell pepper, seeded and diced	½ cup chopped basil
	Salt, to taste (optional)
1 small zucchini,	Freshly ground black pepper, to taste

1. Put the onion in a medium saucepan over medium heat and sauté for 10 minutes, stirring occasionally, or until the onion is tender. Add water 1 to 2 tablespoons at a time to keep it from sticking.
2. Add the garlic, red pepper, zucchini, and eggplant and stir well. Cover and cook for 15 minutes, stirring occasionally.

3. Mix in the tomatoes and basil, then sprinkle with salt (if desired) and pepper. Serve immediately.

Per Serving
Calories: 76 | fat: 0.5g | carbs: 15.3g | protein: 2.7g | fiber: 5.9g

Baked Spaghetti Squash with Swiss Chard

Prep time: 10 minutes | Cook time: 1 hour | Serves 4

2 small spaghetti squash, halved	deseeded and diced small
Salt, to taste (optional)	4 cloves garlic, peeled and minced
Freshly ground black pepper, to taste	2 teaspoons ground coriander
½ cup water	2 teaspoons ground cumin
1 large bunch red-ribbed Swiss chard	½ teaspoon crushed red pepper flakes
1 medium yellow onion, peeled and diced small	½ teaspoon paprika
1 red bell pepper,	Zest and juice of 1 lemon

1. Preheat the oven to 350ºF (180ºC).
2. Season the cut sides of the squash with salt (if desired) and pepper. Place the squash halves, cut-side down, on a rimmed baking pan. Add the water to the pan and bake the squash for 45 to 55 minutes, or until very tender.
3. Meanwhile, remove the stems from the chard and chop them. Chop the leaves into bite-size pieces and set them aside.
4. Place the onion, red pepper, and chard stems in a large saucepan over medium heat and sauté for 5 minutes.
5. Add the garlic, coriander, cumin, crushed red pepper flakes and paprika and cook for 3 minutes.
6. Add the chard leaves and lemon zest and juice. Season with salt (if desired) and pepper and cook for about 5 minutes, or until the chard is wilted. Remove from the heat.
7. When the squash is finished baking, scoop out the flesh and stir it into the warm chard mixture.
8. Serve warm.

Per Serving
Calories: 60 | fat: 0.8g | carbs: 12.2g | protein: 3.7g | fiber: 3.8g

Baingan Bharta (Indian Spiced Eggplant)

Prep time: 15 minutes | Cook time: 25 minutes | Serves 4

2 medium onions, peeled and diced
1 large red bell pepper, deseeded and diced
Water, as needed
2 large tomatoes, finely chopped
2 medium eggplants, stemmed, peeled, and cut into ½-inch dices
3 tablespoons grated ginger

1 teaspoon coriander seeds, toasted and ground
2 teaspoons cumin seeds, toasted and ground
½ teaspoon crushed red pepper flakes
Pinch cloves
Salt, to taste (optional)
½ bunch cilantro, leaves and tender stems, finely chopped

1. Combine the onions and red pepper in a large saucepan and cook over medium heat for about 10 minutes. Add water 1 to 2 tablespoons at a time to keep them from sticking to the pan.
2. Stir in the tomatoes, eggplant, ginger, coriander, cumin, crushed red pepper flakes, and cloves and cook for about 15 minutes or until the vegetables are tender.
3. Sprinkle with the salt, if desired. Garnish with the cilantro and serve warm.

Per Serving
Calories: 140 | fat: 1.1g | carbs: 27.9g | protein: 4.7g | fiber: 10.9g

Easy Baked Potatoes

Prep time: 5 minutes | Cook time: 50 minutes | Makes 5 potatoes

5 medium Russet potatoes, washed and patted dry
1 to 2 tablespoons aquafaba

¼ teaspoon salt (optional)
¼ teaspoon freshly ground black pepper

1. Preheat the oven to 400ºF (205ºC).
2. Using a fork or a knife to pierce each potato several times. Transfer the potatoes to a medium bowl, add the aquafaba, salt (if desired), and pepper. Toss together until the potatoes are well coated on both sides.

3. Arrange the potatoes on a baking sheet and bake in the preheated oven for about 50 minutes until fork-tender, flipping the potatoes halfway through to ensure even cooking.
4. Transfer to a wire rack to cool completely, then serve.

Per Serving
Calories: 172 | fat: 3.1g | carbs: 34.1g | protein: 4.2g | fiber: 5.1g

Stuffed Peppers with Bulgur

Prep time: 30 minutes | Cook time: 30 to 35 minutes | Serves 4

4 green or red bell peppers
1 cup bulgur
1 teaspoon minced fresh thyme
1 teaspoon minced fresh marjoram
1 teaspoon minced

fresh rosemary
1½ cups low-sodium vegetable broth
1 cup cooked black beans (any kind)
4 scallions, finely chopped
1 tomato, chopped

1. Cut a ½- to ¾-inch cap off the top of each bell pepper and scoop out the insides. Keep the caps.
2. Bring a large pot of water to a boil. Cook the peppers and caps in boiling water for 5 minutes. Remove from the heat and drain on paper towels. Set aside.
3. In a medium saucepan, add the bulgur, fresh herbs, and broth. Bring to a boil, and then remove from the heat, cover, and let stand for 30 minutes. Fold in the cooked beans, scallions, and tomato and stir well.
4. Preheat the oven to 350ºF (180ºC).
5. Stuff the peppers with the bulgur mixture loosely to within ¼ inch of the top. Put caps on top.
6. Arrange the peppers in a baking dish. Add about ½ inch of water to the bottom Cover the dish with aluminum foil.
7. Bake in the preheated oven for 25 to 30 minutes, or until the peppers have softened.
8. Allow to cool to room temperature and serve.

Per Serving
Calories: 158 | fat: 0.9g | carbs: 30.0g | protein: 7.4g | fiber: 8.0g

Vegetable Hash with White Beans

Prep time: 15 minutes | Cook time: 23 minutes | Serves 4

1 leek (white part only), finely chopped
1 red bell pepper, deseeded and diced
Water, as needed
2 teaspoons minced rosemary
3 cloves garlic, peeled and minced
1 medium sweet potato, peeled and diced
1 large turnip, peeled and diced
2 cups cooked white beans, or 1 (15-ounce / 425-g) can, drained and rinsed
Zest and juice of 1 orange
1 cup chopped kale
Salt, to taste (optional)
Freshly ground black pepper, to taste

1. Put the leek and red pepper in a large saucepan over medium heat and sauté for 8 minutes, stirring occasionally. Add water, 1 to 2 tablespoons at a time, to keep them from sticking to the bottom of the pan.
2. Stir in the rosemary and garlic and cook for 1 minute more.
3. Add the sweet potato, turnip, beans, and orange juice and zest, and stir well. Cook for an additional 10 minutes, or until the vegetables are softened.
4. Add the kale and sprinkle with salt (if desired) and pepper. Cook for about 5 minutes until the kale is wilted.
5. Remove from the heat and serve on a plate.

Per Serving
Calories: 245 | fat: 0.6g | carbs: 48.0g | protein: 11.9g | fiber: 9.3g

Stuffed Mushrooms with Kale

Prep time: 15 minutes | Cook time: 28 minutes | Serves 4

16 large white button mushrooms, stemmed
2 teaspoons olive oil (optional)
1 teaspoon bottled minced garlic
½ cup finely chopped sweet onion
2 cups finely shredded kale
1 cup chopped water-packed canned artichoke hearts
1 teaspoon chopped fresh oregano
1 teaspoon chopped fresh basil
⅛ Teaspoon sea salt (optional)

1. Preheat the oven to 375ºF (190ºC).
2. Place the mushroom caps on a baking sheet, hollow-side up.
3. Heat the olive oil (if desired) in a large skillet over medium-high heat.
4. Stir in the onion and garlic and sauté for about 3 minutes, or until the garlic is fragrant.
5. Add the kale, artichoke hearts, oregano, basil, and sea salt (if desired) and stir to combine. Sauté for another 5 minutes until the kale is wilted.
6. Using the back of a spoon to squeeze the liquid out of the filling into the skillet. Spoon the mixture evenly into the mushroom caps.
7. Bake in the preheated oven for about 20 minutes, or until the mushrooms are tender and well browned. Cool for 5 minutes and serve.

Per Serving
Calories: 77 | fat: 3.2g | carbs: 11.1g | protein: 4.7g | fiber: 2.9g

Tofu Sloppy Joes

Prep time: 15 minutes | Cook time: 20 minutes | Serves 8

1 green bell pepper, chopped
1 onion, chopped
2 cloves garlic, chopped
1 pound (454 g) tofu, frozen and thawed
1 tablespoon Dijon mustard
½ cup low-sodium soy sauce
2 teaspoons cider vinegar
1 tablespoon maple syrup (optional)
Dash cayenne pepper
1 to 2 teaspoons grated fresh ginger

1. In a saucepan, add the green pepper, onion, garlic, and a little water. Sauté until the green pepper and onion are softened, stirring occasionally.
2. Squeeze the excess liquid out of the tofu and crumble.
3. Add the tofu and the remaining ingredients to the saucepan and stir well. Sauté for another 10 to 15 minutes until thickened, stirring periodically.
4. Serve warm.

Per Serving
Calories: 120 | fat: 6.2g | carbs: 9.0g | protein: 7.1g | fiber: 1.0g

Crispy Baked Cauliflower

Prep time: 10 minutes | Cook time: 40 minutes | Serves 6

1 cup unsweetened oat milk
¾ cup whole-wheat flour
2 teaspoons onion powder
2 teaspoons garlic powder
½ teaspoon paprika
¼ teaspoon freshly ground black pepper
1 head cauliflower, cut into bite-sized florets

1. Preheat the oven to 425ºF (220ºC) and line a baking sheet with parchment paper. Set aside.
2. Combine the oat milk, flour, onion powder, garlic powder, paprika, and pepper in a large bowl, and whisk well. Add the cauliflower florets and gently toss until the florets are thoroughly coated.
3. Arrange the cauliflower florets on the prepared baking sheet in an even layer. Bake in the preheated oven for 40 minutes, flipping the cauliflower florets halfway through, or until the cauliflower is golden brown and crispy.
4. Remove from the oven and serve on a plate.

Per Serving
Calories: 98 | fat: 5.1g | carbs: 2.1g | protein: 3.1g | fiber: 2.1g

Stuffed Zucchini Boats

Prep time: 30 minutes | Cook time: 1 hour | Serves 2 to 4

1 large zucchini (big enough to stuff), halved
¹/₃ cup water
1 cup finely chopped celery
1 cup finely chopped onion
1 to 2 cloves garlic, pressed
1 medium tomato, chopped
3 tablespoons chopped fresh parsley
1 cup whole wheat bread crumbs

1. Bring a large pot of water to a boil. Cook the zucchini in boiling water for 2 to 3 minutes. Remove from the heat and immediately dunk in cold water. Drain on paper towels.
2. Hollow out the flesh with a spoon, leaving a ¼-inch-thick shell on each half. Chop the flesh and set it aside with the shells.
3. Preheat the oven to 325ºF (163ºC).
4. Heat ¹/₃ cup water in a skillet over medium heat until it starts to sputter.
5. Add the celery, onion, and garlic and cook for 5 minutes. Stir in the zucchini flesh, tomato, and parsley. Cook for an additional 5 minutes.
6. Spoon the mixture into the zucchini shells in a casserole and scatter the bread crumbs on top.
7. Cover with aluminum foil and bake in the preheated oven for 30 minutes.
8. Remove the foil and continue to bake for 15 minutes or until the zucchini is soft. Allow to cool to room temperature and serve.

Per Serving
Calories: 47 | fat: 0.3g | carbs: 9.5g | protein: 1.7g | fiber: 2.0g

Veggie Tofu Stir-Fry

Prep time: 15 minutes | Cook time: 7 to 10 minutes | Serves 4

¹/₃ cup water
2 cloves garlic, minced
1½ Teaspoons grated fresh ginger
3 tablespoons low-sodium soy sauce
½ pound (227 g) firm tofu, cut into strips
3 small yellow squash, sliced
2 small zucchini, sliced
1 small baby bok choy, sliced
½ pound (227 g) snow peas, trimmed
¼ pound (113 g) oyster mushrooms, sliced
½ cup bean sprouts
1 bunch scallions, sliced into 1-inch pieces

1. In a large pan, add the water, garlic, ginger, and soy sauce and bring to a boil.
2. Add the tofu, squash, zucchini, bok choy, and snow peas to the pan and sauté for 4 to 5 minutes. Fold in the mushrooms, bean sprouts, and scallions. Sauté for an additional 3 to 5 minutes until the veggies are tender.
3. Remove from the heat and serve.

Per Serving
Calories: 130 | fat: 5.1g | carbs: 10.9g | protein: 9.8g | fiber: 5.1g

Grilled Eggplant Slices

Prep time: 10 minutes | Cook time: 8 to 10 minutes | Serves 4

3 tablespoons balsamic vinegar
2 tablespoons low-sodium soy sauce
Juice of 1 lemon

Freshly ground black pepper, to taste
1 large eggplant, stemmed and cut into ¾-inch slices

1. Preheat the grill to medium heat.
2. Make the marinade: In a small bowl, stir together the balsamic vinegar, soy sauce, lemon juice, and pepper.
3. Brush both sides of the eggplant slices with the prepared marinade.
4. Arrange the eggplant slices on the grill and cook for 4 to 5 minutes per side, brushing the eggplant periodically with the remaining marinade.
5. Let the eggplant cool for 5 minutes and serve hot.

Per Serving
Calories: 56 | fat: 0.3g | carbs: 11.3g | protein: 2.0g | fiber: 4.2g

Grilled Eggplant Slices

Prep time: 10 minutes | Cook time: 8 to 10 minutes | Serves 1

2 tablespoons low-sodium soy sauce
3 tablespoons balsamic vinegar
Juice of 1 lemon

Freshly ground black pepper, to taste
1 large eggplant, stemmed and cut into ¾-inch slices

1. Prepare the grill to medium-high heat.
2. Make the marinade: In a small bowl, stir together the soy sauce, balsamic vinegar, lemon juice, and pepper until well combined.
3. Brush both sides of the eggplant slices generously with the prepared marinade.
4. Arrange the eggplant on the preheated grill and cook for 4 to 5 minutes per side, brushing the eggplant slices with the remaining marinade every few minutes.
5. Remove from the heat and serve hot.

Per Serving
Calories: 54 | fat: 0.3g | carbs: 11.3g | protein: 2.0g | fiber: 4.2g

Stuffed Delicata Squash with Spinach

Prep time: 15 minutes | Cook time: 1 hour 15 minutes | Serves 4

2 delicata squash, halved and deseeded
Sea salt, to taste (optional)
Freshly ground black pepper, to taste
1 shallot, peeled and minced
½ red bell pepper, seeded and diced small
6 cups chopped spinach
1 tablespoon minced sage

2 cloves garlic, peeled and minced
2 cups cooked cannellini beans, or 1 (15-ounce / 425-g) can, drained and rinsed
¾ cup whole-grain bread crumbs
Zest of 1 lemon
3 tablespoons pine nuts, toasted
3 tablespoons nutritional yeast (optional)

1. Preheat the oven to 350ºF (180ºC). Line a baking sheet with parchment paper.
2. Sprinkle the cut sides of the squash halves with salt (if desired) and pepper. Lay the squash halves on the prepared baking sheet, cut sides down. Bake for about 45 minutes, or until the squash is softened.
3. Meanwhile, in a large saucepan, add the shallot and red pepper and sauté over medium heat for 2 to 3 minutes. Add 1 to 2 tablespoons of water, at a time, to keep the vegetables from sticking to the bottom of the saucepan, if needed.
4. Stir in the spinach, sage, and garlic and cook for 4 to 5 minutes, or until the spinach is wilted. Add the beans and sprinkle with salt (if desired) and pepper. Cook for an additional 2 to 3 minutes.
5. Turn off the heat. Fold in the bread crumbs, lemon zest, pine nuts, nutritional yeast (if desired) and stir well.
6. Spoon the filling into the baked squash halves. Arrange the stuffed squash on a baking dish and wrap in aluminum foil.
7. Bake in the preheated oven until heated through, about 15 to 20 minutes,
8. Remove from the oven and allow the squash to cool for 5 minutes before serving.

Per Serving
Calories: 177 | fat: 2.6g | carbs: 28.6g | protein: 9.9g | fiber: 7.2g

Ratatouille

Prep time: 10 minutes | Cook time: 25 minutes | Serves 4

1 medium red onion, peeled and diced
2 tablespoons water, plus more as needed
1 medium eggplant, stemmed and diced
1 small zucchini, diced
1 medium red bell pepper, seeded and diced
4 cloves garlic, peeled and minced
1 large tomato, diced
½ cup chopped basil
Freshly ground black pepper, to taste
Salt, to taste (optional)

1. Put the diced onions in a medium saucepan over medium heat and sauté for 8 minutes, stirring frequently. Add 1 to 2 tablespoons water at a time to help keep them from sticking to the pan.
2. Stir in the eggplant, zucchini, bell pepper, and garlic. Cover and cook for 15 minutes, stirring occasionally, or until the vegetables are softened.
3. Add the diced tomatoes, basil, and pepper, and stir to combine. Sprinkle with the salt, if desired. Cook for 1 minute more.
4. Remove from the heat to a large plate and serve.

Per Serving
Calories: 76 | fat: 0.5g | carbs: 15.3g | protein: 2.7g | fiber: 5.9g

Spanish Veggie Casserole

Prep time: 20 minutes | Cook time: 50 minutes | Serves 4

1 to 2 tablespoons water
1 clove garlic, minced
1 medium onion, chopped
1 medium red or green bell pepper, chopped
1 medium tomato, cored and chopped
1 potato, peeled and diced
⅛ to ¼ teaspoon cayenne
½ teaspoon paprika
2 cups low-sodium vegetable broth
2 medium carrots, scrubbed and chopped or sliced
1 cup long-grain brown rice
2 cups frozen green peas
1 to 2 zucchini, chopped

1. Heat the water in a large, heavy saucepan over medium heat. Add the garlic and onion and sauté for 1 minute.
2. Fold in the pepper and tomato and sauté for about 3 minutes. Add the potato, cayenne, and paprika, and cook for 2 minutes more, stirring occasionally.
3. Stir in the vegetable broth, carrot, and rice. Reduce the heat and cook for 15 minutes until the mixture bubbles.
4. Add the peas and zucchini and stir well. Let simmer covered for an additional 30 minutes until the veggies are softened. Cool for 5 minutes and serve warm.

Per Serving
Calories: 328 | fat: 1.8g | carbs: 67.9g | protein: 10.0g | fiber: 7.9g

Tofu-Vegetable Gravy Bowl

Prep time: 10 minutes | Cook time: 8 to 10 minutes | Serves 4

Gravy:
6 tablespoons water
¼ cup diced red, white, or yellow onion
2 tablespoons whole wheat or all-purpose flour
1 cup low-sodium vegetable broth
Vegetable Base:
1 cup evenly chopped zucchini, steamed
1 cup chopped carrots, steamed
1 cup evenly sliced broccoli, steamed
½ (14-ounce / 397-g) block extra-firm tofu, pressed and cut into ½-inch cubes

1. Add 6 tablespoons of water and the onion into a medium pan and sauté over medium heat for 3 minutes, or until the onion is soft and translucent.
2. Reduce the heat to low, mix in the flour, and continue to sauté for 2 to 3 minutes until fairly smooth.
3. Add the vegetable broth and boil over low heat for 3 to 4 minutes, or until the gravy is thickened.
4. Arrange the zucchini, carrots, broccoli, and tofu on a plate and drizzle the gravy over the top. Serve immediately.

Per Serving
Calories: 102 | fat: 3.6g | carbs: 10.2g | protein: 7.3g | fiber: 1.8g

Tofu and Vegetable Patties

Prep time: 30 minutes | Cook time: 45 minutes | Serves 6

1 bunch scallions, chopped
1 cup sliced mushrooms
½ cup finely chopped broccoli pieces
½ cup finely chopped cauliflower pieces
¼ cup water
2 tablespoons low-sodium soy sauce, divided
1 pound (454 g) tofu
¼ teaspoon ground turmeric
1 teaspoon baking powder
1 cup whole-wheat flour

1. Preheat the oven to 350ºF (180ºC).
2. In a saucepan, add the vegetables, ¼ cup of water, and 1 tablespoon of the soy sauce and sauté for about 5 minutes, or until the vegetables are crispy and the liquid is absorbed. Turn off the heat and set aside.
3. In a blender, add the tofu, turmeric, and the remaining 1 tablespoon of soy sauce and blend until smooth. Transfer to a bowl.
4. Mix in the baking powder and flour. Add the vegetables and stir until well combined. Shape the mixture into 6 patties, 3 inches in diameter and ½ inch thick. Arrange the patties on a nonstick baking sheet.
5. Bake in the preheated oven for 30 minutes, flip, and bake for an additional 15 minutes.
6. Remove from the oven and allow to cool for 5 minutes before serving.

Per Serving
Calories: 171 | fat: 5.9g | carbs: 18.4g | protein: 11.1g | fiber: 3.0g

Broccoli Casserole with Beans and Walnuts

Prep time: 10 minutes | Cook time: 35 to 40 minutes | Serves 4

¾ cup vegetable broth
2 broccoli heads, crowns and stalks finely chopped
1 teaspoon salt (optional)
2 cups cooked pinto or navy beans
1 to 2 tablespoons brown rice flour or arrowroot flour
1 cup chopped walnuts

1. Preheat the oven to 350ºF (180ºC).
2. Warm the vegetable broth in a large ovenproof pot over medium heat.
3. Add the broccoli and season with salt, if desired. Cook for 6 to 8 minutes, stirring occasionally, or until the broccoli is bright green.
4. Add the pinto beans and brown rice flour to the skillet and stir well. Cook for another 5 minutes, or until the liquid thickens slightly. Scatter the top with the walnuts.
5. Transfer the pot to the preheated oven and bake until the walnuts are toasted, 20 to 25 minutes.
6. Let the casserole cool for 5 to 10 minutes in the pot before serving.

Per Serving
Calories: 412 | fat: 20.2g | carbs: 43.3g | protein: 21.6g | fiber: 13.1g

Spicy Marinated Tofu Crumbles

Prep time: 1 hour 10 minutes | Cook time: 40 minutes | Serves 4

1 (14-ounce / 397-g) package tofu, frozen and thawed
½ cup low-sodium soy sauce
2 teaspoons dry mustard
2 teaspoons cider vinegar
1 tablespoon maple syrup (optional)
2 teaspoons onion powder
2 cloves garlic, crushed
1 to 2 teaspoons grated fresh ginger
Dash cayenne

1. Slice the tofu into ¼-inch-thick strips. Arrange the tofu in a medium baking dish, avoiding overlap.
2. Make the marinade by mixing together the remaining ingredients and stirring to combine.
3. Drizzle the marinade over the tofu. Let sit for 1 hour.
4. Preheat the oven to 350ºF (180ºC).
5. Transfer the tofu to the oven and bake in the marinade for 20 minutes, flip and bake for another 20 minutes.
6. Serve warm.

Per Serving
Calories: 228 | fat: 12.5g | carbs: 15.2g | protein: 13.8g | fiber: 1.4g

Spiced Tofu and Oatmeal Burgers

Prep time: 15 minutes | Cook time: 30 minutes | Serves 8

1 pound (454 g) firm tofu, drained
1½ cup rolled oats
2 tablespoons low-sodium soy sauce
1 tablespoon Dijon mustard
1 tablespoon Worcestershire sauce
¼ teaspoon garlic powder
¼ teaspoon onion powder
¼ teaspoon freshly ground black pepper
2 tablespoons minced fresh parsley (optional)
1 teaspoon grated fresh ginger (optional)

1. Preheat the oven to 350ºF (180ºC).
2. Using a potato masher, mash the tofu in a large bowl.
3. Fold in the remaining ingredients and stir until well mixed. Divide the mixture into 8 equal portions and shape into patties with moist hands. Arrange the patties on a nonstick baking sheet.
4. Bake in the preheated oven for 20 minutes, flip and bake for another 10 minutes, or until the patties are firm to the touch on the outside.
5. Remove from the oven and let cool on a wire rack for 5 minutes before serving.

Per Serving
Calories: 175 | fat: 6.9g | carbs: 15.8g | protein: 12.4g | fiber: 4.2g

Kale and Pinto Bean Enchilada Casserole

Prep time: 10 minutes | Cook time: 30 minutes | Makes 8 pieces

1 teaspoon olive oil (optional)
1 yellow onion, diced
1 bunch kale, stemmed and chopped
2 teaspoons Taco Seasoning
3 cups cooked pinto beans, or 2 (15-ounce / 425-g) cans pinto
beans, drained and rinsed
Sea salt, to taste (optional)
Black pepper, to taste
1 (16-ounce / 454-g) jar salsa (any variety), divided
12 corn tortillas
½ cup cashew queso, or more to taste

1. Preheat the oven to 400ºF (205ºC). Grease a baking dish with the olive oil, if desired.
2. Place the onion, kale, taco seasoning, and beans in the dish. Sprinkle with salt (if desired) and pepper. Drizzle half the salsa over the beans. Place the tortillas on top. Scatter with the remaining salsa and cashew queso.
3. Cover the dish with aluminum foil and bake in the preheated oven for about 30 minutes, or until the vegetables are tender and the salsa bubbles.
4. Remove from the oven and let cool for 10 minutes before slicing and serving.

Per Serving
Calories: 194 | fat: 3.8g | carbs: 29.0g | protein: 10.9g | fiber: 9.4g

Potato and Zucchini Casserole

Prep time: 10 minutes | Cook time: 1 hour | Serves 6

3 large russet potatoes, halved lengthwise and thinly sliced
3 medium zucchini, halved lengthwise and thinly sliced
¾ cup nutritional yeast
¾ cup diced green or red bell pepper (about 1 small bell pepper)
¾ cup diced red,
white, or yellow onion (about 1 small onion)
½ cup dry bread crumbs
¼ cup olive oil (optional)
1½ Teaspoons minced garlic (about 3 small cloves)
Pepper, to taste
Sea salt, to taste (optional)

1. Preheat the oven to 400ºF (205ºC).
2. Mix together all the ingredients in a large bowl.
3. Place the mixture in a large casserole dish.
4. Bake in the preheated oven for 1 hour until heated through, stirring once halfway through.
5. Remove from the oven and allow to cool for 5 minutes before serving.

Per Serving
Calories: 352 | fat: 10.0g | carbs: 51.5g | protein: 14.1g | fiber: 5.5g

Twice-Baked Potatoes

Prep time: 15 minutes | Cook time: 1 hour 30 minutes | Serves 6

6 large russet potatoes, scrubbed
1 medium yellow onion, peeled and diced small
1 red bell pepper, deseeded and diced small
1 jalapeño pepper, deseeded and minced
2 cloves garlic, peeled and minced
1 tablespoon toasted and ground cumin seeds
2 teaspoons ancho chile powder
3 ears corn, kernels removed
2 cups cooked black beans
1 teaspoon salt (optional)
½ cup chopped cilantro
1 (12 ounce / 340-g) package extra firm silken tofu, drained
½ cup chopped green onion, white and green parts

1. Preheat the oven to 350ºF (180ºC).
2. Pierce each potato with a fork a few times so that it will release steam during baking. Place the potatoes on a baking sheet and bake for 60 to 75 minutes, or until tender. Let cool until safe to handle.
3. Place the onion and red pepper in a large skillet and sauté over medium heat for 7 to 8 minutes, or until the onion starts to brown. Add water 1 to 2 tablespoons at a time to keep the vegetables from sticking to the pan. Add the jalapeño pepper, garlic, cumin, and chile powder and sauté for another minute. Add the corn, black beans, salt (if desired) and cilantro and mix well. Remove from the heat.
4. Puree the silken tofu in the blender. Add the pureed tofu to the vegetable mixture in the pan and mix well.
5. Halve each potato lengthwise, and scoop out the flesh, leaving a ¼-inch-thick shell. Reserve the flesh for another use. Divide the vegetable filling evenly among the potato halves. Place the filled potatoes on a baking sheet and bake for 30 minutes.
6. Serve garnished with the chopped green onion.

Per Serving

Calories: 503 | fat: 5.2g | carbs: 99.3g | protein: 21.8g | fiber: 13.3g

Grilled Cauliflower "Steaks"

Prep time: 10 minutes | Cook time: 57 minutes | Serves 4

2 medium heads cauliflower
2 medium shallots, peeled and minced
Water, as needed
1 clove garlic, peeled and minced
½ teaspoon ground fennel
½ teaspoon minced sage
½ teaspoon crushed red pepper flakes
½ cup green lentils, rinsed
2 cups low-sodium vegetable broth
Salt, to taste (optional)
Freshly ground black pepper, to taste
Chopped parsley, for garnish

1. On a flat work surface, cut each of the cauliflower heads in half through the stem, then trim each half so you get a 1-inch-thick "steak".
2. Arrange each piece on a baking sheet and set aside. You can reserve the extra cauliflower florets for other uses.
3. Sauté the shallots in a medium saucepan over medium heat for 10 minutes, stirring occasionally. Add water, 1 to 2 tablespoons at a time, to keep the shallots from sticking.
4. Stir in the garlic, fennel, sage, red pepper flakes, and lentils and cook for 3 minutes.
5. Pour into the vegetable broth and bring to a boil over high heat.
6. Reduce the heat to medium, cover, and cook for 45 to 50 minutes, or until the lentils are very soft, adding more water as needed.
7. Using an immersion blender, purée the mixture until smooth. Sprinkle with salt (if desired) and pepper. Keep warm and set aside.
8. Preheat the grill to medium heat.
9. Grill the cauliflower "steaks" for about 7 minutes per side until evenly browned.
10. Transfer the cauliflower "steaks" to a plate and spoon the purée over them. Serve garnished with the parsley.

Per Serving

Calories: 105 | fat: 1.1g | carbs: 18.3g | protein: 5.4g | fiber: 4.9g

Stuffed Tomatoes with Bulgur

Prep time: 10 minutes | Cook time: 45 to 46 minutes | Serves 4

4 large tomatoes (about 2 pounds / 907 g)
2 leeks (white and light green parts), diced small and rinsed
1 clove garlic, peeled and minced
3 ears corn, kernels removed (about 1½ cups)
1 medium zucchini, diced small
1 cup bulgur, cooked in 2 cups low-sodium vegetable broth
Zest and juice of 1 lemon
½ cup finely chopped basil
Sea salt, to taste (optional)
Freshly ground black pepper, to taste

1. Preheat the oven to 350ºF (180ºC).
2. Cut the tops off the tomatoes and hollow out the flesh with a spoon, leaving a ½-inch wall. Set aside.
3. Sauté the leeks in a large saucepan over medium heat for 7 to 8 minutes, stirring occasionally.
4. Add the garlic and cook for another 3 minutes. Stir in the corn and zucchini and cook for an additional 5 minutes.
5. Add the cooked bulgur, lemon zest, juice, and basil and stir well. Sprinkle with salt (if desired) and pepper.
6. Remove from the heat. Spoon the bulgur mixture evenly into the tomatoes and transfer to a baking dish.
7. Wrap the dish in aluminum foil and bake in the preheated oven for 30 minutes.
8. Remove the foil and let cool for 5 to 8 minutes before serving.

Per Serving
Calories: 348 | fat: 3.6g | carbs: 69.3g | protein: 9.7g | fiber: 9.7g

Eggplant Stuffed with Rice and Herbs

Prep time: 15 minutes | Cook time: 1 hour 37 minutes | Serves 4

2 cups low-sodium vegetable broth
1 cup brown basmati rice
1 cinnamon stick
2 medium eggplants, stemmed and halved lengthwise
1 celery stalk, diced small
1 medium yellow onion, peeled and diced small
1 medium red bell pepper, seeded and diced small
Water, as needed
2 cloves garlic, peeled and minced
¼ cup finely chopped cilantro
¼ cup finely chopped basil
Sea salt, to taste (optional)
Freshly ground black pepper, to taste

1. Pour the vegetable broth into a medium saucepan and bring to a boil.
2. Stir in the rice and cinnamon stick and cook covered over medium heat for 45 minutes, or until the rice is soft. Set aside.
3. Scoop out the eggplant flesh, leaving a ¼-inch-thick shell on each half. Chop the eggplant flesh and set it aside with the shells.
4. Preheat the oven to 350ºF (180ºC).
5. In a large saucepan, add the celery, onion, and red pepper and sauté over medium heat for 7 to 8 minutes, or until the veggies are lightly browned. Add water, 1 to 2 tablespoons at a time, to prevent sticking.
6. Stir in the eggplant fresh and garlic and cook for an additional 5 minutes, or until the eggplant is softened.
7. Turn off the heat. Add the cooked rice, cilantro, and basil to the eggplant mixture. Sprinkle with salt (if desired) and pepper.
8. Spoon the filling into the eggplant shells and arrange the stuffed eggplants in a baking dish. Wrap the dish in aluminum foil and bake for 40 minutes, or until the eggplants are nicely browned.
9. Remove from the oven and let cool for 5 minutes before serving.

Per Serving
Calories: 308 | fat: 2.5g | carbs: 62.9g | protein: 8.3g | fiber: 12.1g

Baked Sweet Potatoes

Prep time: 5 minutes | Cook time: 37 minutes | Serves 4

4 medium sweet potatoes
1 tablespoon avocado oil (optional)
2 garlic cloves, minced
1 small white onion, thinly sliced
12 cherry tomatoes, chopped
1 (14-ounce /397-g) can black beans, drained and rinsed well
½ teaspoon chili powder
¼ teaspoon salt (optional)
¼ teaspoon red pepper flakes
1 large avocado, sliced
Juice of 1 lime

1. Preheat the oven to 400ºF (205ºC).
2. On a flat work surface, poke holes 5 to 6 times into each sweet potato with a fork. Loosely wrap each sweet potato in aluminum foil, then arrange them on a baking sheet.
3. Bake in the preheated oven for 25 minutes until cooked through.
4. Meanwhile, heat the avocado oil (if desired) in a large skillet over medium heat.
5. Add the onion and garlic and sauté for 5 minutes until tender.
6. Stir in the tomatoes, beans, chili powder, salt (if desired), and red pepper flakes. Cook for about 7 minutes. Remove from the heat.
7. When the sweet potatoes are ready, remove from the oven and carefully unwrap the foil. Cut each potato lengthwise, almost through to the bottom.
8. Open the potatoes to create a space for the filling. Spoon equal portions of filling into each of the potato halves.
9. Scatter with avocado slices and top with a generous drizzle of lime juice. Serve immediately.

Per Serving
Calories: 327 | fat: 10.1g | carbs: 51.3g | protein: 9.7g | fiber: 12.9g

Pistachio Crusted Tofu

Prep time: 10 minutes | Cook time: 20 minutes | Makes 8 slices

½ cup roasted, shelled pistachios
¼ cup whole wheat bread crumbs
1 garlic clove, minced
1 shallot, minced
½ teaspoon dried tarragon
1 teaspoon grated lemon zest
Sea salt, to taste (optional)
Black pepper, to taste
1 (16-ounce / 454-g) package sprouted or extra-firm tofu, drained and sliced lengthwise into 8 pieces
1 tablespoon Dijon mustard
1 tablespoon lemon juice

1. Preheat the oven to 375ºF (190ºC). Line a baking sheet with parchment paper.
2. Process the pistachios in a food processor until they are about the size of the bread crumbs. Mix together the pistachios, bread crumbs, garlic, shallot, tarragon, and lemon zest in a shallow dish. Sprinkle with salt (if desired) and pepper. Set aside.
3. Sprinkle the tofu with salt (if desired) and pepper. Mix the mustard and lemon juice in a small bowl and stir well.
4. Brushes all over the tofu with the mustard mixture, then coat each slice with the pistachio mixture.
5. Arrange the tofu on the baking sheet. Scatter any remaining pistachio mixture over the slices.
6. Bake in the preheated oven for about 20 minutes, or until the tofu is browned and crispy.
7. Serve hot.

Per Serving
Calories: 159 | fat: 9.3g | carbs: 8.3g | protein: 10.4g | fiber: 1.6g

Chapter 6 Dinner Recipes

Sweet and Smoky Corn

Prep time: 5 minutes | Cook time: 6 to 11 minutes | Serves 2

3 Medjool dates, pitted and chopped
1 teaspoon low-sodium soy sauce
½ teaspoon smoked paprika
½ teaspoon onion powder
½ teaspoon garlic powder
3 cups fresh sweet corn, cut off the cob

1. Heat a saucepan over medium-low heat. Combine the Medjool dates and soy sauce in the saucepan and sauté for 1 minute, or until the dates are softened.
2. Stir in the spices and corn. Cover and cook for 5 to 10 minutes, stirring constantly.
3. Remove from the saucepan and serve hot.

Per Serving
Calories: 295 | fat: 3.1g | carbs: 69.1g | protein: 8.2g | fiber: 7.2g

Lentil Veg Broth Soup

Prep time: 15 minutes | Cook time: 5 minutes | Serves 6

2 small onions, finely chopped
2 carrots, finely chopped
6 small white potatoes, finely chopped
1 (16-ounce / 454-g) bag brown lentils
1 (15½-ounce / 439-g) can fire roasted tomatoes, diced
8 cups vegetable broth or water
1-2 cups finely chopped spinach
Salt and pepper, to taste

1. Combine all ingredients, except the spinach, and cook on low for 2 hours.
2. Add the spinach about 5 minutes before the soup is done. Season to taste with salt and pepper.

Per Serving
Calories: 830| fat: 3.19g | carbs: 187.77g | protein: 30.95g | fiber: 31.3g

Spicy Beans and Rice

Prep time: 5 minutes | Cook time: 45 minutes | Serves 4 to 6

1½ cups long-grain brown rice
1 (19-ounce / 539-g) can kidney beans, rinsed and drained
2 cups chopped onion
1 cup mild salsa
1 teaspoon ground cumin
16 ounces (454 g) tomatoes, chopped
3 cups water

1. In a pot, bring the water to a boil. Stir in the rice. Bring to a boil again and stir in the remaining ingredients, except for the tomatoes. Return to a boil. Reduce the heat to low. Cover and simmer for 45 minutes.
2. Remove from the heat and stir in the tomatoes. Let sit for 5 minutes, covered.

Per Serving
Calories: 386 | fat: 7.1g | carbs: 71.1g | protein: 11.1g | fiber: 5.8g

Black-Eyed Peas and Corn Salad

Prep time: 30 minutes | Cook time: 50 minutes | Serves 4

2½ cups cooked black-eyed peas
3 ears corn, kernels removed
1 medium ripe tomato, diced
½ medium red onion, peeled and diced small
½ red bell pepper, deseeded and diced small
1 jalapeño pepper, deseeded and minced
½ cup finely chopped cilantro
¼ cup plus 2 tablespoons balsamic vinegar
3 cloves garlic, peeled and minced
1 teaspoon toasted and ground cumin seeds

1. Stir together all the ingredients in a large bowl and refrigerate for about 1 hour, or until well chilled.
2. Serve chilled.

Per Serving
Calories: 247 | fat: 1.8g | carbs: 47.6g | protein: 12.9g | fiber: 11.7g

Spiced Tomato Brown Rice

Prep time: 10 minutes | Cook time: 15 minutes | Serves 4 to 6

1 onion, diced
1 green bell pepper, diced
3 cloves garlic, minced
¼ cup water
15 to 16 ounces (425 to 454g) tomatoes, chopped
1 tablespoon chili powder
2 teaspoons ground cumin
1 teaspoon dried basil
½ teaspoon Parsley Patch seasoning, general blend
¼ teaspoon cayenne
2 cups cooked brown rice

1. Combine the onion, green pepper, garlic and water in a saucepan over medium heat. Cook for about 5 minutes, stirring constantly, or until softened.
2. Add the tomatoes and seasonings. Cook for another 5 minutes. Stir in the cooked rice. Cook for another 5 minutes to allow the flavors to blend.
3. Serve immediately.

Per Serving
Calories: 107 | fat: 1.1g | carbs: 21.1g | protein: 3.2g | fiber: 2.9g

Noodle and Rice Pilaf

Prep time: 5 minutes | Cook time: 33 to 44 minutes | Serves 6 to 8

1 cup whole-wheat noodles, broken into ⅛-inch pieces
2 cups long-grain brown rice
6½ cups low-sodium vegetable broth
1 teaspoon ground cumin
½ teaspoon dried oregano

1. Combine the noodles and rice in a saucepan over medium heat and cook for 3 to 4 minutes, or until they begin to smell toasted.
2. Stir in the vegetable broth, cumin and oregano. Bring to a boil. Reduce the heat to medium-low. Cover and cook for 30 to 40 minutes, or until all water is absorbed.

Per Serving
Calories: 287 | fat: 2.5g | carbs: 58.1g | protein: 7.9g | fiber: 5.0g

Easy Millet Loaf

Prep time: 5 minutes | Cook time: 1 hour 15 minutes | Serves 4

1¼ cups millet
4 cups unsweetened tomato juice
1 medium onion, chopped
1 to 2 cloves garlic
½ teaspoon dried sage
½ teaspoon dried basil
½ teaspoon poultry seasoning

1. Preheat the oven to 350ºF (180ºC).
2. Place the millet in a large bowl.
3. Place the remaining ingredients in a blender and pulse until smooth. Add to the bowl with the millet and mix well.
4. Pour the mixture into a shallow casserole dish. Cover and bake in the oven for 1¼ hours, or until set.
5. Serve warm.

Per Serving
Calories: 315 | fat: 3.4g | carbs: 61.6g | protein: 10.2g | fiber: 9.6g

Walnut-Oat Burgers

Prep time: 5 minutes | Cook time: 20 to 30 minutes | Serves 6 to 8

1 medium onion, finely chopped
2 cups rolled oats
2 cups unsweetened low-fat soy milk
1 cup finely chopped walnuts
1 tablespoon soy sauce
½ teaspoon dried sage
½ teaspoon garlic powder
½ teaspoon onion powder
½ teaspoon dried thyme
¼ teaspoon dried marjoram

1. Stir together all the ingredients in a large bowl. Let rest for 20 minutes.
2. Form the mixture into six or eight patties. Cook the patties on a nonstick griddle over medium heat for 20 to 30 minutes, or until browned on each side.
3. Serve warm.

Per Serving
Calories: 341 | fat: 13.9g | carbs: 42.4g | protein: 13.9g | fiber: 6.8g

Low-sodium Vegetable stock Lentil Sloppy Joes

Prep time: 30 minutes | Cook time: 30 minutes | Makes 6

3 ⅓ cups water or low-sodium vegetable stock
1 onion, chopped
1 red bell pepper, chopped
1 tablespoon chili powder
1 ½ cups dried brown lentil
1 (15-ounce / 425-g) can diced fire roasted tomatoes

2 tablespoons soy sauce
2 tablespoons Dijon mustard
2 tablespoons brown sugar
1 teaspoon rice vinegar
1 teaspoon vegetarian Worcestershire sauce
Salt to taste

1. Place 1 cup of the water or stock in a large pot.
2. Add the onions and bell pepper and cook, stirring occasionally until onions soften slightly, about 5 minutes.
3. Add the chili powder and mix in well. Add the remaining liquid, lentils, tomatoes, and the rest of the seasonings. Mix well, bring to a boil, reduce heat, cover and cook over low heat for one hour, stirring occasionally.
4. Serve on whole-wheat buns, or fresh baked bread, with the trimmings of your choice.

Per Serving
Calories: 1008| fat: 26g | carbs: 155g | protein: 61.2g | fiber: 20.2g

The Best Oil-Free Hummus Smoothie

Prep time: 5 minutes | Cook time: 0 minutes | Serves 4

2 cans chickpeas, rinsed and drained
3 cloves garlic
Juice of 1 lemon
2 teaspoons ground

cumin
2 teaspoons Bragg Liquid Amino
¼ cup water or vegetable broth

1. Blend all ingredients into a thick paste.

Per Serving
Calories: 83| fat: 3.95g | carbs: 11.9g | protein: 2.45g | fiber: 1.4g

Spicy Chickpea Curry with Mango

Prep time: 5 minutes | Cook time: 15 minutes | Serves 6

3 cups chickpeas, cooked
2 cups fresh mango chunks
2 cups unsweetened coconut milk
2 tablespoons maple syrup (optional)
1 tablespoon ground ginger

1 tablespoon curry powder
1 teaspoon garlic powder
1 teaspoon onion powder
1 teaspoon ground coriander
⅛ Teaspoon ground cinnamon

1. Heat a saucepan over medium heat. Add all the ingredients to the saucepan and stir well. Cook for 10 minutes, covered, stirring halfway through to avoid sticking.
2. Uncover and cook for another 5 minutes, stirring constantly.
3. Serve hot.

Per Serving
Calories: 218 | fat: 13.9g | carbs: 7.8g | protein: 8.1g | fiber: 9.2g

Red Jerk Beans

Prep time: 5 minutes | Cook time: 15 minutes | Serves 2 to 4

¼ cup low-sodium vegetable soup
1 large yellow onion, diced
2 tablespoons Jerk spices (no salt or sugar added)
1 (14.5-ounce / 411-

g) can diced tomatoes with juice
1 (15-ounce / 425-g) can red kidney beans, drained and rinsed
1 (14.5-ounce / 411-g) can unsweetened tomato sauce

1. Heat the soup in a saucepan over medium-high heat.
2. Add the onion and sauté for 5 minutes or until translucent. Sprinkle with Jerk spices and sauté for a minute more.
3. Add the tomatoes with juice, beans, then pour the tomato sauce over. Bring to a simmer. Cover the pan and cook for another 10 minutes. Stir periodically.
4. Serve immediately.

Per Serving
Calories: 136 | fat: 4.4g | carbs: 20.7g | protein: 5.2g | fiber: 5.4g

Pecan-Maple Granola

Prep time: 5 minutes | Cook time: 50 minutes | Serves 4

1½ cups rolled oats
¼ cup maple syrup (optional)
¼ cup pecan pieces
1 teaspoon vanilla extract
½ teaspoon ground cinnamon

1. Preheat the oven to 300ºF (150ºC). Line a baking sheet with parchment paper.
2. In a large bowl, stir together all the ingredients until the oats and pecan pieces are completely coated.
3. Spread the mixture on the baking sheet in an even layer. Bake in the oven for 20 minutes, stirring once halfway through cooking.
4. Remove from the oven and allow to cool on the countertop for 30 minutes before serving.

Per Serving
Calories: 221 | fat: 17.2g | carbs: 5.1g | protein: 4.9g | fiber: 3.8g

Smoky Tofu and Bean Bowls

Prep time: 10 minutes | Cook time: 10 minutes | Serves 4

¼ cup water
7 ounces (198 g) smoked tofu, cubed
2 cups fresh tomato, cubed
2 cups cooked black beans
1 cup cooked brown rice
1 tablespoon no-salt-added Cajun seasoning

1. Heat the water in a saucepan over medium-high heat.
2. Add the tofu and tomato cubes to the pan and sauté for 3 minutes or until the tomatoes are tender.
3. Add the beans and rice, then sprinkle with Cajun seasoning. Reduce the heat to low and stir to mix for 5 minutes until heated through.
4. Divide them among 4 bowls and serve immediately.

Per Serving
Calories: 371 | fat: 5.0g | carbs: 60.6g | protein: 19.6g | fiber: 11.9g

Quick and Easy Veggie Pasta Soup

Prep time: 15 minutes | Cook time: 30 minutes | Makes 8 Cups

1 cup chopped onion
1 cup chopped celery
1 cup chopped carrots
6 cups vegetable stock
1 teaspoon low-sodium tamari or soy sauce
½ teaspoon dried
marjoram, crushed
½ teaspoon dried sage, crushed
¼ teaspoon dried thyme, crushed
Freshly ground black pepper, to taste
3 cups whole-wheat pasta, broken

1. Combine the onion, celery, carrots, stock, tamari, marjoram, sage, thyme, and pepper in a 4-quart Dutch oven.
2. Bring to a boil over high heat. Reduce heat to medium-low; cover and simmer for 20 minutes.
3. Stir in the noodles; return to a boil. Cook for 10 minutes more or until noodles are tender.

Per Serving
Calories: 1298| fat: 5.5g | carbs: 261g | protein: 49.57g | fiber: 33.1g

Easy Polenta Squares

Prep time: 35 minutes | Cook time: 30 minutes | Serves 6

4 cups water
1 cup cornmeal
1 teaspoon chili powder
¼ teaspoon ground cumin
1 tablespoon low-sodium soy sauce

1. Preheat the oven to 400ºF (205ºC).
2. Make the polenta: Pour the water in a saucepan. Bring to a boil. Reduce the heat to low and add the remaining ingredients. Simmer for 10 minutes or until the liquid is thickened. Keep stirring during the simmering.
3. Pour the polenta in a single layer on a baking pan, then level with a spatula. Bake in the preheated oven for 20 minutes or until set.
4. Allow to cool for 30 minutes, then slice the polenta into squares and serve.

Per Serving
Calories: 100 | fat: 0.6g | carbs: 21.2g | protein: 2.2g | fiber: 1.2g

Brown Rice with Mushrooms

Prep time: 15 minutes | Cook time: 20 minutes | Serves 6 to 8

½ pound (227 g) mushrooms, sliced
1 green bell pepper, chopped
1 onion, chopped
1 bunch scallions, chopped
2 cloves garlic, minced
½ cup water
5 cups cooked brown rice
1 (16-ounce / 454-g) can chopped tomatoes
1 (4-ounce / 113-g) can chopped green chilies
2 teaspoons chili powder
1 teaspoon ground cumin

1. In a large pot, sauté the mushrooms, green pepper, onion, scallions, and garlic in the water for 10 minutes.
2. Stir in the remaining ingredients. Cook over low heat for about 10 minutes, or until heated through, stirring frequently.
3. Serve immediately.

Per Serving
Calories: 185 | fat: 2.6g | carbs: 34.5g | protein: 6.1g | fiber: 4.3g

Veggie Barley Bowl

Prep time: 10 minutes | Cook time: 1 hour 11 minutes | Serves 8

1 cup barley
3 cups low-sodium vegetable broth
2 cups sliced mushrooms
2 cups broccoli florets
1 cup snow peas, trimmed
½ cup sliced scallion
¼ cup chopped green bell pepper
¼ cup chopped red bell pepper
1 cup bean sprouts
¼ cup soy sauce
¼ cup water
¼ teaspoon ground ginger
1 tablespoon cornstarch, mixed with 2 tablespoons cold water

1. In a saucepan over medium heat, place the barley and vegetable stock. Cover and cook for 1 hour.
2. Combine all the vegetables, except for the bean sprouts, in a large pot with the soy sauce, water and ginger. Cook for 5 minutes, stirring constantly.
3. Add the bean sprouts and cook, stirring, for another 5 minutes. Add the cornstarch mixture and cook for about 1 minute, stirring, or until thickened.
4. Remove from the heat. Toss the vegetables with the cooked barley.
5. Serve hot.

Per Serving
Calories: 190 | fat: 2.6g | carbs: 35.7g | protein: 5.9g | fiber: 6.9g

Butternut Squash with Quinoa and Almonds

Prep time: 20 minutes | Cook time: 25 to 30 minutes | Serves 4

Squash:
1 medium (1½-pound/680-g) butternut squash, deseeded and cut into 1-inch cubes
¼ teaspoon dried chili flakes
1 teaspoon smoked paprika
1 clove garlic, thinly sliced
1 teaspoon fresh thyme leaves (about 2 sprigs)
Salt, to taste (optional)
Ground black or white pepper, to taste
12 green olives
4 lemon slices

Almond Quinoa:
¾ cup cooked quinoa
1/3 cup chopped arugula
1/3 cup chopped fresh flat-leaf parsley
1 teaspoon fresh lemon juice
Salt, to taste (optional)
Ground black or white pepper, to taste
¼ cup toasted and chopped almonds

1. Preheat the oven to 400ºF (205ºC). Line a baking sheet with a parchment paper.
2. Combine the butternut squash with chili flakes, paprika, garlic, thyme, salt (if desired), and pepper in a large bowl. Toss to coat well.
3. Pour the butternut squash mixture in the baking sheet, then top them with olives and lemon slices.
4. Bake in the preheated oven for 25 to 30 minutes or until the butternut squash cubes are soft. Shake the baking sheet every 5 or 10 minutes so the cubes are cooked evenly.
5. Meanwhile, combine the cooked quinoa with arugula, parsley, lemon juice, salt (if desired), and pepper on a large serving plate. Toss to combine well.
6. Top the quinoa with cooked butternut squash and almond before serving.

Per Serving
Calories: 172 | fat: 5.1g | carbs: 30.2g | protein: 5.2g | fiber: 6.0g

Vegetable and Wild Rice Pilaf

Prep time: 10 minutes | Cook time: 48 to 49 minutes | Serves 6

1 potato, scrubbed and chopped
1 cup chopped cauliflower
1 cup chopped scallion
1 cup chopped broccoli
1 to 2 cloves garlic, minced
2 tablespoons soy sauce
3 cups low-sodium vegetable broth
1 cup long-grain brown rice
⅓ cup wild rice
2 small zucchinis, chopped
½ cup grated carrot
⅛ Teaspoon sesame oil (optional)
¼ cup chopped fresh cilantro
½ cup water

1. Bring the water to a boil in a large saucepan. Add the potato, cauliflower, scallion, broccoli and garlic and sauté for 2 to 3 minutes.
2. Add the soy sauce and cook for 1 minute. Add the vegetable broth, brown rice and wild rice. Bring to a boil. Reduce the heat, cover, and cook for 15 minutes.
3. Stir in the zucchinis. After another 15 minutes, stir in the carrot. Continue to cook for 15 minutes. Stir in the sesame oil (if desired) and cilantro.
4. Serve immediately.

Per Serving
Calories: 376 | fat: 3.6g | carbs: 74.5g | protein: 11.8g | fiber: 8.1g

Brown Rice with Spiced Vegetables

Prep time: 10 minutes | Cook time: 16 to 18 minutes | Serves 6

2 teaspoons grated fresh ginger
2 cloves garlic, crushed
½ cup water
¼ pound (113 g) green beans, trimmed and cut into 1-inch pieces
1 carrot, scrubbed and sliced
½ pound (227 g) mushrooms, sliced
2 zucchinis, cut in half lengthwise and sliced
1 bunch scallions cut into 1-inch pieces
4 cups cooked brown rice
3 tablespoons soy sauce

1. Place the ginger and garlic in a large pot with the water. Add the green beans and carrot and sauté for 3 minutes.
2. Add the mushrooms and sauté for another 2 minutes. Stir in the zucchini and scallions. Reduce the heat. Cover and cook for 6 to 8 minutes, or until the vegetables are tender-crisp, stirring frequently.
3. Stir in the rice and soy sauce. Cook over low heat for 5 minutes, or until heated through.
4. Serve warm.

Per Serving
Calories: 205 | fat: 3.0g | carbs: 38.0g | protein: 6.4g | fiber:4.4 g

Vinegary Black Beans

Prep time: 10 minutes | Cook time: 2 hours | Serves 8

1 pound (454 g) black beans, soaked overnight and drained
10½ cups water, divided
1 green bell pepper cut in half
1 onion, finely chopped
1 green bell pepper, finely chopped
4 cloves garlic, pressed
1 tablespoon maple syrup (optional)
1 tablespoon Mrs. Dash seasoning
1 bay leaf
¼ teaspoon dried oregano
2 tablespoons cider vinegar

1. Place the beans, 10 cups of the water, and green bell pepper in a large pot. Cook over medium heat for about 45 minutes, or until the green pepper is tendered. Remove the green pepper and discard.
2. Meanwhile, in a different pot, combine the onion, chopped green pepper, garlic and the remaining ½ cup of the water. Sauté for 15 to 20 minutes, or until soft.
3. Add 1 cup of the cooked beans to the pot with vegetables. Mash the beans and vegetables with a potato masher.
4. Add to the pot with the beans, along with the maple syrup (if desired), Mrs. Dash, bay leaf and oregano. Cover and cook over low heat for 1 hour.
5. Drizzle in the vinegar and continue to cook for another hour.Serve warm.

Per Serving
Calories: 226 | fat: 0.9g | carbs: 42.7g | protein: 12.9g | fiber: 9.9g

Spiced Lentil Burgers

Prep time: 10 minutes | Cook time: 43 minutes | Serves 4

¼ cup minced onion
1 clove garlic, minced
2 tablespoons water
1 cup chopped boiled potatoes
1 cup cooked lentils
2 tablespoons minced

fresh parsley
1 teaspoon onion powder
1 teaspoon minced fresh basil
1 teaspoon dried dill
1 teaspoon paprika

1. Preheat the oven to 350ºF (180ºC).
2. In a pot, sauté the onion and garlic in the water for about 3 minutes, or until soft.
3. Combine the lentils and potatoes in a large bowl and mash together well. Add the cooked onion and garlic along with the remaining ingredients to the lentil-potato mixture and stir until well combined.
4. Form the mixture into four patties and place on a nonstick baking sheet. Bake in the oven for 20 minutes. Turnover and bake for an additional 20 minutes.
5. Serve hot.

Per Serving
Calories: 101 | fat: 0.4g | carbs: 19.9g | protein: 5.5g | fiber: 5.3g

Indian Tomato and Garbanzo Stew

Prep time: 15 minutes | Cook time: 50 minutes | Serves 4 to 6

1 large onion, quartered and thinly sliced
1 inch fresh ginger, peeled and minced
2 cloves garlic, peeled and minced
1 teaspoon curry powder
1 teaspoon cumin seeds
1 teaspoon black mustard seeds
1 teaspoon coriander

seeds,
1½ pounds (680 g) tomatoes, deseeded and puréed
1 red bell pepper, cut into ½-inch dice
1 green bell pepper, cut into ½-inch dice
3 cups cooked garbanzo beans
1 tablespoon garam masala
¹/₃ cup water

1. Heat the water in a medium saucepan over medium-low heat. Add the onion, ginger, garlic, curry powder, and seeds to the pan. Sauté for about 10 minutes or until the onion is tender, stirring frequently.

2. Add the tomatoes and simmer, uncovered, for 10 minutes. Add the peppers and garbanzo beans. Reduce the heat. Cover and simmer for 30 minutes, stirring occasionally. Stir in the garam masala and serve.

Per Serving
Calories: 100 | fat: 1.2g | carbs: 20.9g | protein: 5.1g | fiber: 7.0g

Indian Lentil Dahl

Prep time: 10 minutes | Cook time: 25 minutes | Serves 6

3 cup cooked basmati rice
2 tablespoons olive oil (optional)
6 garlic cloves, minced
2 yellow onions, finely diced
1-inch piece fresh ginger, minced
2 tomatoes, diced
2 tablespoons ground

cumin
1 tablespoon ground coriander
1 tablespoon ground turmeric
1 tablespoon paprika
4 cups water
2 cups uncooked green lentils, rinsed
1 teaspoon salt (optional)

1. In a large pot, heat the olive oil (if desired) over medium heat. Add the garlic, onions, and ginger. Cook for 3 minutes, or until onions are golden.
2. Add the tomatoes and cook for 2 minutes more, stirring occasionally. Stir in the cumin, coriander, turmeric and paprika.
3. Add the water and lentils. Cover and bring to a boil over high heat. Once boiling, stir and reduce the heat to a simmer. Cook, covered, for 20 minutes, stirring every 5 minutes, or until the lentils are fully cooked and beginning to break down. Season with salt (if desired) and stir.
4. Divide the rice evenly among 6 meal prep containers. Add an equal portion of the dahl to each container. Let cool completely before putting on lids and refrigerating.

Per Serving
Calories: 432 | fat: 17.2g | carbs: 58.8g | protein: 10.9g | fiber: 8.9g

Simple Baked Navy Beans

Prep time: 10 minutes | Cook time: 2½ to 3 hours | Serves 8

1½ cups navy beans
8 cups water
1 bay leaf
½ cup finely chopped green bell pepper
½ cup finely chopped onion
1 teaspoon minced

garlic
½ cup unsweetened tomato purée
3 tablespoons molasses
1 tablespoon fresh lemon juice

1. Preheat the oven to 300°F (150°C).
2. Place the beans and water in a large pot, along with the bay leaf, green pepper, onion and garlic. Cover and cook for 1½ to 2 hours, or until the beans are softened. Remove from the heat and drain, reserving the cooking liquid. Discard the bay leaf.
3. Transfer the mixture to a casserole dish with a cover. Stir in the remaining ingredients and 1 cup of the reserved cooking liquid. Bake in the oven for 1 hour, covered. Stir occasionally during baking and add a little more cooking liquid if needed to keep the beans moist.Serve warm.

Per Serving
Calories: 162 | fat: 0.6g | carbs: 31.3g | protein: 9.1g | fiber: 6.4g

Peppery Black Beans

Prep time: 10 minutes | Cook time: 33 to 34 minutes | Serves 4

1 red bell pepper, deseeded and chopped
1 medium yellow onion, peeled and chopped
2 jalapeño peppers, deseeded and minced
4 cloves garlic, peeled and minced
1 tablespoon thyme

1 tablespoon curry powder
1½ Teaspoons ground allspice
1 teaspoon freshly ground black pepper
1 (15-ounce / 425-g) can diced tomatoes
4 cups cooked black beans

1. Add the red bell pepper and onion to a saucepan and sauté over medium heat for 10 minutes, or until the onion is softened. Add water 1 to 2 tablespoons at a time to keep the vegetables from sticking to the pan.

2. Stir in the jalapeño peppers, garlic, thyme, curry powder, allspice and black pepper. Cook for 3 to 4 minutes, then add the tomatoes and black beans. Cook over medium heat for 20 minutes, covered.
3. Serve immediately.

Per Serving
Calories: 283 | fat: 1.7g | carbs: 52.8g | protein: 17.4g | fiber: 19.8g

Walnut, Coconut, and Oat Granola

Prep time: 15 minutes | Cook time: 1 hour 40 minutes | Makes 4¼ cups

1 cup chopped walnuts
1 cup unsweetened, shredded coconut
2 cups rolled oats
1 teaspoon ground cinnamon
2 tablespoons hemp seeds
2 tablespoons ground flaxseeds

2 tablespoons chia seeds
¾ teaspoon salt (optional)
¼ cup maple syrup
¼ cup water
1 teaspoon vanilla extract
½ cup dried cranberries

1. Preheat the oven to 250°F (120°C). Line a baking sheet with parchment paper.
2. Mix the walnuts, coconut, rolled oats, cinnamon, hemp seeds, flaxseeds, chia seeds, and salt (if desired) in a bowl.
3. Combine the maple syrup and water in a saucepan. Bring to a boil over medium heat, then pour in the bowl of walnut mixture.
4. Add the vanilla extract to the bowl of mixture. Stir to mix well. Pour the mixture in the baking sheet, then level with a spatula so the mixture coat the bottom evenly.
5. Place the baking sheet in the preheated oven and bake for 90 minutes or until browned and crispy. Stir the mixture every 15 minutes.
6. Remove the baking sheet from the oven. Allow to cool for 10 minutes, then serve with dried cranberries on top.

Per Serving (4¼ cups)
Calories: 1870 | fat: 115.8g | carbs: 238.0g | protein: 59.8g | fiber: 68.9g

Bean and Summer Squash Sauté

Prep time: 10 minutes | Cook time: 15 to 16 minutes | Serves 4

1 medium red onion, peeled and thinly sliced
4 yellow squash, cut into ½-inch rounds
4 medium zucchinis, cut into ½-inch rounds
1 (15-ounce / 425-g) can navy beans,
drained and rinsed
2 cups corn kernels
Zest of 2 lemons
1 cup finely chopped basil
Salt, to taste (optional)
Freshly ground black pepper, to taste

1. Place the onion in a large saucepan and sauté over medium heat for 7 to 8 minutes. Add water 1 to 2 tablespoons at a time to keep the onion from sticking to the pan.
2. Add the squash, zucchini, beans, and corn and cook for about 8 minutes, or until the squash is softened.
3. Remove from the heat. Stir in the lemon zest and basil. Season with salt (if desired) and pepper.
4. Serve hot.

Per Serving
Calories: 298 | fat: 2.2g | carbs: 60.4g | protein: 17.2g | fiber: 13.6g

Crispy Buckwheat

Prep time: 15 minutes | Cook time: 50 minutes | Makes 5 Cups

1 cup raw buckwheat groats, soaked in water for at least 1 hour, well rinsed
½ cup raw sunflower seeds
1 cup sliced almonds
1 cup large flake coconut
2 tablespoons chia seeds
¼ teaspoon ground ginger
¼ teaspoon ground nutmeg
1½ Teaspoons ground cinnamon
3 tablespoons maple sugar
¼ teaspoon sea salt (optional)
¼ cup maple syrup
1 teaspoon vanilla extract

1. Preheat the oven to 325ºF (163ºC). Line a baking sheet with parchment paper.
2. Combine the buckwheat groats with remaining ingredients in a large bowl. Toss to coat well.
3. Spread the mixture on the baking sheet to coat the bottom evenly. Bake in the preheated oven for 50 minutes or until lightly browned and crispy. Flip them halfway through the cooking time.
4. Remove the crispy buckwheat from the oven and allow to cool before serving.

Per Serving (1 cup)
Calories: 369 | fat: 23.8g | carbs: 34.7g | protein: 9.5g | fiber: 8.3g

Peppers and Black Beans with Brown Rice

Prep time: 15 minutes | Cook time: 20 minutes | Serves 4

2 jalapeño peppers, diced
1 red bell pepper, seeded and diced
1 medium yellow onion, peeled and diced
2 tablespoons low-sodium vegetable broth
1 teaspoon toasted and ground cumin seeds
1½ Teaspoons toasted oregano
5 cloves garlic, peeled and minced
4 cups cooked black beans
Salt, to taste (optional)
Ground black pepper, to taste
3 cups cooked brown rice
1 lime, quartered
1 cup chopped cilantro

1. Add the jalapeño peppers, bell pepper, and onion to a saucepan and sauté for 7 minutes or until the onion is well browned and caramelized.
2. Add vegetable broth, cumin, oregano, and garlic to the pan and sauté for 3 minutes or until fragrant.
3. Add the black beans and sauté for 10 minutes or until the vegetables are tender. Sprinkle with salt (if desired) and black pepper halfway through.
4. Arrange the brown rice on a platter, then top with the cooked vegetables. Garnish with lime wedges and cilantro before serving.

Per Serving
Calories: 426 | fat: 2.6g | carbs: 82.4g | protein: 20.2g | fiber: 19.5g

Rice with Almond, Parsley, and Cranberries

Prep time: 10 minutes | Cook time: 40 minutes | Serves 2

1 cup wild and brown rice blend, rinsed
¼ teaspoon ground sumac
¼ cup chopped almonds, for garnish
¼ cup chopped fresh flat-leaf parsley
¼ cup unsweetened dried cranberries
½ teaspoon ground coriander
1 teaspoon apple cider vinegar
2 green onions, thinly sliced
Salt, to taste (optional)
Ground black or white pepper, to taste

1. Pour the rice blend in a saucepan, then pour in the water to cover the rice by about 1 inch. Bring to a boil over medium-high heat. Reduce the heat to low. Put the pan lid on and simmer for 40 minutes or until the water is absorbed. Transfer the rice to a bowl and allow to cool for 5 minutes.
2. Add the remaining ingredient to the bowl and toss to combine well. Serve immediately.

Per Serving
Calories: 105 | fat: 0.9g | carbs: 21.1g | protein: 3.1g | fiber: 3.0g

Simple Maple Navy Bean Bake

Prep time: 50 minutes | Cook time: 2 hours | Serves 8 to 10

1 pound (454 g) dried navy beans, soaked overnight and drained, cooked
1 medium sweet onion, chopped (about 1 cup)
1 tablespoon grainy mustard
2 teaspoons smoked paprika
¼ cup tomato paste
¼ cup apple cider
vinegar
¼ cup unsulfured molasses
½ cup maple syrup
6 Medjool dates, pitted and chopped
2 cups low-sodium vegetables broth, plus more if necessary
Salt, to taste (optional)
Ground black or white pepper, to taste

1. Preheat the oven to 325ºF (163ºC).
2. Combine all the ingredients in an oven-safe pot. Stir to mix well.

3. Put the pot lid on and cook in the preheated oven for 2 hours or until the mixture is lightly saucy. Stir the mixture and add more vegetable broth if necessary every half an hour.
4. Remove the pot from the oven and serve the beans warm.

Per Serving
Calories: 241 | fat: 1.3g | carbs: 55.9g | protein: 6.6g | fiber: 4.0g

Lemony Farro and Pine Nut Chard Rolls

Prep time: 40 minutes | Cook time: 30 minutes | Serves 4

1 cup semi-pearled farro
¼ cup toasted and chopped pine nuts
1 teaspoon nutritional yeast
1 tablespoon fresh lemon juice
1 teaspoon lemon
zest
Salt, to taste (optional)
Ground black or white pepper, to taste
8 chard leaves
2 cups low-sodium marinara sauce
½ cup water

1. Preheat the oven to 350ºF (180ºC).
2. Combine the cooked farro, pine nuts, nutritional yeast, lemon juice and zest, salt (if desired), and pepper in a mixing bowl. Set aside.
3. Remove the stems of the chard leaves so you have 16 chard leaf halves, then blanch the leaves in a bowl of boiling water for 5 minutes or until wilted.
4. Pour ½ cup of marinara sauce on a baking dish. Take a chard half, then spoon 2 tablespoons of farro mixture in the middle of the leaf half. Fold the leaf over the filling, then tuck the leaf and roll up to wrap the filling. Repeat with remaining chard and farro mixture.
5. Arrange the chard rolls on the baking dish over the marinara sauce, seam side down, then top them with remaining marinara sauce and water.
6. Cover the baking dish with aluminum foil and bake in the preheated oven for 30 minutes or until the sauce bubbles.
7. Remove the chard rolls from the oven and serve immediately.

Per Serving
Calories: 254 | fat: 9.0g | carbs: 39.0g | protein: 7.7g | fiber: 6.5g

Easy Chickpea Salad Sandwiches

Prep time: 15 minutes | Cook time: 0 minutes | Serves 6

15 ounces (425 g) cooked chickpeas
1 tablespoon lemon juice
½ cup vegan mayonnaise
Salt, to taste (optional)
¼ cup water
1/3 cup finely chopped dill pickles
2 celery ribs, finely chopped
2 tablespoons minced fresh parsley
2 scallions, sliced thin
Ground black or white pepper, to taste
12 slices hearty multigrain bread, toasted

1. Add the chickpeas, lemon juice, mayo, salt (if desired), and water to a food processor. Pulse until creamy and smooth. Pour the mixture in a bowl and set aside.
2. Add the pickles, celery, parsley, and scallions to the bowl of chickpea mixture. Sprinkle with salt (if desired) and pepper, then stir to combine well.
3. Assemble the chickpea mixture with bread slices to make 6 sandwiches and serve immediately.

Per Serving
Calories: 344 | fat: 10.2g | carbs: 50.1g | protein: 14.1g | fiber: 8.7g

Falafel with Tahini-Milk Sauce

Prep time: 20 minutes | Cook time: 12 minutes | Serves 6 to 8

Falafel:
12 ounces (340 g) dried chickpeas (about 2 cups), soaked in water overnight
1 cup fresh parsley leaves
1 cup fresh cilantro leaves
10 scallions, chopped coarsely
1/8 Teaspoon ground cinnamon
½ teaspoon ground cumin
6 garlic cloves, minced
½ cup low -sodium vegetable broth
Salt, to taste (optional)
Ground black or white pepper, to taste
Sauce:
1/3 cup tahini
3 tablespoons lemon juice
1 garlic clove, minced
1/3 cup unsweetened coconut milk
Salt, to taste (optional)
Ground black or white pepper, to taste

1. Preheat the oven to 375ºF (190ºC). Line baking sheet with parchment paper.
2. Add the soaked chickpeas, parsley, cilantro, scallions, cinnamon, cumin, garlic, vegetables broth, salt (if desired), and pepper to a food processor. Pulse until smooth and creamy.
3. Make the falafel: Drop 2 tablespoons of chickpea mixture on the baking sheet, then flatten with a spatula to make a ½-inch thick and 1-inch wide disk. Repeat with remaining chickpea mixture.
4. Slide the baking sheet in the preheated oven and bake for 4 to 6 minutes or until crispy and well browned. Flip the falafel halfway through.
5. Meanwhile, make the sauce: Combine all the ingredients for the sauce in a bowl. Stir to mix well.
6. Serve the falafel immediately with the sauce.

Per Serving
Calories: 264 | fat: 9.9g | carbs: 35.3g | protein: 11.8g | fiber: 7.8g

Confetti Bean Bowls

Prep time: 15 minutes | Cook time: 10 minutes | Serves 6

¼ cup water
2 red or green bell peppers, chopped
1 onion, chopped
1 to 2 cloves garlic, pressed
3 cups cooked pinto beans
1 (15-ounce / 425-g) can stewed tomatoes
2 cups frozen corn kernels
1 tablespoon chili powder
Freshly ground black pepper, to taste

1. Heat the water in a saucepan over medium-high heat.
2. Add the bell pepper, onion, and garlic to the pan and sauté for 5 minutes or until tender and fragrant.
3. Stir in the remaining ingredients. Reduce the heat to low, cover, and cook for 5 more minutes. Stir periodically.
4. Divide and pour the bean mixture into 6 bowls and serve immediately.

Per Serving
Calories: 216 | fat: 1.7g | carbs: 41.6g | protein: 10.8g | fiber: 11.8g

Veggie Paella

Prep time: 15 minutes | Cook time: 52 to 58 minutes | Serves 4

1 onion, coarsely chopped
8 medium mushrooms, sliced
2 small zucchinis, cut in half, then sliced ½ inch thick
1 leek, rinsed and sliced
2 large cloves garlic, crushed
1 medium tomato, coarsely chopped
3 cups low-sodium vegetable broth
1¼ cups long-grain brown rice
½ teaspoon crushed saffron threads
Freshly ground black pepper, to taste
½ cup frozen green peas
½ cup water
Chopped fresh parsley, for garnish

1. Pour the water in a large wok. Add the onion and sauté for 5 minutes, or until most of the liquid is absorbed.
2. Stir in the mushrooms, zucchini, leek, and garlic and cook for 2 to 3 minutes, or until softened slightly.
3. Add the tomato, broth, rice, saffron, and pepper. Bring to a boil. Reduce the heat and simmer, covered, for 30 minutes.
4. Add the peas and continue to cook for another 5 to 10 minutes. Remove from the heat and let rest for 10 minutes to allow any excess moisture to be absorbed.
5. Sprinkle with the parsley before serving.

Per Serving
Calories: 418 | fat: 3.9g | carbs: 83.2g | protein: 12.7g | fiber: 9.2g

Black-Eyed Pea, Beet, and Carrot Stew

Prep time: 15 minutes | Cook time: 40 minutes | Serves 2

½ cup black-eyed peas, soaked in water overnight
3 cups water
1 large beet, peeled and cut into ½-inch pieces (about ¾ cup)
1 large carrot, peeled and cut into ½-inch pieces (about ¾ cup)
¼ teaspoon turmeric
¼ teaspoon toasted
and ground cumin seeds
⅛ Teaspoon asafetida
¼ cup finely chopped parsley
¼ teaspoon cayenne pepper
¼ teaspoon salt (optional)
½ teaspoon fresh lime juice

1. Pour the black-eyed peas and water in a pot, then cook over medium heat for 25 minutes.
2. Add the beet and carrot to the pot and cook for 10 more minutes. Add more water if necessary.
3. Add the turmeric, cumin, asafetida, parsley, and cayenne pepper to the pot and cook for an additional 6 minutes or until the vegetables are soft. Stir the mixture periodically. Sprinkle with salt, if desired.
4. Drizzle the lime juice on top before serving in a large bowl.

Per Serving
Calories: 84 | fat: 0.7g | carbs: 16.6g | protein: 4.1g | fiber: 4.5g

Ritzy Fava Bean Ratatouille

Prep time: 15 minutes | Cook time: 40 minutes | Serves 4

1 medium red onion, peeled and thinly sliced
2 tablespoons low-sodium vegetable broth
1 large eggplant, stemmed and cut into ½-inch dice
1 red bell pepper, seeded and diced
2 cups cooked fava beans
2 Roma tomatoes, chopped
1 medium zucchini, diced
2 cloves garlic, peeled and finely chopped
¼ cup finely chopped basil
Salt, to taste (optional)
Ground black pepper, to taste

1. Add the onion to a saucepan and sauté for 7 minutes or until caramelized.
2. Add the vegetable broth, eggplant and red bell pepper to the pan and sauté for 10 more minutes.
3. Add the fava beans, tomatoes, zucchini, and garlic to the pan and sauté for an additional 5 minutes.
4. Reduce the heat to medium-low. Put the pan lid on and cook for 15 minutes or until the vegetables are soft. Stir the vegetables halfway through.
5. Transfer them onto a large serving plate. Sprinkle with basil, salt (if desired), and black pepper before serving.

Per Serving
Calories: 114 | fat: 1.0g | carbs: 24.2g | protein: 7.4g | fiber: 10.3g

Mashed White Beans, Potatoes, and Kale

Prep time: 10 minutes | Cook time: 30 minutes | Serves 4

2 large Russet potatoes, rinsed, quartered, then halve each quarter
½ cup low-sodium vegetable soup
1 (14.5-ounce / 411-g) can great northern beans or other white

beans, rinsed and drained
6 ounces (170 g) kale, torn into bite-size pieces
Salt, to taste (optional)
¼ teaspoon freshly ground black pepper

1. Put the potato pieces in a pot, and then pour in enough water to cover. Bring to a boil over medium-high heat. Reduce the heat to medium, cover, and simmer for 20 minutes or until soft.
2. Transfer the potatoes in a colander and rinse under running water. Drain the potatoes and put them back to the pot. Pour the vegetable soup over.
3. Add the beans and kale to the pot, cover and simmer over low heat for 5 minutes or until the kale is wilted.
4. Pour the mixture into a food processor. Sprinkle with salt (if desired) and pepper and pulse until creamy and smooth.
5. Serve immediately.

Per Serving
Calories: 255 | fat: 1.0g | carbs: 53.0g | protein: 12.0g | fiber: 11.0g

Easy Tahini Green Beans

Prep time: 10 minutes | Cook time: 5 minutes | Serves 2

¼ cup water
1 pound (454 g) green beans, rinsed and trimmed
2 tablespoons organic tahini
Zest and juice of 1 lemon

1 garlic clove, minced
Salt and ground black pepper, to taste (optional)
1 teaspoon toasted black or white sesame seeds

1. Pour the water in a saucepan, and then add the green beans and steam over medium-high heat for 5 minutes or until the green beans are tender.

2. Remove the green beans from the pan and reserve about ¼ cup of juice remains in the pan.
3. Combine the tahini, lemon zest and juice, garlic, salt (if desired), and pepper in a large bowl. Thin with the reserved juice as needed.
4. Toss the green beans with the tahini mixture and sprinkle with sesame seeds to serve.

Per Serving
Calories: 154 | fat: 9.8g | carbs: 15.5g | protein: 5.5g | fiber: 6.0g

Fresh Green Pea Risotto

Prep time: 5 minutes | Cook time: 33 minutes | Serves 4

1 teaspoon coconut butter
4 Teaspoons minced garlic
2 cups low-sodium vegetable soup
1 cup Arborio rice, rinsed and drained
¼ teaspoon sea salt (optional)

3 tablespoons lemon juice
2 tablespoons nutritional yeast
2 cups fresh green peas, cooked
¼ to ½ teaspoon freshly ground black pepper

1. Heat the coconut butter in a skillet over medium-high heat. Add the garlic to the skillet and sauté for about 3 minutes, or until fragrant.
2. Pour the soup and rice into the skillet and season with sea salt (if desired), if desired. Whisk to mix well. Bring to a boil. Reduce the heat to low and cook for about 30 minutes, or until the soup is absorbed and the rice is cooked through.
3. Add the lemon juice and nutritional yeast to the skillet and stir well. Whisk the peas in the rice mixture and season with black pepper.
4. Remove the skillet from the heat and let rest for 5 minutes before dividing the risotto among 4 bowls. Serve warm.

Per Serving
Calories: 143 | fat: 1.8g | carbs: 23.9g | protein: 10.1g | fiber: 7.2g

Fragrant Moroccan Chickpeas

Prep time: 10 minutes | Cook time: 2 hours | Serves 6

2 cups dried chick-peas, soaked in water overnight
8 cups cold water
1 bay leaf
1 cup chopped onion
2 cloves garlic, crushed
1 teaspoon ground turmeric
1 teaspoon ground ginger
2 tablespoons chopped fresh parsley
1 cinnamon stick
¼ teaspoon freshly ground black pepper
½ cup raisins

1. Pour the soaked chickpeas in a pot, then pour in the water and add the bay leaf. Bring to a boil.
2. Reduce the heat to low and simmer for 45 to 60 minutes or until the chickpeas are soft.
3. Add the remaining ingredients, except for the raisins, and cook for another hour, then add the raisins and cook for an additional 15 minutes.
4. Remove the bay leaf and cinnamon stick, then serve the chickpeas immediately.

Per Serving
Calories: 307 | fat: 4.2g | carbs: 56.1g | protein: 14.5g | fiber: 9.5g

Lentil Burgers

Prep time: 40 minutes | Cook time: 30 to 40 minutes | Makes 12 Burgers

1 cup lentils
2½ to 3 cups water
1 small onion, diced
3 carrots, grated
¾ cup almond flour
1½ to 2 teaspoons
curry powder
½ teaspoon sea salt (optional)
Ground black pepper, to taste

1. Put the lentils in a pot, then pour in the water. Bring to a boil, then reduce the heat to low and simmer for 30 minutes or until tender and the water is absorbed.
2. Meanwhile, combine the onion and carrots with flour, curry powder, salt (if desired), and pepper in a large bowl. Toss to coat well.
3. Remove the lentils from the pot and pat dry with paper towels, then add them to the bowl of carrots and onion. Stir to combine well.

4. Make the burgers: Pour the mixture in a food processor and pulse until smooth and sticky. Divide the mixture into 12 patties.
5. Preheat the oven to 350ºF (180ºC). Line a baking sheet with parchment paper.
6. Arrange the burgers on the baking sheet, then bake in the preheated oven for 30 minutes or until browned on both sides. Flip the burgers halfway through the cooking time. You may need to work in batches to avoid overcrowding.
7. Remove the burgers from the oven and serve immediately.

Per Serving (1 burger)
Calories: 114 | fat: 11.0g | carbs: 9.0g | protein: 6.0g | fiber: 7.0g

Red Beans with Cauliflower Rice

Prep time: 15 minutes | Cook time: 17 minutes | Serves 4

1 large head cauliflower
2 tablespoons avocado oil (optional)
½ cup diced celery ribs
½ cup chopped green bell pepper
½ cup chopped sweet onion
1½ cups cooked red beans
1 cup cooked brown rice
2 teaspoons cumin
1 tablespoon minced garlic
1 teaspoon chili powder
½ teaspoon basil
½ teaspoon chopped fresh parsley
1 teaspoon paprika
½ teaspoon ground black pepper
2 cups water

1. Pulse the cauliflower in a food processor to make the cauliflower rice. Set aside.
2. Heat the avocado oil (if desired) in a skillet over medium-high heat.
3. Add the celery, green pepper, and onion to the skillet and sauté for 7 minutes or until tender.
4. Add the remaining ingredients to the skillet and sauté for 10 minutes until well combined and the cauliflower rice is soft.
5. Serve immediately.

Per Serving
Calories: 278 | fat: 8.9g | carbs: 41.9g | protein: 12.0g | fiber: 11.4g

Refried Pinto Beans

Prep time: 10 minutes | Cook time: 3 to 4 hours | Makes 6 cups

2 cups pinto beans
8 cups water
½ teaspoon onion powder

½ teaspoon garlic powder
½ to 1 cup mild or spicy salsa

1. Pour the water into a saucepan over medium-high heat and add the beans. Bring to a boil. Decrease the heat to medium-low. Cover and simmer for 3 to 4 hours, or until the beans become softened. Drain the beans and reserve the cooking liquid for later use.
2. Add the drained beans to a blender and pulse until smooth and creamy. Pour the bean mash back to the saucepan over low heat. Season with the onion powder and garlic powder. Add 1 tablespoon of the cooking liquid and the salsa. Stir constantly until the bean mash is heat through and the flavors are well blended.
3. Serve hot.

Per Serving (1 cup)
Calories: 231 | fat: 0.8g | carbs: 42.1g | protein: 14.2g | fiber: 10.4g

Red Bean with Tomatoes

Prep time: 15 minutes | Cook time: 3 hours | Serves 8 to 10

2 cups red beans
3 onions, chopped
8 cloves garlic, crushed
1 jalapeño pepper, deseeded and chopped
2 stalks celery, chopped
6 bay leaves
1 (4-ounce / 113-g) can chopped green chilies
1 (16-ounce / 454-g) can whole tomatoes, chopped with liquid
1 (15-ounce /425-g) can tomato sauce
6 cups water
2 tablespoons paprika

2 tablespoons chopped fresh parsley
2 teaspoons white pepper
1 teaspoon dried marjoram
1 teaspoon dried savory
1 teaspoon dried tarragon
1 teaspoon dried rosemary
1 teaspoon dried basil
1 teaspoon dried thyme
1 teaspoon dried oregano
1 teaspoon pepper sauce

1. Add all the ingredients to a large saucepan over medium-low heat. Bring to a boil. Cover and simmer for about 3 hours, or until the red beans become softened.
2. Serve hot.

Per Serving
Calories: 256 | fat: 1.2g | carbs: 48.8g | protein: 13.4g | fiber: 13.5g

Brown Rice with Tofu Satay

Prep time: 10 minutes | Cook time: 20 minutes | Serves 4

¾ cup cooked brown rice
2 tablespoons coconut oil (optional)
15 ounces (425 g) extra-firm tofu, pressed and cubed
½ yellow onion, diced
3 garlic cloves, minced
1-inch piece fresh ginger, minced
1 red chile, thinly

sliced
2 tablespoons coconut aminos
¼ cup peanut butter
1 (13.5-ounce / 383-g) can unsweetened coconut milk
½ teaspoon salt (optional)
¼ teaspoon freshly ground black pepper
1 scallions, chopped
1 lime, wedged

1. Heat the coconut oil (if desired) in a skillet over medium-high heat.
2. Add the tofu and cook for 10 minutes or until lightly browned on all sides. Stir constantly.
3. Remove the tofu from the skillet and add the chile, onion, ginger, and garlic. Sauté for 3 minutes or until fragrant.
4. Stir in the peanut butter, coconut amino, and coconut milk. Sprinkle with salt (if desired) and ground black pepper. Keep cooking and stirring for 5 minutes or until the mixture starts to thicken and becomes bubbly.
5. Turn off the heat and add the tofu back to the skillet. Toss to coat well.
6. Divide the cooked brown rice among 4 bowls, then top the rice with the tofu and the sauce mixture. Spread with scallions over and squeeze the lime wedges on top. Serve immediately.

Per Serving
Calories: 621 | fat: 41.0g | carbs: 41.0g | protein: 22.0g | fiber: 6.0g

Brown Rice with Beans and Peas

Prep time: 5 minutes | Cook time: 13 minutes | Serves 4

¼ cup low-sodium vegetable soup
2 cups fresh green beans
2 cups fresh green peas
1 teaspoon onion powder
1 teaspoon garlic powder
4 cups brown rice, cooked

1. Heat the vegetable soup in a saucepan over medium heat. Add the green beans, green peas, onion powder and garlic powder to the saucepan and stir. Cover and cook for 8 minutes, stirring constantly, or until the vegetables become softened. Add 1 to 2 tablespoons of vegetable soup to avoid sticking.
2. Pour the brown rice into the saucepan and stir until well mixed. Cook for another 5 minutes, stirring constantly.
3. Let cool for 5 minutes before serving.

Per Serving
Calories: 232 | fat: 11.8g | carbs: 8.1g | protein: 7.9g | fiber: 6.8g

Super Three-Bean and Grains Bowl

Prep time: 30 minutes | Cook time: 50 minutes | Serves 8

2 tablespoons water
1 medium onion, chopped
1 (15-ounce / 425-g) can black beans, drained and rinsed
1 (15-ounce / 425-g) can kidney beans, drained and rinsed
1 (15-ounce / 425-g) can garbanzo beans, drained and rinsed
2 cups long-grain brown rice
1 (15-ounce / 425-g) can stewed tomatoes
4 cups low-sodium vegetable soup
2 cups frozen corn kernels
1 (4-ounce / 113-g) can chopped green chilies

1. Heat the water in a saucepan over medium-high heat.
2. Add the onion and sauté for 3 minutes or until translucent.
3. Add the beans, rice, and tomatoes. Pour in the vegetable soup. Bring to a boil. Keep stirring.
4. Reduce the heat to low. Cover the pan and simmer for 30 minutes or until the beans and rice are soft. Stir periodically.
5. Add the corn and chilies, simmer for 15 more minutes. Stir periodically.
6. Allow to cool for 15 minutes before serving.

Per Serving
Calories: 688 | fat: 5.5g | carbs: 130.1g | protein: 32.1g | fiber: 27.8g

Easy Mushroom Polenta

Prep time: 5 minutes | Cook time: 25 minutes | Serves 6

4 cups low-sodium vegetable soup
2 cups water
1¾ cups cornmeal
1 teaspoon ground cumin
½ teaspoon ground turmeric
1 teaspoon salt (optional)
1 teaspoon avocado
oil (optional)
2 cups chopped white mushrooms
1 tablespoon lemon juice (about ½ small lemon)
¼ cup nutritional yeast
2 teaspoons vegan butter

1. Make the polenta: Pour the vegetable soup and water in a saucepan. Bring to a boil.
2. Fold in the cornmeal, cumin, turmeric, and salt (if desired). Reduce the heat to low and simmer for 15 minutes or until it has a thick consistency.
3. Meanwhile, heat the avocado oil (if desired) in another saucepan over medium-high heat.
4. Add the mushrooms and sauté for 5 minutes or until tender. Set aside.
5. Remove the polenta from the saucepan, then mix in the remaining ingredients.
6. Divide the polenta among 6 bowls and serve warm.

Per Serving
Calories: 174 | fat: 4.0g | carbs: 32.0g | protein: 5.0g | fiber: 4.0g

Sloppy Black Bean Burgers

Prep time: 20 minutes | Cook time: 5 minutes | Serves 4

¼ cup low-sodium vegetable soup
1 cup fresh tomato, cubed
1 (7-ounce / 198-g) pack textured soya mince
1 cup cooked black beans
¼ cup no-salt-added taco seasoning
4 whole-wheat buns, split in half
1 medium red onion, chopped
2 tablespoons tahini

1. Heat the vegetable soup in a saucepan over medium-high heat.
2. Add the tomato cubes and soya mince and sauté for 3 minutes or until the tomatoes are tender.
3. Add the beans and sprinkle with taco seasoning. Sauté for 2 more minutes.
4. Remove the pan from the heat and allow to cool for 5 minutes, then divide the bean mix over 4 bun halves.
5. Spread the onion and tahini on top of the bean mix and place the remaining halves over to make 4 burgers.
6. Serve immediately.

Per Serving
Calories: 483 | fat: 22.0g | carbs: 62.5g | protein: 10.3g | fiber: 8.5g

Kale and Sweet Potato Quinoa

Prep time: 10 minutes | Cook time: 19 minutes | Serves 4

¼ cup olive oil (optional)
1 yellow onion, diced
2 tablespoons ground coriander
2 tablespoons ground cumin
2 tablespoons mustard powder
2 tablespoons ground turmeric
2 teaspoons ground cinnamon
1 large sweet potato, diced
1¼ cup uncooked quinoa
4 cups water
1 bunch kale, rinsed and chopped
Salt, to taste (optional)
Freshly ground black pepper, to taste

1. In a large pot, heat the oil (if desired) over medium-high heat. Add the onion and sauté for 3 minutes. Stir in the coriander, cumin, mustard powder, turmeric and cinnamon. Cook for about 1 minute, or until fragrant.
2. Add the sweet potatoes and stir until well coated with the spices.
3. Stir in the quinoa and water. Cover with a lid and bring to a boil over high heat, stirring occasionally. Once the liquid is boiling, remove the lid and reduce the heat to medium-low. Simmer for 15 minutes.
4. Once the water is mostly absorbed and the sweet potato is cooked through, stir in the kale. Remove from the heat and cover with a lid. Let sit for 10 to 15 minutes. The residual heat will cook the kale and the quinoa will absorb the remaining water.
5. Taste and season with salt (if desired) and pepper. Divide evenly among 4 meal prep containers and let cool completely before putting on lids and refrigerating.

Per Serving
Calories: 457 | fat: 16.2g | carbs: 67.9g | protein: 10.1g | fiber: 12.2g

Gold Chickpea Poppers

Prep time: 15 minutes | Cook time: 25 minutes | Serves 3

2 cups cooked chickpeas
½ teaspoon garlic powder
¼ teaspoon onion powder
½ teaspoon salt (optional)
1 tablespoon coconut oil (optional)
½ teaspoon chili powder
¼ teaspoon cumin
¼ teaspoon ground cayenne pepper
¼ teaspoon paprika

1. Preheat the oven to 400ºF (205ºC). Line a baking pan with parchment paper.
2. Pour the chickpeas on the baking pan and top with the garlic powder, onion powder, salt (if desired), and coconut oil (if desired). Toss to combine well.
3. Bake in the preheated oven for 25 minutes or until the chickpeas are golden and crispy. Stir the chickpeas every 5 minutes.
4. Transfer the toasted chickpeas to a large bowl and allow to cool for 10 minutes. Sprinkle with remaining spices and serve.

Per Serving
Calories: 192 | fat: 7.8g | carbs: 21.5g | protein: 9.1g | fiber: 12.8g

Vegan Corn on the Cob

Prep time: 5 minutes | Cook time: 20 minutes | Serves 4

4 ears of corn, shucked
$1/_3$ cup almond butter
$1/_3$ cup plant-based sour cream
1 tablespoon finely minced cilantro
2 cloves garlic,
minced
¼ teaspoon sea salt
½ cup crumbled vegan feta cheese
1 teaspoon paprika
1 tablespoon fresh lime juice

1. Preheat oven to 400ºF (205ºC). Line a baking pan with parchment paper.
2. Pour the corn in the baking pan, then roast in the preheated oven for 20 minutes or until the corn is lightly charred.
3. Meanwhile, combine the almond butter, sour cream, cilantro, garlic, and salt (if desired) in a small bowl. Stir to mix well.
4. Transfer the roasted corn on a large plate and spread the mayo mixture over, then scatter with feta cheese. Sprinkle with paprika and drizzle with lime juice to serve.

Per Serving
Calories: 321 | fat: 20.6g | carbs: 30.4g | protein: 8.8g | fiber: 4.1g

Veggie-Packed Quinoa Pilaf

Prep time: 10 minutes | Cook time: 18 to 23 minutes | Serves 4

1 cup dry quinoa, rinsed and drained
2 teaspoons water
1 cup diced carrot
½ cup chopped red onion
1½ cups low-sodium vegetable soup
½ teaspoon dried thyme
½ teaspoon dried parsley
½ teaspoon sea salt (optional)
¼ to ½ cup chopped walnuts

1. Heat the water in a saucepan over medium-high heat. Add the carrot and onion to the saucepan and sauté for 3 minutes.
2. Stir in the quinoa, vegetable soup, thyme, parsley and sea salt (if desired). Bring to a boil. Decrease the heat to low. Cover and simmer for 15 to 20 minutes, or until the soup is absorbed and the quinoa becomes tender.

3. Remove the saucepan from the heat and let cool for 5 minutes. Fluff the quinoa and stir in the chopped walnuts.
4. Divide the cooked quinoa among 4 bowls and serve hot.

Per Serving
Calories: 201 | fat: 4.9g | carbs: 32.8g | protein: 6.8g | fiber: 5.2g

Mexican Quinoa with Beans and Corn

Prep time: 10 minutes | Cook time: 30 minutes | Serves 6

2 cups quinoa
4 cups water
2 tablespoons avocado oil (optional)
1 red onion, diced (about 9-ounce / 255-g)
1 red bell pepper, diced (about 7-ounce / 198-g)
1 (15-ounce / 425-g) can black beans, rinsed and drained
1 (15-ounce / 425-g)
can corn, rinsed and drained
1 bunch cilantro, rinsed
1 teaspoon ground cumin
1 teaspoon salt (optional)
½ teaspoon freshly ground black pepper
1 jalapeño, sliced
6 lime wedges, for serving

1. Pour the quinoa and water in a pot. Cover and bring to a boil over high heat. Reduce the heat to low and simmer for 15 more minutes or until the liquid is almost absorbed. Set the pot aside and fluffy with a fork.
2. Meanwhile, heat the oil (if desired) in a skillet over medium-high heat.
3. Add the onion and sauté for 3 minutes or until translucent. Add the bell pepper and sauté for 2 minutes.
4. Pour the sautéed onion and bell pepper in the pot of quinoa. Stir to mix well, then fold in the beans, corn, cilantro, cumin, salt (if desired), and pepper.
5. Divide the rice mix into 6 bowls, then top with slices jalapeño and squeeze the lime wedges over. Serve immediately.

Per Serving
Calories: 410 | fat: 10.0g | carbs: 66.0g | protein: 14.0g | fiber: 11.0g

Fast Farro Tabbouleh

Prep time: 20 minutes | Cook time: 25 minutes | Serves 4

1 cup farro, soaked overnight and drained
2½ cups water
1 English cucumber, diced
1 red or yellow bell pepper, finely diced
1 bunch flat-leaf parsley, leaves only, chopped
3 scallions, white and light green parts, sliced thinly
Zest and juice of 2 lemons
Handful mint leaves, chopped
¼ cup low-sodium vegetable soup
¼ teaspoon salt (optional)
⅛ Teaspoon ground black pepper

1. Pour the farro and water in a pot. Bring to a boil. Reduce the heat to low. Cover and cook for 25 minutes or until the liquid is almost absorbed. Stir periodically.
2. Allow the farro to cool for 10 minutes, then fluffy with a fork. Divide the farro among 4 or 6 bowls, then toss with remaining ingredients.
3. Serve warm.

Per Serving
Calories: 211 | fat: 1.8g | carbs: 44.4g | protein: 5.4g | fiber: 3.6g

Black Beans and Avocado on Toast

Prep time: 5 minutes | Cook time: 3 minutes | Serves 4

4 (½-inch-thick) slices whole-wheat crusty bread
4 ounces (113 g) cherry tomatoes, quartered
4 Teaspoons avocado oil, divided (optional)
Salt and ground black pepper, to taste (optional)
1 (15-ounce / 425-g) can black beans, rinsed and drained
½ teaspoon lime zest
1 tablespoon lime juice
¼ cup boiling water
1 ripe avocado, halved, pitted, and sliced thinly
¼ cup fresh cilantro leaves

1. Set the oven to boil and line a baking pan with parchment paper.
2. Arrange the bread slices on the baking pan and toast in the oven for 3 minutes or until golden brown on both sides. Flip the bread halfway through.
3. Meanwhile, put the cherry tomatoes in a large bowl. Drizzle with 1 teaspoon avocado oil (if desired) and sprinkle with salt (if desired) and black pepper. Toss to combine well.
4. Combine the black beans with lime zest and juice in a food processor. Pour in the boiling water. Drizzle with 1 tablespoon of avocado oil (if desired) and sprinkle with salt (if desired) and pepper. Pulse to mix well and leave some beans intact.
5. Transfer the toasted bread on a plate, then spread with mashed bean mixture on top. Place the avocado over the bean mixture and top the avocado with cherry tomatoes and cilantro leaves.
6. Serve immediately.

Per Serving
Calories: 513 | fat: 14.2g | carbs: 75.3g | protein: 25.0g | fiber: 20.1g

Cranberry Rice Bowl with Almonds

Prep time: 20 minutes | Cook time: 40 minutes | Serves 4

1 cup uncooked wild and brown rice blend, rinsed
¼ cup unsweetened dried cranberries
¼ cup chopped fresh flat-leaf parsley
2 green onions, thinly sliced
¼ teaspoon ground sumac
½ teaspoon ground coriander
1 teaspoon apple cider vinegar
2 teaspoons avocado oil (optional)
Salt and ground black pepper, to taste (optional)
¼ cup almonds, chopped, for garnish

1. Pour the wild and brown rice blend in a saucepan, then pour in enough water to cover the rice about 1 inch.
2. Bring to a boil. Reduce the heat to low. Cover and simmer for 40 minutes or until the liquid is almost absorbed.
3. Turn off the heat and allow to sit for 5 minutes, then fluff with a fork and divide the rice into 4 serving bowls.
4. Add the remaining ingredients, except for the almonds, to the rice bowls and toss to mix well. Spread with almonds on top for garnish and serve.

Per Serving
Calories: 103 | fat: 5.5g | carbs: 11.5g | protein: 2.8g | fiber: 2.2g

Appetizing Veggie Chili with Onion Toppings

Prep time: 15 minutes | Cook time: 60 minutes | Serves 6

2 cups dried pinto beans, rinsed and drained
1 (14.5-ounce/411 g) can no-salt-added fire-roasted diced tomatoes, undrained
1 cup chopped red onion
1 (1-ounce/28 g) packet vegetarian chili seasoning, such as Simply Organic, or chili seasonings of

your choice
6 cloves garlic, minced
4 cups unsalted vegetable stock
2 cups water
1 cup fresh or frozen whole kernel corn
Toppings such as chopped bell pepper, sliced green onions, and/or snipped fresh cilantro

1. In a cooker, combine the beans, tomatoes, onion, seasoning, and garlic. Add the stock and water.
2. Cover and cook on high heat for 60 minutes; stir in the corn for the last 15 minutes. Serve with toppings.

Per Serving
Calories: 1742| fat: 7.49g | carbs: 318.6g |

protein: 96g | fiber: 78.3g

Authentic Italian Zucchini Onion Sauté

Prep time: 25 minutes | Cook time: 25 minutes | Makes 6 cups

1 onion, chopped (1 cup)
1 large red bell pepper, chopped (1 cup)
6 cloves garlic, minced
1 teaspoon dried oregano
½ teaspoon dried thyme
3 medium zucchini, halved lengthwise and cut into ¼-inch slices

(4 cups)
1 (15-oz./28 g) can chickpeas, rinsed and drained (1½ cups)
1 cup oil-free marinara sauce
1 tablespoon white wine vinegar
Sea salt and freshly ground black pepper, to taste
8 to 10 fresh basil leaves, chopped

1. Heat an extra-large skillet over medium.
2. Add the first five ingredients (through thyme); cook 10 minutes, stirring often and adding water, 1 to 2 Tbsp. at a time, as needed to prevent sticking.

3. Add zucchini; cook 10 minutes more or until zucchini is tender. Stir in chickpeas, marinara sauce, and vinegar.
4. Season with salt and black pepper. Heat through. Serve immediately garnished with basil.

Per Serving
Calories: 973| fat: 11.8g | carbs: 173g | protein: 41.1g | fiber: 46.7g

Creamy Mushroom Wild Rice Soup

Prep time: 20 minutes | Cook time: 30 minutes | Serves 6

4 cups vegetable stock
1 (8-ounce/227 g) package button mushrooms, trimmed and quartered
¾ cup uncooked wild rice, rinsed and drained
½ cup thinly sliced leek (white part only)
4 cloves garlic,

minced
1 cup chopped red bell pepper
½ cup chopped carrot
¼ teaspoon sea salt
¼ cup almond flour
¼ cup chickpea flour
1 tablespoon snipped fresh thyme
1 tablespoon white wine vinegar

1. Combine the stock, mushrooms, wild rice, leek, and garlic in a 5-quart Dutch oven or soup pot.
2. Bring to a boil over high heat; reduce heat to medium-low. Cover and simmer for 35 minutes or until the rice is tender (kernels will start to pop open).
3. Stir in the bell peppers, carrot, and salt. Cover and simmer for 8 minutes more.
4. Combine the almond flour and chickpea flour in a small bowl; stir in ¼ cup water.
5. Stir the mixture into the soup. Cook, stirring constantly, for 1 to 2 minutes or until thick and bubbly.
6. Stir in up to ½ cup more water to reach the desired consistency. Stir in the thyme and vinegar.

Per Serving
Calories: 776| fat: 7.3g | carbs: 123g | protein: 43.34g | fiber: 14.4g

Vegan Baked Potato with Black Beans

Prep time: 20 minutes | Cook time: 30 minutes | Serves 1

1 large baking potato
1½ teaspoons nutritional yeast (optional)
½ cup black beans, either canned or prepared as directed for Black Beans
¼ cup salsa of your choice

¼ to ½ avocado, cubed, sliced, or smashed
Salt and black pepper, to taste
Cilantro for garnish
Lime wedges for garnish

1. Preheat the oven to 450°F (230°C) if baking the potato (rather than microwaving it).
2. Pierce the potato with a fork or knife a few times to allow the steam to escape. Bake in the oven for about 40 minutes, or microwave for 4 to 6 minutes, depending on the size of the potato. Pierce the potato with a fork or knife to check if it is soft and cooked through.
3. When the potato is done, slice it open, and sprinkle on the nutritional yeast, if using.
4. Layer on the black beans, salsa, and avocado. Season with salt and pepper, if using, and garnish with cilantro and lime.
5. Enjoy your yummy, healthy meal!

Per Serving
Calories: 743| fat: 9.57g | carbs: 137g | protein: 32.84g | fiber: 26.6g

Italian Style Tender Zucchini Pepper Sauté

Prep time: 25 minutes | Cook time: 25 minutes | Serves 6

1 onion, chopped (1 cup)
1 large red bell pepper, chopped (1 cup)
6 cloves garlic, minced
1 teaspoon dried oregano
½ teaspoon dried thyme
3 medium zucchini, halved lengthwise and cut into ¼-inch slices

(4 cups)
1 15-oz.(425 g) can chickpeas, rinsed and drained (1½ cups)
1 cup oil-free marinara sauce
1 tablespoon white wine vinegar
Sea salt and freshly ground black pepper, to taste
8 to 10 fresh basil leaves, chopped

1. Heat an extra-large skillet over medium.
2. Add the first five ingredients (through thyme); cook 10 minutes, stirring often and adding water, 1 to 2 tablespoons at a time, as needed to prevent sticking.
3. Add zucchini; cook 10 minutes more or until zucchini is tender. Stir in chickpeas, marinara sauce, and vinegar.
4. Season with salt and black pepper. Heat through. Serve immediately garnished with basil.

Per Serving
Calories: 2617| fat: 229g | carbs: 119g | protein: 34.3g | fiber: 30.6g

Stove-Top Cashew Macaroni Cheese

Prep time: 15minutes | Cook time: 30 minutes | Serves 2

1 large russet potato, peeled and cut into ½-inch cubes (1½ cups)
1 cup chopped carrots
½ cup chopped yellow onion
1 teaspoon ground turmeric or 1 tablespoon finely chopped turmeric root

3 cloves garlic, minced
½ cup raw cashews
½ cup nutritional yeast
1 teaspoon sea salt
4 ounces dried whole-wheat or gluten-free pasta
Freshly ground black pepper, to taste

1. Combine the potato, carrots, onion, turmeric, garlic, and 2 cups water in a medium saucepan. Bring to a boil over high heat. Reduce heat to low and simmer, covered, for 20 minutes.
2. Place the cashews in a small bowl and add enough water to cover them. Soak for at least 10 minutes; drain.
3. Meanwhile, cook the pasta in a large saucepan according to package directions; drain. Rinse with cool water; drain again. Return to the saucepan.
4. Transfer the potato mixture to a blender. Add the cashews, nutritional yeast, salt, and ½ cup water. Blend for 2 minutes or until smooth and creamy.
5. Top the pasta with the desired amount of sauce, and toss to coat. Season with pepper.

Per Serving
Calories: 1666| fat: 78.4g | carbs: 188.5g | protein: 69.5g | fiber: 26.7g

Simple Miso Quinoa

Prep time: 5 minutes | Cook time: 10 to 15 minutes | Serves 4

3 cups quinoa, rinsed
1 tablespoon miso paste
1½ Teaspoons freshly grated ginger
1 teaspoon low-sodium soy sauce
1 tablespoon coconut oil (optional)

1. Heat the water in a pan over medium heat. Add the quinoa to the pan and bring to a boil. Reduce the heat to low and simmer for 10 to 15 minutes, or until the water is absorbed and the quinoa is tender.
2. Remove the pan from the heat and let rest for 5 minutes. Whisk in the miso paste, ginger, soy sauce and coconut oil (if desired).
3. Divide the quinoa among 4 bowls and serve immediately.

Per Serving
Calories: 205 | fat: 5.8g | carbs: 30.9g | protein: 7.1g | fiber: 4.2g

Sweet Potato Lacinato Kale Chili

Prep time: 20 minutes | Cook time: 30 minutes | Serves 6

2 medium sweet potatoes, diced (approximately 2 pounds)
1 large red onion (approximately 10 ounces), finely chopped
2 (15 ounce/425 g) cans salt-free kidney beans
2 red bell peppers, seeded and finely diced
2 pounds (907 g) fresh tomatoes, diced (or 2 (14.5 ounce/411 g) cans of salt-free tomatoes)
1 tablespoon salt-free chili powder
2 teaspoons smoked paprika (makes a difference when it's smoked)
¼ teaspoon chipotle powder (or more to taste)
2 cups lacinato kale finely shredded like coleslaw (around 8(227 g) ounces)
3 cups of orange juice

1. In large pot, sauté onion and bell pepper in half of the orange juice for 8-10 minutes until onion is soft and translucent.
2. Add all remaining ingredients except for the kale.

3. Bring to a boil, and then reduce heat to simmer for 25-30 minutes until the sweet potatoes are soft, but not mushy.
4. Turn off heat and stir in kale so it wilts, then serve.
5. To make in an electric pressure cooker, place all ingredients in the cooker and cook on high pressure for 6 minutes and release pressure.

Per Serving
Calories: 1731| fat: 8.9g | carbs: 351g | protein: 83g | fiber: 69g

Veggie Sunday Avocado Pita Pizzas

Prep time: 5 minutes | Cook time: 10 to 15 minutes | Serves 4

1 cup chopped onion
1 cup chopped bell pepper, any color
2 cloves garlic, minced
½ teaspoon ground cumin
1 (15-ounce / 425-g) can black beans, rinsed and drained
1 cup fresh or frozen corn kernels
6 (6- to 7-inch) whole wheat pita rounds
1 cup chopped avocado
1 cup oil-free salsa
2 tablespoons snipped fresh cilantro

1. Preheat oven to 350°F (177°C). Line two baking sheets with parchment paper.
2. In a large saucepan, bring ¼ cup of water to a boil. Add the onion, sweet pepper, garlic, and cumin; cook over medium-low heat for 10 minutes or until the onion is tender, stirring occasionally and adding additional water, 1 to 2 tablespoons at a time, as needed to prevent sticking. Stir in the beans and corn. Cook for 5 minutes more or until flavors are blended and beans and corn are heated through, stirring occasionally.
3. Meanwhile, place the pita rounds on the prepared baking sheets. Bake for 10 to 15 minutes or until lightly toasted.
4. Mash the avocado. Spread pita rounds with avocado and bean mixture.
5. Top with salsa and sprinkle with cilantro.

Per Serving
Calories: 1118 | fat: 31.25g | carbs: 194.99g | protein: 36.11g | fiber: 41.8g

Simple 8-Ingredient Veggie Chili

Prep time: 25 minutes | Cook time: 30 minutes | Serves 6

2 cups dried pinto beans, rinsed and drained
1 (14.5-ounce/411 g) can no-salt-added fire-roasted diced tomatoes, undrained
1 cup chopped red onion
1 (1-ounce/28 g) packet vegetarian chili seasoning, such as Simply Organic, or chili seasonings of

your choice
6 cloves garlic, minced
4 cups unsalted vegetable stock
2 cups water
1 cup fresh or frozen whole kernel corn
Toppings such as chopped bell pepper, sliced green onions, and/or snipped fresh cilantro

1. In a 4- to 5-quart slow cooker, combine the beans, tomatoes, onion, seasoning, and garlic. Add the stock and water.
2. Cover and cook on high heat for 4 to 5 hours; stir in the corn for the last 15 minutes. Serve with toppings.

Per Serving
Calories: 2148| fat: 8.5g | carbs: 412g | protein: 116g | fiber: 110g

Delicious Worcestershire Lentil Sloppy Joes

Prep time: 10 minutes | Cook time: 60 minutes | Makes 6 Burgers

3 ⅓ cups water or low-sodium vegetable stock
1 onion, chopped
1 red bell pepper, chopped
1 tablespoon chili powder
1 ½ cups dried brown lentil
1 (15-ounce/ 425 g) can diced fire roasted tomatoes

2 tablespoons soy sauce
2 tablespoons Dijon mustard
2 tablespoons brown sugar
1 teaspoon rice vinegar
1 teaspoon vegetarian Worcestershire sauce
Salt to taste

1. Place 1 cup of the water or stock in a large pot.
2. Add the onions and bell pepper and cook, stirring occasionally until onions soften slightly, about 5 minutes.

3. Add the chili powder and mix in well. Add the remaining liquid, lentils, tomatoes, and the rest of the seasonings. Mix well, bring to a boil, reduce heat, cover and cook over low heat for one hour, stirring occasionally.
4. Serve on whole-wheat buns, or fresh baked bread, with the trimmings of your choice.

Per Serving
Calories: 1008| fat: 26g | carbs: 155g | protein: 61.2g | fiber: 20.2g

Diced Pickle Chick Pea Salad Sandwich

Prep time: 10 minutes | Cook time: 10 minutes | Makes 4 sandwiches

Salad:
1 (15-ounce/ 425 g) can chickpeas, rinsed and drained
3 tablespoons tahini
1 teaspoon Dijon or spicy brown mustard
1 tablespoon maple syrup or agave nectar
¼ cup diced red onion
¼ cup diced celery
¼ cup diced pickle
1 teaspoon capers, drained and loosely chopped

Healthy pinch each sea salt and black pepper
1 tablespoon roasted unsalted sunflower seeds (optional)
Serving:
8 slices whole-wheat bread
Dijon or spicy brown mustard
Romaine lettuce
Tomato, sliced
Red onion, sliced

1. Place the chickpeas in a mixing bowl and mash with a fork, leaving only a few beans whole.
2. Add tahini, mustard, maple syrup, red onion, celery, pickle, capers, salt and pepper, and sunflower seeds (if using) to mixing bowl. Mix to incorporate. Taste and adjust seasonings as needed.
3. Toast bread if desired, and prepare any other desired sandwich toppings (such as lettuce, tomato, and onion).
4. Scoop a healthy amount of the chickpea mixture (about ½ cup) onto one slice of bread, add desired toppings and top with second slice of bread. Repeat for additional sandwiches.

Per Serving
Calories: 813| fat: 40.8g | carbs: 91.8g | protein: 30.6g | fiber: 24.3g

Sumptuous Quinoa Primavera

Prep time: 20 minutes | Cook time: 15 minutes | Serves 4 to 6

Citrus Shallots:
2 large shallots, sliced into half-moons
2 tablespoons orange juice
½ teaspoon apple cider vinegar
½ teaspoon salt (optional)
Pinch of sugar (optional)
Quinoa:
1 cup quinoa, soaked in water for at least 2 hours, rinsed and drained
2 cups water
1 (14-ounce / 397-g) can artichoke hearts packed in water, halved
1 teaspoon dried tar-ragon
2 garlic cloves, minced
¼ teaspoon dried dill
½ teaspoon dried thyme
½ teaspoon salt (optional)
¼ teaspoon black pepper
2 cups frozen peas, thawed
1 yellow bell pepper, chopped
2 carrots, diced
3 scallions, white and light green parts, sliced thinly
Zest and juice of 1 lemon
½ cup raw sunflower seeds

1. Combine the ingredients of the citrus shallots in a small bowl. Stir to mix well. Refrigerate until ready to serve.
2. Pour the quinoa and water in a pot, then bring to a boil over high heat.
3. Reduce the heat to medium-low and add the artichoke hearts, tarragon, garlic, dill, thyme, salt (if desired), and pepper. Stir to combine well and cover the lid of the pot. Simmer for 10 minutes.
4. Reduce the heat to low and add the peas, bell pepper, carrots, and scallions. Stir to combine well and cover the lid. Simmer for another 5 minutes or until the vegetables are tender.
5. Turn off the heat, and then sprinkle with lemon zest and sunflower seeds. Drizzle with lemon juice. Fluff the quinoa with a fork, then divide among 4 or 6 bowls. Serve with the citrus shallots on top.

Per Serving
Calories: 263 | fat: 8.2g | carbs: 40.2g | protein: 11.2g | fiber: 9.8g

Koshari

Prep time: 15 minutes | Cook time: 2 hours 10 minutes | Serves 6

1 cup green lentils, rinsed
3 cups water
Salt, to taste (optional)
1 large onion, peeled and minced
2 tablespoons low-sodium vegetable broth
4 cloves garlic, peeled and minced
½ teaspoon ground allspice
1 teaspoon ground coriander
1 teaspoon ground cumin
2 tablespoons tomato paste
½ teaspoon crushed red pepper flakes
3 large tomatoes, diced
1 cup cooked medium-grain brown rice
1 cup whole-grain elbow macaroni, cooked, drained, and kept warm
1 tablespoon brown rice vinegar

1. Put the lentils and water in a saucepan, and sprinkle with salt, if desired. Bring to a boil over high heat. Reduce the heat to medium, then put the pan lid on and cook for 45 minutes or until the water is mostly absorbed. Pour the cooked lentils in the bowl and set aside.
2. Add the onion to a nonstick skillet, then sauté over medium heat for 15 minutes or until caramelized.
3. Add vegetable broth and garlic to the skillet and sauté for 3 minutes or until fragrant.
4. Add the allspice, coriander, cumin, tomato paste, and red pepper flakes to the skillet and sauté for an additional 3 minutes until aromatic.
5. Add the tomatoes to the skillet and sauté for 15 minutes or until the tomatoes are wilted. Sprinkle with salt, if desired.
6. Arrange the cooked brown rice on the bottom of a large platter, then top the rice with macaroni, and then spread the lentils over. Pour the tomato mixture and brown rice vinegar over before serving.

Per Serving
Calories: 201 | fat: 1.6g | carbs: 41.8g | protein: 6.5g | fiber: 3.6g

Harissa Lentils with Riced Cauliflower

Prep time: 50 minutes | Cook time: 6 to 10 minutes | Serves 4

Harissa:
3 tablespoons cumin seeds
3 tablespoons caraway seeds
3 tablespoons coriander seeds
2 tablespoons tomato paste
1/3 cup fresh lemon juice
1 tablespoon lemon zest
2 cloves garlic, chopped
3 to 4 small red chili peppers, seeded and chopped
Salt, to taste (optional)
Ground black or white pepper, to taste

2 tablespoons low-sodium vegetable broth
1 cup cooked French or black beluga lentils
Cauliflower Rice:
5 cups chopped cauliflower florets
1 tablespoon low-sodium vegetable broth
Salt, to taste (optional)
Ground black or white pepper, to taste
1/4 cup chopped fresh mint leaves
1/4 cup chopped fresh flat-leaf parsley
2 teaspoons fresh lemon juice
2 green onions, thinly sliced

1. Heat a skillet over medium heat, then adds and sauté the seeds to toast for 2 minutes or until lightly browned.
2. Make the harissa: Pour the toasted seeds in a food processor, then add the tomato paste, lemon juice and zest, garlic, chili peppers, salt (if desired), and pepper. Process until the mixture is creamy and smooth. Pour the harissa in a bowl and set aside until ready to use.
3. Heat the vegetable broth in a saucepan over medium heat. Add the cooked lentils and ¾ cup of harissa to the pan and simmer for 5 to 10 minutes until the mixture is glossy and smooth and has a thick consistency. Keep stirring during the simmering.
4. Put the cauliflower florets in a food processor, then process to rice the cauliflower.
5. Heat the vegetable broth in a nonstick skillet over medium heat. Add the riced cauliflower, then sprinkle with salt (if desired) and pepper. Sauté for 1 minute or until lightly softened.
6. Transfer the cooked cauliflower rice to a large bowl, then add the mint, parsley, lemon juice, and green onions. Toss to combine well.
7. Serve the riced cauliflower with harissa lentils on top.

Per Serving
Calories: 176 | fat: 3.4g | carbs: 32.2g | protein: 11.2g | fiber: 12.4g

Green Onion Millet Polenta

Prep time: 15 minutes | Cook time: 10 minutes | Serves 4

1/3 cup plus 2 teaspoons grape seed oil, divided (optional)
½ cup green onions, white and green parts, chopped
Salt, to taste (optional)

1 cup millet
2 leeks, white and light-green parts only, chopped
2 teaspoons miso
3 cups low-sodium vegetable soup

1. Heat 1/3 cup of the grape seed oil (if desired) in a medium saucepan over medium heat.
2. Add the green onions and sauté for 30 seconds or until fragrant.
3. Pour the sautéed onions and oil (if desired) in a food processor. Sprinkle with salt (if desired) and pulse until creamy and smooth. Pour the mixture in a bowl and set aside.
4. Pour the millet in the food processor and pulse to grind until it has a coarse consistency. Pour the ground millet in a separate bowl and set aside.
5. Heat 2 teaspoons of the grape seed oil (if desired) in the now empty saucepan over medium heat.
6. Add the leeks and sauté for 5 minutes or until tender.
7. Add the miso and vegetable soup. Bring to a boil. Stir constantly. Fold in the ground millet. Keep stirring until the mixture has a thick consistency.
8. Pour the millet polenta in a large serving bowl and drizzle with green onion oil before serving.

Per Serving
Calories: 516 | fat: 23.2g | carbs: 66.9g | protein: 10.8g | fiber: 9.3g

Nasi Goreng

Prep time: 20 minutes | Cook time: 20 minutes | Serves 4

2 shallots, finely sliced
Sea salt, to taste (optional)
1 cup peas
5 baby courgettes, sliced at an angle
Handful of fine green beans, chopped
1 cup tofu cubes
1 red bell pepper, finely sliced
1 red onion, finely sliced
2 tablespoons low-sodium vegetable broth
2 cups basmati, soaked in water for 1 hour, cooked
Handful of toasted cashew nuts
3 tablespoons kecap manis

Sambal:
3 red chilies
1 tablespoon tomato purée
1 tablespoon lemongrass paste
3 garlic cloves
Juice and zest of 1 lime
1 teaspoon sea salt (optional)

1. Heat a nonstick skillet over high heat, then add the shallot and sprinkle with salt, if desired. Sauté for 5 minutes or until caramelized. Transfer the shallots in a bowl and set aside until ready to serve.
2. Put the ingredients for the sambal in a blender, then process until smooth.
3. Pour the sambal in the cleaned skillet, then sauté over high heat for 1 minutes.
4. Add the peas, baby courgettes, green beans, tofu cubes, bell peppers, red onion, and vegetable broth to the skillet and sauté for 6 minutes or until tender.
5. Add the cooked basmati to the skillet and sauté with the vegetables for 4 minutes until well mixed. Add the cashew nuts and kecap manis halfway through the cooking time.
6. Transfer the basmati and vegetables onto a large plate, and serve with caramelized shallots on top.

Per Serving
Calories: 658 | fat: 19.1g | carbs: 100.3g | protein: 25.7g | fiber: 7.1g

Bibimbap

Prep time: 1 hour 30 minutes | Cook time: 20 minutes | Makes 1 Bowl

2 tablespoons tamari, divided
½ cup chickpeas, soaked in water overnight, cooked
¾ cup cooked quinoa
3 tablespoons low-sodium vegetable broth, divided
1 carrot, scrubbed or peeled, and julienned
2 garlic cloves, minced, divided
½ cup asparagus, cut into 2-inch pieces
½ cup chopped spinach
½ cup bean sprouts
3 tablespoons gochujang
1 scallion, chopped
1 tablespoon toasted sesame seeds

1. Add 1 tablespoon of tamari in a small bowl, then dunk the chickpeas in the tamari and set aside to marinade until ready to use.
2. Put the cooked quinoa in a large serving bowl.
3. Heat 1 tablespoon of vegetable broth in a nonstick skillet over medium heat. Add the carrot and 1 garlic clove and sauté for 5 minutes or until tender. Transfer the cooked carrots and garlic to the serving bowl and place over the quinoa.
4. Add the asparagus and 1 tablespoon of vegetable broth and sauté for 5 minutes or until soft. Transfer the asparagus to the serving bowl and place beside the carrot.
5. Add spinach, the other garlic clove, and 1 tablespoon of vegetable broth to the skillet, then sauté for 5 minutes or until wilted. Drizzle with remaining tamari and transfer the spinach to the serving bowl and place beside the asparagus.
6. Add the bean sprouts and sauté for 1 minute, then transfer to the serving bowl and place beside the spinach.
7. Put the marinated chickpeas in the serving bowl and place beside the bean sprouts.
8. Top them with gochujang, chopped scallion, and sesame seeds. Stir to mix them well and enjoy.

Per Serving
Calories: 665 | fat: 33.0g | carbs: 32.0g | protein: 22.0g | fiber: 16.0g

Roasted Lime Tofu and Broccoli Rice Bowl

Prep time: 20 minutes | Cook time: 35 minutes | Serves 4

2 tablespoons fresh lime juice
2 teaspoons lime zest
½ teaspoon chili flakes
½ teaspoon garlic powder
2 tablespoons grape seed oil (optional)
Salt and ground black pepper, to taste (optional)
14 ounces (397 g) extra-firm tofu, rinsed and drained, cut into 1-inch cubes
2 cups broccoli florets
2 cups cooked brown rice
¼ cup chopped fresh basil leaves
½ cup fresh sunflower sprouts
¼ cup toasted sunflower seeds

1. Preheat the oven to 400°F (205°C). Line a baking pan with parchment paper.
2. Combine the lime juice and zest, chili flakes, garlic powder, grapeseed oil (if desired), salt (if desired), and ground black pepper in a bowl. Stir to mix well.
3. Add the tofu to the bowl and toss to coat well, then transfer the tofu to a single layer on the baking pan. Roast the tofu in the preheated oven for 15 minutes.
4. Meanwhile, add the broccoli to the bowl of lime mixture, then toss to coat well.
5. Remove the baking pan from the oven and add the well-coated broccoli to the baking pan. Put the pan back to the oven and roast for 20 more minutes or until the tofu and broccoli are browned on all sides.
6. In the meantime, divide the cooked brown rice into 4 bowls. Mix the basil in lime mixture.
7. Divide the roasted tofu and broccoli over the brown rice bowls, and then spread with sunflower sprouts and sunflower seeds. Drizzle with basil-lime mixture and toss to serve.

Per Serving
Calories: 326 | fat: 18.4g | carbs: 28.8g | protein: 15.7g | fiber: 3.8g

Cauliflower, Navy Bean, and Quinoa Risotto

Prep time: 15 minutes | Cook time: 45 minutes | Serves 4

5 to 6 cups cauliflower, cut into 1- to 1½-inch florets
Salt, to taste (optional)
Ground black or white pepper, to taste
2 cups cooked navy beans
2¹/₃ cups low-sodium vegetable broth, divided
1 tablespoon fresh lemon juice
Pinch of nutritional yeast
4 to 5 shallots, finely diced
2 teaspoons minced fresh thyme leaves (about 4 sprigs)
1 cup quinoa
½ cup chopped fresh flat-leaf parsley

1. Preheat the oven to 400°F (205°C). Line a baking sheet with parchment paper.
2. Arrange the cauliflower florets on the baking sheet. Sprinkle with salt (if desired) and pepper. Toss to coat well.
3. Roast in the preheated oven for 25 minutes or until golden brown. Flip the florets every 5 minutes to roast evenly.
4. Meanwhile, put the navy beans, ¹/₃ cup of the vegetable broth, lemon juice, and nutritional yeast in a food processor. Pulse to purée until creamy and smooth. Set aside.
5. Heat a saucepan over medium heat. Add the shallots and sauté for 4 minutes or until lightly browned.
6. Add the thyme to the pan and sauté for 1 minute or until aromatic.
7. Make the risotto: Add the quinoa and remaining vegetable broth to the pan. Stir to combine well. Bring to a boil, then reduce the heat to medium-low and simmer for 14 minutes or until the liquid is mostly absorbed.
8. Mix in the navy bean purée. Sprinkle with salt (if desired) and pepper. Spread the parsley and roasted cauliflower florets over the risotto. Serve warm.

Per Serving
Calories: 456 | fat: 5.1g | carbs: 84.9g | fiber: 20.8g | protein: 21.7g

Creamy Polenta with Veggies and Tofu

Prep time: 10 minutes | Cook time: 29 to 40 minutes | Serves 2

Polenta:
½ cup polenta
1 cup water
¾ cup unsweetened coconut milk
½ tablespoon nutritional yeast
¼ teaspoon garlic powder
¼ teaspoon sea salt (optional)
1 teaspoon avocado oil (optional)
2 handfuls of kale, chopped
12 Brussels sprouts, cut in half
5 ounces (142 g) extra firm tofu, cut into cubes
Balsamic Glaze Sauce:
2 tablespoons balsamic vinegar
1 tablespoon maple syrup (optional)
2 tablespoons water

1. Combine the water, coconut milk, polenta, nutritional yeast, garlic powder and sea salt (if desired) in a pot over medium heat. Bring to a boil. Reduce the heat to low. Cover and simmer for 15 to 20 minutes, or until tender and creamy.
2. Heat the avocado oil (if desired) in a saucepan over low heat. Add the kale and Brussels sprouts to the saucepan. Cover and cook for 8 to 11 minutes, or until tender and wilted. Transfer the veggies to a bowl.
3. Add the tofu to the saucepan over low heat and cook for 3 to 5 minutes, or until lightly browned.
4. In a small bowl, whisk together all the ingredients for the balsamic glaze sauce.
5. Place the cook veggies and the balsamic glaze sauce into the pan with tofu. Continue to cook for 3 to 4 minutes, or until all the flavors are well blended.
6. Pour the cooked polenta into a bowl. Spread the tofu and veggie mixture on top. Serve immediately.

Per Serving
Calories: 433 | fat: 8.2g | carbs: 69.6g | protein: 24.7g | fiber: 8.7g

Foxtail Millet Fried Rice

Prep time: 20 minutes | Cook time: 30 minutes | Serves 4

1 cup foxtail millet, rinsed and drained, soaked in water for 30 minutes
$1/3$ cup avocado oil (optional)
2 medium onions, sliced
4 green chillies, sliced
20 French beans, chopped
½ medium red bell pepper, chopped
½ head medium cabbage, chopped
1 medium carrot, chopped
3 Teaspoons Italian seasoning (no salt added)
3 Teaspoons paprika
Salt, to taste (optional)
2 teaspoons ground black pepper
20 twigs medium spring onions

1. Pour the millet in a pot, then pour in enough water to cover the millet about 1 inch. Bring to a boil, then cook for 15 more minutes.
2. Strain the cooked millet in a colander and put the millet in a skillet and simmer for 5 minutes with the lid covered.
3. Remove the millet from the skillet and fluffy with a fork. Heat the avocado oil (if desired) in the skillet over medium heat.
4. Add the onions and green chilies and sauté for 3 minutes or until the onions are translucent.
5. Add the French beans, bell pepper, cabbage, and carrots to the skillet. Sauté for 3 minutes, then sprinkle with Italian seasoning, paprika, salt (if desired), and black pepper. Sauté for 3 more minutes or until the vegetables are tender.
6. Fold in the spring onions and cooked foxtail millet and sauté for 1 more minutes to combine well.
7. Serve immediately.

Per Serving
Calories: 556 | fat: 19.0g | carbs: 82.6g | protein: 19.7g | fiber: 25.7g

Chapter 7 Sauces, Broths, Dip and Dressings

Garlic Mushroom Sauce

Prep time: 10 minutes | Cook time: 6 minutes | Makes 2 cups

1¾ cups water, divided
1 cup sliced mushrooms
2 tablespoons low-sodium soy sauce
1 clove garlic, crushed
1 teaspoon grated

fresh ginger
2½ tablespoons cornstarch, dissolved in ¼ cup water
Dash sesame oil (optional)
Freshly ground pepper, to taste

1. Combine ¼ cup of water and mushrooms in a saucepan. Stir in the soy sauce, garlic, and ginger and sauté for about 4 minutes, or until the mushrooms are lightly softened.
2. Whisk in the remaining 1½ cups of water and cornstarch mixture and continue stirring until the sauce begins to thicken and bubble.
3. Drizzle with the sesame oil, if desired. Season with the pepper to taste before serving.

Per Serving

Calories: 25.6 | fat: 1.2g | carbs: 3.4g | protein: 0.3g | fiber: 0.1g

Cilantro-Chili Dressing

Prep time: 5 minutes | Cook time: 0 minutes | Makes ¾ cups

1 (4-ounce / 113-g) can chopped green chilies
1 to 2 cloves garlic
¼ cup fresh lime juice
¼ cup water

¼ cup chopped fresh cilantro
2 teaspoons maple syrup (optional)
Freshly ground pepper, to taste

1. Combine all the ingredients in a food processor and pulse until creamy and smooth.

Per Serving

Calories: 50 | fat: 2.1g | carbs: 5.5g | protein: 2.3g | fiber: 0.3g

Homemade Tomato Sauce

Prep time: 20 minutes | Cook time: 40 minutes | Makes about 6 cups

4 pounds (1.8 kg) tomatoes, coarsely chopped
2 to 3 cloves garlic, minced
1 large onion, chopped
1 tablespoon chopped fresh thyme

1 tablespoon chopped fresh oregano
1 bay leaf
¼ teaspoon crushed red pepper flakes
¼ cup chopped fresh basil
Freshly ground pepper, to taste

1. Combine all the ingredients except the basil and pepper in a large saucepan and bring to a boil over medium-high heat.
2. When it starts to boil, reduce the heat, and simmer uncovered for about 30 minutes, stirring occasionally.
3. Discard the baby leaf and stir in the basil and pepper. Serve warm.

Per Serving

Calories: 35.1 | fat: 0.3g | carbs: 6.2g | protein: 1.9g | fiber: 1.6g

Creamy Spinach and Avocado Dressing

Prep time: 10 minutes | Cook time: 0 minutes | Makes about 1 cup

2 ounces (57 g) spinach leaves (about 1 cup chopped and packed)
¼ medium, ripe avocados
¼ cup water, plus

more as needed
1 small clove garlic
1 tablespoon Dijon mustard
1 green onion, white and green parts, sliced

1. Blitz all the ingredients in a blender until thoroughly mixed. Add a little more water if a thinner consistency is desired.
2. Refrigerate in an airtight container for 3 days and shake before using.

Per Serving

Calories: 14.6 | fat: 1.0g | carbs: 1.0g | protein: 0.4g | fiber: 0.7g

Homemade Tzatziki Sauce

Prep time: 20 minutes | Cook time: 0 minutes | Makes about 1 cup

2 ounces (57 g) raw, unsalted cashews (about ½ cup)
2 tablespoons lemon juice
¹/₃ cup water

1 small clove garlic
1 cup chopped cucumber, peeled
2 tablespoons fresh dill

1. In a blender, add the cashews, lemon juice, water, and garlic. Keep it aside for at least 15 minutes to soften the cashews.
2. Blend the ingredients until smooth. Stir in the chopped cucumber and dill, and continue to blend until it reaches your desired consistency. It doesn't need to be totally smooth. Feel free to add more water if you like a thinner consistency.
3. Transfer to an airtight container and chill for at least 30 minutes for best flavors.
4. Bring the sauce to room temperature and shake well before serving.

Per Serving
Calories: 208 | fat: 13.5g | carbs: 15.0 g | protein: 6.7g | fiber: 2.8g

Tamari Vinegar Sauce

Prep time: 10 minutes | Cook time: 0 minutes | Makes about 1¼ cups

¼ cup tamari
½ cup nutritional yeast
2 tablespoons balsamic vinegar
2 tablespoons apple cider vinegar
2 tablespoons Worcestershire sauce

2 teaspoons Dijon mustard
1 tablespoon plus 1 teaspoon maple syrup
½ teaspoon ground turmeric
¼ teaspoon black pepper

1. Place all the ingredients in an airtight container, and whisk until everything is well incorporated. Store in the refrigerator for up to 3 weeks.

Per Serving
Calories: 216 | fat: 9.9g | carbs: 18.0g | protein: 13.7g | fiber: 7.7g

Hot Buffalo Sauce

Prep time: 5 minutes | Cook time: 15 minutes | Makes 2 cups

¼ cup olive oil (optional)
1 small red onion, roughly chopped
4 garlic cloves, roughly chopped
6 cayenne chiles, roughly chopped

1 cup water
½ cup apple cider vinegar
½ teaspoon salt (optional)
½ teaspoon freshly ground black pepper

1. In a large sauté pan over medium-high heat, heat the olive oil, if desired. Add the onion, garlic and chiles to the pan and sauté for 5 minutes, or until the onion is tender.
2. Pour in the water and bring to a boil. Cook for about 10 minutes, or until the water has nearly evaporated.
3. Transfer the cooked onion and chile mixture to a blender and blend briefly to combine.
4. Add the apple cider vinegar, salt (if desired), and pepper to the blender. Blend again for 30 seconds.
5. Using a mesh sieve, strain the sauce into a bowl. Use a spoon to scrape and press all the liquid from the pulp.
6. Serve immediately or refrigerate in an airtight container for up to 2 weeks.

Per Serving (2 tablespoons)
Calories: 76 | fat: 7.1g | carbs: 2.9g | protein: 1.1g | fiber: 1.2g

Fresh Strawberry Vinaigrette

Prep time: 5 minutes | Cook time: 0 minutes | Makes 1 cup

1 cup fresh strawberries
2 tablespoons red wine vinegar

1 teaspoon maple syrup (optional)
Freshly ground pepper, to taste

1. Place all the ingredients in a food processor and pulse until creamy and smooth.

Per Serving
Calories: 15 | fat: 0.1g | carbs: 3.8g | protein: 0.2g | fiber: 0.7g

Hearty Vegetable Broth

Prep time: 15 minutes | Cook time: 3 to 4 hours | Makes about 6 quarts

5 quarts water
4 to 5 cloves garlic, peeled
4 large carrots, scrubbed and thickly sliced
4 stalks celery, thickly sliced
2 large potatoes, scrubbed and coarsely chopped
2 large onions, peeled and quartered
2 leeks, white parts only, washed and thickly sliced
2 bay leaves
4 tablespoons low-sodium soy sauce
10 whole peppercorns
Several large sprigs fresh parsley, for garnish

1. Combine all the ingredients in a large soup pot or stockpot and bring to a boil.
2. When it starts to boil, reduce the heat to low, cover, and let simmer for 3 to 4 hours, stirring occasionally, or until the broth is pale golden.
3. Strain the broth through a colander, then once more through a fine-mesh strainer. Discard the vegetables. Allow the broth to cool uncovered at room temperature for 1 hour.
4. Refrigerate in an airtight container for up to 3 days or freeze for up to 3 months.

Per Serving
Calories: 104 | fat: 1.3g | carbs: 20.5g | protein: 2.6g | fiber: 2.8g

Creamy Avocado Cilantro Lime Dressing

Prep time: 5 minutes | Cook time: 0 minutes | Makes about 2 cups

1 avocado, diced
½ cup water
¼ cup cilantro leaves
¼ cup fresh lime or lemon juice (about 2 limes or lemons)
½ teaspoon ground cumin
¼ teaspoon salt (optional)

1. Put all the ingredients in a blender, and pulse until well combined. Taste and adjust the seasoning as needed. It is best served within 1 day.

Per Serving
Calories: 94 | fat: 7.4g | carbs: 5.7g | protein: 1.1g | fiber: 3.5g

Enchilada Sauce

Prep time: 10 minutes | Cook time: 25 minutes | Makes 2 ½ cups

1 (8-ounce / 227-g) can tomato sauce
1½ cups water
2 cloves garlic, minced
1 large onion, chopped
1 tablespoon chili powder
½ teaspoon dried oregano
½ teaspoon ground cumin
2 tablespoons cornstarch, mixed with $1/_4$ cup cold water

1. Combine all the ingredients except the cornstarch mixture in a small saucepan and bring to a boil over medium-high heat.
2. Reduce the heat to low, cover, and allow to simmer for 20 minutes, whisking occasionally.
3. Stir in the cornstarch mixture and cook for about 5 minutes until the sauce thickens, whisking constantly.
4. Remove from the heat and allow the sauce to cool to room temperature. Serve warm.

Per Serving
Calories: 21 | fat: 0.2g | carbs: 4.3g | protein: 0.5g | fiber: 1.0g

Citrus Tahini Dressing

Prep time: 5 minutes | Cook time: 0 minutes | Makes about 1 cup

½ cup orange juice
¼ cup tahini
¼ cup lemon juice
1 small clove garlic
1 teaspoon grated or finely chopped fresh ginger

1. Put all the ingredients in a blender and pulse until smooth.
2. Chill for an hour in the refrigerator to thicken and blend the flavors.
3. Refrigerate in an airtight container for up to 5 days.

Per Serving
Calories: 57.6 | fat: 4.0g | carbs: 4.0g | protein: 1.4g | fiber: 0.8g

Mild Harissa Sauce

Prep time: 5 minutes | Cook time: 20 minutes | Makes 3 to 4 cups

1 large red bell pepper, deseeded, cored, and cut into chunks
4 garlic cloves, peeled
1 yellow onion, cut into thick rings
1 cup no-sodium vegetable broth or water

2 tablespoons tomato paste
4 garlic cloves, peeled
1 tablespoon low-sodium soy sauce or tamari
1 teaspoon ground cumin

1. Preheat the oven to 450ºF (235ºC). Line a baking sheet with aluminum foil or parchment paper.
2. Put the bell pepper, flesh-side up, on the baking sheet and spread the garlic and onion around the bell pepper.
3. Roasted in the preheated oven for 20 minutes until the pepper is lightly charred.
4. Remove from the heat and let it cool for a few minutes.
5. Place the bell pepper in a blender, along with the remaining ingredients, and process until smoothly puréed.
6. Serve immediately or store in a sealed container in the refrigerator for up to 2 weeks or in the freezer for up to 6 months.

Per Serving
Calories: 16 | fat: 0.9g | carbs: 3.1g | protein: 1.1g | fiber: 1.3g

Vinegary Maple Syrup dressing

Prep time: 5 minutes | Cook time: 0 minutes | Makes 2/3 cup

¼ cup rice vinegar
¼ cup balsamic vinegar
2½ tablespoons maple syrup (optional)

1½ tablespoons Dijon mustard
Freshly ground pepper, to taste

1. Combine all the ingredients in a jar. Cover and shake until well blended.

Per Serving
Calories: 49 | fat: 0.2g | carbs: 11.5g | protein: 0.3g | fiber: 0.2g

Satay Sauce

Prep time: 5 minutes | Cook time: 8 minutes | Makes 2 cups

½ yellow onion, diced
3 garlic cloves, minced
1 fresh red chile, thinly sliced (optional)
1-inch (2.5-cm) piece fresh ginger, peeled and minced
¼ cup smooth peanut butter

2 tablespoons coconut amino
1 (13.5-ounce / 383-g) can unsweetened coconut milk
¼ teaspoon freshly ground black pepper
¼ teaspoon salt (optional)

1. Heat a large nonstick skillet over medium-high heat until hot.
2. Add the onion, garlic cloves, chile (if desired), and ginger to the skillet, and sauté for 2 minutes.
3. Pour in the peanut butter and coconut amino and stir well. Add the coconut milk, black pepper, and salt (if desired) and continue whisking, or until the sauce is just beginning to bubble and thicken.
4. Remove the sauce from the heat to a bowl. Taste and adjust the seasoning if necessary.

Per Serving (½ cup)
Calories: 322 | fat: 28.8g | carbs: 9.4g | protein: 6.3g | fiber: 1.8g

Homemade Chimichurri

Prep time: 5 minutes | Cook time: 0 minutes | Makes about 1 cup

1 cup finely chopped flat-leaf parsley leaves
Zest and juice of 2 lemons

¼ cup low-sodium vegetable broth
4 garlic cloves
1 teaspoon dried oregano

1. Place all the ingredients into a food processor, and pulse until it reaches the consistency you like.
2. Refrigerate the chimichurri in an airtight container for up to 5 days. It's best served within 1 day.

Per Serving
Calories: 19 | fat: 0.2g | carbs: 3.7g | protein: 0.7g | fiber: 0.7g

Tahini BBQ Sauce

Prep time: 10 minutes | Cook time: 0 minutes | Makes about ¾ cups

½ cup water
¼ cup red miso
3 cloves garlic, minced
1-inch (2.5 cm) piece ginger, peeled and minced
2 tablespoons rice

vinegar
2 tablespoons tahini
2 tablespoons chili paste or chili sauce
1 tablespoon date sugar
½ teaspoon crushed red pepper (optional)

1. Place all the ingredients in a food processor, and purée until thoroughly mixed and smooth. You can thin the sauce out by stirring in ½ cup of water, or keep it thick.
2. Transfer to the refrigerator to chill until ready to serve.

Per Serving
Calories: 206 | fat: 10.2g | carbs: 21.3g | protein: 7.2g | fiber: 4.4g

Avocado-Dill Dressing

Prep time: 20 minutes | Cook time: 0 minutes | Makes about 1 cup

2 ounces (57 g) raw, unsalted cashews (about ½ cup)
½ cup water
3 tablespoons lemon juice
½ medium, ripe

avocado, chopped
1 medium clove garlic
2 tablespoons chopped fresh dill
2 green onions, white and green parts, chopped

1. Put the cashews, water, lemon juice, avocado, and garlic into a blender. Keep it aside for at least 15 minutes to soften the cashews.
2. Blend until everything is fully mixed. Fold in the dill and green onions, and blend briefly to retain some texture.
3. Store in an airtight container in the fridge for up to 3 days and stir well before serving.

Per Serving
Calories: 312 | fat: 21.1g | carbs: 22.6g | protein: 8.0g | fiber: 7.1g

Light Vegetable Broth

Prep time: 30 minutes | Cook time: 3 to 4 hours | Makes about 8 quarts

6½ quarts water
2 cups white wine or unsweetened apple juice
6 carrots, scrubbed and coarsely chopped
6 stalks celery, thickly sliced
3 medium zucchini, thickly sliced
2 large potatoes, scrubbed and coarsely chopped
2 large onions, chopped

½ pound (227 g) mushrooms, cleaned and left whole
1 leek, white part only, cleaned and thickly sliced
2 bay leaves
5 to 6 cloves garlic, crushed
10 whole peppercorns
Several large sprigs fresh thyme
Several large sprigs fresh parsley

1. Combine all the ingredients in a large soup pot or stockpot and bring to a boil.
2. When it starts to boil, reduce the heat to low, cover, and allow to simmer for 3 to 4 hours, stirring occasionally, or until the vegetables are very soft.
3. Strain the broth through a fine-mesh strainer and discard the vegetables.
4. Let the broth cool to room temperature and refrigerate until ready to use.

Per Serving
Calories: 194 | fat: 0.5g | carbs: 42.8g | protein: 4.6g | fiber: 6.1g

Orange-Mango Dressing

Prep time: 5 minutes | Cook time: 0 minutes | Makes ¾ cup

1 medium mango, peeled and cut into chunks
1 clove garlic, crushed

½ cup orange juice
1 teaspoon soy sauce
¼ teaspoon curry powder

1. Place all the ingredients in a blender and blend until creamy and smooth.

Per Serving
Calories: 51 | fat: 0.5g | carbs: 11.3g | protein: 0.7g | fiber: 1.0g

Easy Lemon Tahini Dressing

Prep time: 5 minutes | Cook time: 0 minutes | Makes 1¼ cups

½ cup tahini
¼ cup fresh lemon juice (about 2 lemons)
1 teaspoon maple syrup
1 small garlic clove,
chopped
⅛ Teaspoon black pepper
¼ teaspoon salt (optional)
¼ to ½ cup water

1. Process the tahini, lemon juice, maple syrup, garlic, black pepper, and salt (if desired) in a blender (high-speed blenders work best for this). Gradually add the water until the mixture is completely smooth.
2. Store in an airtight container in the fridge for up to 5 days.

Per Serving
Calories: 128 | fat: 9.6g | carbs: 6.8g | protein: 3.6g | fiber: 1.9g

Creamy Black Bean Dip

Prep time: 10 minutes | Cook time: 0 minutes | Serves: 3

4 cups cooked black beans, rinsed and drained
2 tablespoons Italian seasoning
2 tablespoons minced garlic
2 tablespoons low-so-
dium vegetable broth
2 tablespoons onion powder
1 tablespoon lemon juice, or more to taste
¼ teaspoon salt (optional)

1. In a large bowl, mash the black beans with a potato masher or the back of a fork until mostly smooth.
2. Add the remaining ingredients to the bowl and whisk to combine.
3. Taste and add more lemon juice or salt, if needed. Serve immediately, or refrigerate for at least 30 minutes to better incorporate the flavors.

Per Serving
Calories: 387 | fat: 6.5g | carbs: 63.0g | protein: 21.2g | fiber: 16.0g

Maple Dijon Dressing

Prep time: 5 minutes | Cook time: 0 minutes | Makes ½ cups

¼ cup apple cider vinegar
2 teaspoons Dijon mustard
2 tablespoons maple syrup
2 tablespoons low-sodium vegetable broth
¼ teaspoon black pepper
Salt, to taste (optional)

1. Mix together the apple cider vinegar, Dijon mustard, maple syrup, vegetable broth, and black pepper in a resealable container until well incorporated. Season with salt, if desired.
2. The dressing can be refrigerated for up to 5 days.

Per Serving
Calories: 82 | fat: 0.3g | carbs: 19.3g | protein: 0.6g | fiber: 0.7g

Avocado-Chickpea Dip

Prep time: 15 minutes | Cook time: 0 minutes | Makes about 2 cups

1 (15-ounce / 425-g) can cooked chickpeas, drained and rinsed
2 large, ripe avocados, chopped
¼ cup red onion, finely chopped
1 tablespoon Dijon
mustard
1 to 2 tablespoons lemon juice
2 teaspoons chopped fresh oregano
½ teaspoon garlic clove, finely chopped

1. In a medium bowl, mash the cooked chickpeas with a potato masher or the back of a fork, or until the chickpeas pop open (a food processor works best for this).
2. Stir in the remaining ingredients and continue to mash until completely smooth.
3. Place in the refrigerator to chill until ready to serve.

Per Serving
Calories: 101 | fat: 1.9g | carbs: 16.2g | protein: 4.7g | fiber: 4.6g

Easy Cucumber Dip

Prep time: 5 minutes | Cook time: 0 minutes | Makes 1½ cups

1 cucumber, peeled, cut in half lengthwise, deseeded and coarsely chopped	crushed
	1 cup plain soy yogurt
	¼ teaspoon white pepper
3 to 4 cloves garlic,	

1. In a blender, blend the cucumber until finely chopped. Remove from the blend and place in a very fine strainer. Press out as much water as possible. Return to the blender.
2. Add the remaining ingredients and process until smooth.
3. Refrigerate for several hours before serving.

Per Serving
Calories: 48 | fat: 1.0g | carbs: 6.2g | protein: 3.6g | fiber: 0.4g

Lemony Hummus with Tahini

Prep time: 10 minutes | Cook time: 0 minutes | Serves 6

1 (15-ounce / 425-g) can no-salt-added chickpeas, drained and rinsed	lemon juice (from 1 lemon)
	3 garlic cloves
½ cup tahini	1 teaspoon ground cumin
¼ cup low-sodium vegetable broth	½ teaspoon sea salt (optional)
3 tablespoons fresh	Dash of paprika

1. Process the chickpeas in a food processor until finely chopped.
2. Add the tahini, vegetable broth, lemon juice, garlic cloves, cumin, and sea salt (if desired) to the processor. Continue processing until everything is well combined and smooth.
3. Transfer the hummus to a serving bowl and sprinkle with the paprika. Serve chilled.

Per Serving
Calories: 222 | fat: 12.2g | carbs: 20.1g | protein: 8.2g | fiber: 6.0g

Tangy Cashew Mustard Dressing

Prep time: 20 minutes | Cook time: 0 minutes | Makes about 1 cup

2 ounces (57 g) raw, unsalted cashews (about ½ cup)	2 teaspoons apple cider vinegar
½ cup water	2 tablespoons Dijon mustard
3 tablespoons lemon juice	1 medium clove garlic

1. Put all the ingredients in a food processor and keep it aside for at least 15 minutes.
2. Purée until the ingredients are combined to a smooth and creamy mixture. Thin the dressing with a little extra water as needed to achieve your preferred consistency.
3. Store in an airtight container in the refrigerator for up to 5 days.

Per Serving
Calories: 187 | fat: 13.0g | carbs: 11.5g | protein: 5.9g | fiber: 1.7g

Creamy Lentil Dip

Prep time: 10 minutes | Cook time: 15 minutes | Makes 3 cups

2½ cups water, divided	$1/3$ cup tahini
	1 garlic clove
1 cup dried green or brown lentils, rinsed	½ teaspoon salt (optional)

1. Stir together 2 cups of water and dried lentils in a medium pot and bring to a boil over high heat.
2. When it starts to boil, reduce the heat to low, cover, and let simmer for 15 minutes until the lentils are soft, stirring occasionally. Drain any excess liquid.
3. Transfer the lentils to a food processor, along with the remaining ½ cup of water, tahini, garlic, and salt (if desired), and pulse until smooth and creamy.
4. Serve immediately.

Per Serving (¼ cup)
Calories: 101 | fat: 4.2g | carbs: 10.8g | protein: 5.0g | fiber: 6.0g

Sweet Mango and Orange Dressing

Prep time: 5 minutes | Cook time: 0 minutes | Makes about 1½ cups

1 cup (165 g) diced mango, thawed if frozen
½ cup orange juice
2 tablespoons rice vinegar
2 tablespoons fresh lime juice
¼ teaspoon salt (optional)
1 teaspoon date sugar (optional)
2 tablespoons chopped cilantro

1. Pulse all the ingredients except for the cilantro in a food processor until it reaches the consistency you like. Add the cilantro and whisk well.
2. Store in an airtight container in the fridge for up to 2 days.

Per Serving
Calories: 32 | fat: 0.1g | carbs: 7.4g | protein: 0.3g | fiber: 0.5g

Broccoli Dip

Prep time: 5 minutes | Cook time: 0 minutes | Makes 2 cups

1½ cups cooked broccoli stems, tough outer layers peeled off
1½ tablespoons lemon juice
¼ teaspoon ground cumin
⅛ Teaspoon garlic powder
1 canned green chili, chopped
1 scallion, sliced
½ tomato, diced

1. In a blend, combine the broccoli stems, lemon juice, cumin and garlic powder and blend until completely smooth. Add the remaining ingredients and mix well by hand, but do not blend.
2. Serve chilled.

Per Serving
Calories: 7.3 | fat: 0.1g | carbs: 1.2g | protein: 0.4g | fiber: 0.5g

Ranch Cauliflower Dip

Prep time: 15 minutes | Cook time: 0 minutes | Serves 8

2 cups frozen cauliflower, thawed
½ cup unsweetened almond milk
2 tablespoons apple cider vinegar
2 tablespoons extra-virgin olive oil (Optional)
1 garlic clove, peeled
2 teaspoons finely chopped fresh parsley
2 teaspoons finely chopped scallions, both white and green parts
1 teaspoon finely chopped fresh dill
½ teaspoon onion powder
½ teaspoon Dijon mustard
½ teaspoon salt (optional)
¼ teaspoon freshly ground black pepper

1. Pulse all the ingredients in a blender until smooth and combined.
2. Serve immediately or store in a sealed container in the refrigerator for up to 3 days.

Per Serving (2 tablespoons)
Calories: 51 | fat: 4.2g | carbs: 2.1g | protein: 1.2g | fiber: 1.1g

Guacamole

Prep time: 15 minutes | Cook time: 0 minutes | Makes 2 cups

3 medium ripe avocados, peeled and chopped
½ cup chopped fresh cilantro
½ cup finely chopped yellow or white onion
2 small garlic cloves, finely chopped
3 tablespoons lime juice
½ teaspoon ground cumin

1. In a medium bowl, mash the chopped avocados with a potato masher or the back of a fork, until it reaches the consistency you like.
2. Add the cilantro, onion, garlic cloves, lime juice, and cumin. Stir to combine.
3. Chill for at least 30 minutes in the refrigerator to let the flavors blend.

Per Serving
Calories: 276 | fat: 22.2g | carbs: 15.8g | protein: 3.4g | fiber: 10.5g

Sweet and Tangy Ketchup

Prep time: 5 minutes | Cook time: 15 minutes | Makes 2½ cups

1 cup water
¼ cup maple syrup
1 cup tomato paste
3 tablespoons apple cider vinegar
1 teaspoon onion powder
1 teaspoon garlic powder

1. Add the water to a medium saucepan and bring to a rolling boil over high heat.
2. Reduce the heat to low, stir in the maple syrup, tomato paste, vinegar, onion powder, and garlic powder. Cover and bring to a gently simmer for about 10 minutes, stirring frequently, or until the sauce begins to thicken and bubble.
3. Let the sauce rest for 30 minutes until cooled completely. Transfer to an airtight container and refrigerate for up to 1 month.

Per Serving (¼ CUP)
Calories: 46 | fat: 5.2g | carbs: 1.0g | protein: 1.1g | fiber: 1.0g

Cilantro Coconut Pesto

Prep time: 5 minutes | Cook time: 0 minutes | Makes about 2 cups

1 (13.5-ounce / 383-g) can unsweetened coconut milk
2 jalapeños, seeds and ribs removed
1 bunch cilantro leaves only
1 tablespoon white miso
1-inch (2.5 cm) piece ginger, peeled and minced
Water, as needed

1. Pulse all the ingredients in a blender until creamy and smooth.
2. Thin with a little extra water as needed to reach your preferred consistency.
3. Store in an airtight container in the fridge for up t0 2 days or in the freezer for up to 6 months.

Per Serving
Calories: 141 | fat: 13.7g | carbs: 2.8g | protein: 1.6g | fiber: 0.3g

Raw Cashew Pesto

Prep time: 5 minutes | Cook time: 0 minutes | Makes 1 cup

$1/_3$ red onion, about 2 ounces (57 g)
Juice of 1 lemon
2 garlic cloves
4 cups packed basil leaves
1 cup wheatgrass
¼ cup raw cashews
soak in boiling water for 5 minutes and drained
¼ cup water
1 tablespoon olive oil (optional)
¼ teaspoon salt (optional)

1. Place all the ingredients in a food processor and pulse for 2 to 3 minutes, or until fully combined.
2. Serve immediately or refrigerate in an airtight container for up to 2 days.

Per Serving (¼ cup)
Calories: 98 | fat: 7.3g | carbs: 6.1g | protein: 3.2g | fiber: 1.1g

Fresh Mango Salsa

Prep time: 10 minutes | Cook time: 0 minutes | Serves: 6

2 small mangoes, diced
1 red bell pepper, finely diced
½ red onion, finely diced
Juice of ½ lime, or more to taste
2 tablespoons low-sodium vegetable broth
Handful cilantro, chopped
Freshly ground black pepper, to taste
Salt, to taste (optional)

1. Stir together all the ingredients in a large bowl until well incorporated.
2. Taste and add more lime juice or salt, if needed.
3. Store in an airtight container in the fridge for up to 5 days.

Per Serving
Calories: 86 | fat: 1.9g | carbs: 13.3g | protein: 1.2g | fiber: 0.9g

Beer "Cheese" Dip

Prep time: 10 minutes | Cook time: 7 minutes | Makes about 3 cups

¾ cup water
¾ cup brown ale
½ cup raw walnuts, soaked in hot water for at least 15 minutes, then drained
½ cup raw cashews, soaked in hot water for at least 15 minutes, then drained
2 tablespoons tomato paste

2 tablespoons fresh lemon juice
1 tablespoon apple cider vinegar
½ cup nutritional yeast
½ teaspoon sweet or smoked paprika
1 tablespoon arrowroot powder
1 tablespoon red miso

1. Place the water, brown ale, walnuts, cashews, tomato paste, lemon juice, and apple cider vinegar into a high-speed blender, and purée until thoroughly mixed and smooth.
2. Transfer the mixture to a saucepan over medium heat. Add the nutritional yeast, paprika, and arrowroot powder, and whisk well. Bring to a simmer for about 7 minutes, stirring frequently, or until the mixture begins to thicken and bubble.
3. Remove from the heat and whisk in the red miso. Let the dip cool for 10 minutes and refrigerate in an airtight container for up to 5 days.

Per Serving
Calories: 113 | fat: 5.1g | carbs: 10.4g | protein: 6.3g | fiber: 3.8g

Creamy Mushroom Sauce

Prep time: 10 minutes | Cook time: 22 minutes | Makes 2 cups

¼ pound (113 g) mushrooms, sliced
1 leek, rinsed and sliced
2 cups water, divided
1 tablespoon soy sauce
1 teaspoon parsley flakes

¼ teaspoon dried oregano
¼ teaspoon dried sage
⅛ Teaspoon paprika
Freshly ground white pepper, to taste
2 tablespoons cornstarch

1. In a medium saucepan over medium-high heat, heat ½ cup of the water. Add the mushrooms and leek to the pan and sauté for 5 minutes.

2. Pour in 1 cup of the water and stir in all the seasonings. Reduce to low heat and continue to cook for 15 minutes.
3. In a small bowl, mix the cornstarch in the remaining ½ cup of the water. Slowly add to the sauce while stirring. Cook for 2 more minutes, or until thickened and clear, stirring constantly.
4. Serve immediately.

Per Serving
Calories: 35 | fat: 0.6g | carbs: 6.5g | protein: 0.8g | fiber: 0.9g

Creamy Alfredo Pasta Sauce

Prep time: 5 minutes | Cook time: 6 minutes | Makes 4 cups

2 tablespoons olive oil (optional)
6 garlic cloves, minced
3 cups unsweetened almond milk
1 head cauliflower, cut into florets, about

1 pound (454 g) total
1 teaspoon salt (optional)
¼ teaspoon freshly ground black pepper
4 tablespoons nutritional yeast
Juice of 1 lemon

1. In a medium saucepan over medium-high heat, heat the olive oil, if desired. Add the garlic to the pan and sauté for 1 minute, or until fragrant. Stir in the almond milk and bring to a boil.
2. Gently fold in the cauliflower florets. Stir in the salt (if desired) and pepper and return to a boil. Cook over medium-high heat for an additional 5 minutes, or until the cauliflower is tender, stirring constantly.
3. Carefully transfer the cauliflower along with the cooking liquid to a blender. Add the nutritional yeast and lemon and blend for 1 to 2 minutes, or until smooth and creamy.
4. Store in an airtight container and refrigerate for up to 5 days.

Per Serving (½ cup)
Calories: 108 | fat: 7.1g | carbs: 6.9g | protein: 4.2g | fiber: 3.1g

Pineapple Mint Salsa

Prep time: 10 minutes | Cook time: 0 minutes | Makes about 3 cups

1 pound (454 g) fresh pineapple, finely diced and juices reserved
1 bunch mint, leaves only, chopped
1 minced jalapeño
(optional)
1 white or red onion, finely diced
Salt, to taste (optional)

1. In a medium bowl, mix the pineapple with its juice, mint, jalapeño (if desired), and onion, and whisk well. Season with salt to taste, if desired.
2. Refrigerate in an airtight container for at least 2 hours to better incorporate the flavors.

Per Serving
Calories: 58 | fat: 0.1g | carbs: 13.7g | protein: 0.5g | fiber: 1.0g

Spicy and Tangy Black Bean Salsa

Prep time: 15 minutes | Cook time: 0 minutes | Makes about 3 cups

1 (15-ounce / 425-g) can cooked black beans, drained and rinsed
1 cup chopped tomatoes
1 cup corn kernels, thaw if frozen
½ cup cilantro or parsley, chopped
¼ cup finely chopped red onion
1 tablespoon lemon juice
1 tablespoon lime juice
1 teaspoon chili powder
½ teaspoon ground cumin
½ teaspoon regular or smoked paprika
1 medium clove garlic, finely chopped

1. Put all the ingredients in a large bowl and stir with a fork until well incorporated.
2. Serve immediately, or chill for 2 hours in the refrigerator to let the flavors blend.

Per Serving
Calories: 83 | fat: 0.5g | carbs: 15.4g | protein: 4.3g | fiber: 4.6g

Slow-Cooker Applesauce

Prep time: 10 minutes | Cook time: 4 to 5 hours | Makes about 4 cups

6 large apples, peeled, cored, and chopped into 1- to 2-inch pieces
½ cup water
1 tablespoon freshly
squeezed lemon juice
2 (3-inch) cinnamon sticks
¼ teaspoon salt (optional)

1. Add the apple pieces, water, lemon juice, cinnamon sticks, and salt (if desired) to a slow cooker and stir to combine.
2. Cover and cook on High for about 4 to 5 hours, stirring twice during cooking, or until the apples are very softened.
3. If you prefer a smooth applesauce, you can pureé the applesauce with an immersion blender until the desired consistency is reached.
4. Allow the applesauce to cool for 5 minutes and serve hot.

Per Serving
Calories: 173 | fat: 0.4g | carbs: 41.6g | protein: 0.8g | fiber: 4.2g

Chapter 8 Smoothies, Beverages and Desserts

Kale Smoothie

Prep time: 5 minutes | Cook time: 0 minutes | Serves 1

2 cups chopped kale leaves	1 cup unsweetened almond milk
1 banana, peeled	4 Medjool dates, pitted and chopped
1 cup frozen strawberries	

1. Put all the ingredients in a food processor, then blitz until glossy and smooth.
2. Serve immediately or chill in the refrigerator for an hour before serving.

Per Serving
Calories: 663 | fat: 10.0g | carbs: 142.5g | protein: 17.4g | fiber: 19.0g

Oat Cookies

Prep time: 30 minutes | Cook time: 15 to 20 minutes | Makes 40 cookies

2 cups rolled oats	cinnamon
1 cup whole-wheat flour	½ cup unsweetened pineapple juice
¼ cup soy flour	½ cup fresh apple juice
¼ cup wheat bran	
¼ cup oat bran	½ cup raisins
1 teaspoon baking soda	½ cup chopped dates
1 tablespoon baking powder	2 teaspoons vanilla extract
2 teaspoons ground	¾ cup maple syrup (optional)

1. Preheat the oven to 350ºF (180ºC).
2. Combine the dry ingredients in a large bowl. Fold in the remaining ingredients. Stir to mix well.
3. Drop 1 tablespoon of the mixture on a baking sheet to make a cookie. Repeat with remaining mixture.
4. Bake in the preheated oven for 15 to 20 minutes, or until golden brown.
5. Serve immediately.

Per Serving (1 cookie)
Calories: 57 | fat: 0.6g | carbs: 14.1g | protein: 1.7g | fiber: 1.7g

Orange and Cranberry Quinoa Bites

Prep time: 10 minutes | Chill time: 15 minutes | Makes 12 bites

2 tablespoons almond butter	¼ cup ground almonds
2 tablespoons maple syrup (optional)	1 tablespoon chia seeds
Zest of 1 orange	¼ cup sesame seeds, toasted
1 tablespoon dried cranberries	½ teaspoon vanilla extract
¾ cup cooked quinoa	

1. In a medium bowl, mix the almond butter and maple syrup (if desired) until smooth.
2. Stir in the remaining ingredients, and mix to hold together in a ball.
3. Divide and form the mixture into 12 balls. Put them on a baking sheet lined with parchment paper.
4. Put in the fridge to set for about 15 minutes. Serve chilled.

Per Serving
Calories: 109 | fat: 11.0g | carbs: 5.0g | protein: 3.0g | fiber: 3.0g

Orange Glazed Bananas

Prep time: 10 minutes | Cook time: 4 minutes | Serves 6 to 8

$^1/_3$ cup fresh orange juice	1 teaspoon vanilla extract
6 ripe bananas, peeled and sliced	½ teaspoon ground cinnamon

1. Put the orange juice in a saucepan and warm over medium heat. Add the sliced bananas and cook for 2 minutes.
2. Add the vanilla and cinnamon and continue to cook until the moisture is absorbed, about another 2 minutes.
3. Serve warm.

Per Serving
Calories: 98 | fat: 0.4g | carbs: 24.7g | protein: 1.2g | fiber: 2.8g

Hot Tropical Smoothie

Prep time: 5 minutes | Cook time: 0 minutes | Serves 1

1 cup frozen mango chunks	peeled and pitted
1 cup frozen pineapple chunks	2 cups spinach leaves
1 small tangerine,	1 cup coconut water
	¼ teaspoon cayenne pepper (optional)

1. Add all the ingredients in a food processor, then blitz until the mixture is smooth and combine well.
2. Serve immediately or chill in the refrigerator for an hour before serving.

Per Serving
Calories: 283 | fat: 1.9g | carbs: 67.9g | protein: 6.4g | fiber: 10.4g

Pecan, Coconut, and Chocolate Bars

Prep time: 15 minutes | Cook time: 10 minutes | Makes 8 Bars

1 cup pitted dates, soaked in hot water for 10 minutes and drained	$1/_3$ cup plus ¼ cup chopped pecans
¼ cup maple syrup	$1/_3$ cup unsweetened shredded coconut
1½ cups rolled oats	$1/_3$ cup mini chocolate chips

1. Preheat the oven to 300ºF (150ºC). Line a baking dish with parchment paper.
2. Put the dates in a blender and process to make the date paste, then combine the date paste with maple syrup in a bowl.
3. Put ½ cup of the oats and ¼ cup of the pecans in the blender and process to grind. Mix them in the bowl of date mixture.
4. Stir in the remaining oats and pecans, coconut, and chocolate chips.
5. Pour the mixture in the baking dish and bake in the preheated oven for 10 minutes or until lightly browned.
6. Remove the baking dish from the oven and slice the chunk into 8 bars. Serve immediately.

Per Serving (8 bars)
Calories: 2347 | fat: 81.0g | carbs: 407.0g | protein: 26.0g | fiber: 31.0g

No-Bake Green Energy Super Bars

Prep time: 15 minutes | Cook time: 0 minutes | Makes 36 Energy Bars

1½ cups pitted dates, soaked in hot water for 5 minutes and drained	2 tablespoons spirulina powder
½ cup roasted, unsalted cashews	¼ cup carob
½ cup raw sunflower seeds	2 tablespoons unsweetened shredded coconut
	Pinch of salt (optional)

1. Put the dates in a blender and process to make the date paste. Add the cashews, sunflower seeds, spirulina powder, and carob. Pulse until dough-like and thick.
2. Pour the mixture in a baking dish lined with parchment paper, then sprinkle with coconut and salt (if desired).
3. Let stand for 5 minutes, then pull the parchment paper with the mixture out of the container and cut the mixture into 36 bars. Serve immediately.

Per Serving (36 energy bars)
Calories: 1729 | fat: 79.0g | carbs: 231.0g | protein: 33.0g | fiber: 18.0g

Prune, Grapefruit, and Orange Compote

Prep time: 10 minutes | Cook time: 4 minutes | Serves 4

1 cup pitted prunes	grapefruit sections, drained
¾ cup fresh orange juice	2 (11-ounce / 312-g) cans unsweetened mandarin oranges, drained
1 tablespoon maple syrup (optional)	
2 (1-pound / 454-g) cans unsweetened	

1. Put the prunes, orange juice, and maple syrup (if desired) in a saucepan. Bring to a boil, reduce the heat, and cook gently for 1 minute. Remove from the heat and cool.
2. Combine the mixture with the grapefruit and mandarin oranges. Stir to mix.
3. Cover and refrigerate for at least 2 hours before serving.

Per Serving
Calories: 303 | fat: 0.7g | carbs: 77.2g | protein: 4.3g | fiber: 4.8g

Coconut and Pineapple Pudding

Prep time: 10 minutes | Cook time: 30 minutes | Serves 2

2 tablespoons ground flaxseeds
2 cups unsweetened almond milk
1 tablespoon maple syrup
¼ cup chia seeds
1 teaspoon vanilla ex-
tract
2 tablespoons shred-ded, unsweetened co-conut
1 Medjool date, pitted and chopped
2 cups sliced pineap-ple

1. Put the flaxseeds, almond milk, maple syrup, chia seeds, and vanilla extract in a bowl. Stir to mix well.
2. Put the bowl in the refrigerator for 20 minutes, then remove from the refrigera-tor and stir again. Place the bowl back to the refrigerator for 30 minutes or over-night to make the pudding.
3. Mix in the coconut, and spread the date and pineapple on top before serving.

Per Serving
Calories: 513 | fat: 22.9g | carbs: 66.4g | protein: 16.2g | fiber: 17.0g

Sweet Potato Toast with Blueberries

Prep time: 10 minutes | Cook time: 30 minutes | Makes 10 Slices

1 large sweet potato, rinsed and cut into 10 slices
20 blueberries
2 tablespoons almond butter

1. Preheat the oven to 350ºF (180ºC). Put a wire rack on a baking sheet.
2. Arrange the sweet potato slices on the wire rack, then cook in the preheated oven for 15 or until soft. Flip the sweet potato slices for every 5 minutes to make sure evenly cooked. Then toast immedi-ately or store in the refrigerator.
3. To make the sweet potato toast, put the cooked sweet potato slices in a toaster in batches and toast over medium for 15 minutes or until crispy and golden brown.
4. Serve the toast with blueberries and al-mond butter.

Per Serving (10 slices)
Calories: 374 | fat: 18.1g | carbs: 47.2g | protein: 10.5g | fiber: 9.9g

Pumpkin Smoothie

Prep time: 5 minutes | Cook time: 0 min-utes | Serves 1

½ cup pumpkin purée
4 Medjool dates, pit-ted and chopped
1 cup unsweetened almond milk
¼ teaspoon vanilla
extract
¼ teaspoon ground cinnamon
½ cup ice
Pinch ground nutmeg

1. Add all the ingredients in a blender, then process until the mixture is glossy and well mixed.
2. Serve immediately.

Per Serving
Calories: 417 | fat: 3.0g | carbs: 94.9g | pro-tein: 11.4g | fiber: 10.4g

Apple Toast

Prep time: 5 minutes | Cook time: 20 minutes | Makes 2 slices

½ teaspoon ground cinnamon
1 Teaspoons coconut oil (optional)
1 tablespoon maple
syrup (optional)
1 apple, cored and thinly sliced
2 slices whole-grain bread

1. Preheat the oven to 350ºF (180ºC).
2. In a large bowl, mix the cinnamon, coco-nut oil (if desired), and maple syrup (if desired). Add the apple slices and toss to coat well.
3. Put the apple slices in a skillet over me-dium-high heat and cook for 5 minutes, or until soft. Transfer the apple slices to a plate.
4. Cook in the skillet for 4 minutes. Flip halfway through. Top the toast with the apples. Rub each slice of bread with cin-namon mixture on both sides.
5. Lay the bread slices on a baking sheet, top the slices with the apples. Cook in the oven for 15 minutes, or until softened.
6. Serve immediately.

Per Serving (1 slice)
Calories: 187 | fat: 18.0g | carbs: 7.0g | pro-tein: 4.0g | fiber: 4.0g

Strawberry Sushi

Prep time: 20 minutes | Cook time: 25 minutes | Makes 24 Sushi

3 cups cooked white sushi rice
3 tablespoons fresh lemon juice
½ teaspoon vanilla extract
½ cup maple sugar

2 cups strawberries, hulled and quartered
3 tablespoons chia seeds
Salt, to taste (optional)

1. Combine the cooked sushi rice, lemon juice, vanilla extract, and maple sugar in a large bowl. Stir to mix well.
2. Cover a sushi mat with plastic wrap, then arrange 1 cup of rice on top and press into ½-inch thick.
3. Arrange a row of strawberries on the rice and leave a 1-inch gap from the bottom side. Sprinkle with 1 teaspoon of chia seeds.
4. Use the plastic wrap and sushi mat to help to roll the rice into a cylinder. When you roll, pull the plastic wrap and sushi mat away from the rice at the same time. Repeat with the remaining rice and chia seeds.
5. Sprinkle the rolls with salt, if desired. Let stand for 5 minutes and slice each roll into 8 sushi. Serve immediately.

Per Serving (24 sushi)
Calories: 3081 | fat: 13.0g | carbs: 699.0g | protein: 72.0g | fiber: 34.0g

Pineapple Smoothie

Prep time: 5 minutes | Cook time: 0 minutes | Serves 1 to 2

¾ cup pineapple chunks
½ cup frozen straw-

berries
½ cup unsweetened apple juice

1. Put all the ingredients in a blender and pulse until smooth.
2. Serve immediately.

Per Serving
Calories: 134 | fat: 0.2g | carbs: 32.4g | protein: 0.6g | fiber: 2.3g

Graham Pancakes

Prep time: 20 minutes | Cook time: 4 minutes each | Serves 4 to 6

2 cups whole-wheat flour (about 11 ounces / 312 g)
2 teaspoons baking powder
½ teaspoon baking soda
2 tablespoons date sugar
¾ teaspoon salt (op-

tional)
2½ cups unsweetened oat milk
2 tablespoons lemon juice
¼ cup unsweetened applesauce
2 teaspoons vanilla extract

1. Combine the flour, baking powder and soda, date sugar, and salt (if desired) in a large bowl.
2. Make a well in the center of the flour mixture, then add the oat milk, lemon juice, applesauce, and vanilla extract. Whisk the mixture until smooth and thick.
3. Make a pancake: Pour ¼ cup of the mixture in a nonstick skillet, then cook for 4 minutes. Flip the pancake halfway through the cooking time or until the first side is golden brown. Repeat with the remaining mixture.
4. Transfer the pancakes on a plate and serve warm.

Per Serving
Calories: 208 | fat: 3.1g | carbs: 38.9g | protein: 8.7g | fiber: 4.4g

Berry Smoothie

Prep time: 5 minutes | Cook time: 0 minutes | Serves 1

1 cup berry mix (strawberries, blueberries, and cranberries)
4 Medjool dates, pit-

ted and chopped
1½ cups unsweetened almond milk, plus more as needed

1. Add all the ingredients in a blender, then process until the mixture is smooth and well mixed.
2. Serve immediately or chill in the refrigerator for an hour before serving.

Per Serving
Calories: 473 | fat: 4.0g | carbs: 103.7g | protein: 14.8g | fiber: 9.7g

Cranberry and Banana Smoothie

Prep time: 5 minutes | Cook time: 0 minutes | Serves 1

1 cup frozen cranberries
1 large banana, peeled
4 Medjool dates, pitted and chopped
1½ cups unsweetened almond milk

1. Add all the ingredients in a food processor, then process until the mixture is glossy and well mixed.
2. Serve immediately or chill in the refrigerator for an hour before serving.

Per Serving
Calories: 616 | fat: 8.0g | carbs: 132.8g | protein: 15.7g | fiber: 14.6g

Raisin Oat Cookies

Prep time: 20 minutes | Cook time: 8 to 10 minutes | Makes 24 Cookies

$1/3$ cup almond butter
½ cup maple sugar
¼ cup unsweetened applesauce
1 teaspoon vanilla extract
$1/3$ cup sorghum flour
$2/3$ cups oat flour
½ teaspoon baking soda
½ cup raisins
1 cup rolled oats
½ teaspoon ground cinnamon
¼ teaspoon salt (optional)

1. Preheat the oven to 350°F (180°C). Line two baking sheets with parchment paper.
2. Whisk together the almond butter, maple sugar, and applesauce in a large bowl until smooth.
3. Mix in the remaining ingredients and keep whisking until a stiff dough form.
4. Divide and roll the dough into 24 small balls, then arrange the balls in the baking sheets. Keep a little space between each two balls. Bash them with your hands to make them form like cookies.
5. Bake in the preheated oven for 9 minutes or until crispy. Flip the cookies halfway through the cooking time.
6. Remove them from the oven and allow to cool for 10 minutes before serving.

Per Serving (24 cookies)
Calories: 1400 | fat: 56.0g | carbs: 224.1g | protein: 45.5g | fiber: 30.5g

Super Smoothie

Prep time: 5 minutes | Cook time: 0 minutes | Makes 3 to 4 Cups

1 banana, peeled
1 cup chopped mango
1 cup raspberries
¼ cup rolled oats
1 carrot, peeled
1 cup chopped fresh kale
2 tablespoons
chopped fresh parsley
1 tablespoon flaxseeds
1 tablespoon grated fresh ginger
½ cup unsweetened soy milk
1 cup water

1. Put all the ingredients in a food processor, then blitz until glossy and smooth.
2. Serve immediately or chill in the refrigerator for an hour before serving.

Per Serving
Calories: 550 | fat: 39.0g | carbs: 31.0g | protein: 13.0g | fiber: 15.0g

Overnight Oats

Prep time: 5 minutes | Cook time: 5 minutes | Serves 1

½ cup rolled oats
1 tablespoon ground flaxseeds
1 tablespoon maple syrup
¼ teaspoon ground cinnamon
Topping Options:
1 pear, chopped and
1 tablespoon cashews
1 apple, chopped and
1 tablespoon walnuts
1 banana, sliced, and
1 tablespoon peanut
butter
1 cup sliced grapes and 1 tablespoon sunflower seeds
1 cup berries and 1 tablespoon unsweetened coconut flakes
2 tablespoons raisins and 1 tablespoon hazelnuts
2 tablespoons dried cranberries and 1 tablespoon pumpkin seeds

1. Combine the ground flaxseeds, oats, cinnamon, and maple syrup in a bowl, and then pour the water into the bowl to submerge. Stir to mix well.
2. Leave them to soak for at least 1 hour, or overnight, then serve with the topping you choose.

Per Serving
Calories: 244 | fat: 16.0g | carbs: 10.0g | protein: 7.0g | fiber: 6.0g

Kiwi and Strawberry Smoothie

Prep time: 5 minutes | Cook time: 0 minutes | Serves 1

1 kiwi, peeled
5 medium strawberries
½ frozen banana
1 cup unsweetened almond milk
2 tablespoons hemp seeds
2 tablespoons peanut butter
1 to 2 teaspoons maple syrup
½ cup spinach leaves
Handful broccoli sprouts

1. Put all the ingredients in a food processor, then blitz until creamy and smooth.
2. Serve immediately or chill in the refrigerator for an hour before serving.

Per Serving
Calories: 562 | fat: 28.6g | carbs: 63.6g | protein: 23.3g | fiber: 15.1g

Cashew and Lemon Meltaways

Prep time: 1 hour 10 minutes | Cook time: 0 minutes | Makes 36 meltaways

½ cup finely ground raw cashews
½ cup organic virgin coconut oil (optional)
2 tablespoons fresh lemon juice
2 tablespoons pure maple syrup (optional)
Pinch of sea salt (optional)

1. Put a piece of wax paper in a baking pan and place the pan into the refrigerator.
2. Combine all the ingredients in a blender and blitz until the mixture becomes creamy and smooth.
3. Scoop up ½ tablespoon of the cashew mixture and drop onto the cold baking pan. Repeat with remaining mixture, leaving enough space between each drop.
4. Put the pan back into the refrigerator to set for about 1 hour, or until the drops become solid. You may need to work in batches to avoid overcrowding.
5. Remove the solid meltaways from the wax paper and serve immediately.

Per Serving (1 meltaway)
Calories: 40 | fat: 3.8g | carbs: 1.3g | protein: 0.3g | fiber: 0.1g

Banana and Chai Chia Smoothie

Prep time: 5 minutes | Cook time: 0 minutes | Makes 3 Cups

1 banana
1 cup alfalfa sprouts
1 tablespoon chia seeds
½ cup unsweetened coconut milk
1 to 2 soft Medjool dates, pitted
¼ teaspoon ground cinnamon
1 tablespoon grated fresh ginger
1 cup water
Pinch ground cardamom

1. Add all the ingredients in a blender, then process until the mixture is smooth and creamy. Add water or coconut milk if necessary.
2. Serve immediately.

Per Serving (3 cups)
Calories: 477 | fat: 41.0g | carbs: 31.0g | protein: 8.0g | fiber: 14.0g

Belgian Gold Waffles

Prep time: 15 minutes | Cook time: 5 to 6 minutes | Makes 4 Waffles

2 cups soy flour (about 10 ounces / 284 g)
1 tablespoon baking powder
¼ teaspoon baking soda
3 tablespoons cornstarch
2 tablespoons date sugar
½ teaspoon salt (optional)
2 cups unsweetened soy milk
1 tablespoon lemon juice
1 teaspoon vanilla extract
¼ cup unsweetened applesauce

1. Preheat the waffle iron.
2. Combine the soy flour, baking powder and soda, cornstarch, date sugar, and salt (if desired) in a large bowl.
3. Make a well in the center of the flour mixture, then add the soy milk, lemon juice, vanilla extract, and applesauce. Whisk the mixture until smooth and thick.
4. Add 1 cup of the mixture to the preheated waffle iron and cook for 5 to 6 minutes or until golden brown. Serve immediately. Repeat with the remaining mixture.

Per Serving (1 waffle)
Calories: 292 | fat: 8.0g | carbs: 34.6g | protein: 23.9g | fiber: 7.4g

Chocolate and Peanut Butter Smoothie

Prep time: 5 minutes | Cook time: 0 minutes | Makes 3 to 4 Cups

1 tablespoon unsweetened cocoa powder	½ cup unsweetened soy milk
1 tablespoon peanut butter	¼ cup rolled oats
1 banana	1 tablespoon flaxseeds
1 teaspoon maca powder	1 tablespoon maple syrup
	1 cup water

1. Add all the Ingredients in a blender, then process until the mixture is smooth and creamy. Add water or soy milk if necessary.
2. Serve immediately.

Per Serving (3 to 4 cups)
Calories: 474 | fat: 16.0g | carbs: 27.0g | protein: 13.0g | fiber: 18.0g

Chewy Salted Caramel Bites

Prep time: 1 hour 10 minutes | Cook time: o minutes | Makes 18 bites

1 cup finely chopped raw cashews	1 teaspoon pure vanilla extract
1 cup soft Medjool dates, cored	¼ teaspoon sea salt (optional)
½ cup tahini	

1. Line a baking pan with wax paper and place the pan into the refrigerator.
2. Combine the cashews and the Medjool dates in a food processor and process until finely chopped and well mixed. Add the tahini, vanilla, and salt (if desired) and pulse until the mixture has broken down into a chunky paste consistency.
3. Scoop up a Teaspoonful of the mixture and roll into a ball. Repeat to make 18 balls. Arrange them on the prepared baking pan and freeze in the refrigerator for about 1 hour, or until firm.
4. Serve immediately.

Per Serving (1 bite)
Calories: 75 | fat: 3.6g | carbs: 10.9g | protein: 1.4g | fiber: 1.5g

Vanilla Milk Steamer

Prep time: 5 minutes | Cook time: 5 minutes | Serves 1

1 cup unsweetened almond milk	½ teaspoon pure vanilla extract
2 teaspoons pure maple syrup (optional)	Pinch ground cinnamon

1. Warm the almond milk in a small saucepan over medium heat for 5 minutes until steaming, stirring constantly (don't allow it to boil).
2. Carefully pour the hot milk into your blender and mix in the maple syrup (if desired) and vanilla. Blend on low speed for 10 seconds, then increase the speed to high and blend until well combined and frothy.
3. Serve sprinkled with the cinnamon.

Per Serving
Calories: 184 | fat: 7.9g | carbs: 20.7g | protein: 7.6g | fiber: 0g

Apple Chips

Prep time: 25 minutes | Cook time: 30 minutes | Serves 8 to 10

½ cup old-fashioned rolled oats	¼ teaspoon ground nutmeg
½ cup unsweetened apple juice, divided	½ teaspoon ground cinnamon
2 pounds (907 g) apples, sliced	1 tablespoon whole-wheat flour

1. Preheat the oven to 425ºF (220ºC).
2. Combine the rolled oats and 1 tablespoon of the apple juice in a food processor. Pulse to mix well. Set aside.
3. Put the apples in a mixing bowl and mix with the remaining apple juice. Add the nutmeg, cinnamon, and flour. Toss to coat.
4. Put the apples in a baking pan. Sprinkle the oat mixture over the apples.
5. Bake in the preheated oven for 30 minutes, or until golden brown.
6. Serve immediately.

Per Serving
Calories: 68 | fat: 0.5g | carbs: 17.7g | protein: 1.2g | fiber: 3.1g

Golden Milk

Prep time: 5 minutes | Cook time: 0 minutes | Serves 1

¼ teaspoon ground cinnamon
½ teaspoon ground turmeric
½ teaspoon grated fresh ginger
1 teaspoon maple syrup
1 cup unsweetened coconut milk
Ground black pepper, to taste
2 tablespoons water

1. Combine all the ingredients in a saucepan. Stir to mix well.
2. Heat over medium heat for 5 minutes. Keep stirring during the heating.
3. Allow to cool for 5 minutes, then pour the mixture in a blender. Pulse until creamy and smooth. Serve immediately.

Per Serving
Calories: 577 | fat: 57.3g | carbs: 19.7g | protein: 5.7g | fiber: 6.1g

Creamy Dreamy Mango Banana Smoothie

Prep time: 5 minutes | Cook time: 0 minutes | Serves 4

1 banana
¼ cup rolled oats, or 1 scoop plant protein powder
1 tablespoon flaxseed or chia seeds
1 cup berries
1 cup chopped mango (frozen or fresh)
½ cup non-dairy milk (optional)
1 cup water
2 tablespoons fresh parsley, or basil, chopped
1 cup chopped fresh kale, spinach, collards, or other green
1 carrot, peeled
1 tablespoon grated fresh ginger

1. Purée everything in a blender until smooth, adding more water (or non-dairy milk) if needed.
2. Add none, some, or all of the bonus boosters, as desired. Purée until blended.

Per Serving
Calories: 550 | fat: 39g | carbs: 16g | protein: 13g | fiber: 15g

Alfalfa Sprouts Banana Smoothie

Prep time: 5 minutes | Cook time: 0 minutes | Serves 3

1 banana
½ cup coconut milk
1 cup water
1 cup alfalfa sprouts
1 to 2 soft Medjool dates, pitted
1 tablespoon chia
seeds or ground flax or hemp hearts
¼ teaspoon ground cinnamon
Pinch ground cardamom

1. 1 tablespoon grated fresh ginger, or ¼ teaspoon ground ginger
2. Purée everything in a blender until smooth, adding more water (or coconut milk) if needed.

Per Serving
Calories: 477 | fat: 41g | carbs: 17g | protein: 8g | fiber: 14g

Golden Milk

Prep time: 5 minutes | Cook time: 5 minutes | Serves 1

½ teaspoon ground turmeric
½ teaspoon grated fresh ginger
¼ teaspoon ground cinnamon
Pinch ground black pepper
1 cup canned full-fat coconut milk
1 tablespoon extra-virgin coconut oil (optional)
1 teaspoon maple syrup (optional)

1. Combine the turmeric, ginger, cinnamon, and black pepper in a small saucepan over medium heat.
2. Add the milk, oil, and maple syrup (if desired) and whisk well.
3. Let the mixture heat for 5 minutes until very hot but not boiling.
4. Carefully pour hot milk into a blender and blend on low speed until it becomes frothy. Serve immediately.

Per Serving
Calories: 641 | fat: 61.9g | carbs: 16.7g | protein: 5.6g | fiber: 1.4g

Rhubarb and Strawberry Pie

Prep time: 45 minutes | Cook time: 30 minutes | Serves 6 to 8

Crust:
2 cups whole-wheat pastry flour
¾ cup finely ground almonds
1 cup unsweetened apple juice
Filling:
2 cups chopped rhu-
barb
2 cups sliced strawberries
¼ cup fresh orange juice
¼ cup maple syrup (optional)
3 tablespoons arrowroot

1. Pour the flour and ground almonds into a food processor. Add the apple juice slowly while processing until the mixture forms a ball. Refrigerate for ½ hour.
2. Roll out half of the crust into ⅛-inch thick and place in a lightly oiled pie pan. Make strips for the top out of the remaining dough, or roll out a top crust.
3. Preheat the oven to 350ºF (180ºC).
4. Mix the ingredients for the filling in a bowl. Pour the mixture over the pie crust. Cover with top crust.
5. Bake in the preheated oven for 30 minutes until liquid oozes out.
6. Allow to cool before cutting and serving.

Per Serving
Calories: 228 | fat: 5.4g | carbs: 41.7g | protein: 6.5g | fiber: 5.9g

Mango Agua Fresca

Prep time: 5 minutes | Cook time: 0 minutes | Serves 2

2 fresh mangoes, diced
1½ cups water
1 teaspoon fresh lime juice
Maple syrup, to taste
2 cups ice
2 slices fresh lime, for garnish
2 fresh mint sprigs, for garnish

1. Put the mangoes, lime juice, maple syrup, and water in a blender. Process until creamy and smooth.
2. Divide the beverage into two glasses, then garnish each glass with ice, lime slice, and mint sprig before serving.

Per Serving
Calories: 230 | fat: 1.3g | carbs: 57.7g | protein: 2.8g | fiber: 5.4g

Light Ginger Tea

Prep time: 5 minutes | Cook time: 10 to 15 minutes | Serves 2

1 small ginger knob, sliced into four 1-inch chunks
4 cups water
Juice of 1 large lemon
Maple syrup, to taste

1. Add the ginger knob and water in a saucepan, then simmer over medium heat for 10 to 15 minutes.
2. Turn off the heat, then mix in the lemon juice. Strain the liquid to remove the ginger, then fold in the maple syrup and serve.

Per Serving
Calories: 32 | fat: 0.1g | carbs: 8.6g | protein: 0.1g | fiber: 0.1g

Banana Smoothie

Prep time: 5 minutes | Cook time: 0 minutes | Serves 1 to 2

1 banana
½ cup frozen peaches
½ cup unsweetened apple juice

1. Process all the ingredients in a blender until fully mixed and smooth.
2. Serve immediately.

Per Serving
Calories: 149 | fat: 0.3g | carbs: 35.4g | protein: 1.1g | fiber: 2.8g

Classic Switchel

Prep time: 5 minutes | Cook time: 0 minutes | Makes 4¼ cups

1-inch piece ginger, minced
2 tablespoons apple cider vinegar
2 tablespoons maple
syrup
4 cups water
¼ teaspoon sea salt (optional)

1. Combine all the ingredients in a glass. Stir to mix well.
2. Serve immediately or chill in the refrigerator for an hour before serving.

Per Serving (4¼ cups)
Calories: 110 | fat: 0g | carbs: 28.0g | protein: 0g | fiber: 0g

Lime and Cucumber Electrolyte Drink

Prep time: 5 minutes | Cook time: 0 minutes | Makes 4¼ cups

¼ cup chopped cucumber
1 tablespoon fresh lime juice
1 tablespoon apple cider vinegar
2 tablespoons maple syrup
¼ teaspoon sea salt (optional)
4 cups water

1. Combine all the ingredients in a glass. Stir to mix well.
2. Refrigerate overnight before serving.

Per Serving (4¼ cups)
Calories: 114 | fat: 0.1g | carbs: 28.9g | protein: 0.3g | fiber: 0.3g

Apricot and Pear Bars

Prep time: 15 minutes | Cook time: 25 minutes | Makes 24 bars

3 cups packed dried apricots
2 (1-pound / 454-g) cans pears, with juice
½ cup oat flour
1 cup whole-wheat flour
1¹/₃ cups rolled oats
1¹/₃ cups quick oats
1 cup fresh orange juice
1 teaspoon vanilla extract
¼ cup maple syrup (optional)

1. Put the apricots and the pears with juices in a saucepan. Cook for 5 minutes over medium heat or until soft.
2. Pour in a food processor and process to purée. Set aside.
3. Preheat the oven to 300ºF (150ºC).
4. Combine the flours and oats in a large bowl. Make a well in the center of the dry ingredients.
5. Combine the remaining ingredients in the well and stir to mix well with the oat mixture.
6. Press ¾ of the mixture into the bottom of a baking pan. Pour the apricot mixture over. Spread the remaining mixture on top.
7. Bake in the preheated oven for 20 minutes, or until firm. Cool and cut into 24 bars before serving.

Per Serving (1 bar)
Calories: 129 | fat: 1.1g | carbs: 28.7g | protein: 3.0g | fiber: 4.2g

Crispy Graham Crackers

Prep time: 30 minutes | Cook time: 11 minutes | Makes 12 Crackers

1½ cups spelt flour, plus additional for dusting
½ teaspoon baking soda
¼ cup date sugar
1 teaspoon ground cinnamon
½ teaspoon salt (optional)
2 tablespoons molasses
1 teaspoon vanilla extract
¼ cup unsweetened applesauce
1 tablespoon ground flaxseeds
¼ cup unsweetened soy milk
1 tablespoon maple sugar

1. Preheat the oven to 350ºF (180ºC). Line a baking sheet with parchment paper.
2. Combine the flour, baking soda, date sugar, ½ teaspoon of the cinnamon, and salt (if desired) in a large bowl. Stir to combine well.
3. Make a well in the center of the flour mixture, then add the molasses, vanilla, and applesauce to the well. Whisk to combine.
4. Mix in the flaxseeds and soy milk, then knead the mixture to form a smooth dough. Add a dash of water if necessary.
5. On a clean work surface, dust with a touch of flour, then flatten the dough into a ⅛-inch-thick rectangle with a rolling pin on this surface.
6. Cut the dough into 8 equal-sized rectangles to make the crackers, then arrange the crackers on the baking sheet.
7. Sprinkle the crackers with maple sugar and remaining cinnamon. Poke holes into each cracker with a fork.
8. Bake in the preheated oven for 11 minutes or until crispy and golden brown. Flip the crackers halfway through the cooking time.
9. Remove them from the oven and allow to cool for 10 minutes before serving.

Per Serving (12 crackers)
Calories: 1266 | fat: 10.4g | carbs: 268.6g | protein: 41.2g | fiber: 32.0g

Easy and Fresh Mango Madness

Prep time: 5 minutes | Cook time: 0 minutes | Makes 3 to 4 Cups

1 cup chopped mango
1 cup chopped peach
1 banana
1 cup strawberries
1 carrot, peeled and chopped
1 cup water

1. Put all the ingredients in a food processor, then blitz until glossy and smooth.
2. Serve immediately or chill in the refrigerator for an hour before serving.

Per Serving (3 to 4 cups)
Calories: 376 | fat: 22.0g | carbs: 19.0g | fiber: 14.0g | protein: 5.0g

Brown Rice Pudding

Prep time: 10 minutes | Cook time: 45 minutes | Serves 4

2 cups cooked brown rice
1 cup raisins
¾ cup soy milk
2 teaspoons ground cinnamon
1 teaspoon vanilla extract
2 tablespoons maple syrup (optional)
¾ cup water

1. Preheat the oven to 325ºF (163ºC).
2. Combine all the ingredients and pour into a casserole dish| cover and bake in the preheated oven for 45 minutes, or until set.
3. Serve hot.

Per Serving
Calories: 284 | fat: 1.8g | carbs: 65.2g | protein: 5.1g | fiber: 4.1g

Chia Pudding with Coconut and Fruits

Prep time: 20 minutes | Cook time: 0 minutes | Serves 4

2 cups unsweetened soy milk
1½ Teaspoons vanilla extract
½ cup chia seeds
2 tablespoons maple syrup
¼ teaspoon salt (optional)
¼ cup flaked coconut, toasted
2 cups strawberries, avocado slices, and banana slices mix

1. Make the pudding: Combine the soy milk, vanilla extract, chia seeds, maple syrup, and salt (if desired) in a bowl. Stir to mix well. Wrap the bowl in plastic and refrigerate for at least 8 hours.
2. Serve the pudding with coconut flakes and fruit mix on top.

Per Serving
Calories: 303 | fat: 14.7g | carbs: 36.0g | protein: 9.5g | fiber: 13.1g

Peach and Mango Sorbet

Prep time: 1 hour 5 minutes | Cook time: o minutes | Serves 4

2 cups frozen peaches
2 cups frozen mango
1 cup fresh orange juice

1. In a food processor, combine the peaches, mango and orange juice and pulse until puréed and smooth.
2. Transfer the fruit mixture to an airtight container and freeze in the refrigerator for about 1 hour, or until firm.
3. Serve cold.

Per Serving
Calories: 107 | fat: 0.6g | carbs: 26.2g | protein: 1.8g | fiber: 2.6g

Cinnamon Apple Bites

Prep time: 15 minutes | Cook time: 15 minutes | Serves 4

4 apples cut into bite-size chunks
½ cup raisins
½ cup unsweetened
apple juice
Pinch ground cinnamon, for sprinkling

1. Put all the ingredients in a saucepan. Cook over medium-low heat for 15 minutes or until the apples are tender, stirring occasionally.
2. Serve immediately.

Per Serving
Calories: 172 | fat: 0.5g | carbs: 45.5g | protein: 1.2g | fiber: 5.5g

Matcha Limeade

Prep time: 10 minutes | Cook time: 0 minutes | Makes 4 Cups

2 tablespoons matcha powder
¼ cup raw agave syrup

3 cups water, divided
1 cup fresh lime juice
3 tablespoons chia seeds

1. Lightly simmer the matcha, agave syrup, and 1 cup of water in a saucepan over medium heat. Keep stirring until no matcha lumps.
2. Pour the matcha mixture in a large glass, then add the remaining ingredients and stir to mix well.
3. Refrigerate for at least an hour before serving.

Per Serving (1 cup)
Calories: 152 | fat: 4.5g | carbs: 26.8g | protein: 3.7g | fiber: 5.3g

Pear Squares

Prep time: 40 minutes | Cook time: 50 minutes | Makes 24 squares

Filling:
1 (1-pound / 454-g) can pears, with juice
2 cups chopped dried pears
¾ cup pitted dates
¼ cup tapioca
1 teaspoon orange extract
Crust:
½ cup pitted dates
1½ cups water

½ cup whole-wheat flour
1½ cups regular rolled oats
⅛ Teaspoon salt (optional)
1 teaspoon vanilla extract
Topping:
1 cup regular rolled oats

1. Put the canned pears and juice in a food processor and process until puréed.
2. Transfer to a saucepan. Add the dried pears, dates, and tapioca. Simmer, covered, for 20 minutes. Add the orange extract and set aside.
3. Preheat the oven to 375ºF (190ºC).
4. Combine the dates and water in a food processor and process until finely ground.
5. In a bowl, combine the date water (reserve ¼ cup), flour, oats, salt (if desired), and vanilla. Press into a baking dish and bake for 10 minutes.

6. Meanwhile, toss the remaining rolled oats with the reserved date water.
7. Spoon the filling over the crust. Sprinkle, the oat topping over the filling.
8. Bake in the preheated oven for 20 minutes, or until firm. Cool and cut into 2-inch squares before serving.

Per Serving (1 square)
Calories: 112 | fat: 0.8g | carbs: 27.5g | protein: 2.2g | fiber: 3.8g

Green Smoothie

Prep time: 5 minutes | Cook time: 0 minutes | Serves 2

2 cups shredded kale
1 cup unsweetened almond milk
½ Granny Smith apple, unpeeled,

cored, and chopped
½ avocado, diced
¼ cup coconut yogurt
3 ice cubes

1. Process all the ingredients in a blender until creamy and smooth, scraping down the sides as needed. If the smoothie is too thick, you can add more almond milk to thin.
2. Divide the smoothie between two glasses and serve.

Per Serving
Calories: 175 | fat: 7.1g | carbs: 19.8g | protein: 8.0g | fiber: 4.0g

Chia Fresca

Prep time: 5 minutes | Cook time: 0 minutes | Serves 1

1 cup unsweetened coconut water
1 tablespoon chia seeds
1 tablespoon fresh

lime juice
½ teaspoon pure maple syrup (optional)
¼ cup strawberries
¼ cup diced peaches

1. Stir together all the ingredients in a glass and allow to sit for 5 to 10 minutes, or until some liquid is absorbed, and the chia seeds become gelatinous.
2. Serve chilled.

Per Serving
Calories: 105 | fat: 3.1g | carbs: 22.2g | protein: 3.7g | fiber: 6.7g

Tropical Fruit Smoothie Bowl

Prep time: 5 minutes | Cook time: 0 minutes | Serves 1 to 2

2 cups frozen mango chunks
1 frozen banana
½ cup frozen pineapple chunks
½ to 1 cup plant-based milk
¼ cup chopped fruit of your choice

2 tablespoons chopped nuts of your choice
Toppings:
1½ tablespoons coconut shreds
1 tablespoon flaxseed meal

1. Place all the ingredients except the toppings into a blender and process until smoothly blended.
2. Serve topped with the coconut shreds and flaxseed meal.

Per Serving
Calories: 343 | fat: 8.7g | carbs: 66.4g | protein: 6.8g | fiber: 7.0g

Berry Smoothie

Prep time: 5 minutes | Cook time: 0 minutes | Makes 3 cups

1 cup strawberries
1 cup cranberries or raspberries
1 cup chopped melon (any kind)

1 cup water
½ cup unsweetened coconut milk
1 tablespoon chia seeds

1. Blend all the ingredients in a blender until smoothly puréed. If you prefer a thinner smoothie, you can add more water or coconut milk if needed.
2. Serve immediately.

Per Serving
Calories: 175 | fat: 13.0g | carbs: 16.8g | protein: 3.1g | fiber: 5.3g

Simple Date Shake

Prep time: 10 minutes | Cook time: 0 minutes | Serves 2

5 Medjool dates, pitted, soaked in boiling water for 5 minutes
¾ cups unsweetened coconut milk
1 teaspoon vanilla ex-

tract
½ teaspoon fresh lemon juice
¼ teaspoon sea salt (optional)
1½ cups ice

1. Put all the ingredients in a food processor, then blitz until it has a milkshake and smooth texture.
2. Serve immediately.

Per Serving
Calories: 380 | fat: 21.6g | carbs: 50.3g | protein: 3.2g | fiber: 6.0g

Beet and Clementine Protein Smoothie

Prep time: 10 minutes | Cook time: 0 minutes | Serves 1

1 small beet, peeled and chopped
1 clementine, peeled and broken into segments
½ ripe banana
½ cup raspberries
1 tablespoon chia seeds

2 tablespoons almond butter
¼ teaspoon vanilla extract
1 cup unsweetened almond milk
⅛ Teaspoon fine sea salt (optional)

1. Combine all the ingredients in a food processor, then pulse on high for 2 minutes or until glossy and creamy.
2. Refrigerate for an hour and serve chilled.

Per Serving
Calories: 526 | fat: 25.4g | carbs: 61.9g | protein: 20.6g | fiber: 17.3g

Date Rice Balls

Prep time: 30 minutes | Cook time: 5 minutes | Makes 12 to 15 balls

1 teaspoon vanilla extract
3 cups chopped dates

1 cup water
2 cups puffed rice

1. Cook the vanilla, dates, and water over low heat for 5 minutes in a saucepan or until smooth, keep stirring.
2. Allow to cool under room temperature. Add the puffed rice.
3. Form the mixture into 1½-inch balls and place on a baking pan and refrigerate for 2 hours.
4. Serve chilled.

Per Serving (1 ball)
Calories: 133 | fat: 3.4g | carbs: 29.9g | protein: 2.8g | fiber: 5.7g

Fruity Rice Pudding

Prep time: 15 minutes | Cook time: 30 minutes | Serves 4

1 cup crushed pineapple with juice, drained
2 cups cooked brown rice
2 tablespoons raisins
1 banana, peeled and chopped
¼ cup fresh orange juice
1 tablespoon vanilla extract
¾ cup water

1. Preheat the oven to 350ºF (180ºC).
2. Mix the pineapple, rice, and raisins in a bowl.
3. Put the remaining ingredients in a food processor and process until smooth. Fold the mixture into the rice mixture.
4. Pour into a casserole dish. Cover and bake in the preheated oven for 30 minutes, or until set.
5. Serve immediately.

Per Serving
Calories: 210 | fat: 1.1g | carbs: 46.8g | protein: 3.4g | fiber: 3.3g

Vanilla Frosting

Prep time: 10 minutes | Cook time: 0 minutes | Makes about 1½ cups

1 teaspoon vanilla extract (or seeds from 1 vanilla bean)
3 ounces (85 g) raw, unsalted cashews (about ¾ cup)
5 ounces (142 g)
pitted dates (8 to 9 Medjool or 16 to 18 Deglet Noor), chopped
¾ cup water, plus more as needed

1. In a blender, add the vanilla, cashews, dates, and ¾ cup water. If the cashews and dates aren't covered completely, add more water as needed. Let sit for at least 45 minutes, or until the nuts and dates are thoroughly softened.
2. Blitz until the mixture is smooth and creamy. You'll need to stop the blender occasionally to scrape down the sides. Add a little more water if a thinner consistency is desired.
3. Serve chilled.

Per Serving (1½ cups)
Calories: 875 | fat: 37.5g | carbs: 132.5g | protein: 18.1g | fiber: 12.3g

Bread and Walnut Pudding

Prep time: 15 minutes | Cook time: 40 minutes | Serves 6 to 8

9 slices whole-grain bread (about 4 cups), cubed into 1-inch pieces
1 cup vanilla soy milk
1 cup water
½ cup raisins
½ cup unsweetened pineapple juice
¼ cup chopped walnuts
1½ tablespoons cornstarch
1 teaspoon ground cinnamon
½ cup maple syrup (optional)

1. Preheat the oven to 350ºF (180ºC).
2. Combine the bread pieces, soy milk and water in a large mixing bowl. Set aside.
3. Mix the remaining ingredients into the bowl. Pour the mixture into a baking dish and bake for 40 minutes, or until a knife inserted in the center comes out clean.
4. Serve immediately.

Per Serving
Calories: 249 | fat: 4.1g | carbs: 46.9g | protein: 7.8g | fiber: 4.2g

Date and Almond Balls

Prep time: 5 minutes | Chill time: 15 minutes | Makes 24 balls

1 cup dates, pitted
¾ cup ground almonds
1 cup unsweetened
shredded coconut
¼ cup non-dairy chocolate chips
¼ cup chia seeds

1. Combine all the ingredients in a food processor and purée until crumbly and sticking together.
2. Divide and shape the mixture into 24 balls and place them on a baking sheet lined with parchment paper.
3. Put the balls in the fridge to set for about 15 minutes.
4. Serve chilled.

Per Serving (1 ball)
Calories: 152 | fat: 11.0g | carbs: 3.0g | protein: 3.0g | fiber: 5.0g

Easy Blueberry Cobbler

Prep time: 20 minutes | Cook time: 45 minutes | Serves 4 to 6

²/₃ cup whole-wheat pastry flour
1½ Teaspoons baking powder
Salt, to taste (optional)
²/₃ cup low-fat vanilla soy milk
3 tablespoons maple syrup (optional)
2 cups blueberries

1. Preheat the oven to 350ºF (180ºC).
2. Combine the flour, baking powder, and salt (if desired) in a large bowl. Stir in the soy milk and maple syrup (if desired), and mix until smooth.
3. Pour the batter into a square baking pan. Spread the berries over. Bake in the preheated oven for 45 minutes or until golden brown.
4. Serve immediately.

Per Serving
Calories: 158 | fat: 0.7g | carbs: 37.1g | protein: 3.3g | fiber: 2.8g

Easy Pumpkin Pie Squares

Prep time: 20 minutes | Cook time: 30 minutes | Makes 16 squares

1 cup unsweetened almond milk
1 teaspoon vanilla extract
7 ounces (198 g) dates, pitted and chopped
1¼ cups old-fashioned rolled oats
2 teaspoons pumpkin pie spice
1 (15-ounce / 425-g) can pure pumpkin

1. Preheat the oven to 375ºF (190ºC). Put the parchment paper in a baking pan.
2. Stir together the milk and vanilla in a bowl. Soak the dates in it for 15 minutes, or until the dates become softened.
3. Add the rolled oats to a food processor and pulse the oats into flour. Remove the oat flour from the food processor bowl and whisk together with the pumpkin pie spice in a different bowl.
4. Place the milk mixture into the food processor and process until smooth. Add the flour mixture and pumpkin to the food processor and pulse until the mixture has broken down into a chunky paste consistency.

5. Transfer the batter to the prepared pan and smooth the top with a silicone spatula. Bake for 30 minutes, or until a toothpick inserted in the center of the pie comes out clean.
6. Let cool completely before cutting into squares. Serve cold.

Per Serving (1 square)
Calories: 68 | fat: 0.9g | carbs: 16.8g | protein: 2.3g | fiber: 2.1g

Oat Scones

Prep time: 15 minutes | Cook time: 22 minutes | Makes 12 Scones

1 teaspoon apple cider vinegar
½ cup unsweetened soy milk
1 teaspoon vanilla extract
3 cups oat flour
2 tablespoons baking
powder
½ cup maple sugar
½ teaspoon salt (optional)
¹/₃ cup almond butter
½ cup unsweetened applesauce

1. Preheat the oven to 350ºF (180ºC). Line a baking sheet with parchment paper.
2. Combine cider vinegar and soy milk in a bowl. Stir to mix well. Let stand for a few minutes to curdle, then mix in the vanilla.
3. Combine the flour, baking powder, sugar, and salt (if desired) in a second bowl. Stir to mix well.
4. Combine the almond butter and applesauce in a third bowl. Stir to mix well.
5. Gently fold the applesauce mixture in the flour mixture, then stir in the milk mixture.
6. Scoop the mixture on the baking sheet with an ice-cream scoop to make 12 scones. Drizzle them with a touch of water.
7. Bake in the preheated oven for 22 minutes or until puffed and lightly browned. Flip the scones halfway through the cooking time.
8. Remove them from the oven and allow to cool for 10 minutes before serving.

Per Serving (1 scone)
Calories: 177 | fat: 6.0g | carbs: 26.6g | protein: 5.4g | fiber: 2.5g

Garlicky Toast

Prep time: 5 minutes | Cook time: 5 minutes | Makes 1 slice

1 Teaspoons nutritional yeast
1 teaspoon coconut oil (optional)
Sea salt, to taste (optional)
1 small garlic clove, pressed
1 slice whole-grain bread

1. In a small bowl, mix the nutritional yeast, oil (if desired), salt (if desired), and garlic.
2. Brush the mixture on the bread and put it in a toaster oven to bake for 5 minutes until golden brown.
3. Serve immediately.

Per Serving (1 slice)
Calories: 138 | fat: 16.0g | carbs: 5.0g | protein: 7.0g | fiber: 4.0g

Godlen Muffins

Prep time: 15 minutes | Cook time: 30 minutes | Makes 6 muffins

1 orange, peeled
2 tablespoons chopped dried apricots
1 carrot, coarsely chopped
2 tablespoons almond butter
¼ cup unsweetened almond milk
2 tablespoons ground flaxseeds
3 tablespoons molasses
½ teaspoon ground cinnamon
¼ teaspoon ground
nutmeg
½ teaspoon ground ginger
1 teaspoon apple cider vinegar
1 teaspoon vanilla extract
¼ teaspoon allspice
¾ cup rolled oats
½ teaspoon baking soda
1 teaspoon baking powder
2 tablespoons raisins
2 tablespoons sunflower seeds

1. Preheat the oven to 350ºF (180ºC). Line a 6-cup muffin tin with parchment paper.
2. Add the orange, apricots, carrot, almond butter, almond milk, flaxseeds, molasses, cinnamon, nutmeg, ginger, vinegar, vanilla, and allspice to a food processor and process until creamy and smooth.
3. Add the rolled oats to a blender and pulse until well ground. Combine the ground oat with baking soda and baking powder in a bowl. Stir to mix well.
4. Pour the orange mixture in the oat mixture, then mix in the raisins and sunflower seeds. Stir to mix well.
5. Divide the mixture into the muffin cups, then bake in the preheated oven for 30 minutes or until puffed and lightly browned.
6. Remove them from the oven and allow to cool for 10 minutes before serving.

Per Serving (1 muffin)
Calories: 287 | fat: 23.0g | carbs: 17.0g | protein: 8.0g | fiber: 6.0g

Hearty Sweet Potato Biscuits

Prep time: 60 minutes | Cook time: 10 minutes | Makes 12 biscuits

1 medium sweet potato
3 tablespoons melted coconut oil, divided (optional)
1 tablespoon maple
syrup (optional)
1 cup whole-grain flour
2 teaspoons baking powder

1. Preheat the oven to 350ºF (180ºC).
2. Bake the sweet potato in the preheated oven for 45 minutes or until tender. Allow to cool, then remove the flesh and mash.
3. Raise the temperature of the oven up to 375ºF (190ºC) and line a baking sheet with parchment paper.
4. In a medium bowl, combine 1 cup of the mashed sweet potato with 1½ tablespoons of the coconut oil (if desired) and the maple syrup (if desired).
5. Mix the flour and baking powder in a separate medium bowl, then add the flour mixture to the potato mixture and blend well.
6. On a floured cutting board, pat the mixture out into a ½-inch-thick circle, then cut the circle into 1-inch rounds.
7. Put the rounds on the baking sheet. Brush the top with remaining coconut oil, if desired.
8. Bake in the oven for 10 minutes, or until lightly golden. Serve hot.

Per Serving (1 biscuit)
Calories: 116 | fat: 14.0g | carbs: 9.0g | protein: 3.0g | fiber: 3.0g

Crispy Almond Biscotti

Prep time: 20 minutes | Cook time: 40 minutes | Makes 18 Slices

2 tablespoons ground flaxseeds
$^1/_3$ cup unsweetened soy milk
¼ cup unsweetened applesauce
½ teaspoon vanilla extract
½ teaspoon almond extract
¼ cup almond butter
¾ cup maple sugar
$1^2/_3$ cups whole wheat pastry flour
2 teaspoons baking powder
1 cup slivered almonds
2 tablespoons cornstarch
2 teaspoons anise seeds
½ teaspoon salt (optional)

1. Preheat the oven to 350ºF (180ºC). Line a baking sheet with parchment paper.
2. Combine the flaxseeds, soy milk, applesauce, vanilla, almond extract, almond butter, and maple sugar in a large bowl. Stir to mix well.
3. Mix in the remaining ingredients and knead the mixture until a stiff dough form.
4. Shape the dough into a 9-inch-long rectangle in the baking sheet. Bake in the preheated oven for 27 minutes or until golden brown.
5. Remove the baking sheet from the oven. Allow to cool for 20 minutes, and then slice the loaf into ½-inch-thick slices.
6. Put the biscotti back to the baking sheet and increase the temperature of the oven to 375ºF (190ºC).
7. Bake in the oven for 11 minutes or until crispy. Flip the biscotti halfway through the cooking time.
8. Transfer the biscotti onto a plate and serve.

Per Serving (18 slices)
Calories: 2338 | fat: 104.4g | carbs: 315.9g | protein: 69.1g | fiber: 48.8g

Roasted Beets & Carrot with Avocado Dip

Prep time: 10 minutes | Cook time: 30 minutes | Serves 2

Avocado Dip:
1 avocado
1 tablespoon apple cider vinegar
¼ to ½ cup water
2 tablespoons nutritional yeast
1 teaspoon dried dill, or 1 tablespoon fresh dill
Pinch sea salt
Roasted Veg:
1 small sweet potato, peeled and cubed
2 small beets, peeled and cubed
2 small carrots, peeled and cubed
1 teaspoon sea salt
1 teaspoon dried oregano
¼ teaspoon cayenne pepper
Pinch freshly ground black pepper

1. In a blender, purée the avocado with the other dip ingredients, using just enough water to get a smooth, creamy texture.
2. Alternately, you can mash the avocado thoroughly in a large bowl, then stir in the rest of the dip ingredients.
3. Preheat the oven to 350°F.
4. Put the sweet potato, beets, and carrots in a large pot with a small amount of water, and bring to a boil over high heat. Boil for 15 minutes, until they're just barely soft, and then drain.
5. Sprinkle the salt, oregano, cayenne, and pepper over them and stir gently to combine. (Use more or less cayenne depending on your taste.)
6. Spread the vegetables on a large baking sheet and roast them in the oven 10 to 15 minutes, until they've browned around the edges.
7. Serve the veg with the avocado dip on the side.

Per Serving
Calories: 335 | fat: 32g | carbs: 11g | protein: 11g | fiber: 16g

Peach and Raspberry Crisp

Prep time: 50 minutes | Cook time: 30 to 35 minutes | Serves 6

Filling:
2½ pounds (1.1 kg) peaches, peeled, halved, pitted, and cut into ½-inch wedges
¼ cup maple sugar (about 1¾ ounces / 50 g)
⅛ Teaspoon salt (optional)
1 tablespoon lemon juice
2 tablespoons ground tapioca
1 teaspoon vanilla extract
2 cups raspberries (about 10 ounces / 284 g)
Topping:
½ cup soy flour
(about 2½ ounces / 71 g)
¼ teaspoon ground cinnamon
¼ teaspoon ground ginger
¼ cup date sugar (about 1¾ ounces / 50 g)
¼ cup maple sugar (about 1¾ ounces / 50 g)
¼ teaspoon salt (optional)
¼ cup unsweetened applesauce
½ cup chopped pecans
½ cup rolled oats (about 1½ ounces / 43 g)
2 tablespoons water

Make the Filling
1. Preheat the oven to 400ºF (205ºC). Line a baking dish with parchment paper.
2. Put the peaches, maple sugar, and salt in a large bowl. Toss to combine well. Let stand for 30 minutes. Toss periodically.
3. Drain the peaches in a colander. Reserve 2 tablespoons of juice remain in the bowl and discard the extra juice.
4. Move the drained peaches back to the bowl. Add the lemon juice, tapioca, vanilla, and reserved peach juice. Toss to combine well.
5. Arrange the peaches and raspberries in the single layer on the baking dish.
Make the Topping
6. Put the soy flour, cinnamon, ginger, date sugar, maple sugar, and salt (if desired) in a food processor. Blitz for 15 seconds to combine well.
7. Add the applesauce to the mixture and blitz for 10 times until it becomes wet sand. Add the pecans, oats, and water and blitz for 15 times until smooth. Pour the mixture in a large bowl then refrigerate for 20 minutes.
8. Spread the topping over the peaches and raspberries in the baking dish, then bake

in the preheated oven for 30 to 35 minutes or until crispy and golden brown. Flip the peaches and raspberries halfway through the cooking time.
9. Remove the dish from the oven. Allow to cool for 30 minutes and serve.

Per Serving
Calories: 294 | fat: 7.9g | carbs: 55.9g | protein: 7.7g | fiber: 8.9g

Banana French Toast with Raspberry Syrup

Prep time: 10 minutes | Cook time: 30 minutes | Makes 8 Slices

Banana French Toast:
1 banana
¼ teaspoon ground nutmeg
1½ Teaspoons arrowroot flour
1 cup unsweetened coconut milk
1 teaspoon vanilla extract
½ teaspoon ground
cinnamon
Pinch sea salt (optional)
8 slices whole-grain bread
Raspberry Syrup:
1 cup fresh raspberries
2 tablespoons water
1 to 2 tablespoons maple syrup

1. Preheat the oven to 350ºF (180ºC). Line a baking sheet with parchment paper.
2. Purée the banana in a blender, then pour the banana purée in a bowl and mix in the nutmeg, arrowroot flour, coconut milk, vanilla, cinnamon, and salt, if desired.
3. Dredge the bread slices into the mixture to coat, then arrange them in the single layer on the baking sheet. Pour the remaining banana mixture over.
4. Bake in the preheated oven for 30 minutes or until golden brown. Flip the bread slices at least three times during the baking time.
5. Put the raspberries, maple syrup, and water in a saucepan, then simmer over medium heat for 15 to 20 minutes or until it has a thick consistency. Keep stirring during the simmering and mash the raspberries with a spatula.
6. Serve the banana toast with raspberry syrup.

Per Serving (1 slice)
Calories: 166 | fat: 15.0g | carbs: 11.0g | protein: 5.0g | fiber: 4.0g

Chickpea and Chocolate Squares

Prep time: 1 hour 20 minutes | Cook time: 20 minutes | Makes 16 squares

Chickpea Layer:
1 (15-ounce / 425-g) can chickpeas, drained and rinsed
1/3 cup pure maple syrup (optional)
2 teaspoons pure vanilla extract
½ cup almond butter
½ teaspoon baking soda
1 teaspoon baking powder
¼ teaspoon ground cinnamon
½ teaspoon sea salt (optional)
½ cup gluten-free

rolled oats
Almond Butter Layer:
½ cup almond butter
1 tablespoon pure maple syrup (optional)
Pinch of sea salt (optional)
1 tablespoon organic virgin coconut oil, melted (optional)
Chocolate Topping:
2 tablespoons unsweetened almond milk
4 ounces (113 g) vegan dark chocolate, chopped

1. Preheat the oven to 350°F (180°C). Line a baking pan with parchment paper.
2. Make the chickpea layer: Pour the chickpeas and maple syrup (if desired) in a food processor. Pulse to mix until it has a thick consistency.
3. Add the vanilla extract, almond butter, baking soda, baking powder, cinnamon, and salt (if desired) to the food processor and pulse until smooth and creamy.
4. Add the rolled oats to the food processor and pulse to break the oats. Pour the mixture in the prepared baking pan.
5. Bake in the preheated oven for 20 minutes or until a toothpick inserted in the center comes out dry. Remove the baking pan from the oven and allow to cool for 10 minutes.
6. Combine the ingredients for the almond butter in a large bowl. Stir to mix well. Spread the mixture in a single layer over the cooled chickpea layer. Transfer the baking pan in the refrigerator and chill for 30 minutes.
7. Microwave the almond milk and chocolate in a medium bowl until melted. Stir to mix well. Pour the chocolate milk over the chilled almond butter layer. Place the baking pan back to the refrigerator to chill for another 30 minutes or until firm.

8. Remove the baking pan from the refrigerator and cut the chunk into squares, then serve.

Per Serving (1 square)
Calories: 213 | fat: 13.4g | carbs: 19.8g | protein: 6.3g | fiber: 4.5g

Spicy Fruit Energy Bars

Prep time: 10 minutes | Cook time: 30 to 35 minutes | Makes 8 bars

1 cup barley flour
1 cup whole-wheat pastry flour
1 tablespoon baking powder
1 teaspoon ground ginger
1 teaspoon ground cinnamon
¼ teaspoon ground cloves
¼ teaspoon sea salt (optional)

1 cup maple syrup (optional)
¾ cup unsweetened applesauce
1 teaspoon almond extract
1 teaspoon orange zest
½ cup raisins
½ cup chopped dried apricots
½ cup chopped Medjool dates

1. Preheat the oven to 350°F (180°C). Line a baking sheet with the parchment paper.
2. In a large bowl, combine the barley flour, pastry flour, baking powder, ginger, cinnamon, cloves and sea salt (if desired) until well mixed.
3. In a medium bowl, whisk together the maple syrup (if desired), applesauce, almond extract and orange zest. Add the raisins, apricots and dates to the bowl and stir well.
4. Pour the date syrup mixture into the flour mixture to combine until well blended.
5. Place the batter on the baking sheet and smooth the top with a silicone spatula. Bake for 30 to 35 minutes, or until a knife inserted in the center comes out clean.
6. Let rest for 5 minutes before cutting into bars. Serve immediately.

Per Serving (1 bar)
Calories: 318 | fat: 0.9g | carbs: 77.9g | protein: 4.8g | fiber: 5.9g

Chapter 9 Snacks and Sides

Roasted Tamari Almonds

Prep time: 5 minutes | Cook time: 10 to 15 minutes | Serves 8

1 pound (454 g) raw almonds
3 tablespoons tamari
1 tablespoon nutri-
tional yeast
1 to 2 teaspoons chili powder

1. Preheat the oven to 400ºF (205ºC). Line a large baking tray with parchment paper and set aside.
2. Mix the almonds and tamari in a medium bowl and toss to coat.
3. Arrange the almonds on the prepared baking tray in a single layer.
4. Roast in the preheated oven until browned, about 10 t0 15 minutes. Stir the almonds halfway through the cooking time.
5. Let the almonds cool for 10 minutes in the baking tray. Sprinkle with the nutritional yeast and chili powder. Serve immediately, or store in the fridge for up to 2 weeks.

Per Serving
Calories: 91 | fat: 28.3g | carbs: 13.2g | protein: 12.2g | fiber: 7.4g

Veggie Hummus Pinwheels

Prep time: 10 minutes | Cook time: 0 minutes | Serves 3

3 gluten-free tortillas
3 large Swiss chard leaves
¾ cup store-bought
hummus
¾ cup shredded carrots

1. Lay the tortillas on your cutting board. Top each tortilla with 1 Swiss chard leaf and spread the hummus evenly over the leaves. Place ¼ cup of shredded carrots on top of the hummus.
2. Make the pinwheels: Roll up each tortilla tightly and cut crosswise into pinwheels with a sharp knife. Serve immediately.

Per Serving
Calories: 256 | fat: 8.2g | carbs: 39.1g | protein: 10.2g | fiber: 8.1g

Easy Kale Chips

Prep time: 5 minutes | Cook time: 20 minutes | Serves 4

¼ cup low-sodium vegetable broth
1 tablespoon nutritional yeast
½ teaspoon onion powder
½ teaspoon garlic powder
6 ounces (170 g) kale, stemmed and cut into 2- to 3-inch pieces

1. Preheat the oven to 300ºF (150ºC). Line a baking tray with parchment paper and set aside.
2. Stir together the vegetable broth, nutritional yeast, onion powder, and garlic powder in a small bowl.
3. Add the kale and massage the vegetable broth mixture thoroughly all over the leaves.
4. Arrange the kale on the prepared baking tray in an even layer. Bake in the preheated oven for 20 minutes, flipping the kale halfway through, or until the kale is crispy.
5. Remove from the oven and serve warm.

Per Serving
Calories: 142 | fat: 10.2g | carbs: 7.1g | protein: 4.2g | fiber: 2.1g

Strawberry and Mashed Avocado Toast

Prep time: 5 minutes | Cook time: 0 minutes | Serves 4

1 avocado, mashed
4 whole-wheat bread slices, toasted
4 ripe strawberries
cut into ¼-inch slices
1 tablespoon balsamic glaze

1. Spread ¼ of mashed avocado on top of each toasted bread slice.
2. Top the bread slices evenly with strawberry slices, finished by a drizzle of balsamic glaze. Serve immediately.

Per Serving
Calories: 153 | fat: 8.2g | carbs: 17.2g | protein: 5.1g | fiber: 5.2g

Cashew Queso

Prep time: 5 minutes | Cook time: 0 minutes | Serves 5

1 cup raw cashews, soaked in water for 6 hours
1 cup water
1 teaspoon nutritional yeast
1 teaspoon garlic powder
½ teaspoon salt (optional)

1. Drain the cashews and transfer to a food processor.
2. Add the water, nutritional yeast, garlic powder, and salt (if desired) to the cashews. Pulse until the mixture is creamy and has a spreadable consistency.
3. Serve immediately or refrigerate to chill for at least 2 hours for best flavor.

Per Serving
Calories: 152 | fat: 10.8g | carbs: 8.7g | protein: 4.7g | fiber: 1.1g

Matcha Pistachio Balls

Prep time: 15 minutes | Cook time: 0 minutes | Serves 4

½ cup pistachios
1 cup raw cashews
½ cup pitted dates
½ cup vegan protein powder (vanilla flavor)
¼ cup finely shredded coconut
1 tablespoon maple syrup
1 tablespoon matcha powder
¼ cup crushed hazelnuts

1. In a food processor, add all the ingredients except for the hazelnuts and pulse until finely chopped.
2. Scoop tablespoon-sized mounds of the mixture onto a baking sheet lined with parchment paper and shape into balls with your hands.
3. In a bowl, add the hazelnuts. Roll the balls in the nut mixture, pressing so the balls are nicely coated.
4. Transfer the baking sheet to the freezer and let the balls chill for about 30 minutes until solid. Serve immediately, or store in the fridge for up to 1 week.

Per Serving
Calories: 336 | fat: 21.3g | carbs: 21.4g | protein: 14.7g | fiber: 4.8g

Chocolate and Almond Balls

Prep time: 10 minutes | Cook time: 0 minutes | Serves 3

1 cup almonds
1½ tablespoons cocoa powder
1 tablespoon maple syrup (optional)
⅛ Teaspoon pink Himalayan salt (optional)
10 Medjool dates, pitted and chopped

1. Process the almonds in a food processor until they become a rough, grainy powder. Add the remaining ingredients and process until smoothly blended.
2. Shape the mixture into 1½-inch balls with your hands and serve. You can store the balls in the refrigerator for up to 7 days.

Per Serving
Calories: 518 | fat: 24.3g | carbs: 75.8g | protein: 12.2g | fiber: 11.8g

Apple Nachos

Prep time: 10 minutes | Cook time: 0 minutes | Serves 4

1 cup pitted Medjool dates
½ cup unsweetened plant-based milk
1 teaspoon vanilla extract
⅛ Teaspoon pink Himalayan salt (optional)
4 Granny Smith apples, cored and cut into ¼-inch slices
¼ cup chopped pecans
2 tablespoons vegan dark chocolate chips
1 teaspoon hemp seeds

1. Pulse the dates in a food processor until they resemble a paste. Add the milk, vanilla, and salt (if desired), and pulse until smooth. Set aside.
2. On a plate, lay out 1 sliced apple (use 1 apple Per Serving on individual plates). Drizzle 1 tablespoon of the date sauce over the apple. Top with 1 tablespoon of chopped pecans, ½ tablespoon of chocolate chips, and finish with ¼ teaspoon of hemp seeds. Repeat with the remaining apples and toppings.
3. Serve immediately.

Per Serving
Calories: 319 | fat: 8.6g | carbs: 65.1g | protein: 3.2g | fiber: 10.1g

5-Minute Almond Butter Bites

Prep time: 5 minutes | Cook time: 0 minutes | Makes 9 bites

½ cup almond or peanut butter
½ cup rolled oats
3 tablespoons maple syrup (optional)
¼ cup ground chia
seeds
1 tablespoon pumpkin seeds
1 tablespoon ground flaxseed

1. Pulse all the ingredients in a food processor until very small bits of the seeds are still visible.
2. Shape the mixture into small balls with your hands. Serve immediately.

Per Serving
Calories: 156 | fat: 10.5g | carbs: 13.3g | protein: 6.2g | fiber: 4.1g

Seed and Nut Bars

Prep time: 10 minutes | Cook time: 0 minutes | Serves 4

¼ cup chia seeds, soaked in water for 20 minutes
1/3 cup raw cashews
¼ cup pecan
1/3 cup sunflower seeds
2 cups pitted dates
2 tablespoons freshly squeezed lemon juice
¼ teaspoon salt (optional)
½ cup vegan protein powder (vanilla flavor)

1. Drain the chia seeds and put in a food processor, along with the cashews, pecans, and sunflower seeds. Pulse until everything is well combined and crumbly.
2. Add the dates, lemon juice, and salt (if desired) to the chia seed mixture. Continue pulsing while adding the protein powder until the ingredients are a bit chunky but doughy.
3. Line a baking sheet with parchment paper and add the dough. Using a rolling pin, press the dough out to form a square, about ½ inch thick.
4. Put the baking sheet in the freezer for about 1 hour until solid.
5. With a sharp knife, cut the square into 8 uniform bars and serve.

Per Serving
Calories: 273 | fat: 10.8g | carbs: 34.8g | protein: 9.1g | fiber: 6.6g

Strawberry and Date Syrup

Prep time: 20 minutes | Cook time: 0 minutes | Serves 4

4 ounces (113 g) pitted dates, chopped
½ cup sliced
strawberries
1½ cups water

1. In a blender, add the dates, strawberries, and water. Set aside for at least 15 minutes to soften the dates.
2. Blend the ingredients until a smooth and pourable consistency is achieved.
3. Transfer the syrup to a bowl. If your syrup gets too thick, you can add more water to thin it (the syrup will thicken as it sits). Serve immediately, or refrigerate to chill until ready to use.

Per Serving
Calories: 94 | fat: 0.1g | carbs: 22.6g | protein: 0.8g | fiber: 2.6g

Oil-Free Green Beans with Almonds

Prep time: 5 minutes | Cook time: 10 minutes | Serves 4

1 pound (454 g) green beans, washed and trimmed
2 to 3 tablespoons water
1½ cup raw almonds, roughly chopped
Juice of 1 lemon
Salt, to taste (optional)

1. Heat a large nonstick skillet over medium heat until hot. Add the green beans, cover, and sauté for 5 minutes, stirring frequently.
2. Add 2 to 3 tablespoons water to keep them from sticking to the pan.
3. Add the almonds and stir to combine. Cook for 3 minutes until the nuts are lightly toasted.
4. Transfer the green beans and almonds to a bowl. Drizzle with the lemon juice. Season with salt to taste, if desired.
5. Let them cool for 5 minutes and serve.

Per Serving
Calories: 156 | fat: 3.2g | carbs: 10.2g | protein: 4.1g | fiber: 6.2g

Garlicky Broccoli

Prep time: 5 minutes | Cook time: 6 to 7 minutes | Serves 4

2 heads broccoli, cut into small florets
2 to 3 tablespoons water

8 garlic cloves, minced
¼ cup coconut amino

1. Heat a large nonstick frying pan over medium heat until hot.
2. Add the broccoli florets, cover, and sauté for 4 to 5 minutes, stirring frequently. Add 2 to 3 tablespoons water to keep them from sticking to the pan.
3. Fold in the minced garlic and coconut amino. Stir well and continue cooking for 2 minutes until fork-tender.
4. Remove from the heat and cool for 5 minutes before serving.

Per Serving
Calories: 176 | fat: 11.2g | carbs: 14.3g | protein: 5.2g | fiber: 5.1g

Roasted Root Veggies with Maple Syrup

Prep time: 15 minutes | Cook time: 40 to 45 minutes | Serves 8

4 russet potatoes, diced
1 sweet potato, diced
1 rutabaga, diced
2 carrots, diced
2 beets, diced
¼ cup low-sodium vegetable broth

3 tablespoons maple syrup
5 sprigs rosemary leaves only, minced
¼ teaspoon freshly ground black pepper
1 teaspoon salt (optional)

1. Preheat the oven to 400ºF (205ºC).
2. Combine all the ingredients in a large bowl and toss until the root veggies are coated thoroughly.
3. Arrange the root veggies on two baking sheets and transfer to the oven.
4. Roast in the preheated oven for 40 to 45 minutes until browned and tender. Stir the root veggies halfway through the cooking time.
5. Remove from the oven and serve warm.

Per Serving
Calories: 229 | fat: 4.2g | carbs: 44.1g | protein: 4.2g | fiber: 6.1g

Baked Pears and Yams

Prep time: 15 minutes | Cook time: 25 to 30 minutes | Serves 6 to 8

2 pounds (907 g) Bosc pears (about 4 medium), peeled, cored, and cut into 1-inch chunks
1½ pounds (680 g)

yams, peeled and cut into 1-inch chunks
1 teaspoon cinnamon
⅛ Teaspoon ground cloves
1 cup water

1. Preheat the oven to 375ºF (190ºC).
2. Put the pear and yam chunks in a baking dish. Add the cinnamon, ground cloves, and water, and stir well until the pears and yams are nicely coated. Cover the baking dish with aluminum foil.
3. Bake in the preheated oven for about 25 to 30 minutes until golden brown and tender.
4. Remove from the oven and serve on a plate.

Per Serving
Calories: 232 | fat: 0.4g | carbs: 54.9g | protein: 2.3g | fiber: 9.6g

Persimmon and Cranberry Relish

Prep time: 15 minutes | Cook time: 0 minutes | Serves 6

2 medium, ripe Fuyu persimmons, chopped
1½ cups fresh cranberries
2 tangerines, peeled, seeded, and chopped

1 medium apple, peeled, cored, and chopped
½ teaspoon ground nutmeg
½ teaspoon cinnamon

1. Make the relish: Add all the ingredients to a food processor and pulse 10 to 15 times, or until the relish resembles chunky salsa.
2. Transfer to a bowl and give the relish a good stir until completely mixed.
3. Serve immediately, or refrigerate to chill for later.

Per Serving
Calories: 93 | fat: 0.35g | carbs: 21.8g | protein: 0.7g | fiber: 4.6g

Crispy Roasted Chickpeas

Prep time: 5 minutes | Cook time: 20 to 25 minutes | Makes 1 cup

1 (14-ounce / 397-g) can chickpeas, rinsed and drained, or 1½ cups cooked
2 tablespoons tamari or soy sauce
1 tablespoon nutri-
tional yeast
1 teaspoon onion powder
1 teaspoon paprika
½ teaspoon garlic powder

1. Preheat the oven to 400ºF (205ºC).
2. Toss the chickpeas with all the other ingredients, and spread them out on a baking sheet.
3. Roast in the preheated oven for 20 to 25 minutes, tossing the chickpeas halfway through the cooking time.
4. Let rest for 5 to 10 minutes before serving.

Per Serving
Calories: 124 | fat: 10.3g | carbs: 5.1g | protein: 7.9g | fiber: 6.1g

Crunchy Maple Granola

Prep time: 5 minutes | Cook time: 25 minutes | Serves 4

2 cups rolled oats
1 cup maple syrup (optional)
¼ cup chopped almonds
¼ cup chopped walnuts
¼ cup chopped pecans
2 tablespoons pumpkin seeds
2 tablespoons sunflower seeds
1 tablespoon hemp seeds
1 teaspoon vanilla extract

1. Preheat the oven to 350ºF (180ºC). Line a baking sheet with parchment paper.
2. Stir together all the ingredients in a large bowl until completely mixed.
3. Spread out the mixture on the prepared baking sheet and bake for 25 minutes, stirring the granola halfway through, or until lightly browned.
4. Remove from the oven and let cool for 5 to 10 minutes before serving.

Per Serving
Calories: 557 | fat: 21.5g | carbs: 85.6g | protein: 11.2g | fiber: 7.1g

Creamy Green Beans with Mushrooms

Prep time: 5 minutes | Cook time: 15 minutes | Serves 4

1 small yellow onion, diced
3 or 4 garlic cloves, minced
1 cup vegetable broth, divided
1 cup sliced mushrooms
1 cup unsweetened plant-based milk
2 tablespoons nutritional yeast
2 tablespoons gluten-free flour
3 cups fresh green beans
Pink Himalayan salt (optional)
Freshly ground black pepper, to taste

1. In a large nonstick pan over medium heat, sauté the onion and garlic in ¼ cup of broth until the onion is softened.
2. Add the mushrooms, milk, remaining ¾ cup of broth, flour, and nutritional yeast, whisking until there are no clumps.
3. Add the green beans, cover, and cook over medium-low heat for 10 to 15 minutes, or until the beans are tender. Add salt (if desired) and pepper to taste. Serve warm.

Per Serving
Calories: 103 | fat: 2.0g | carbs: 19.8g | protein: 6.2g | fiber: 7.0g

Easy Baked Sweet Potato Fries

Prep time: 10 minutes | Cook time: 30 to 45 minutes | Serves 2

1 medium sweet potato, peeled and cut into thin sticks
1 teaspoon olive oil (optional)
1 teaspoon dried basil
¼ teaspoon sea salt (optional)
½ teaspoon dried oregano

1. Preheat the oven to 350ºF (180ºC).
2. Toss the potato sticks with all the other ingredients, and spread them out on a large baking sheet.
3. Bake in the preheated oven for 30 to 45 minutes, flipping them halfway through the cooking time, or until crisp-tender.
4. Cool for 5 minutes before serving.

Per Serving
Calories: 259 | fat: 22.3g | carbs: 18.3g | protein: 4.6g | fiber: 11.1g

Crisp Onion Rings

Prep time: 5 minutes | Cook time: 10 to 12 minutes | Serves 2

1 cup vegan bread crumbs
½ teaspoon paprika
¼ teaspoon garlic powder
¼ teaspoon pink Himalayan salt (optional)
¼ teaspoon freshly ground black pepper
¾ cup water
½ cup whole wheat flour
2 large yellow onions, cut into ½-inch rings

1. Preheat the oven to 400ºF (205ºC). Line a baking sheet with parchment paper.
2. Combine the bread crumbs, paprika, garlic powder, salt (if desired), and pepper in a bowl.
3. In another bowl, whisk the water and flour to combine.
4. Dip each onion ring in the flour, then coat in the bread crumb mixture. Arrange the coated onion rings on the prepared baking sheet.
5. Bake in the preheated oven for 10 to 12 minutes, or until lightly browned.
6. Serve immediately.

Per Serving
Calories: 328 | fat: 1.1g | carbs: 72.6g | protein: 10.2g | fiber: 8.0g

Red Onion Cucumber Dill Bowl

Prep time: 5 minutes | Cook time: 0 minutes | Serves 2

¼ cup water
3 tablespoons white wine vinegar
2 tablespoons chopped fresh dill
½ teaspoon coconut sugar
¼ teaspoon pink
Himalayan salt
¼ teaspoon freshly ground black pepper
1 cucumber, cut into ¼-inch-thick rounds
1 red onion, thinly sliced

1. In a medium bowl, combine the water, vinegar, dill, coconut sugar, salt, and pepper and mix well.
2. Add the cucumber and red onion and stir to mix with the dressing. Chill in the refrigerator for 10 minutes before serving.

Per Serving:
Calories: 50| Total fat: <1g| Carbohydrates: 10g| Fiber: 2g| Protein: 2g

Roasted Balsamic Beets

Prep time: 8 minutes | Cook time: 40 minutes | Serves 4

4 medium beets, peeled and diced
2 tablespoons balsamic vinegar
2 tablespoons olive oil
(optional)
½ teaspoon salt (optional)
¼ teaspoon freshly ground black pepper

1. Preheat the oven to 400ºF (205ºC). Line a baking sheet with parchment paper.
2. Toss the beets with the olive oil (if desired), vinegar, salt (if desired), and black pepper in a medium bowl.
3. Spread the beets on the prepared baking sheet and roast for 40 minutes until fork-tender.
4. Cool for 5 minutes before serving.

Per Serving
Calories: 178 | fat: 8.1g | carbs: 21.3g | protein: 3.9g | fiber: 5.2g

Sautéed Leeks and Tomatoes

Prep time: 10 minutes | Cook time: 10 minutes | Serves 4

3 leeks, white parts only
1 tablespoon olive oil (optional)
1 yellow onion, diced
4 Roma tomatoes, diced
1 tablespoon Dijon mustard
Salt, to taste (optional)
Freshly ground black pepper, to taste

1. Slice the leeks lengthwise down the middle and wash very well to remove any dirt. Then cut them into ½-inch pieces.
2. Heat the olive oil (if desired) in a saucepan over medium heat until it shimmers.
3. Add the onion and sauté for 2 minutes until translucent.
4. Add the leeks, stir, and cook for 5 minutes, stirring occasionally.
5. Stir in the tomatoes, mustard, salt (if desired), and pepper. Continue to cook for about 3 minutes, stirring occasionally, or until the tomatoes have broken down a little.
6. Serve warm.

Per Serving
Calories: 168 | fat: 4.3g | carbs: 28.9g | protein: 4.2g | fiber: 5.1g

Lemony Edamame

Prep time: 5 minutes | Cook time: 5 minutes | Serves 2

2 tablespoons freshly squeezed lemon juice
Zest of 1 lemon
¼ teaspoon freshly ground black pepper

⅛ Teaspoon pink Himalayan salt (optional)
2 cups edamame, unshelled

1. Combine the lemon juice, lemon zest, pepper, and salt (if desired) in a small bowl. Set aside.
2. Steam or boil the edamame for 5 minutes. Remove from the heat and place in a large bowl.
3. Pour the lemon mixture over the edamame and toss until fully coated. Serve warm.

Per Serving
Calories: 368 | fat: 15.1g | carbs: 29.6g | protein: 30.2g | fiber: 9.2g

Simple Mustard Greens

Prep time: 8 minutes | Cook time: 18 minutes | Serves 4 to 6

4 pounds (1.8 kg) mustard greens, stemmed and washed
1 large onion, diced
2 cloves garlic,

minced
Sea salt, to taste (optional)
Black pepper, to taste

1. Bring a large pot of water to a boil, add the mustard greens in batches, and let them cook for 5 minutes.
2. Remove the greens from the water and transfer them to a large bowl with ice water to stop their cooking and help them keep their color.
3. Sauté the onion in a large skillet for 7 to 8 minutes over medium heat. Add the water, 1 to 2 tablespoons, at a time to keep the onion from sticking.
4. Add the garlic and cook for another 1 minute. Add the greens and cook for 5 minutes. Season with salt (if desired) and pepper. Serve immediately.

Per Serving
Calories: 170 | fat: 1.9g | carbs: 25.1g | protein: 13.4g | fiber: 15.2g

Cheesy Kale Chips

Prep time: 10 minutes | Cook time: 10 minutes | Serves 4

6 tablespoons Parmesan Cheese
3 tablespoons freshly squeezed lemon juice
Pinch freshly ground

black pepper
Pinch pink Himalayan salt
1 bunch kale stems removed, chopped

1. Preheat the oven to 350°F. Line a baking sheet with parchment paper or a silicone liner.
2. In a bowl, mix the cheese, lemon juice, pepper, and salt. Rub the mixture into the kale.
3. Spread out the kale on the prepared baking sheet, making sure the pieces aren't overlapping. Bake for 8 to 12 minutes, or until crispy. Keep your eye on the chips while they're baking so they don't burn.

Per Serving
Calories: 109| Total fat: 6g| Carbohydrates: 12g| Fiber: 4g| Protein: 5g

Nutty Chocolate Balls

Prep time: 10 minutes | Cook time: 0 minutes | Serves 3

1 cup almonds
1½ tablespoons cocoa powder
⅛ Teaspoon pink Himalayan salt

1 tablespoon maple syrup
10 Medjool dates, pitted and chopped

1. In a food processor, blend the almonds until they become a rough, grainy powder.
2. Add the cocoa, salt, and maple syrup and blend well. Add the dates and blend until completely smooth.
1. Using your hands, shape the mixture into individual 1½-inch balls. Enjoy immediately or store in a reusable container at room temperature or in the refrigerator for up to 7 days.

Per Serving (3 balls)
Calories: 517| Total fat: 24g| Carbohydrates: 76g| Fiber: 12g| Protein: 12g|

Garlic Roasted Brussels Sprouts

Prep time: 10 minutes | Cook time: 30 to 40 minutes | Serves 4

2 pounds (907 g) Brussels sprouts, halved
8 to 12 garlic cloves (1 head garlic), unpeeled

2 tablespoons olive oil (optional)
2 tablespoons balsamic vinegar
½ teaspoon salt (optional)

1. Preheat the oven to 400ºF (205ºC).
2. On a baking sheet, toss the Brussels sprouts and garlic cloves with the olive oil (if desired), vinegar, and salt (if desired) until well coated.
3. Roast in the preheated oven for 30 to 40 minutes, shaking the pan halfway through the cooking time, or until crisp.
4. Serve hot.

Per Serving
Calories: 178 | fat: 8.6g | carbs: 19.5g | protein: 6.2g | fiber: 6.1g

One Pan Vegetable Bread Mix

Prep time: 10 minutes | Cook time: 40 minutes | Serves 6

1½ (20-ounce) loaves whole wheat bread, broken into small pieces
2 cups vegetable broth

5 celery stalks, chopped
1 large yellow onion, chopped
3 tablespoons vegan poultry seasoning

1. Preheat the oven to 350°F.
2. In a large roasting pan, combine all the ingredients and stir together until everything is well mixed and the bread is evenly moistened.
3. Cover the pan with aluminum foil and bake for 40 minutes.
4. You can serve this stuffing immediately or store in a reusable container in the refrigerator.

Per Serving
Calories: 608| Total fat: 11g| Carbohydrates: 113g| Fiber: 14g| Protein: 18g

Simple Showtime Popcorn

Prep time: 1 minute | Cook time: 5 minutes | Serves 2

¼ cup popcorn kernels
1 tablespoon nutritional yeast

¼ teaspoon onion powder
¼ teaspoon garlic powder

1. Place the popcorn kernels in a paper lunch bag, folding over the top of the bag so the kernels won't spill out.
2. Microwave on high for 2 to 3 minutes, or until you hear a pause of 2 seconds in between kernels popping.
3. Remove the bag from the microwave, and add the nutritional yeast, onion powder, and garlic powder. Fold the top of the bag back over and shake to thoroughly coat.
4. Pour into a bowl and serve immediately.

Per Serving
Calories: 49 | fat: 2.1g | carbs: 5.7g | protein: 4.2g | fiber: 1.9g

Simple Lemony Edamame

Prep time: 5 minutes | Cook time: 5 minutes | Serves 2

Zest of 1 lemon
2 tablespoons freshly squeezed lemon juice
¼ teaspoon freshly ground black pepper

⅛ Teaspoon pink Himalayan salt
2 cups edamame, unshelled

1. In a small bowl, combine the lemon zest, lemon juice, pepper, and salt.
2. Steam or boil the edamame for 5 minutes. Remove from the heat and place in a big bowl. Pour the lemon-pepper mixture over the edamame and toss until covered thoroughly.
3. Enjoy warm or store in a reusable container in the refrigerator for up to 5 days.

Per Serving
Calories: 366| Total fat: 15g| Carbohydrates: 29g| Fiber: 9g| Protein: 30g

Creamy Mushroom Green Beans Bowl

Prep time: 5 minutes | Cook time: 15 minutes | Serves 4

1 small yellow onion, diced
3 or 4 garlic cloves, minced
1 cup vegetable broth, divided
1 cup sliced mushrooms
1 cup unsweetened plant-based milk
2 tablespoons gluten-free flour
2 tablespoons B12-fortified nutritional yeast
3 cups fresh green beans
Pink Himalayan salt
Freshly ground black pepper

1. In a large nonstick pan over medium heat, sauté the onion and garlic in ¼ cup of broth until the onion is soft.
2. Add the mushrooms, milk, and remaining ¾ cup of broth, flour, and nutritional yeast. Whisk until there are no clumps.
3. Add the green beans, cover the pan with a lid, and cook on medium-low heat for 10 to 15 minutes, or until the beans are soft.
4. Add salt and pepper to taste.
5. Serve immediately or store in a reusable container in the refrigerator for up to 5 days.

Per Serving
Calories: 102| Total fat: 2g| Carbohydrates: 20g| Fiber: 7g| Protein: 6g|

Creamy Garlic Cauliflower Mashed Potatoes

Prep time: 10 minutes | Cook time: 25 minutes | Serves 4

5 medium yellow potatoes, chopped
¾ cup unsweetened plant-based milk
Pink Himalayan salt (optional)
Freshly ground black pepper, to taste
½ medium cauliflowers
6 garlic cloves, minced
¼ cup vegetable broth

1. In a large pot over medium-high heat, boil the potatoes for 15 minutes until soft.
2. When cooked, drain and return the potatoes to the pot. Mash the potatoes while beating in the milk. Season with salt (if desired) and pepper.
3. In a vegetable steamer, steam the cauliflower for 10 minutes. Transfer it to a food processor and blend until roughly smooth.
4. In a nonstick pan over medium heat, sauté the garlic in the broth for 5 minutes, or until tender.
5. Transfer the cauliflower and garlic to the large pot with the mashed potatoes. Combine by using a potato masher or stirring well. Serve warm.

Per Serving
Calories: 170 | fat: 1.0g | carbs: 37.8g | protein: 5.9g | fiber: 5.0g

Lentil Energy Bites

Prep time: 15 minutes | Cook time: 20 to 25 minutes | Serves 9

1 cup water
½ cup lentils, rinsed and drained
2 cups quick-cooking oats
½ cup dairy-free chocolate chips
¼ cup raw shelled
hemp seeds
¼ cup sunflower seed kernels
¼ cup unsweetened shredded coconut
½ cup maple syrup (optional)
½ cup almond butter

1. Combine the water and lentils in a large saucepan and bring to a boil over high heat.
2. Once it starts to boil, reduce the heat to medium-high and cook for 20 to 25 minutes, or until the lentils are softened. All the water should be absorbed. Set aside to cool.
3. Mix together the oats, chocolate chips, hemp seeds, sunflower seeds, and coconut in a large bowl. Stir in the cooled lentils. Whisk in the maple syrup (if desired) and almond butter until combined. Shape the mixture into thirty-six balls and place in a glass container with a lid.
4. Let sit in the refrigerator for about 30 minutes. Serve immediately or store in the refrigerator for up to 5 days or in the freezer for up to 6 months.

Per Serving
Calories: 245 | fat: 12.9g | carbs: 25.6g | protein: 6.8g | fiber: 3.6g

Tomato Garlic Swiss Chard

Prep time: 5 minutes | Cook time: 10 minutes | Serves 4

1 bunch Swiss chard, about 18 ounces (510 g)
1 tablespoon olive oil (optional)
6 garlic cloves, diced
1½ cups marinara sauce
½ teaspoon salt (optional)
¼ teaspoon freshly ground black pepper

1. Strip the chard leaves from the stalks and finely dice the stalks. Slice the leaves into thin strips. (Keep the stalks and leaves separate.)
2. Heat the olive oil (if desired) in a large, nonstick skillet over medium heat until shimmering.
3. Add the garlic and diced chard stalks and sauté for 2 to 3 minutes until slightly golden.
4. Add the chard leaves, stir, and cook for 3 minutes until they start to wilt.
5. Stir in the marinara sauce and simmer for an additional 3 minutes, or until the leaves are fully cooked.
6. Season with salt (if desired) and pepper, then serve.

Per Serving
Calories: 128 | fat: 7.3g | carbs: 10.8g | protein: 4.2g | fiber: 3.2g

Skillet Asparagus With Caramelized Onion

Prep time: 5 minutes | Cook time: 15 minutes | Serves 4

1 tablespoon olive oil (optional)
1 medium yellow onion, sliced
Pinch of salt (optional)
1 bunch asparagus, about 14 ounces (397 g), trimmed and cut in half
Splash of vinegar, any variety

1. In a large, nonstick sauté pan, heat the olive oil (if desired) over medium-high heat.
2. Once hot, add the sliced onions and a pinch of salt (if desired). Cook for 10 minutes, stirring occasionally, until golden brown.
3. Add the asparagus to the pan with the onions. Cover and cook for another 5 minutes.
4. Turn the heat off and add a splash of vinegar to deglaze the pan. As the vinegar sizzles, use a spatula to stir the onion and asparagus, scraping the browned bits from the bottom of the pan.
5. Serve warm.

Per Serving
Calories: 153 | fat: 11.6g | carbs: 10.2g | protein: 3.2g | fiber: 3.1g

Peanut Butter Snack Squares

Prep time: 10 minutes | Cook time: 20 minutes | Serves 8

1 cup creamy peanut butter
½ cup coconut sugar (optional)
1 teaspoon vanilla extract
¼ cup garbanzo flour
¾ cup whole wheat flour
1 teaspoon baking
soda
½ teaspoon baking powder
1 cup old-fashioned oats
½ cup unsweetened plant-based milk
½ cup pitted and chopped small dates
½ cup peanuts

1. Preheat the oven to 350ºF (180ºC). Lightly grease a square baking dish and set aside.
2. Mix the peanut butter and sugar (if desired) with a hand or stand mixer on medium speed for 5 minutes. Fold in the vanilla.
3. Add the flours, baking soda, and baking powder and mix on medium speed. Add the oats and mix for a few seconds until stiff. Whisk in the milk until just incorporated. Fold in the dates and peanuts and stir until well combined.
4. Lightly press the dough into the prepared dish. Bake in the preheated oven for 15 to 20 minutes until lightly golden brown.
5. Remove from the oven and place on a wire rack to cool. Cut into squares and serve.

Per Serving
Calories: 420 | fat: 22.0g | carbs: 41.3g | protein: 14.7g | fiber: 7.2g

Spicy Thai Vegetables

Prep time: 10 minutes | Cook time: 10 minutes | Serves 2

5 baby bok choy
5 broccoli florets
½ red bell pepper
½ cup edamame, shelled
¼ cup rice vinegar
¼ cup plus 1 tablespoon water, divided
3 garlic cloves, minced

4 Teaspoons red pepper flakes
½ tablespoon low-sodium soy sauce
1 tablespoon maple syrup (optional)
¼ teaspoon garlic powder
1 teaspoon gluten-free flour

1. Steam the bok choy, broccoli, bell pepper, and edamame for 10 minutes, or until softened.
2. In a small saucepan, combine the vinegar, ¼ cup of water, garlic, red pepper flakes, soy sauce, maple syrup (if desired), and garlic powder.
3. In a bowl, mix the flour with the remaining 1 tablespoon of water, then add the slurry to the saucepan. Whisk the sauce until it is thickened.
4. Remove the vegetables from the steamer and transfer to a large bowl. Pour the sauce over the vegetables and stir until thoroughly covered. Serve immediately.

Per Serving
Calories: 150 | fat: 1.0g | carbs: 25.9g | protein: 17.1g | fiber: 2.0g

Gluten Free Oats Walnut Granola

Prep time: 5 minutes | Cook time: 25 minutes | Serves 4

2 cups rolled oats (check label for gluten-free)
1 cup maple syrup
¼ cup chopped walnuts
¼ cup chopped almonds
¼ cup chopped

pecans
2 tablespoons sunflower seeds
2 tablespoons pumpkin seeds
1 tablespoon hemp seed
1 teaspoon vanilla extract

1. Preheat the oven to 350°F. Line a baking sheet with parchment paper or a silicone liner.
2. In a large bowl, stir together all the ingredients until thoroughly mixed.
3. Spread out the mixture on the prepared baking sheet and bake for 25 minutes, or until lightly browned. Stir the granola at the halfway mark to ensure an even bake.
4. Remove from the oven and allow it to cool before serving.

Per Serving
Calories: 553| Total fat: 21g| Carbohydrates: 85g| Fiber: 7g| Protein: 11g|

Garlicky Spinach Dip

Prep time: 15 minutes | Cook time: 25 minutes | Serves 6

3 garlic cloves, crushed
1 cup cashews, soaked in hot water for at least 1 hour
½ cup water
2 teaspoons Dijon mustard
2 teaspoons pink Himalayan salt
2 teaspoons freshly squeezed lemon juice
1½ Teaspoons freshly

ground black pepper
1½ Teaspoons red pepper flakes
1 teaspoon white vinegar
1 (14-ounce) can artichoke hearts, drained and chopped
1 cup frozen spinach, thawed and strained
Parmesan Cheese, for topping (optional)

1. Preheat the oven to 350°F.
2. In a pot over medium-high heat, boil the cauliflower and garlic in water for 10 minutes, or until the garlic has softened. Remove from the heat, strain, and set aside to cool.
3. Once cooled, in a food processor, combine the cauliflower and garlic with the cashews, water, mustard, salt, lemon juice, black pepper, red pepper flakes, and vinegar. Blend until smooth.
4. Transfer the mixture to a large bowl and stir in the artichoke hearts and spinach.
5. Transfer the mixture to an 8-inch square casserole dish and bake for 15 minutes, or until lightly browned on the top and edges.

Per Serving:
Calories: 260| Total fat: 16g| Carbohydrates: 24g| Fiber: 6g| Protein: 10g

Spicy Baked Onions

Prep time: 5 minutes | Cook time: 10 minutes | Serves2

1 cup vegan bread crumbs
½ teaspoon paprika
¼ teaspoon garlic powder
¼ teaspoon freshly ground black pepper

¼ teaspoon pink Himalayan salt
¾ cup water
½ cup whole wheat flour
2 large yellow onions cut into ½-inch rings

1. Preheat the oven to 400°F. Line a baking sheet with parchment paper or a silicone liner.
2. In a bowl, blend the bread crumbs, paprika, garlic powder, pepper, and salt.
3. In a separate bowl, blend the water and flour.
4. Dip each onion ring first into the wet ingredients and then into the dry ingredients, coating well. Place the coated onions rings on the prepared baking sheet and bake for 10 to 12 minutes, or until light brown. These are best enjoyed immediately after baking.

Per Serving
Calories: 327| Total fat: 1g| Carbohydrates: 72g| Fiber: 8g| Protein: 10g|

Spinach and Artichoke Dip

Prep time: 15 minutes | Cook time: 25 minutes | Serves 6

2 cups chopped cauliflower
3 garlic cloves, crushed
1 cup cashews, soaked in hot water for at least 1 hour
½ cup water
2 teaspoons Dijon mustard
2 teaspoons freshly squeezed lemon juice
2 teaspoons pink Hi-

malayan salt (optional)
1½ Teaspoons red pepper flakes
1½ Teaspoons freshly ground black pepper
1 teaspoon white vinegar
1 cup frozen spinach, thawed and drained
1 (14-ounce / 397-g) can artichoke hearts, drained and chopped

1. Preheat the oven to 350ºF (180ºC).
2. In a pot over medium-high heat, boil the chopped cauliflower and garlic in water for 10 minutes, or until the garlic is tender.
3. Remove from the heat, drain, and set aside to cool.
4. Once cooled, combine the cauliflower and garlic with the cashews, water, mustard, lemon juice, salt (if desired), red pepper flakes, black pepper, and vinegar in a food processor. Pulse until smooth.
5. Transfer the mixture to a large bowl and add the spinach and artichoke hearts, stirring well.
6. Place the mixture in a casserole dish and bake for 15 minutes, or until lightly browned on the top and edges.
7. Let rest for 5 minutes before serving.

Per Serving
Calories: 263 | fat: 16.1g | carbs: 24.6g | protein: 10.2g | fiber: 6.1g

One Pan Baked Sweet Potatoes

Prep time: 5 minutes | Cook time: 30 minutes | Serves 2

2 sweet potatoes
2 cups fresh kale
1 cup cooked black beans (drained and rinsed, if canned)
½ cup corn, frozen or canned
½ small red onion, diced

¼ cup vegetable broth or water
¾ cup chopped fresh tomatoes
Fresh cilantro, chopped
Creamy Avocado Dressing

1. Preheat the oven to 400°F.
2. Poke several holes all over the sweet potatoes with a fork. Bake on a baking sheet for 50 minutes, or until tender.
3. While the potatoes are cooking, warm the kale, beans, corn, and onion in a nonstick pan over medium heat with the broth, covered with a lid but stirring frequently, for 10 minutes, or until the onion has softened.
4. Remove the potatoes from the oven, cut down the center of each, and push the ends

Per Serving
Calories: 600 | fat: 5.89g | carbs: 116.06g | protein: 26.53g

Roasted Red Pepper Hummus

Prep time: 20 minutes | Cook time: 0 minutes | Serves 8

1 (15-ounce / 425-g) can chickpeas, 3 tablespoons aquafaba (chickpea liquid from the can) reserved, remaining liquid drained, and rinsed
¼ cup tahini
1 tablespoon freshly
squeezed lemon juice
1 teaspoon paprika
½ teaspoon ground cumin
¼ teaspoon freshly ground black pepper
2 garlic cloves, peeled and stemmed
2 roasted red peppers

1. Pour the chickpeas into a bowl and fill the bowl with water. Gently rub the chickpeas between your hands until you feel the skins coming off. Add more water to the bowl and let the skins float to the surface. Using your hand, scoop out the skins. Drain some of the water and repeat this step once more to remove as many of the chickpea skins as possible. Drain to remove all the water. Set the chickpeas aside.
2. In a food processor or high-speed blender, combine the reserved Aquafina, tahini, and lemon juice. Process for 2 minutes.
3. Add the paprika, cumin, black pepper, garlic, and red peppers. Purée until the red peppers are incorporated.
4. Add the chickpeas and blend for 2 to 3 minutes, or until the hummus is smooth.
5. Serve chilled.

Per Serving
Calories: 100 | fat: 5.1g | carbs: 11.8g | protein: 4.2g | fiber: 3.1g

Creamy Dreamy Mayo Potato Bowl

Prep time: 10 minutes | Cook time: 15 minutes | Serves 4

6 medium potatoes, cubed and boiled
¾ cup Mighty Mayo
2 celery stalks, diced
2 or 3 scallions, chopped
2 dill pickles, chopped
2 tablespoons yellow mustard
Freshly ground black pepper
Pink Himalayan salt
Ground paprika (optional)

1. Cook the potatoes in boiling water for 15 minutes, or until tender but still a little firm. Drain and rinse the potatoes in cool water.
2. In a bowl, combine the potatoes, mayo, celery, scallions, pickles, and mustard and season with pepper and salt to taste.
3. Mix until thoroughly coated. Sprinkle with paprika (if using).
4. Enjoy immediately or store in a reusable container in the refrigerator for up to 5 days.

Per Serving
Calories: 375| Total fat: 13g| Carbohydrates: 63g| Fiber: 9g| Protein: 9g

Steamed Garlic Vegetables

Prep time: 10 minutes | Cook time: 20 minutes | Serves 4

5 medium yellow potatoes, chopped
¾ cup unsweetened plant-based milk
Pink Himalayan salt
Freshly ground black
pepper
½ medium cauliflowers
6 garlic cloves, minced
¼ cup vegetable broth

1. In a big pot over medium-high heat, boil the potatoes for 15 minutes, or until soft. When cooked, drain and return the potatoes to the pot.
2. Mash the potatoes while beating in the milk. Season with salt and pepper.
3. In a vegetable steamer, steam the cauliflower for 10 minutes. Transfer it to a food processor and blend until roughly smooth.
4. In a nonstick pan over medium heat, sauté the garlic in the broth for 5 minutes, or until soft.
5. Transfer the cauliflower and garlic to the big pot with the mashed potatoes. Combine by using a potato masher or stirring well.
6. Serve warm. This store well in a reusable container in the refrigerator for up to 5 days.

Per Serving
Calories: 169| Total fat: 1g| Carbohydrates: 38g| Fiber: 5g| Protein: 6g|

Low Fat Nutty Cookies

Prep time: 10 minutes | Cook time: 0 minutes | Serves 9

½ cup almond or peanut butter
½ cup rolled oats (check label for gluten-free)
¼ cup ground chia seeds

3 tablespoons maple syrup
1 tablespoon ground flaxseed
1 tablespoon pumpkin seeds

1. Combine all the ingredients in a food processor and blend well, until very small bits of the seeds are still visible.
2. Using your hands, shape the mixture into small balls and enjoy immediately or store in a reusable container at room temperature or in the refrigerator for up to 10 days.

Per Serving
Calories: 154| Total fat: 10g| Carbohydrates: 13g| Fiber: 4g| Protein: 6g

Authentic Spicy Veggies

Prep time: 10 minutes | Cook time: 10 minutes | Serves 2

5 broccoli florets
5 baby bok choy
½ red bell pepper
½ cup edamame, shelled
¼ cup rice vinegar
¼ cup water, plus 1 tablespoon
3 garlic cloves, minced
4 Teaspoons red pep-

per flakes
½ tablespoon low-sodium soy sauce (or tamari, which is a gluten-free option)
1 tablespoon maple syrup
¼ teaspoon garlic powder
1 teaspoon gluten-free flour

1. Steam the broccoli, bok choy, bell pepper, and edamame for 10 minutes, or until tender.
2. In a small saucepan, combine the vinegar, ¼ cup of water, garlic, red pepper flakes, soy sauce, maple syrup, and garlic powder.
3. In a bowl, mix the flour with the remaining 1 tablespoon of water, then add the slurry to the saucepan.
4. Stir the sauce until it thickens.

5. Remove the vegetables from the steamer and transfer to a large bowl. Pour the sauce over the vegetables and mix until thoroughly covered
6. Serve immediately or store in a reusable container in the refrigerator for up to 5 days.

Per Serving
Calories: 151| Total fat: 1g| Carbohydrates: 26g| Fiber: 2g| Protein: 17g

Easy Tasty Homemade Pastry

Prep time: 30 minutes | Cook time: 25 minutes | Serves 8

2¼ Teaspoons active dry yeast
1 tablespoon sugar
1½ cups warm water
2½ cups whole wheat flour

¼ cup vital wheat gluten
10 cups water
⅔ Cup baking soda
Pink Himalayan salt (optional)

1. Stir the yeast and sugar into the warm water and let it sit for 10 to 15 minutes.
2. In a large bowl, combine the flour and wheat gluten. Add the yeast mixture and mix well.
3. Knead the dough by hand for 5 minutes. Form the dough into a ball and place it in a clean bowl. Cover the bowl and let it sit for 50 to 60 minutes to allow the dough to rise.
4. Preheat the oven to 450°F. Line a baking sheet with parchment paper.
5. Remove the dough from the bowl and cut it into 8 equal pieces. Roll the pieces into ropes 15 to 18 inches long. Shape the ropes into pretzels.
6. Pour 10 cups of water into a pot. Set over high heat and add the baking soda. Bring to a boil and cook each pretzel, one at a time, for 30 to 45 seconds.
7. Place the pretzels on the prepared baking sheet. Bake for 12 to 14 minutes, or until lightly browned. Sprinkle with salt (if using). Enjoy warm or store in a reusable container at room temperature for 3 to 5 days.

Per Serving
Calories: 158| Total fat: 1g| Carbohydrates: 31g| Fiber: 5g| Protein: 7g

Cashew Potato Casserole

Prep time: 10 minutes | Cook time: 40 minutes | Serves 4

1 cup cashews, soaked in hot water for at least 1 hour
¾ cup vegetable broth
½ cup unsweetened plant-based milk
2 tablespoons B*12*-fortified nutritional yeast

2 teaspoons pink Himalayan salt
1 teaspoon paprika
1 teaspoon freshly ground black pepper
½ teaspoon onion powder
5 small yellow potatoes, peeled and thinly sliced

1. Preheat the oven to 400°F. In a food processor, combine the cashews and broth and blend until completely smooth.
2. Add the milk, nutritional yeast, salt, paprika, pepper, and onion powder. Blend until mixed well.
3. In an 8-inch square glass casserole dish, spread a thin layer of sauce. Lay half the potatoes on top and pour half of the remaining sauce evenly over them. Layer the rest of the potatoes on top, and cover with the rest of the sauce.
4. Cover with aluminum foil and cook for 30 minutes. Uncover and cook for another 10 minutes.
5. Serve warm or store in a reusable container in the refrigerator for up to 7 days.

Per Serving
Calories: 320| Total fat: 16g| Carbohydrates: 37g| Fiber: 5g| Protein: 11g

Purple Green Coleslaw

Prep time: 10 minutes | Cook time: 0 minutes | Serves 4

½ cup cashews, soaked in hot water for at least 1 hour
2½ tablespoons white wine vinegar
¾ tablespoon coconut sugar
½ teaspoon pink Himalayan salt
¼ teaspoon freshly

ground black pepper
2 cups shredded green cabbage
1 cup shredded purple cabbage
1 cup shredded carrots
1 cup shredded Brussels sprouts
½ cup water

1. In a food processor, combine the cashews, vinegar, coconut sugar, salt, water, and pepper. Blend well until creamy and smooth.
2. In a large bowl, combine the green cabbage, purple cabbage, carrots, and Brussels sprouts.
3. Add the dressing and mix well. Serve immediately or store in a reusable container in the refrigerator for up to 5 days.

Per Serving
Calories: 194| Total fat: 11g| Carbohydrates: 22g| Fiber: 5g| Protein: 6g

Homemade Soft Pretzels

Prep time: 15 minutes | Cook time: 25 minutes | Serves 8

2¼ Teaspoons active dry yeast
1 tablespoon coconut sugar (optional)
1½ cups warm water
2½ cups whole wheat flour

¼ cup vital wheat gluten
10 cups water
²/₃ cup baking soda
Pink Himalayan salt (optional)

1. Stir the yeast and sugar (if desired) into the warm water and let sit for 10 to 15 minutes.
2. Combine the flour and wheat gluten in a large bowl. Add the yeast mixture and stir until well incorporated.
3. Knead the dough by hand for 5 minutes. Shape the dough into a ball and place it in a clean bowl. Cover and sit for 50 to 60 minutes to allow the dough to rise.
4. Preheat the oven to 450ºF (235ºC). Line a baking sheet with parchment paper and set aside.
5. Remove the dough from the bowl and cut it into 8 equal pieces. Roll the pieces into ropes, about 15 to 18 inches long. Shape the ropes into pretzels.
6. Pour the water into a pot over high heat and add the baking soda. Bring to a boil and cook each pretzel, one at a time, for 30 to 45 seconds.
7. Arrange the pretzels on the prepared baking sheet and bake for 12 to 14 minutes, or until lightly browned.
8. Season with salt, if desired. Serve warm.

Per Serving
Calories: 159 | fat: 1.7g | carbs: 31.3g | protein: 7.2g | fiber: 5.1g

Vanilla flavoured Apple Bowl

Prep time: 10 minutes | Cook time: 0 minutes | Serves 4

1 cup Medjool dates, pitted
½ cup unsweetened plant-based milk
1 teaspoon vanilla extract
⅛ Teaspoon pink Himalayan salt
4 Granny Smith ap-
ples, cored and cut into ¼-inch slices
¼ cup pecans, chopped
2 tablespoons vegan dark chocolate chips
1 teaspoon hemp seeds

1. Blend the dates in a food processor until they resemble a paste.
2. Add the milk, vanilla, and salt, and blend until smooth. Set aside.
3. On a plate, lay out 1 sliced apple (use 1 apple Per Serving on individual plates). Drizzle 1 tablespoon of the date sauce over the apple.
4. Top with 1 tablespoon of pecans, ½ tablespoon of chocolate chips, and ¼ teaspoon of hemp seeds. Repeat with the remaining apples and toppings.

Per Serving
Calories: 318| Total fat: 9g| Carbohydrates: 64g| Fiber: 9g| Protein: 3g|

Buffalo Cauliflower

Prep time: 10 minutes | Cook time: 40 minutes | Serves 4

¼ cup plus 2 tablespoons olive oil, divided (optional)
4 garlic cloves, roughly chopped
6 red chiles, such as cayenne, roughly chopped (more if you like it super spicy)
1 yellow onion,
roughly chopped
1 cup water
½ cup apple cider vinegar
½ teaspoon salt (optional)
½ teaspoon freshly ground black pepper
1 head cauliflower, cut into florets

1. In a large nonstick sauté pan, heat ¼ cup of olive oil (if desired) over medium-high heat.
2. Once hot, add the garlic, chiles, and onion. Cook for 5 minutes, stirring occasionally, until the onions are golden brown.
3. Add the water and bring to a boil. Let this cook for about 10 minutes until the water has almost evaporated.
4. Preheat the oven to 450ºF (235ºC). Line a baking sheet with foil or parchment

paper.
5. Spread the cauliflower florets in a single layer on the prepared baking sheet.
6. Transfer the cooked garlic mixture to a food processor or blender and blend briefly to combine.
7. Add the vinegar, salt (if desired), and pepper. Blend again for 30 seconds.
8. Using a fine-mesh sieve, strain the sauce into a bowl. Use a spoon or spatula to scrape and press all the liquid from the pulp.
9. Pour half of the sauce over the cauliflower florets and toss to coat.
10. Transfer the remaining sauce to an airtight container and refrigerate until ready to serve.
11. Place the cauliflower in the oven and bake for 15 minutes. Remove from the oven, drizzle the remaining 2 tablespoons of olive oil (if desired) over the top, and stir. Return to the oven to bake for 10 minutes more.
12. Serve the baked cauliflower with extra sauce, if desired.

Per Serving
Calories: 234 | fat: 14.5g | carbs: 19.3g | protein: 7.2g | fiber: 14.1g

Slow Cooker Tender Saucy Beans

Prep time: 5 minutes | Cook time: 30 minutes | Serves 4

1½ cups water
1 cup tomato sauce
⅓ Cup molasses
¼ cup brown sugar
1 tablespoon apple cider vinegar
1 tablespoon mustard
½ teaspoon pink
Himalayan salt
½ teaspoon freshly ground black pepper
2 cups dried navy beans, soaked overnight and drained
1 medium yellow onion, chopped

1. In a mixing bowl, combine the water, tomato sauce, molasses, brown sugar, vinegar, mustard, salt, and pepper.
2. In a slow cooker, combine the beans, onion, and the sauce. Set the slow cooker for 6 to 8 hours on Low, until the beans are tender.
3. Enjoy warm or store in a reusable container in the refrigerator for up to 7 days.

Per Serving
Calories: 325| Total fat: 1g| Carbohydrates: 82g| Fiber: 20g| Protein: 17g

Chapter 10 Pastas and Noodles

Cannellini Pesto Spaghetti

Prep time: 5 minutes | Cook time: 10 minutes | Serves 4

12 ounces (340 g) whole-grain spaghetti, cooked, drained, and kept warm, ½ cup cooking liquid reserved
1 cup pesto
2 cups cooked cannellini beans, drained and rinsed

1. Put the cooked spaghetti in a large bowl and add the pesto.
2. Add the reserved cooking liquid and beans and toss well to serve.

Per Serving
Calories: 549 | fat: 34.9g | carbs: 45.2g | protein: 18.3g | fiber: 10.1g

Ponzu Pea Rice Noodle Salad

Prep time: 5 minutes | Cook time: 10 minutes | Serves 4

16 cups water
1 pound (454 g) brown rice noodles
½ pound (227 g) snow peas, trimmed and cut into matchsticks
3 medium carrots, peeled and cut into matchsticks
½ cup unsweetened Ponzu sauce
3 green onions, white and green parts, cut into ¾-inch pieces
½ cup coarsely chopped cilantro

1. Bring water to a boil in a large pot, add the rice noodles and cook for 10 minutes or until al dente.
2. Add the snow peas and carrots during the last minute of cooking.
3. Drain and rinse the mixture until cooled and place them in a large bowl.
4. Add the ponzu sauce, green onions, and cilantro. Toss well before serving.

Per Serving
Calories: 179 | fat: 0.5g | carbs: 39.0g | protein: 4.8g | fiber: 4.8g

Tomato Spaghetti

Prep time: 5 minutes | Cook time: 10 minutes | Serves 4

3 medium tomatoes, chopped
Zest and juice of 2 lemons
1 cup finely chopped basil
6 cloves garlic, peeled and minced
3 ears corn, kernels removed (about 2 cups)
1 pound (454 g) spaghetti, cooked, drained
Salt and freshly ground black pepper, to taste (optional)

1. Combine the tomatoes, lemon zest and juice, basil, garlic, and corn in a large bowl.
2. Add the cooked spaghetti and toss well. Season with salt (if desired) and pepper. Serve immediately.

Per Serving
Calories: 263 | fat: 2.4g | carbs: 57.0g | protein: 10.9g | fiber: 8.6g

Teriyaki Noodles

Prep time: 20 minutes | Cook time: 12 to 15 minutes | Serves 6 to 8

½ pound (227 g) whole-wheat spaghetti
5 cups boiling water
3 medium zucchini, cut into julienne strips
3 medium carrots, scrubbed and cut into julienne strips
½ pound (227 g) mushrooms, sliced
½ cup teriyaki sauce

1. In a pot, cook the spaghetti in the boiling water for 10 minutes, uncovered.
2. Add the veggies into the pot with the spaghetti. Cook for another 2 to 5 minutes until the spaghetti is tender. Drain.
3. Drizzle the teriyaki sauce over the spaghetti and veggies and toss until well combined.
4. Serve immediately.

Per Serving
Calories: 104 | fat: 1.7g | carbs: 19.1g | protein: 4.7g | fiber: 3.5g

Indonesia Green Noodle Salad

Prep time: 10 minutes | Cook time: 8 minutes | Serves 4

12 ounces (340 g) brown rice noodles, cooked, drained, and rinsed until cool
1 cup snow peas, trimmed and sliced in half on the diagonal
2 medium cucumbers, peeled, halved, deseeded, and sliced thinly
2 heads baby bok choy, trimmed and thinly sliced

4 green onions, green and white parts, trimmed and thinly sliced
3 tablespoons sambal oelek
½ cup chopped cilantro
2 tablespoons soy sauce
¼ cup fresh lime juice
¼ cup finely chopped mint

1. Combine all the ingredients in a large bowl and toss to coat well.
2. Serve immediately.

Per Serving
Calories: 288 | fat: 1.1g | carbs: 64.6g | protein: 12.1g | fiber: 18.7g

Kimchi Green Rice Noodle Salad

Prep time: 10 minutes | Cook time: 8 minutes | Serves 4

1 pound (454 g) brown rice noodles, cooked, drained, and rinsed until cool
2½ cups chopped kimchi
3 to 4 tablespoons gochujang
1 cup mung bean

sprouts
1 medium cucumber, halved, deseeded and thinly sliced
4 green onions, white and green parts, thinly sliced
2 tablespoons sesame seeds, toasted

1. Combine the rice noodles, kimchi, gochujang, and mung bean sprouts in a large bowl and toss to mix well.
2. Divide the mixture among 4 serving plates and garnish with the cucumber slices, green onions, and sesame seeds. Serve immediately.

Per Serving
Calories: 186 | fat: 2.7g | carbs: 35.6g | protein: 6.1g | fiber: 4.0g

Quick and Spicy Soba Noodles with Marinated Tofu

Prep time: 15 minutes | Cook time: 30 minutes | Serves 6

Marinated Tofu:
8 ounces firm tofu, pressed and drained
2 tablespoons olive oil
1/4 cup finely chopped cilantro
1/4 cup finely chopped mint
1 inch grated fresh ginger
Soba Noodles
8 ounces soba noodles:
3/4 cup edamame
2 thin-skinned cucumbers (like Persian), peeled and julienned
1 large carrot, peeled and julienned

1–2 tablespoons black sesame seeds
1–2 tablespoons white sesame seeds (or one or the other)
2 scallions, chopped
Ginger-Soy Sauce
2 tablespoons fresh lime juice
2 tablespoons soy sauce (preferably low-sodium)
1 tablespoon brown sugar
1 tablespoon grated fresh ginger
2 tablespoons sesame oil
½ tablespoon garlic chili sauce

1. Prepare the tofu. Whisk together the olive oil, herbs ginger and salt/pepper in a food processor or mortar and pestle.
2. Finely mash the herbs with the oil to form a thick paste. Add the herbed mixture to the tofu and toss to combine. Set aside for 30 minutes.
3. Bring a large pot of salted water to a boil and add the soba noodles. Cook according to package instructions, then remove and rinse with cold water.
4. While the noodles are cooking, whisk together the ingredients for the dressing in the bottom of a large bowl.
5. Add in the cooked and slightly-cooled noodles, vegetables, scallions, sesame seeds and marinated tofu.
6. Toss well to combine. Season to taste, as needed, and set aside to let merry for at least 20-30 minutes.

Per Serving
Calories: 2170 | fat: 102.55g | carbs: 244.67g | protein: 102.33g

Cold Orange Soba Noodles

Prep time: 10 minutes | Cook time: 8 minutes | Serves 4

3 tablespoons mellow white miso
Zest of 1 orange and juice of 2 oranges
3 tablespoons grated ginger
½ teaspoon crushed red pepper flakes
1 pound (454 g) soba noodles, cooked, drained, and rinsed until cool
¼ cup chopped cilantro
4 green onions, white and green parts, chopped

1. Put the miso, orange zest and juice, ginger, and crushed red pepper flakes in a large bowl and whisk well to combine.
2. Add water as needed to make the sauce pourable. Add the cooked noodles and toss to coat well.
3. Serve garnished with the cilantro and green onions.

Per Serving
Calories: 166 | fat: 1.1g | carbs: 34.2g | protein: 7.9g | fiber: 1.3g

Crispy Tofu and Vegetable Noodles

Prep time: 35 minutes | Cook time: 30 minutes | Serves 4 to 6

12 ounces (340 g) rice noodles
14 ounces (397 g) firm tofu, cut into ¾-inch pieces
Salt and ground black pepper, to taste (optional)
6 Thai, Serrano chiles, stemmed and deseeded
4 shallots, peeled
6 garlic cloves, peeled
2 cups vegetable broth
¼ cup soy sauce
¼ cup date sugar (optional)
3 tablespoons lime juice (2 limes)
⅓ cup cornstarch
5 tablespoons vegetable oil, divided (optional)
4 (4-ounce / 113-g) heads baby bok choy, stalks sliced into ¼ inch thick, greens sliced into ½ inch thick
1 red bell pepper, stemmed, deseeded, sliced into ¼ inch thick, and halved crosswise
2 cups fresh Thai basil leaves

1. Cover the noodles with hot water in a large bowl and stir to separate. Let noodles soak until softened, about 35 minutes. Drain noodles.

2. Meanwhile, spread tofu on a paper towel lined baking sheet and let drain for 20 minutes. Gently pat dry with paper towels and season with salt (if desired) and pepper.
3. Meanwhile, pulse chiles, shallots, and garlic in a food processor to smooth paste.
4. Whisk the broth, soy sauce, sugar (if desired), and lime juice together in a medium bowl. Set aside.
5. Toss drained tofu with cornstarch in a separate large bowl, then transfer to fine-mesh strainer and shake gently to remove excess cornstarch.
6. Heat 2 tablespoons of vegetable oil (if desired) in a skillet over medium-high heat until shimmering.
7. Add tofu and cook, turning constantly, until crisp and well browned on all sides, 14 minutes. Transfer the tofu to a paper towel lined plate to drain.
8. Heat 1 tablespoon of vegetable oil (if desired) in the skillet over high heat until shimmering.
9. Add the bok choy stalks and bell pepper and cook until tender and lightly browned, 3 minutes.
10. Stir in bok choy leaves and cook until lightly wilted, about 30 seconds| transfers to a medium bowl.
11. Heat the remaining vegetable oil (if desired) in the skillet over medium-high heat until shimmering.
12. Add the processed chile mixture and cook until moisture evaporates and color deepens, 4 minutes.
13. Add the noodles and broth mixture to skillet and cook, tossing gently, until sauce has thickened slightly and noodles are well coated and tender, about 5 minutes.
14. Stir in the browned vegetables and basil and cook until warmed through, about 1 minute.
15. Top with crispy tofu and serve.

Per Serving
Calories: 375 | fat: 18.3g | carbs: 42.0g | protein: 15.4g | fiber: 5.5g

Lemony Broccoli Penne

Prep time: 25 minutes | Cook time: 15 minutes | Serves 4

1 medium yellow onion, peeled and thinly sliced
1 pound (454 g) broccoli rabe, trimmed and cut into 1-inch pieces
¼ cup golden raisins
Zest and juice of 2 lemons
4 cloves garlic, peeled and minced
½ teaspoon crushed

red pepper flakes
1 pound (454 g) whole-grain penne, cooked, drained, and kept warm, ¼ cup cooking liquid reserved
Salt and freshly ground black pepper, to taste (optional)
¼ cup pine nuts, toasted
½ cup chopped basil

1. Put the onion in a large skillet over medium-high heat and sauté for 10 minutes, or until the onion is lightly browned.
2. Add the broccoli rabe and cook, stirring frequently, until the rabe is tender, about 5 minutes.
3. Add the raisins, lemon zest and juice, garlic, crushed red pepper flakes, and the cooked pasta and reserved cooking water.
4. Remove from the heat. Mix well and season with salt (if desired) and pepper. Serve garnished with the pine nuts and basil.

Per Serving
Calories: 278 | fat: 7.4g | carbs: 49.6g | protein: 8.8g | fiber: 9.9g

Spinach and Chickpea Penne

Prep time: 20 minutes | Cook time: 15 minutes | Serves 4

1 medium yellow onion, peeled and diced
4 cloves garlic, minced
½ cup dry white wine
6 sun-dried tomatoes, soaked for 15 minutes in hot water, drained, and chopped
½ pound (227 g) baby spinach

¼ cup chopped dill
2 cups cooked chickpeas, drained and rinsed
12 ounces (340 g) whole-grain penne, cooked, drained, and kept warm
Salt and freshly ground black pepper, to taste (optional)

1. Put the onion in a skillet and sauté over medium heat for 10 minutes.
2. Add the garlic and cook for 3 minutes. Add the white wine and sun-dried tomatoes and cook until the liquid has evaporated.
3. Add the spinach, dill, and chickpeas and cook until the spinach is wilted.
4. Remove from the heat. Add the cooked pasta, mix well, and season with salt (if desired) and pepper. Serve hot.

Per Serving
Calories: 280 | fat: 3.1g | carbs: 53.9g | protein: 12.2g | fiber: 12.5g

Spring Penne Salad

Prep time: 10 minutes | Cook time: 5 minutes | Serves 4

8 cups water
½ pound (227 g) asparagus, trimmed and cut into ½-inch pieces
½ pound (227 g) sugar snap peas, trimmed
12 ounces (340 g) whole-grain penne, cooked, drained, and rinsed until cool
1 (15-ounce / 425-g) can artichoke hearts (oil-free), drained and

quartered
4 green onions, white and green parts, thinly sliced
¼ cup finely chopped chives
1 tablespoon Dijon mustard
¼ cup plus 2 tablespoons balsamic vinegar
Salt and freshly ground black pepper, to taste (optional)

1. Prepare an ice bath by filling a large bowl with ice and cold water.
2. Bring the water to a boil in a pot and add the asparagus and sugar snap peas, and cook for 3 minutes, then drain and plunge them into the ice bath.
3. Drain the vegetables and combine them with the cooked pasta, artichoke hearts, green onions, and chives. Set aside.
4. In a small bowl, combine the balsamic Dijon mustard, vinegar, and salt (if desired) and pepper.
5. Pour the dressing over the pasta mixture and toss well before serving warm.

Per Serving
Calories: 230 | fat: 1.3g | carbs: 49.1g | protein: 8.9g | fiber: 16.7g

Spinach Rotelle Provençale

Prep time: 8 minutes | Cook time: 12 minutes | Serves 6

2 (15-ounce / 425-g) cans unsweetened stewed tomatoes
1 (19-ounce / 539-g) can white beans, drained and rinsed
20 cups water
1 (10-ounce / 283-g) package spinach rotelle
¼ cup chopped fresh parsley

1. Put the beans and tomatoes in a saucepan and heat over medium heat for 8 minutes or until the mixture thickened and has a sauce consistency.
2. Meanwhile, bring the water to a boil in a large pot. Add the spinach rotelle and cook, uncovered, for 12 minutes.
3. Drain the rotelle and transfer into a large bowl. Add the tomato-bean sauce and toss to coat.
4. Sprinkle with fresh parsley before serving.

Per Serving
Calories: 40 | fat: 0.7g | carbs: 8.2g | protein: 2.1g | fiber: 4.2g

Cold Noodle Salad with Spinach

Prep time: 15 minutes | Cook time: 10 minutes | Serves 2

8 ounces (227 g) spaghetti
1 teaspoon toasted sesame oil (optional)
Sauce:
1 garlic clove, finely chopped
2 tablespoons sesame oil (optional)
¼ cup almond butter
3 tablespoons low-sodium soy sauce
2 tablespoons mirin
2 tablespoons unseasoned rice vinegar
1½ tablespoons maple syrup (optional)
½ tablespoon fresh lime juice
⅛ Teaspoon sriracha
Serving:
3 cups baby spinach
1 cup thinly sliced English cucumber
½ red bell pepper, thinly sliced
2 scallions, thinly sliced
1/ ₃ cup coarsely chopped mint leaves
¼ cup coarsely chopped roasted peanuts

1. Bring a large pot of water to a boil over medium-high heat. Add the spaghetti to the pot and cook for 10 minutes, or until al dente, stirring constantly.
2. Drain the spaghetti and rinse in cold water. Transfer to a large bowl and toss with the sesame oil (if desired).
3. In a blender, combine all the ingredients for the sauce and blend until smooth. Pour the sauce over the spaghetti and stir until well mixed. Set in a refrigerator for 15 minutes.
4. Add all the ingredients for the serving to the bowl with the spaghetti. Toss to combine well. Serve immediately.

Per Serving
Calories: 678 | fat: 43.4g | carbs: 60.6g | protein: 21.6g | fiber: 12.4g

Rice Noodle Salad with Tofu

Prep time: 10 minutes | Cook time: 2 to 3 minutes | Serves 2 to 3

½ package vermicelli rice noodles
8 lettuce leaves, shredded
2 cucumbers, julienned
1 large carrot, julienned
1 block smoked tofu, cubed
¼ cup chopped roasted peanuts
½ cup coarsely chopped mint leaves
½ cup coarsely chopped cilantro
Dressing:
3 tablespoons rice vinegar
¼ cup lime juice
¼ cup vegan fish sauce
2 tablespoons maple syrup (optional)
2 garlic cloves, finely minced
1 red chilli, deseeded and sliced

1. Soak the rice noodles in a large bowl of water for 15 minutes, or until softened.
2. In a small bowl, combine all the ingredients for the dressing until well mixed.
3. Add the rice noodles and a bit of the soaking water to a pot over medium heat and cook for 2 to 3 minutes. Drain the rice noodles and rinse in cold water. Transfer to a large bowl.
4. Place the remaining ingredients and the dressing into the bowl with the vermicelli noodles. Toss to combine well. Serve immediately.

Per Serving
Calories: 537 | fat: 14.4g | carbs: 77.3g | protein: 24.1g | fiber: 6.2g

Corn and Tomato Pasta Salad

Prep time: 10 minutes | Cook time: 10 to 15 minutes | Serves 4 to 6

8 ounces (227 g) pasta
1¼ cups frozen corn, thawed
¾ cup coconut butter
Juice of 1 medium lime
½ tablespoon taco seasoning

1½ cups cherry tomatoes, sliced
1¼ cups black beans, rinsed well
¼ cup red onion, finely diced
2 tablespoons cilantro stems, finely chopped

1. Bring a large pot of water to boil over medium heat. Add the pasta to the pot and cook for 10 to 15 minutes, or until just softened. Drain the pasta and rinse the pasta with cold water to bring it down to room temperature.
2. In a large mixing bowl, whisk together the coconut butter, lime juice and taco seasoning.
3. Add the cooked pasta, thawed corn, cherry tomatoes, black beans, onion and cilantro stems to the bowl. Toss to combine well.
4. Divide the pasta salad among serving bowls and serve immediately.

Per Serving
Calories: 440 | fat: 24.3g | carbs: 46.3g | protein: 11.4g | fiber: 9.5g

Rotini Salad with Tofu

Prep time: 10 minutes | Cook time: 10 minutes | Serves 4 to 6

8 ounces (227 g) pressed tofu, cut into cubes
Marinade:
2 tablespoons extra virgin olive oil (optional)
1 tablespoon Dijon mustard
Juice of 1 medium lemon
1 clove garlic, finely minced
½ teaspoon dried oregano
½ teaspoon sea salt (optional)

Ground black pepper, to taste
Rotini Salad:
8 ounces (227 g) gluten-free rotini
8.5 ounces (241 g) canned quartered artichoke hearts, drained
1 cup sliced Persian cucumbers
$1/_3$ cup kalamata olives, sliced in half
¼ cup sun-dried tomatoes, sliced
½ cup fresh basil, coarsely chopped

1. In a medium bowl, whisk together all the ingredients for the marinade. Transfer the tofu to the bowl and use a spatula to gently fold the tofu into the marinade until every cube is coated. Let marinate at room temperature for at least 20 minutes.
2. Bring a large pot of water to a boil. Add the rotini to the pot and cook for 10 minutes, or until al dente. Drain the rotini and rinse with cold water. Transfer the cooled rotini to a large mixing bowl.
3. Add the marinated tofu along with the marinade, artichoke hearts, cucumbers, olives and sun-dried tomatoes to the mixing bowl. Gently stir everything together until well blended.
4. Serve topped with fresh basil.

Per Serving
Calories: 161 | fat: 7.9g | carbs: 18.3g | protein: 7.8g | fiber: 4.3g

Pasta with Orange and Walnut

Prep time: 10 minutes | Cook time: 10 to 15 minutes | Serves 3

7 ounces (198 g) whole-grain pasta
Zest and juice of 1 orange
2 tablespoons olive oil (optional)
1 clove garlic, pressed
Pinch sea salt (optional)

2 to 3 tablespoons fresh parsley, finely chopped
10 olives, pitted and chopped
¼ cup walnuts, chopped
2 to 3 tablespoons nutritional yeast

1. Bring a pot of water to boil over medium heat. Add the pasta to the pot and cook for 10 to 15 minutes, or until just softened. Drain the pasta.
2. In a large bowl, whisk together the orange zest and juice, olive oil (if desired), garlic and salt (if desired). Add the pasta to the bowl and toss until well combined.
3. Spread the fresh parsley, chopped olives, walnuts and nutritional yeast on top. Serve immediately.

Per Serving
Calories: 259 | fat: 15.4g | carbs: 26.2g | protein: 6.1g | fiber: 5.1g

Ritzy Thai Tofu Noodles

Prep time: 30 minutes | Cook time: 20 minutes | Serves 4

Sauce:
3 tablespoons tamarind paste
¾ cup boiling water
¼ cup soy sauce
2 tablespoons rice vinegar
3 tablespoons date sugar (optional)
1 tablespoon vegetable oil (optional)
⅛ Teaspoon cayenne pepper
Noodles:
8 ounces (227 g) rice noodles
14 ounces (397 g) extra-firm tofu, cut into ¾-inch cubes

⅓ cup cornstarch
¼ cup vegetable oil, divided (optional)
1 shallot, minced
3 garlic cloves, minced
6 ounces (170 g) bean sprouts
4 scallions, sliced thinly
Salt, to taste (optional)
¼ cup minced fresh cilantro
2 tablespoons chopped dry-roasted peanuts
Lime wedges, for garnish

1. Soak the tamarind paste in boiling water until softened, about 10 minutes.
2. Strain the mixture through fine-mesh strainer, pressing on solids to extract as much pulp as possible, then discard the solids.
3. Whisk the soy sauce, vinegar, sugar (if desired), oil (if desired), and cayenne into tamarind liquid.
4. Cover the noodles with hot water in a large bowl and stir to separate. Let noodles soak until softened, about 20 minutes. Drain noodles.
5. Meanwhile, spread tofu on a paper towel lined baking sheet and let drain for 20 minutes. Gently pat dry with paper towels.
6. Toss the drained tofu with cornstarch in a medium bowl, then transfer to fine-mesh strainer and shake gently to remove excess cornstarch.
7. Heat 3 tablespoons of vegetable oil (if desired) in a skillet over medium-high heat until just smoking.
8. Add tofu and cook, turning constantly, until crisp and browned on all sides, 12 minutes. Transfer the tofu to a paper towel lined plate to drain.
9. Heat remaining 1 tablespoon oil (if desired) in the skillet over medium heat until shimmering.
10. Add shallot and garlic and cook until lightly browned, about 2 minutes. Whisk sauces to recombine. Add noodles and sauce to skillet, increase heat to high, and cook, tossing gently, until noodles are evenly coated, about 1 minute.
11. Add the browned tofu, bean sprouts, and scallions and cook, tossing gently, until tofu is warmed through and noodles are tender, about 2 minutes.
12. Season with salt (if desired), sprinkle with cilantro and peanuts, and serve with lime wedges.

Per Serving
Calories: 523 | fat: 25.4g | carbs: 62.4g | protein: 15.6g | fiber: 3.5g

Veggie Pasta

Prep time: 15 minutes | Cook time: 15 minutes | Serves 6 to 8

Crushed red pepper flakes, to taste
5 to 6 cloves garlic, finely chopped
1 to 2 tablespoons soy sauce
½ to ¾ cup finely chopped fresh basil
24 cups water

¾ pound (340 g) vegetable fusilli pasta
4 cups rinsed and drained frozen mixed veggies (no corn)
2 large red potatoes, scrubbed, cooked, and cubed

1. In a saucepan, add the red pepper, garlic, soy sauce, and basil. Set aside.
2. Bring the water to a boil in a pot. Drop the pasta into the boiling water and cook for 5 minutes until slightly soft. Stir in the mixed veggies and cook for another 5 minutes.
3. Drain the pasta and veggies and save a few cups of the cooking water. Add 1 cup of the cooking water into the saucepan with the mixture and heat until thickened.
4. Pour the heated mixture over the pasta and veggies. Fold in the cooked potatoes. Stir together all the ingredients. You may need to add reserved cooking water for desired moisture.

Per Serving
Calories: 190 | fat: 4.3g | carbs: 33.7g | protein: 8.4g | fiber: 5.2g

Sesame Soba Noodles with Vegetables

Prep time: 15 minutes | Cook time: 8 minutes | Serves 4

Sauce:
3 tablespoons toasted sesame seeds
1½ tablespoons rice vinegar
¼ cup soy sauce
3 tablespoons peanut butter
1 tablespoon grated fresh ginger
1 garlic clove, minced
1½ tablespoons date sugar (optional)
¾ teaspoon unsweetened hot sauce
Noodles and Vegetables:
16 cups water
12 ounces (340 g)

soba noodles
Salt, to taste (optional)
6 ounces (170 g) snow peas, strings removed and halved lengthwise
10 radishes, trimmed, halved, and sliced thin
1 celery rib, sliced thinly
2 tablespoons toasted sesame oil (optional)
½ cup fresh cilantro leaves
1 tablespoon toasted sesame seeds

1. Process sesame seeds, vinegar, soy sauce, peanut butter, ginger, garlic, sugar (if desired), and hot sauce in a blender until smooth.
2. Bring 16 cups water to a boil in a large pot. Add noodles and 1 tablespoon salt (if desired) and cook, stirring often, for 8 minutes or until al dente.
3. Drain noodles, rinse with cold water, and drain again.
4. Transfer noodles to large bowl and toss with snow peas, radishes, celery, the sauce, and oil (if desired) to coat well.
5. Sprinkle with cilantro and sesame seeds and serve.

Per Serving
Calories: 512 | fat: 17.6g | carbs: 77.3g | protein: 19.3g | fiber: 3.9g

Shiitake and Bean Sprout Ramen

Prep time: 20 minutes | Cook time: 1 hour 15 minutes | Serves 4

4 ounces (113 g) bean sprouts
3 tablespoons soy sauce, divided
4 Teaspoons toasted sesame oil, divided (optional)

1 tablespoon rice vinegar
1 onion, chopped
1 (3-inch) piece ginger, peeled and sliced into ¼-inch thick
5 garlic cloves,

smashed
8 ounces (227 g) shiitake mushrooms, stems removed and reserved, caps sliced thin
½ ounce (14 g) kombu
¼ cup mirin
4 cups vegetable broth
20 cups water, divid-

ed
2 tablespoons red miso
Salt, to taste (optional)
12 ounces (340 g) dried ramen noodles
2 scallions, sliced thinly
1 tablespoon toasted black sesame seeds

1. Combine the bean sprouts, 1 teaspoon soy sauce, 1 teaspoon sesame oil (if desired), and vinegar in a small bowl| set aside.
2. Heat remaining 1 tablespoon sesame oil (if desired) in a large saucepan over medium-high heat until shimmering.
3. Stir in onion and cook until softened and lightly browned, about 6 minutes. Add ginger and garlic and cook until lightly browned, about 2 minutes.
4. Stir in mushroom stems, kombu, mirin, broth, 4 cups of water, and remaining soy sauce and bring to boil.
5. Reduce heat to low, cover, and simmer for 1 hour.
6. Strain broth through fine-mesh strainer into a large bowl. Wipe the saucepan clean and return the strained broth to the saucepan.
7. Whisk miso into broth and bring to gentle simmer over medium heat, whisking to dissolve miso completely.
8. Stir in mushroom caps and cook until warmed through, about 1 minute| season with salt, if desired. Remove from heat and cover to keep warm.
9. Meanwhile, bring 16 cups of water to a boil in a large pot. Add the ramen noodles and 1 tablespoon salt (if desired) and cook, stirring often, until al dente, about 2 minutes.
10. Drain the noodles and divide evenly among serving bowls. Ladle soup over noodles, garnish with bean sprouts, scallions, and sesame seeds. Serve hot.

Per Serving
Calories: 237 | fat: 5.6g | carbs: 37.8g | protein: 8.4g | fiber: 4.1g

Sumptuous Shiitake Udon Noodles

Prep time: 20 minutes | Cook time: 21 minutes | Serves 4 to 6

1 tablespoon vegetable oil (optional)
8 ounces (227 g) shiitake mushrooms, stemmed and sliced thinly
½ ounce (14 g) dried shiitake mushrooms, rinsed and minced
¼ cup mirin
3 tablespoons rice vinegar
3 tablespoons soy sauce
2 garlic cloves, smashed and peeled
1 (1-inch) piece ginger, peeled, halved, and smashed
1 teaspoon toasted sesame oil (optional)
18 cups water, divided
1 teaspoon unsweetened Asian chili-garlic sauce
1 pound (454 g) mustard greens, stemmed and chopped into 2-inch pieces
Salt and ground black pepper, to taste (optional)
1 pound (454 g) fresh udon noodles

1. Heat the vegetable oil (if desired) in a Dutch oven over medium-high heat until shimmering.
2. Add the mushrooms and cook, stirring occasionally, until softened and lightly browned, about 5 minutes.
3. Stir in the dried mushrooms, mirin, vinegar, soy sauce, garlic, ginger, sesame oil (if desired), 2 cups of water, and chili-garlic sauce and bring to a simmer.
4. Reduce the heat to medium-low and simmer until liquid has reduced by half, 8 minutes. Turn off the heat, discard the garlic and ginger| cover pot to keep warm.
5. Meanwhile, bring 16 cups water to a boil in a large pot. Add mustard greens and 1 tablespoon salt (if desired) and cook until greens are tender, about 5 minutes.
6. Add noodles and cook until greens and noodles are tender, about 2 minutes.
7. Reserve ¹/₃ cup cooking water, drain noodles and greens, and return them to pot.
8. Add sauce and reserved cooking water, and toss to combine.
9. Cook over medium-low heat, tossing constantly, until sauce clings to noodles, about 1 minute.
10. Season with salt (if desired) and pepper, and serve.

Per Serving
Calories: 184 | fat: 3.6g | carbs: 32.6g | protein: 6.7g | fiber: 3.6g

Lentil Bolognese with Spaghetti

Prep time: 10 minutes | Cook time: 35 minutes | Serves 6

12 ounces (340 g) brown rice spaghetti
1 tablespoon olive oil (optional)
1 yellow onion, about 9 ounces (250 g), finely diced
6 garlic cloves, minced
6 celery stalks, about 5 ounces (150 g) total, finely diced
3 carrots, about 9 ounces (250 g) total, finely diced
½ teaspoon salt (optional)
¼ teaspoon freshly ground black pepper
3 cups water, plus more as needed
4 cups marinara sauce
3 (14.5-ounces / 420-g) cans cooked lentils, drained and rinsed
1 tablespoon ground cumin
1 tablespoon dried oregano

1. Bring a large pot of salted water to a boil over high heat. Add the spaghetti into the boiling water and cook for 10 minutes until al dente, stirring occasionally to prevent sticking.
2. Remove from the pot. Drain and rinse with cold water for 30 to 60 seconds and then return it to the pot. Set aside.
3. Meanwhile, heat the olive oil (if desired) over medium-high heat in a large pan.
4. Add the onion and garlic and sauté until golden brown, about 2 minutes. Stir in the celery and carrots and continue to cook for 3 minutes. Sprinkle with salt (if desired) and pepper.
5. Add 3 cups of water and sauté for about 8 minutes, or until the pan is nearly dry and the celery and carrots are tender.
6. Add more water, ½ cup at a time, until the celery and carrots soften, if needed.
7. Reduce the heat to medium-low and mix in the marinara sauce, lentils, cumin, and oregano. Stir well and let simmer for 10 minutes.
8. Spoon the mixture on top of the spaghetti and serve immediately.

Per Serving
Calories: 558 | fat: 10.8g | carbs: 91.7g | protein: 23.3g | fiber: 22.1g

Tomato and Artichoke Rigatoni

Prep time: 20 minutes | Cook time: 25 minutes | Serves 4

5 cloves garlic, peeled and minced
2 large tomatoes, diced small
½ cup dry white wine
2 tablespoons unsweetened tomato paste
1 tablespoon oregano
1 (15-ounce / 425-g) can artichoke hearts (oil-free), drained and halved
1 cup kalamata olives, pitted and halved
1 pound (454 g) whole-grain rigatoni, cooked, drained, and kept warm
Salt and freshly ground black pepper, to taste (optional)
Chopped parsley, for garnish

1. Put the garlic in a skillet and sauté over low heat for 5 minutes.
2. Raise the heat to medium and add the tomatoes, white wine, tomato paste, and oregano and cook for 15 minutes, or until the liquid is reduced by half.
3. Add the artichokes, olives, and cooked rigatoni, mix well, and cook for another 5 minutes.
4. Season with salt (if desired) and pepper. Serve garnished with the parsley.

Per Serving
Calories: 272 | fat: 5.1g | carbs: 54.0g | protein: 8.0g | fiber: 17.7g

One Pot Pumpkin Pasta

Prep time: 0 minutes | Cook time: 25 minutes | Serves 4

1 tablespoon olive oil (optional)
2 sprigs rosemary or a few sage leaves, roughly chopped
16 ounces (454g) brown rice pasta, such as penne
4 cups water
1¼ cups pumpkin purée
1 teaspoon ground nutmeg
1 teaspoon salt (optional)

1. Heat the olive oil (if desired) in a large pot over medium-high heat. Add the rosemary or sage and cook for 1 minute until fragrant.
2. Add the pasta, water, pumpkin purée, nutmeg, and salt (if desired).
3. Stir until the pumpkin has dissolved into the water. Cover and bring to a boil. Stir again and reduce the heat to medium.
4. Let simmer uncovered for 20 to 25 minutes, or until the water is absorbed, stirring occasionally to prevent sticking.
5. Divide the pasta evenly among 4 bowls and serve warm.

Per Serving
Calories: 475 | fat: g | carbs: 91.2g | protein: 9.0g | fiber: 5.1g

Olive and Cannellini Bean Pasta

Prep time: 10 minutes | Cook time: 20 minutes | Serves 1

½ cup whole-grain pasta
Pinch sea salt (optional)
1 teaspoon olive oil, or 1 tablespoon vegetable broth
¼ cup thinly sliced zucchini
¼ cup thinly sliced
red bell pepper
½ cup cooked cannellini beans
½ cup spinach
1 tablespoon balsamic vinegar
1 tablespoon nutritional yeast
2 or 3 black olives, pitted and chopped

1. Bring a pot of salted water to a boil. Add the pasta into the boiling water and cook for 10 minutes until chewy, stirring occasionally to prevent sticking.
2. Remove from the pot. Drain and rinse with cold water for 30 to 60 seconds and then return it to the pot. Set aside.
3. Meantime, heat the oil (if desired) in a large skillet. Add the zucchini and bell pepper and lightly sauté for 7 to 8 minutes, or until the veggies are tender.
4. Fold in the beans to warm for 2 minutes and then add the spinach. Once the spinach is wilted, drizzle the vinegar over the top.
5. Add the bean mixture to the cooked pasta and toss to combine.
6. Serve scattered with the nutritional yeast and olives.

Per Serving
Calories: 386 | fat: 16.8g | carbs: 3.9g | protein: 18.2g | fiber: 19.1g

Zucchini Noodles with Jackfruit

Prep time: 10 minutes | Cook time: 19 minutes | Serves 2

Dressing:
2 tablespoons low-sodium soy sauce
1 tablespoon vegan fish sauce
2 tablespoons rice vinegar
1 tablespoon maple syrup (optional)
2 garlic cloves, minced
½ tablespoon ginger
½ teaspoon red pepper flakes
3 tablespoons water
¼ cup almond butter
Juice of 1 lime

Zucchini Noodle Salad:
1 can jackfruit, drained, rinsed and shredded
1 medium carrot, spiralized
2 medium zucchini, spiralized
1 cup red pepper, thinly sliced
2 scallions, green parts only
¼ cup peanuts, crushed
¼ cup cilantro, chopped

1. Preheat the oven to 400ºF (205ºC). Line a baking sheet with the parchment paper.
2. In a small bowl, combine all the ingredients for the dressing, except for the almond butter and lime juice, until well mixed. Add 3 tablespoons water to thin the dressing as needed.
3. In a medium bowl, place the jackfruit and pour 2 tablespoons dressing into the bowl. Toss to coat well. Spread the coated jackfruit on the prepared baking sheet. Bake for 15 minutes, or until lightly browned.
4. Add the almond butter and lime juice to the dressing bowl and stir until well combined.
5. In a saucepan over medium-high heat, add the carrots and sauté for 1 minute. Stir in the zucchini and bell pepper. Continue to sauté for 3 minutes. Let it sit for a couple minutes and drain any excess liquid.
6. Add the dressing and baked jackfruit to the saucepan and stir to mix well. Top with the green scallions, peanuts and cilantro and serve.

Per Serving
Calories: 519 | fat: 27.1g | carbs: 62.8g | protein: 15.1g | fiber: 8.7g

Sweet Potato Mac and Cheese

Prep time: 0 minutes | Cook time: 30 minutes | Serves 10

3 (12-ounce / 340-g) packages brown rice pasta
Sauce:
1 sweet potato, peeled and roughly chopped, about 9 ounces (250 g)
1 yellow onion, roughly chopped, about 9 ounces (250 g)
5 carrots, roughly chopped, about 12 ounces (350 g) total
5 garlic cloves
¾ cup raw cashews (omit for a nut-free version)
1 teaspoon salt (optional)
2 tablespoons nutritional yeast
½ to 2 cups water

1. Bring a large pot of salted water to a boil. Add the pasta into the boiling water and cook for 10 minutes until al dente, stirring occasionally to prevent sticking.
2. Remove from the pot. Drain and rinse with cold water for 30 to 60 seconds and then return it to the pot. Set aside.
3. Meanwhile, make the sauce: Place the potato, onion, carrots, garlic, and cashews in a medium pot over high heat. Add enough water to cover and bring to a boil.
4. Reduce the heat to medium and cook for 15 minutes, or until the largest pieces of carrot and potato can be easily pierced with a fork.
5. Drain the cooked veggies and transfer to a food processor. Add the salt and nutritional yeast. Add the water, ½ cup at a time, stirring to combine after each addition. You may need 2 cups of water to reach desired creaminess.
6. Add the sauce to the cooked pasta and stir until well coated.
7. Divide evenly among the bowls. Serve immediately.

Per Serving
Calories: 486 | fat: 6.8g | carbs: 94.7g | protein: 11.2g | fiber: 7.3g

Vegan Mushroom Stroganoff

Prep time: 10 minutes | Cook time: 20 minutes | Serves 4

8 ounces (227 g) gluten-free pasta
2 tablespoons olive oil, divided (optional)
2 shallots, diced (about ½ cup)
1 pound (454 g) button mushrooms
1 tablespoon fresh thyme, plus additional for garnish
3 garlic cloves, minced (about 2 tablespoons)
3 tablespoons quinoa flour
2½ cups vegetable broth
$1/3$ cup nutritional yeast
½ cup coconut yogurt (or vegan yogurt of choice)
Sea salt, to taste (optional)
Pepper, to taste

1. Bring a large pot of salted water to a boil. Add the pasta into the boiling water and cook for 10 minutes until al dente, stirring occasionally to prevent sticking.
2. Remove from the pot. Drain and rinse with cold water for 30 to 60 seconds and then return it to the pot. Set aside.
3. Meanwhile, in a large pan, heat 1 tablespoon of olive oil, if desired. Add the shallot and sauté for about 2 minutes until nicely browned.
4. Add the remaining 1 tablespoon of oil, mushrooms, thyme, and garlic, and sauté for about 5 minutes, or until the mushrooms are tender.
5. Sprinkle with salt (if desired) and pepper and stir well. Fold in the quinoa flour and sauté until well incorporated.
6. Mix in the vegetable broth and stir to combine.
7. Let the mixture simmer for about 5 to 7 minutes until thickened. Add the nutritional yeast and coconut yogurt and stir well.
8. Add the pasta and toss until well mixed. Taste and add more salt and pepper if desired.
9. Serve garnished with additional thyme.

Per Serving
Calories: 384 | fat: 16.9g | carbs: 45.5g | protein: 21.2g | fiber: 10.0g

Easy Pasta Primavera

Prep time: 30 minutes | Cook time: 45 minutes | Serves 6

Sauce:
½ cup water
2 cloves garlic, crushed
2 stalks celery, chopped
1 onion, chopped
1 (8-ounce / 227-g) can tomato sauce
1 tablespoon chopped fresh oregano
1 tablespoon chopped fresh basil
¼ cup chopped fresh parsley
1 (28-ounce / 794-g) can whole tomatoes, chopped, with liquid

Vegetables:
½ cup water
1 cup asparagus or green beans, cut into 1-inch pieces
1 cup broccoli florets
2 cups sliced mushrooms
1 cup sliced zucchini or yellow squash
1 tablespoon soy sauce
Freshly ground black pepper, to taste
1 pound (454 g) uncooked whole-wheat or spinach pasta
8 cups water

1. To make the sauce: In a medium saucepan. Add the water, garlic, celery, and onion and sauté over medium heat for 6 minutes. Add the remaining ingredients. Reduce the heat to medium-low and let simmer for 30 minutes.
2. To cook the vegetables: Place the water in a pan and bring to a boil. Stir in the asparagus and broccoli and steam covered for 4 minutes until soft. Fold in the mushrooms, zucchini, soy sauce, and pepper. Stir and continue to cook for another 4 minutes, uncovered. Remove from the heat.
3. Meanwhile, cook the pasta: Bring a large pot of water to a boil. Add the pasta into the boiling water, stir occasionally to make sure all the strands are separated. Cook for about 8 minutes until al dente. Drain.
4. Transfer the pasta to a plate and top with the vegetables and then with a generous drizzle of the sauce.

Per Serving
Calories: 197 | fat: 4.4g | carbs: 32.4g | protein: 8.8g | fiber: 9.5g

Eggplant Bolognese

Prep time: 15 minutes | Cook time: 1 hour | Serves 4

1 large eggplant, diced into ½-inch cubes
Sea salt, to taste (optional)
Pepper, to taste
¼ cup + 1 tablespoon olive oil, divided (optional)
5 cloves garlic, minced
¼ teaspoon dried oregano
½ teaspoon chili flakes
1 cup water or vege-table stock
1 can (28-ounce / 794-g) crushed tomatoes
¾ pound (341 g) whole-grain or gluten-free long pasta of your choice, such as spaghetti or linguini
6 whole fresh basil leaves, plus extra chopped, for garnish
½ cup pitted Kalamata olives, finely chopped

1. Preheat the oven to 400ºF (205ºC). Line a baking sheet with parchment paper.
2. Add the eggplant cubes in a large bowl and sprinkle with salt. Let stand to release some of its water, about 10 minutes, then transfer to a colander, and rinse with fresh water.
3. Drain as much liquid from the eggplant cubes as possible with a kitchen towel. Place them on the prepared baking sheet.
4. Add the salt (if desired), pepper, and 1 tablespoon of the olive oil (if desired) and toss to coat. Spread the eggplant cubes out into a single layer.
5. Transfer to the oven and roast for about 20 minutes, or until the eggplant is softened and starts to brown. Set aside.
6. Heat the remaining ¼ cup of olive oil (if desired) in a large skillet over medium heat. Add the garlic and sauté for about 30 seconds until fragrant.
7. Stir in the oregano and chili flakes, then add the vegetable stock and tomatoes, and stir again until well mixed. Bring to a boil, uncovered. Reduce the heat and simmer the sauce until thickened, about 30 minutes.
8. Meantime, cook the pasta in a large pot of boiling, salted water until tender, stirring occasionally to prevent sticking.
9. Remove from the pot. Drain and rinse with cold water for 30 to 60 seconds and then return it to the pot. Set aside.
8. Add the basil leaves to the tomato sauce and submerge the leaves. Continue to cook covered for another 10 minutes.
9. Remove the basil leaves from the sauce and sprinkle with salt (if desired) and pepper. Stir in the roasted eggplant and chopped olives.
10. Add the cooked pasta into the skillet with the sauce and toss until well coated.
11. Serve hot topped with the chopped basil.

Per Serving
Calories: 355 | fat: 18.6g | carbs: 44.2g | protein: 9.1g | fiber: 13.4g

Vegetable and Tofu Soba Noodles

Prep time: 15 minutes | Cook time: 8 minutes | Serves 4 to 6

6 cups low-sodium vegetable soup
2 tablespoons wakame
1 teaspoon minced or grated fresh ginger
1 teaspoon toasted sesame seeds
¼ teaspoon crushed red pepper
1 small yellow onion, diced
8 ounces (227 g) extra-firm tofu, cubed
2 carrots, finely chopped
2 cups shredded red cabbage
2 cups broccoli florets
½ cup kimchi
2 (2.8-ounce / 79-g) packages soba noodles
2 tablespoons red miso
2 scallions, white and light green parts, thinly sliced
2 nori sheets, cut into strips
2 tablespoons chopped cilantro

1. Bring the vegetable soup to a boil in a large pot over medium-high heat. Stir in the wakame, ginger, sesame seeds, red pepper and onion. Reduce the heat to medium and add the tofu, carrots, cabbage, broccoli and kimchi. Cook for 3 minutes.
2. Add the noodles to the pot. Increase the heat to medium-high and cook for 5 minutes, or until the noodles are tender.
3. Remove the pot from the heat and whisk in the miso. Transfer to the bowls and sprinkle scallions, nori and cilantro on top. Serve immediately.

Per Serving
Calories: 383 | fat: 6.5g | carbs: 67.6g | protein: 19.1g | fiber: 8.2g

Creamy Broccoli Pasta

Prep time: 10 minutes | Cook time: 30 minutes | Serves 6

1½ cups raw cashews
2 (12-ounce / 340-g) packages brown rice pasta
2 heads broccoli, cut into florets, about 3½ pound (1.6 kg) total
Juice of ½ lemons, plus more to taste
½ teaspoon salt, plus more to taste
1 garlic clove
¼ cup nutritional yeast
2 cups almond milk
Freshly ground black pepper, to serve

1. In a bowl, place the cashews and boiling water to cover and soak for at least 10 minutes. Drain and set aside.
2. Bring a large pot of salted water to a boil. Add the pasta into the boiling water and cook for 10 minutes until tender, stirring occasionally to prevent sticking.
3. Remove from the pot. Drain and rinse with cold water for 30 to 60 seconds and then return it to the pot. Set aside.
4. Meanwhile, steam the broccoli in a pot with a steamer insert for about 5 minutes, or until the broccoli is bright green.
5. Remove from the heat, squeeze a little lemon juice on top, and lightly sprinkle with salt (if desired). Set aside.
6. Add the soaked cashews, nutritional yeast, almond milk, garlic, ½ teaspoon salt, and juice of ½ lemon in a blender and blitz until smooth.
7. Add the mixture and steamed broccoli into the pasta and stir until well mixed.
8. Top with black pepper and serve immediately

Per Serving
Calories: 769 | fat: 21.8g | carbs: 116.9g | protein: 26.1g | fiber: 14.3g

Carrot and Miso Soba Bowl

Prep time: 15 minutes | Cook time: 8 to 9 minutes | Makes 2 bowls

4 ounces (113 g) uncooked soba noodles
½ cup frozen, shelled edamame
10 to 20 snow peas, vertically sliced
¼ cup vegetable soup
2 teaspoons sesame oil (optional)
1 teaspoon miso paste
1 teaspoon grated fresh ginger
¼ teaspoon pure ma-
ple syrup (optional)
¼ teaspoon sea salt (optional)
1 teaspoon olive oil (optional)
1 large carrots, shaved into ribbons
1 cup thinly sliced red cabbage
4 rehydrated dried shiitake mushrooms, stems removed and sliced
4 scallions, sliced

1. Bring a medium saucepan of water to a boil over medium-high heat. Add the soba noodles and edamame to the saucepan and cook for 2 minutes.
2. Add in the snow peas and cook for 1 minute, or until the noodles are tender. Drain and rinse with cold water. Set aside.
3. In a small bowl, stir together the vegetable soup, sesame oil (if desired), miso paste, ginger, maple syrup (if desired) and salt (if desired). Set aside.
4. Heat the olive oil (if desired) in a skillet over medium heat. Add the carrots, cabbage, mushrooms and scallions to the skillet. Toss and cook for 3 minutes, or until just softened.
5. Add the noodles, edamame, snow peas and sesame sauce to the skillet and sauté for 2 to 3 minutes, or until the dish is heated through.
6. Serve hot.

Per Serving (1 bowl)
Calories: 388 | fat: 9.7g | carbs: 66.4g | protein: 16.1g | fiber: 6.8g

Chapter 11 Wraps and Spreads and Sauces

Chickpea and Mango Wraps

Prep time: 15 minutes | Cook time: 0 minutes | Makes 3 wraps

3 tablespoons tahini
1 tablespoon curry powder
¼ teaspoon sea salt (optional)
Zest and juice of 1 lime
3 to 4 tablespoons water
1½ cups cooked

chickpeas
1 cup diced mango
½ cup fresh cilantro, chopped
1 red bell pepper, de-seeded and diced
3 large whole-wheat wraps
1½ cups shredded lettuce

1. In a large bowl, stir together the tahini, curry powder, lime zest, lime juice and sea salt (if desired) until smooth and creamy. Whisk in 3 to 4 tablespoons water to help thin the mixture.
2. Add the cooked chickpeas, mango, cilantro and bell pepper to the bowl. Toss until well coated.
3. On a clean work surface, lay the wraps. Divide the chickpea and mango mixture among the wraps. Spread the shredded lettuce on top and roll up tightly.Serve immediately.

Per Serving (1 wrap)
Calories: 436 | fat: 17.9g | carbs: 8.9g | protein: 15.2g | fiber: 12.1g

Quick White Bean Spread

Prep time: 15 minutes | Cook time: 0 minutes | Serves 4

2 cups cooked cannellini beans
4 cloves garlic
Zest and juice of 1 lemon

1 teaspoon cooked fresh rosemary
Sea salt, to taste (optional)
Black pepper, to taste

1. In a food processor, combine all the ingredients and process until creamy and smooth. Use a silicone spatula to scrape down the sides of the processor bowl as needed.

Per Serving
Calories: 137 | fat: 0.6g | carbs: 26.1g | protein: 7.8g | fiber: 10.0g

Fresh Herbs filled Hummus Wraps

Prep time: 10 minutes | Cook time: 0 minutes | Serves 4

1 batch Hummus
8 romaine lettuce leaves
1 batch Basic Vegeta-

ble Stir fry
1 cup chopped herbs, such as chives, basil, or cilantro

1. Spoon 3 tablespoons hummus into one of the lettuce leaves.
2. Top with some of the stir-fried vegetables and garnish with the fresh herbs.
3. Fold the leaf in from the sides and roll it up like a cigar. Repeat for the remaining lettuce leaves.

Per Serving
Calories: 597 | fat: 27.24g | carbs: 58.45g | protein: 30.12g

Carrot Celery Stock

Prep time: 10 minutes | Cook time: 5 minutes | Makes 6 cups

1 large onion, peeled
2 large carrots, peeled
2 celery stalks
8 cloves garlic, peeled

and smashed
8 sprigs parsley
½ cup green lentils, rinsed

1. Scrub the vegetables and chop them roughly into 1-inch chunks.
2. In a large pot, add the onion, carrots, celery, garlic, parsley, and lentils and cook them over high heat for 5 to 10 minutes, stirring frequently.
3. Add water 1 to 2 tablespoons at a time to keep the vegetables from sticking to the pot.
4. Add 2 quarts of water and bring to a boil. Lower the heat and simmer, uncovered, for 30 minutes.
5. Strain the stock carefully and discard the solids.

Per Serving
Calories: 204| fat: 0.95g | carbs: 45.78g | protein: 8.44g

Eggplant and Red Pepper Sauce

Prep time: 20 minutes | Cook time: 30 minutes | Serves 4 to 6

4 large red bell pep-
pers
1 large eggplant
4 cloves garlic, finely
chopped

Zest and juice of 1
lemon
Sea salt, to taste (op-
tional)
Black pepper, to taste

1. Preheat the oven to 475ºF (245ºC). Line a baking pan with the parchment paper.
2. Arrange the bell peppers and eggplant in the baking pan and roast for 30 minutes or until the skins blister and blacken.
3. Transfer the eggplant to a plate and let rest for 5 minutes. Cut the eggplant crosswise and spoon the flesh into a food processor.
4. Transfer the bell peppers to a plastic bag and let steam for 15 minutes, or until the skins are loosened. Remove the stem and core of the peppers and peel off the skins. Place the remaining flesh into the food processor.
5. Add the remaining ingredients to the food processor bowl and process until the mixture has broken down into a chunky paste consistency.
6. Serve immediately or kept in an airtight container in the refrigerator for up to 1 week.

Per Serving
Calories: 94 | fat: 0.8g | carbs: 20.4g | pro-
tein: 3.3g | fiber: 8.1g

Coriander Mushroom Wraps

Prep time: 10 minutes | Cook time: 5 minutes | Serves 4

½ cup Spicy Cilantro
Pesto or Coriander
Chutney
8 romaine lettuce
leaves
2 cups cooked brown

rice
1 batch Grilled Por-
tobello Mushrooms,
cut into ¾-inch-wide
strips

1. Spread 1 tablespoon of the pesto in the bottom of one of the lettuce leaves and top with ¼ cup of the rice and about half of a grilled mushroom.
2. Roll the lettuce leaf up around the filling. Repeat for the remaining lettuce leaves

Per Serving
Calories: 115 | fat: 1.39g | carbs: 21.92g |
protein: 6.21

Ginger Mango Spread

Prep time: 10 minutes | Cook time: 15 minutes | Makes 2 cups

2 to 3 mangoes,
peeled and diced
(about 2 cups)
1 small yellow onion,
peeled and minced
½ cup golden raisins
1 jalapeño pepper,

seeded and minced
2 tablespoons brown
rice syrup
Zest of 1 lime and
juice of 2 limes
2 teaspoons grated
ginger

1. Combine all ingredients in a large sauce-pan with ½ cup of water and bring to a boil over high heat.
2. Reduce the heat to medium-low and sim-mer, uncovered, until thickened, about 15 minutes.

Per Serving
Calories: 309 | fat: 0.6g | carbs: 80.81g |
protein: 4.72g

Garlicky Pineapple Spread

Prep time: 10 minutes | Cook time: 5 minutes | Makes 2 cups

1½ cups unsweet-
ened pineapple juice
¼ cup apple cider
vinegar
¼ cup low-sodium
soy sauce
1 clove garlic, peeled
and minced

¼ cup plus 2
tablespoons brown
rice syrup, more to
taste
2 tablespoons ar-
rowroot powder, dis-
solved in ¼ cup of
cold water

1. Combine the pineapple juice, vinegar, low-sodium soy sauce, garlic, and brown rice syrup in a saucepan.
2. Bring the pot to a boil, and whisk in the arrowroot mixture. Cook until thickened, about 1 minute.

Per Serving
Calories: 351 | fat: 0.6g | carbs: 84.31g |
protein: 7.64g

Chilled Lemony Tofu Spread

Prep time: 10 minutes | Cook time: 5 minutes | Makes 1 ½ cups

One 12-ounce package extra firm silken tofu, drained
1 tablespoon fresh

lemon juice
1 tablespoon red wine vinegar
Salt to taste

1. Combine all ingredients in a blender and puree until smooth and creamy.
2. Chill until ready to serve.

Per Serving
Calories: 316| fat: 19.87g | carbs: 7.9g | protein: 33.71g

Spicy Onion Spread

Prep time: 10 minutes | Cook time: 5 minutes | Makes 1 ½ cups

2 pounds yellow onions, peeled and diced small
9 cloves garlic, peeled and minced
1 tablespoon grated ginger
½ tablespoon turmeric

¼ teaspoon ground cardamom
½ teaspoon ground cinnamon
⅛ Teaspoon ground cloves
⅛ Teaspoon ground nutmeg

1. Place the onions in a large skillet over medium heat. Stir frequently, adding water only as needed to keep the onions from sticking to the pan, and cook for about 20 minutes, or until the onions are browned.
2. Add the garlic, ginger, turmeric, cardamom, cinnamon, cloves, and nutmeg and cook for 5 minutes.
3. Add ¼ cup of water and scrape the bottom of the pan with a spatula to pick up and incorporate the bits on the bottom of the pan.
4. Transfer the mixture to a blender and puree, adding water as needed to make a smooth and creamy consistency. This will keep, refrigerated, for up to 7 days.

Per Serving
Calories: 356| fat: 1.22g | carbs: 83.18g | protein: 9.66g

Refried Bean Taquitos

Prep time: 5 minutes | Cook time: 21 to 22 minutes | Serves 4

2 cups pinto beans, cooked
1 teaspoon chili powder
1 teaspoon ground cumin
½ teaspoon garlic

powder
½ teaspoon onion powder
¼ teaspoon red pepper flakes
12 corn tortillas

1. Preheat the oven to 400ºF (205ºC). Line a baking pan with the parchment paper.
2. In a blender, combine all the ingredients, except for the tortillas, and blend until creamy and smooth.
3. Arrange the tortillas in the baking pan and bake for 1 to 2 minutes, or until softened and pliable.
4. Transfer the tortillas to a clean work surface. Spoon the mashed beans into the center of each tortilla and spread over. Roll up tightly and secure with toothpicks.
5. Arrange the stuffed tortillas in the baking pan and bake for 20 minutes, or until golden brown and crispy, flipping halfway through.
6. Let rest for 5 minutes before serving.

Per Serving
Calories: 285 | fat: 13.1g | carbs: 5.8g | protein: 12.2g | fiber: 12.9g

Brown Rice Lettuce Wraps

Prep time: 10 minutes | Cook time: 5 minutes | Serves 4

1 batch Potato Samosa Filling
8 romaine lettuce leaves

3 cups cooked brown rice
Coriander Chutney

1. Place some of the samosa filling on the bottom of one of the lettuce leaves. Top with some brown rice and a spoonful of the coriander chutney.
2. Roll the leaf up around the filling. Repeat for the remaining lettuce leaves.

Per Serving
Calories: 284 | fat: 0.33g | carbs: 64.46g | protein: 7.45

Low Sodium Soy Vinegar Sauce

Prep time: 10 minutes | Cook time: 5 minutes | Makes 1 ¾ cups

Zest and juice of 2 lemons
Zest and juice of 2 limes
¼ cup brown rice vinegar

¾ cup low-sodium soy sauce
¼ cup sake
¼ cup date molasses or brown rice syrup

1. Combine all ingredients in a bowl and whisk until smooth.
2. Store refrigerated in an airtight container for up to 1 week.

Per Serving
Calories: 230| fat: 0.87g | carbs: 27.64g | protein: 18.31g

Toasted Cashew Sauce

Prep time: 10 minutes | Cook time: 5 minutes | Makes 2 ½ cups

1 large yellow onion, peeled and coarsely chopped
1 large red bell pepper, seeded and coarsely chopped
3 tablespoons ca-

shews toasted optional
1 tablespoon tahini, optional
1 cup nutritional yeast
Salt to taste

1. Combine all ingredients in a blender in the order given and puree until smooth and creamy, adding up to ½ cup of water if necessary to achieve a smooth consistency.

Per Serving
Calories: 1045| fat: 45.58g | carbs: 87.09g | protein: 78.63g

Chilled Garlicky Soy Sauce

Prep time: 10 minutes | Cook time: 5 minutes | Makes ¾ cups

⅓ Cup low-sodium soy sauce
⅓ Cup veg stock low-sodium vegetable broth
¼ cup date molasses or brown rice syrup

2 teaspoons grated ginger
2 cloves garlic, peeled and minced
2 teaspoons arrowroot powder

1. Combine all ingredients in a medium saucepan and cook over medium heat until thickened, about 5 minutes.
2. Store refrigerated in an airtight container for up to 1 week.

Per Serving
Calories: 95| fat: 0.59g | carbs: 15.28g | protein: 8.85g

Instant Peanut Sauce with Curry Roasted Carrots

Prep time: 5 minutes | Cook time: 0 minutes | Serves 2

½ cup salted creamy peanut butter
1 to 2 tablespoons gluten-free tamari (if not gluten-free sub soy sauce
1 to 2 tablespoons maple syrup (or other

sweetener of choice)
1 teaspoon chili garlic sauce
2-3 tablespoons lime juice
1/4 cup water (to thin)

1. To a medium mixing bowl add (starting with the amount at the lower end of the measurement range where applicable) peanut butter, tamari (or soy sauce or coconut amino), maple syrup, lime juice, chili sauce (or chili or red pepper), and whisk to combine.
2. Add water a little at a time until a thick but pourable sauce is achieved.
3. Taste and adjust seasonings as needed, adding more maple syrup for sweetness, chili garlic sauce (or red chili or red pepper) for heat, lime juice for acidity, or tamari for saltiness.
4. If your sauce has become too thin, add more nut butter. If it's too thick, thin with more water. For a fun flavor twist, add some fresh grated ginger to taste.
5. Store leftovers covered in the refrigerator up to 1 week.

Per Serving
Calories: 633 | fat: 61.32g | carbs: 21.77g | protein: 2.6g

Creamy Cauliflower Chipotle Spread

Prep time: 10 minutes | Cook time: 20 minutes | Makes 1 cup

1½ cups cauliflower florets
2 chipotle peppers in adobo sauce
½ cup low-sodium vegetable soup
Sea salt and black

pepper, to taste (optional)
3 shallots, minced
2 cloves garlic, minced
¼ cup dry white wine

1. Cook the cauliflower in a steamer for 10 minutes or until soft.
2. Transfer the cauliflower in a food processor. Add the chipotle peppers, then pour in the vegetable soup and sprinkle with salt (if desired). Pulse to purée until creamy and smooth. Set aside.
3. Add the shallots in a skillet and sauté over medium heat for 5 minutes or until translucent.
4. Add the garlic and sauté for 1 more minute or until fragrant.
5. Pour the wine in the skillet and cook until the liquid is almost absorbed.
6. Reduce the heat to medium-low and pour in the puréed cauliflower and chipotle peppers. Cover and simmer for 5 minutes until it becomes thick. Stir occasionally.
7. Smear on the fillings of the tortillas or pitas to serve.

Per Serving (1 cup)
Calories: 235 | fat: 1.8g | carbs: 39.7g | protein: 8.8g | fiber: 8.2g

Chilled Pine Apple Tomato Sauce

Prep time: 10 minutes | Cook time: 5 minutes | Makes 2 cups

One 6-ounce cans tomato paste
½ cup pineapple juice
¼ cup 100% pure maple syrup
3 tablespoons low-sodium soy sauce, or Bragg Liquid Amino
2 tablespoons apple cider vinegar
2 tablespoons stone-ground mustard
1 tablespoon minced

ginger
1 to 2 cloves garlic, peeled and minced
½ teaspoon chipotle powder
½ teaspoon paprika or smoked paprika
½ teaspoon freshly ground black pepper
¼ teaspoon onion powder
¼ teaspoon cayenne pepper

1. Combine all ingredients in a blender and blend on high until smooth.
2. Serve immediately or keep in an airtight container in the refrigerator for up to 4 or 5 days.

Per Serving
Calories: 530| fat: 5.95g | carbs: 114.21g | protein: 15.64g

Homemade Garlic Tomato Spicy Sauce

Prep time: 10 minutes | Cook time: 5 minutes | Makes 4 cups

3 large ripe tomatoes, diced small
1 small red onion, peeled and diced small
½ cup chopped cilantro
1 to 2 jalapeño pep-

pers, minced (for less heat, remove the seeds)
2 cloves garlic, peeled and minced
3 tablespoons fresh lime juice
Salt to taste

1. Combine all ingredients in a large bowl and mix well.
2. Store refrigerated until ready to serve.

Per Serving
Calories: 179| fat: 2.73g | carbs: 38.18g | protein: 7.23g

Best Ever Lettuce Wraps

Prep time: 10 minutes | Cook time: 0 minutes | Serves 4

½ Cup Spicy Cilantro Pesto
8 romaine lettuce leaves

2 cups hummus
2 cups quinoa Tabbouleh

1. Spread 1 tablespoon of pesto on one of the lettuce leaves.
2. Top with 2 tablespoons of hummus and 2 tablespoons of the tabbouleh.
3. Fold the leaf in from the sides and roll it up like a cigar.
4. Repeat for the remaining lettuce leaves.

Per Serving
Calories: 2124 | fat: 62.94g | carbs: 317.43g | protein: 72.09

Navy Beans, Spinach, and Artichoke Spread

Prep time: 5 minutes | Cook time: 0 minutes | Serves 6

1 (15-ounce / 425-g) can navy beans, rinsed and drained
1 (14-ounce / 397-g) can artichoke hearts packed in water, drained
1 (10-ounce / 284-g) package frozen spinach, thawed and

drained
¼ cup nutritional yeast
6 cloves garlic, minced
Sea salt, to taste (optional)
Pinch of ground nutmeg

1. Combine all the ingredients in a food processor. Pulse to mix until creamy and smooth.
2. Smear on the fillings of the tortillas to serve.

Per Serving
Calories: 296 | fat: 2.1g | carbs: 53.2g | protein: 21.1g | fiber: 18.9g

Quinoa and Black Bean Lettuce Wraps

Prep time: 30 minutes | Cook time: 15 minutes | Serves 6

2 tablespoons avocado oil (optional)
¼ cup deseeded and chopped bell pepper
½ onion, chopped
2 tablespoons minced garlic
1 teaspoon salt (optional)
1 teaspoon pepper

(optional)
½ cup cooked quinoa
1 cup cooked black beans
½ cup almond flour
½ teaspoon paprika
½ teaspoon red pepper flakes
6 large lettuce leaves

1. Heat 1 tablespoon of the avocado oil (if desired) in a skillet over medium-high heat.
2. Add the bell peppers, onions, garlic, salt (if desired), and pepper. Sauté for 5 minutes or until the bell peppers are tender.
3. Turn off the heat and allow to cool for 10 minutes, then pour the vegetables in a food processor. Add the quinoa, beans, flour. Sprinkle with paprika and red pepper flakes. Pulse until thick and well combined.

4. Line a baking pan with parchment paper, then shape the mixture into 6 patties with your hands and place on the baking pan.
5. Put the pan in the freezer for 5 minutes to make the patties firm.
6. Heat the remaining avocado oil (if desired) in the skillet over high heat.
7. Add the patties and cook for 6 minutes or until well browned on both sides. Flip the patties halfway through.
8. Arrange the patties in the lettuce leaves and serve immediately.

Per Serving
Calories: 200 | fat: 10.6g | carbs: 40.5g | protein: 9.5g | fiber: 8.2g

Onion Mushroom Wraps

Prep time: 10 minutes | Cook time: 5 minutes | Serves 4

1 tablespoon grated ginger
2 cloves garlic, peeled and minced
Zest and juice of 1 lime
3 tablespoons low-sodium soy sauce
1 teaspoon crushed red pepper flakes
2 large shallots, diced small
1 pound Porto-

bello mushrooms, stemmed and finely chopped
½ cup coarsely chopped cilantro
3 tablespoons finely chopped mint
4 green onions (white and green parts), thinly sliced
4 large romaine lettuce leaves or 8 small ones

1. Combine the ginger, garlic, lime zest and juice, soy sauce, and crushed red pepper flakes in a small bowl and set aside.
2. Heat a large skillet over high heat. Add the shallots and mushrooms and stir-fry for 3 to 4 minutes.
3. Add water 1 to 2 tablespoons at a time to keep the vegetables from sticking to the pan.
4. Add the ginger mixture and cook for another minute. Add the cilantro, mint, and green onions and remove from the heat.
5. To serve, place some of the mushroom mixture on the bottom of one the lettuce leaves and fold the lettuce over the filling. Repeat for the remaining lettuce leaves.

Per Serving
Calories: 3225 | fat: 62.15g | carbs: 541.15g | protein: 206.58g

Guacamole Lettuce Wraps

Prep time: 10 minutes | Cook time: 0 minutes | Serves 6

1 batch Black Beans and Rice
1 large head romaine lettuce leaves sepa-

rated
1 batch Not-So-Fat Guacamole

1. Place some of the black beans and rice into the center of one of the lettuce leaves. Top with some of the guacamole.
2. Fold the leaf in from the sides and roll it up like a cigar.
3. Repeat for any remaining lettuce leaves until the beans and rice and guacamole are used up.

Per Serving
Calories: 3586 | fat: 357.09g | carbs: 19.04g | protein: 77.51g

Avocado and Dulse Pitas

Prep time: 15 minutes | Cook time: 10 minutes | Serves 4

2 teaspoons coconut oil (optional)
½ cup dulse
¼ teaspoon liquid smoke
Salt and ground black pepper, to taste (optional)
2 avocados, sliced
¼ cup chopped cilantro
2 scallions, white and

light green parts, sliced
2 tablespoons lime juice
4 (8-inch) whole wheat pitas, sliced in half
4 cups chopped romaine
4 plum tomatoes, sliced

1. Heat the coconut oil (if desired) in a skillet over medium heat.
2. Add the dulse and drizzle with liquid smoke. Cook for 5 minutes or until crispy. Stir constantly. Turn off the heat and sprinkle with ground black pepper. Transfer on a plate and set aside.
3. Put the avocado, cilantro, and scallions in a food processor, then drizzle with lime juice and sprinkle with salt (if desired) and ground black pepper. Pulse to combine well and mash the avocado.
4. Toast the pita halves in the skillet for 4 minutes or until lightly browned on both sides. Set aside until cool enough to handle.

5. Stuff the pita halves with the avocado mixture, romaine, plum tomatoes, and crispy dulse. Serve immediately.

Per Serving
Calories: 434 | fat: 18.9g | carbs: 61.0g | protein: 9.6g | fiber: 13.5g

Tempeh and Vegetable Wraps

Prep time: 10 minutes | Cook time: 16 minutes | Serves 4

1 pound (454 g) tempeh
1 cup water
¼ cup maple syrup (optional)
2 teaspoons extra-virgin olive oil (optional)
1 teaspoon low-sodium soy sauce
1 teaspoon ground cayenne pepper

⅛ Teaspoon liquid smoke
Cooking spray (optional)
4 whole-wheat tortillas
2 large tomatoes cut into 8 slices total
8 lettuce leaves
½ cup almond butter

1. Heat the water in a pot over medium heat and bring to a boil. Put a steam basket in the pot and place the tempeh in the basket.
2. Cover and steam for 10 minutes. Transfer the tempeh to a plate and let rest for 5 minutes. Slice into 16 strips. Set aside.
3. Stir together the maple syrup (if desired), olive oil (if desired), soy sauce, cayenne pepper and liquid smoke in a small bowl.
4. Spritz a pan over medium-high heat with cooking spray.
5. Place the tempeh slices in the pan. Spread the sauce over the tempeh and cook for 6 minutes, flipping halfway through. Transfer the tempeh back to the plate.
6. On a clean work surface, lay the tortillas. Place 4 tempeh slices, 2 tomato slices, 2 lettuce leaves and 2 tablespoons of almond butter on each tortilla. Roll up tightly and serve.

Per Serving
Calories: 433 | fat: 22.8g | carbs: 40.9g | protein: 23.2g | fiber: 3.1g

Tomato Salad Lettuce Wraps

Prep time: 10 minutes | Cook time: 5 minutes | Serves 4

1½ cups Fava Bean Spread
8 romaine lettuce leaves

1 batch Tomato, Cucumber and Mint Salad

1. Place some of the fava bean spread in the center of one of the lettuce leaves. Top with some of the tomato salad.
2. Fold the leaf in from the sides and roll it up like a cigar.
3. Repeat for the remaining lettuce leaves.

Per Serving
Calories: 789 | fat: 3.69g | carbs: 135.94g | protein: 59.85g

Tofu and Pineapple in Lettuce

Prep time: 2 hours 20 minutes | Cook time: 15 minutes | Serves 4

¼ cup low-sodium soy sauce
1 garlic clove, minced
2 tablespoons sesame oil (optional)
1 tablespoons coconut sugar (optional)
1 (14-ounce / 397-g) package extra firm tofu, drained, cut into ½-inch cubes

1 small white onion, diced
½ pineapple, peeled, cored, cut into cubes
Salt and ground black pepper, to taste (optional)
4 large lettuce leaves
1 tablespoon roasted sesame seeds

1. Combine the soy sauce, garlic, sesame oil (if desired), and coconut sugar in a bowl. Stir to mix well.
2. Add the tofu cubes to the bowl of soy sauce mixture, then press to coat well. Wrap the bowl in plastic and refrigerate to marinate for at least 2 hours.
3. Pour the marinated tofu and marinade in a skillet and heat over medium heat. Add the onion and pineapple cubes to the skillet and stir to mix well.
4. Sprinkle with salt (if desired) and pepper and sauté for 15 minutes or until the onions are lightly browned and the pineapple cubes are tender.

5. Divide the lettuce leaves among 4 plates, then top the leaves with the tofu and pineapple mixture. Sprinkle with sesame seeds and serve immediately.

Per Serving
Calories: 259 | fat: 15.4g | carbs: 20.5g | protein: 12.1g | fiber: 3.2g

Oil-Free Mushroom and Tofu Burritos

Prep time: 15 minutes | Cook time: 28 to 45 minutes | Serves 4

1½ cups shiitake mushrooms, stemmed and sliced
2 large leeks, white and light green parts only, diced
1 medium red bell pepper, diced
3 cloves garlic, minced
3 tablespoons nutritional yeast
2 tablespoons low-sodium soy sauce

2 teaspoons ground coriander
2 teaspoons turmeric
2 teaspoons ground cumin
Black pepper, to taste
1 pound (454 g) lite firm tofu, pressed and mashed
½ cup chopped cilantro
4 whole-wheat tortillas
1 cup salsa

1. Preheat the oven to 350ºF (180ºC). Line a baking pan with the parchment paper.
2. Add the mushrooms, leeks and red bell pepper to a saucepan over medium-high heat. Sauté for 8 to 10 minutes, or until the vegetables are softened.
3. Add the garlic, nutritional yeast, soy sauce, coriander, turmeric, cumin and black pepper to the saucepan. Reduce the heat to medium-low. Sauté for 5 minutes. Stir in the tofu mash.
4. Spread the mixture in an even layer in the prepared pan. Bake for 25 to 30 minutes. Transfer the mixture to a large bowl and mix with the cilantro to combine well.
5. On a clean work surface, lay the tortillas. Spoon the mixture into the tortillas and spread all over. Drizzle the salsa over the filling. Roll up the tortillas tightly.
6. Serve immediately.

Per Serving
Calories: 411 | fat: 15.1g | carbs: 48.9g | protein: 28.1g | fiber: 12.4g

Rice and Bean Lettuce Burgers

Prep time: 1 hour 25 minutes | Cook time: 45 minutes | Serves 8

1 cup uncooked medium-grain brown rice
2 cups water
½ cup grated carrots
¾ cup chopped red onion
½ cup raw sunflower seeds
¾ cup cooked pinto beans
5 cloves garlic, peeled
2 tablespoons oat flour
2 teaspoons arrowroot powder
2 tablespoons nutri-tional yeast
¼ cup chopped fresh basil
4 Teaspoons ground cumin
4 Teaspoons low-sodium soy sauce
2 tablespoons low-sodium tomato paste
Salt and ground black pepper, to taste (optional)
1 to 2 tablespoons water
8 large lettuce leaves, for serving

1. Pour the rice and water in a pot. Bring to a boil over medium heat. Reduce the heat to low and simmer for 15 more minutes or until the rice is tender. Transfer the rice in a large bowl. Allow the rice to cool and fluff with a fork.
2. Put the carrots, onions, sunflower seeds, beans, and garlic in a food processor and pulse until well combined and chunky. Pour the mixture over the rice.
3. Add the remaining ingredients, except for the lettuce, to the bowl of rice, then toss to combine well. Shape the mixture into 8 patties and arrange them on a parchment-lined baking pan. Refrigerate for an hour until firm.
4. Preheat the oven to 350°F (180°C).
5. Place the baking pan in the oven and bake for 30 minutes or until well browned on both sides. Flip the patties halfway through.
6. Unfold the lettuce leaves on 8 plates, then top each leaf with a patty. Wrap and serve.

Per Serving
Calories: 197 | fat: 5.9g | carbs: 30.5g | protein: 7.4g | fiber: 4.7g

Bulgur and Pinto Bean Lettuce Wraps

Prep time: 30 minutes | Cook time: 10 minutes | Serves 8

1½ cups plus 2 tablespoons water, divided
Salt and ground black pepper, to taste (optional)
²/₃ cup bulgur, rinsed
¾ cup walnuts
½ cup fresh basil leaves
2 garlic cloves, minced
1 large beet (about 9 ounces / 255 g), peeled and shredded
1 (15-ounce / 425-g) can pinto beans, rinsed
1 (4-ounce / 113-g) jar carrot
1 tablespoon Dijon mustard
1½ cups panko bread crumbs
6 tablespoons avocado oil (optional)
8 large lettuce leaves

1. Pour 1½ cups of water in a pot and sprinkle with salt (if desired) to taste. Bring to a boil, then turn off the heat. Pour the bulgur in the boiling water. Cover the lid and let sit for 15 minutes or until the bulgur is soft. Drain the bulgur and spread it on a baking pan to cool.
2. Meanwhile, combine the walnuts, basil, garlic, and beet in a food processor. Pulse to mix well. Then add the beans, carrot, 2 tablespoons of water, Dijon mustard, salt (if desired) and pepper. Pulse to combine well.
3. Pour the mixture in a large bowl and fold in the cooked bulgur and panko. Shape the mixture into 8 patties.
4. Heat the avocado oil (if desired) in the skillet over medium-high heat.
5. Arrange the patties in a skillet and cook for 8 minutes or until well browned on both sides. Flip the patties halfway through. Work in batches to avoid overcrowding.
6. Unfold the lettuce leaves on 8 plates, then top the leaves with the patties and wrap to serve.

Per Serving
Calories: 317 | fat: 17.2g | carbs: 33.9g | protein: 8.9g | fiber: 6.5g

Cannellini Bean and Bell Pepper Burger

Prep time: 15 minutes | Cook time: 35 minutes | Serves 6

¾ cup quinoa
1½ cups water
2 (15-ounce / 425-g) cans cannellini beans, rinsed and drained
½ cup ground flaxseeds
1 cup walnuts, finely chopped
1 tablespoon ground cumin
3 tablespoons Italian seasoning
1 tablespoon minced garlic
2 tablespoons almond butter

1 teaspoon salt (optional)
½ teaspoon freshly ground black pepper
3 tablespoons Dijon mustard
1½ tablespoons avocado oil (optional)
4 to 5 large red bell peppers cut into thirds
Topping:
1 cucumber, sliced
2 to 3 tomatoes, sliced
½ small red onion, sliced

1. In a saucepan, combine the quinoa and water. Bring to a boil over high heat, then cover and reduce heat to medium-low. Simmer for 20 minutes or until all the water has absorbed. Set aside.
2. On a large cutting board, spread out the beans. Pat dry with paper towels. Then press down firmly with the beans between the paper towel and cutting board, using your knuckles to mash them. When you remove the paper towel, you should have a layer of semi-smashed beans. Using a chef's knife, chop the beans a little bit more, leaving a few larger chunks.
3. Transfer the mashed beans to a medium bowl. Add the cooked quinoa, flaxseeds, walnuts, cumin, Italian seasoning, garlic, almond butter, salt (if desired), pepper, and mustard. Mix until well combined.
4. Dip your fingers in water to prevent the burger mixture from sticking and form 12 burger patties.
5. In a nonstick skillet, heat ½ tablespoon olive oil (if desired) over medium heat. Once hot, add 4 patties. Cook for 3 minutes, then flip to the other side and cook for 3 minutes more.
6. To serve, cutting bell peppers into thirds and sandwiching a burger patty between two pieces of pepper. Top with sliced cucumber, tomatoes, and onion.

Per Serving
Calories: 304 | fat: 16.1g | carbs: 27.9g | protein: 12.2g | fiber: 11.8g

Spicy Garlic Pepper Sauce

Prep time: 5 minutes | Cook time: 0 minutes | Makes 2 cups

2 cups cooked great northern beans, or one (15-ounce / 425-g) can, drained and rinsed
1 red bell pepper, roasted, seeded, and coarsely chopped

3 cloves garlic, peeled and minced
3 tablespoons finely chopped dill
Zest and juice of 1 lemon
Salt to taste
Pinch cayenne pepper

1. Combine all ingredients in the bowl of a food processor and puree until smooth and creamy.

Per Serving
Calories: 170 | fat: 3.44g | carbs: 33.63g | protein: 9.3g

Garlic Cumin Bean Spread

Prep time: 5 minutes | Cook time: 17 minutes | Makes 3 ½ cups

4 cups cooked fava beans, or two (15-ounce / 425-g) cans, drained and rinsed
8 cloves garlic, peeled and chopped

Zest of 1 lemon and juice of 2 lemons
1 teaspoon cumin seeds, toasted and ground
Salt, to taste

1. Combine the fava beans, garlic, lemon zest and juice, cumin, salt, and 1 cup of water in the bowl of a food processor and puree until smooth and creamy.
2. Add more water as needed to achieve a smooth consistency.

Per Serving
Calories: 154 | fat: 1.53g | carbs: 32.17g | protein: 11.05g

Appendix 1 Measurement Conversion Chart

VOLUME EQUIVALENTS(DRY)

US STANDARD	METRIC (APPROXIMATE)
1/8 teaspoon	0.5 mL
1/4 teaspoon	1 mL
1/2 teaspoon	2 mL
3/4 teaspoon	4 mL
1 teaspoon	5 mL
1 tablespoon	15 mL
1/4 cup	59 mL
1/2 cup	118 mL
3/4 cup	177 mL
1 cup	235 mL
2 cups	475 mL
3 cups	700 mL
4 cups	1 L

VOLUME EQUIVALENTS(LIQUID)

US STANDARD	US STANDARD (OUNCES)	METRIC (APPROXIMATE)
2 tablespoons	1 fl.oz.	30 mL
1/4 cup	2 fl.oz.	60 mL
1/2 cup	4 fl.oz.	120 mL
1 cup	8 fl.oz.	240 mL
1 1/2 cup	12 fl.oz.	355 mL
2 cups or 1 pint	16 fl.oz.	475 mL
4 cups or 1 quart	32 fl.oz.	1 L
1 gallon	128 fl.oz.	4 L

TEMPERATURES EQUIVALENTS

FAHRENHEIT(F)	CELSIUS(C) (APPROXIMATE)
225 °F	107 °C
250 °F	120 °C
275 °F	135 °C
300 °F	150 °C
325 °F	160 °C
350 °F	180 °C
375 °F	190 °C
400 °F	205 °C
425 °F	220 °C
450 °F	235 °C
475 °F	245 °C
500 °F	260 °C

WEIGHT EQUIVALENTS

US STANDARD	METRIC (APPROXIMATE)
1 ounce	28 g
2 ounces	57 g
5 ounces	142 g
10 ounces	284 g
15 ounces	425 g
16 ounces (1 pound)	455 g
1.5 pounds	680 g
2 pounds	907 g

Appendix 2 The Dirty Dozen and Clean Fifteen

The Environmental Working Group (EWG) is a nonprofit, nonpartisan organization dedicated to protecting human health and the environment Its mission is to empower people to live healthier lives in a healthier environment. This organization publishes an annual list of the twelve kinds of produce, in sequence, that have the highest amount of pesticide residue-the Dirty Dozen-as well as a list of the fifteen kinds ofproduce that have the least amount of pesticide residue-the Clean Fifteen.

THE DIRTY DOZEN	THE CLEAN FIFTEEN
• The 2016 Dirty Dozen includes the following produce. These are considered among the year's most important produce to buy organic:	• The least critical to buy organically are the Clean Fifteen list. The following are on the 2016 list:

THE DIRTY DOZEN		THE CLEAN FIFTEEN	
Strawberries	Spinach	Avocados	Papayas
Apples	Tomatoes	Corn	Kiw
Nectarines	Bell peppers	Pineapples	Eggplant
Peaches	Cherry tomatoes	Cabbage	Honeydew
Celery	Cucumbers	Sweet peas	Grapefruit
Grapes	Kale/collard greens	Onions	Cantaloupe
Cherries	Hot peppers	Asparagus	Cauliflower
		Mangos	

• *The Dirty Dozen list contains two additional itemskale/collard greens and hot peppers-because they tend to contain trace levels of highly hazardous pesticides.*

• *Some of the sweet corn sold in the United States are made from genetically engineered (GE) seedstock. Buy organic varieties of these crops to avoid GE produce.*

Appendix 3 Index

Made in the USA
Coppell, TX
05 August 2021